Computational Linguistics for Linguistic Complexity (CL4LC 2016)

Osaka, Japan
11 December 2016

ISBN: 978-1-5108-3321-0

Preface

Welcome to the first edition of the "Computational Linguistics for Linguistic Complexity" workshop (CL4LC)! CL4LC aims at investigating "processing" aspects of linguistic complexity with the objective of promoting a common reflection on approaches for the detection, evaluation and modelling of linguistic complexity.

What has motivated such a focus on linguistic complexity? Although the topic of linguistic complexity has attracted researchers for quite some time, this concept is still poorly defined and often used with different meanings. Linguistic complexity indeed is inherently a multidimensional concept that must be approached from various perspectives, ranging from natural language processing (NLP), second language acquisition (SLA), psycholinguistics and cognitive science, as well as contrastive linguistics. In 2015, a one-day workshop dedicated to the question of *Measuring Linguistic Complexity* was organized at the catholic University of Louvain (UCL) with the aim of identifying convergent approaches in diverse fields addressing linguistic complexity from their specific viewpoint. Not only did the workshop turn out to be a great success, but it strikingly pointed out that more in–depth thought is required in order to investigate how research on linguistic complexity and its processing aspects could actually benefit from the sharing of definitions, methodologies and techniques developed from different perspectives.

CL4LC stems from these reflections and would like to go a step further towards a more multifaceted view of linguistic complexity. In particular, the workshop would like to investigate processing aspects of linguistic complexity both from a machine point of view and from the perspective of the human subject in order to pinpoint possible differences and commonalities.

We are glad to see that our expectations have been met since the workshop has generated great enthusiasm both within the Program Committee, whose members from various disciplines have wholeheartedly agreed to serve, and within authors, as we received 33 paper submissions in all, out of which eight were selected as oral presentations and seventeen as posters.

The multidisciplinary approach assumed by the workshop is reflected in the submissions that we received. We can classify them following one major "theoretical" distinction between absolute complexity (i.e. the formal properties of linguistic systems) and relative complexity (i.e. covering issues such as cognitive cost, difficulty, level of demand for a user/learner). Several papers that we received focused on language complexity per se, which is typically addressed comparing the structural complexity of different languages. Bentz et al. (a) thus compare typical measures of language complexity across 519 languages. In Bentz et al. (b), they also discuss language evolution, with a special focus on morphological complexity, in the light of learning pressures. Another approach is to assess document complexity and Chen and Meurers propose a web-based tool to this aim. Papers focusing deeper on a specific aspect of linguistic complexity were also proposed, such as Zaghouani et al., who report a method to detect lexical ambiguity, which is one of the major sources of language complexity, and on its impact on human annotation. Bjerva and Börstell investigate the impact of morphological complexity and animacy features on the order of verb and object in Swedish Sign Language. Takahira et al. adopt a broader approach and compare the entropy rates of six different languages by means of a state-of-the-art compression method. Finally, Shi et al. investigate the impact of polysemy on automatic word representation in order to improve the performance of word embeddings.

We also got very interesting papers on the relative complexity of language, i.e. the difficulty perceived by humans when processing linguistic input. Some of them are concerned with modeling human sentence processing through experimental and computational metrics to capture linguistic clues of sentence processing difficulty. Other papers address relative complexity from a more applicative point of view. The first is the case of van Schijndel and Schuler, who revisit the question of using eye-tracking data to predict the level of surprisal of sentences, showing that taking into consideration a word skipped during reading improves n-gram surprisal, but not surprisal measures based on PCFG. The work of Bloem also uses the construct of surprisal to investigate the relation between processing cost and the choice between near-synonymous verbal constructions in Dutch. The contribution of Shain et al. investigates the existence of a latency effect during sentence processing due to memory access. On their side, Li et al. regress various measures of textual complexity on fMRI timecourses while listening to a story to discuss the role of various regions of interest (ROI) in the humain brain. Chersoni et al. propose a very relevant contribution suggesting a Distributional Model for computing semantic complexity that is based on the MUC (Memory, Unification and Control) model for sentence comprehension. Heilmann and Neumann explore a completely different horizon and make use of keylogs to better model language complexity and the cognitive load it produces during the translation process. Finally, Becerra-Bonache and Jimenez-Lopez adopt a developmental approach of linguistic complexity that uses grammatical inference algorithms to simulate the acquisition of language by a native speaker.

The second more applicative point of view to relative complexity is addressed by Falkenjack and Jönsson, who are concerned with the scarcity of available texts for training readability models in languages other than English and suggest using a Bayesian Probit model coupled with a ranking classification strategy. Ströbel et al. suggest another approach to text readability based on a sliding-window that is used to create the distribution of linguistic complexity for a text. Wagner Filho et al. compare the efficiency of various machine learning algorithms and engineered features to automatically build a large corpus for readability assessment. Vajjala et al. provide an interesting example of a integrated view of text readability that correlates text characteristics with reader's language ability reflected in reading comprehension experiments. The paper by Deep Singh et al. also addresses readability prediction from a psycholinguistic point of view, using eye-tracking measures instead of grade level to train their model. Gonzalez-Dios et al. carry out an interesting in-depth analysis combining readability and text simplification, retaining the most predictive syntactic structures from a readability model and analysing how human writers simplify the syntactic structures concerned. Similarly, with the goal of connecting text simplification practises with real needs of readers, Gala et al. experiment with dyslexic children to verify the effects of lexical simplification on reading comprehension. Albertsson et al. on their part detect paraphrased segments between two corpora (one comprised of simple texts, while the other includes more advanced materials) for text simplification purposes. Finally, Pilan et al. use coursebook-based lists of vocabulary to improve the proficiency prediction of learner essays in Swedish.

A further perspective is assumed by those papers more focused on linguistic complexity from the automatic processing point of view, investigating differences and similarities with human sentence processing. This is the case of Delmonte's paper, which is concerned with syntactic complexity for a syntactic parser focusing in particular on those syntactic structures which are known to be difficult for human parsing. Mirzaei et al. use errors made by an automatic speech recognition system as indicators of second language learners's listening difficulties.

To conclude this nice programme, we wish to thank everyone who submitted a paper, all of the authors for their contributions, the members of the Program Committee for their thoughtful reviews, and everyone who attended this workshop for sharing time and thoughts on this increasingly important research topic.

Sincerely,

Dominique Brunato
Felice Dell'Orletta
Giulia Venturi
Thomas François
Philippe Blache

Organisers

Dominique Brunato, ItaliaNLP Lab, Istituto di Linguistica Computazionale "A. Zampolli", Pisa, Italy

Felice Dell'Orletta, ItaliaNLP Lab, Istituto di Linguistica Computazionale "A. Zampolli", Pisa, Italy

Giulia Venturi, ItaliaNLP Lab, Istituto di Linguistica Computazionale "A. Zampolli", Pisa, Italy

Thomas François, CENTAL, IL&C Université catholique de Louvain, Louvain-la-Neuve, Belgium

Philippe Blache, Laboratoire Parole et Langage, CNRS & Université de Provence, Aix-en-Provence, France

Programme Committee

Mohammed Attia (George Washington University, USA)

Delphine Bernhard (LilPa, Université de Strasbourg, France)

Joachim Bingel (University of Copenhagen, Denmark)

Nicoletta Calzolari (Istituto di Linguistica Computazionale "A. Zampolli", ILC-CNR, Italy - European Language Resources Association (ELRA), France)

Angelo Cangelosi, (Centre for Robotics and Neural Systems at the University of Plymouth, UK)

Benoît Crabbé (Université Paris 7, INRIA, France)

Scott Crossley (Georgia State University, USA)

Rodolfo Delmonte (Department of Computer Science, Università Ca' Foscari, Italy)

Piet Desmet (KULeuven, Belgium)

Arantza Díaz de Ilarraza (IXA NLP Group, University of the Basque Country)

Cédrick Fairon (Université catholique de Louvain, Belgium)

Marcello Ferro (Istituto di Linguistica Computazionale "A. Zampolli", ILC-CNR, Italy)

Nuria Gala (Aix-Marseille Université, France)

Ted Gibson (MIT, USA)

Itziar Gonzalez-Dios (IXA NLP Group, University of the Basque Country)

Alex Housen (Vrije Universiteit Brussel, Belgium)

Frank Keller (University of Edinburgh, UK)

Kristopher Kyle (Georgia State University, USA)

Alessandro Lenci (Università di Pisa, Italy)

Annie Louis (University of Essex, UK)

Xiaofei Lu (Pennsylvania State University, USA)

Shervin Malmasi (Harvard Medical School)

Ryan Mcdonald (Google Inc.)

Detmar Meurers (University of Tübingen, Germany)

Simonetta Montemagni (Istituto di Linguistica Computazionale "A. Zampolli", ILC-CNR, Italy)

Alexis Neme (Université Paris-Est, France)

Frederick J. Newmeyer (University of Washington, USA, University of British Columbia, Simon Fraser University, CA)

Joakim Nivre (Uppsala University, Sweden)

Gabriele Pallotti (Università di Modena e Reggio Emilia, Italy)

Magali Paquot (Université catholique de Louvain, Belgium)

Vito Pirrelli (Istituto di Linguistica Computazionale "A. Zampolli", ILC-CNR, Italy)

Barbara Plank (University of Groningen, Netherlands)
Massimo Poesio (University of Essex, UK)
Horacio Saggion (Universitat Pompeu Fabra, Spain)
Paul Smolensky (John Hopkins University, USA)
Kaori Sugiyama (Department of Literature, Seinan Gakuin University, Japan)
Benedikt Szmrecsanyi (KULeuven, Belgium)
Kumiko Tanaka-Ishii (University of Tokyo, Japan)
Joel Tetreault (Grammarly Inc.)
Sara Tonelli (FBK, Trento, Italy)
Sowmya Vajjala (Iowa State University, USA)
Aline Villavicencio (Institute of Informatics Federal University of Rio Grande do Sul, Brazil)
Elena Volodina (University of Gothenburg, Sweden)
Patrick Watrin (CENTAL, IL&C, Université catholique de Louvain, Louvain-la-Neuve, Belgium)
Daniel Wiechmann (University of Amsterdam, Netherlands)
Victoria Yaneva (University of Wolverhampton, UK)
Leonardo Zilio (CENTAL, IL&C, Université catholique de Louvain, Louvain-la-Neuve, Belgium)

Table of Contents

This page intentionally left blank.

Conference Program

Sunday December 11, 2016 (Room 1002)

09:00–09:15   **Opening Remarks**

09:15–10:30   **Session 1 – Oral presentations**

09:15–09:40   *Could Machine Learning Shed Light on Natural Language Complexity?*
Maria Dolores Jimenez Lopez and Leonor Becerra-Bonache

09.40–10.05   *Towards a Distributional Model of Semantic Complexity*
Emmanuele Chersoni, Philippe Blache and Alessandro Lenci

10.05–10.30   *CoCoGen - Complexity Contour Generator: Automatic Assessment of Linguistic Complexity Using a Sliding-Window Technique*
Ströbel Marcus, Elma Kerz, Daniel Wiechmann and Stella Neumann

10:30–10:50   **Break**

10:50–12:05   **Session 2 – Oral presentations**

10:50–11:15   *Addressing surprisal deficiencies in reading time models*
Marten van Schijndel and William Schuler

11:15–11:40   *Towards grounding computational linguistic approaches to readability: Modeling reader-text interaction for easy and difficult texts*
Sowmya Vajjala, Detmar Meurers, Alexander Eitel and Katharina Scheiter

11:40–12:05   *Memory access during incremental sentence processing causes reading time latency*
Cory Shain, Marten van Schijndel, Richard Futrell, Edward Gibson and William Schuler

12:05–14:00   **Lunch Break**

14:00–15:20   **Poster session**

Reducing lexical complexity as a tool to increase text accessibility for children with dyslexia
Nuria Gala and Johannes Ziegler

A Preliminary Study of Statistically Predictive Syntactic Complexity Features and Manual Simplifications in Basque
Itziar Gonzalez-Dios, María Jesús Aranzabe and Arantza Díaz de Ilarraza

Dynamic pause assessment of keystroke logged data for the detection of complexity in translation and monolingual text production
Arndt Heilmann and Stella Neumann

Could Machine Learning Shed Light on Natural Language Complexity?

Leonor Becerra-Bonache
Laboratoire Hubert Curien
Jean Monnet University
Saint-Etienne, France
`leonor.becerra@univ-st-etienne.fr`

M. Dolores Jiménez-López
Research Group on Mathematical Linguistics
Universitat Rovira i Virgili
Tarragona, Spain
`mariadolores.jimenez@urv.cat`

Abstract

In this paper, we propose to use a subfield of machine learning –grammatical inference– to measure linguistic complexity from a developmental point of view. We focus on relative complexity by considering a child learner in the process of first language acquisition. The relevance of grammatical inference models for measuring linguistic complexity from a developmental point of view is based on the fact that algorithms proposed in this area can be considered computational models for studying first language acquisition. Even though it will be possible to use different techniques from the field of machine learning as computational models for dealing with linguistic complexity –since in any model we have algorithms that can learn from data–, we claim that grammatical inference models offer some advantages over other tools.

1 Introduction

Complexity has become an important concept in several scientific disciplines (biology, physics, chemistry, philosophy, psychology and sociology) (Mitchell, 2009). There has been a lot of research on complexity and complex systems in the natural sciences, economics, social sciences and, now, also increasingly in linguistics. From McWhorther's (2001) pioneering work, there have been many seminars, conferences, articles, monographs (Dahl, 2004; Kusters, 2003) and collective volumes (Miestamo et al., 2008; Sampson et al., 2009; Newmeyer and Preston, 2014) that have dealt with linguistic complexity and have challenged the so-called *equi-complexity dogma*. In fact, we can say that, nowadays, complexity figures prominently in linguistics.

However, despite the interest it has generated, there is no agreement in the literature on the definition of *complexity*. In a recent article, Pallotti (2015) underlines the polysemy of the term complexity in the linguistic literature and summarizes the different notions of complexity in this field by referring to three main meanings:

- *Structural complexity*, a formal property of texts and linguistic systems having to do with the number of their elements and their relational patterns.

- *Cognitive complexity*, having to do with the processing costs associated with linguistic structures.

- *Developmental complexity*, the order in which linguistic structures emerge and are mastered in second (and, possibly, first) language acquisition.

The above three meanings cover the two conceptions that, according to Crystal (1997), the concept has in linguistics, where 'complexity refers to both the internal structuring of linguistic units and psychological difficulty in using or learning them'. This distinction is directly reflected in the two main types of complexity found in the literature (Miestamo, 2006; Miestamo, 2009a; Miestamo, 2009b):

- The *absolute complexity* approach that defines complexity as an objective property of the system and it is measured in terms of the number of parts of the system, the interrelations between the parts

Proceedings of the Workshop on Computational Linguistics for Linguistic Complexity,
pages 1–11, Osaka, Japan, December 11-17 2016.

or the length of the description of the phenomenon. It is a usual complexity notion in cross-linguistic typology studies (McWhorter, 2001; Dahl, 2004).

- The *relative complexity* approach that takes into account the users of language and identifies complexity with difficulty/cost of processing, learning or acquisition. This type of approach is very common in the fields of sociolinguistics and psycholinguistics (Kusters, 2003).

Differences in the definition led to abundance of complexity measures. Edmonds (1999), for example, identifies forty-eight different metrics used in natural and social sciences. In linguistics, there is no conventionally agreed metric for measuring the complexity of natural languages. The measures proposed are varied and could be grouped into two blocs:

- *Measures of absolute complexity.* The number of categories or rules, length of the description, ambiguity, redundancy, etc. (Miestamo, 2009a).

- *Measures of relative complexity.* When the relative approach of complexity is adopted the problem that has to be faced is the answer to the question: Difficult/costly to whom? This means that it is necessary to determine what kind of task –learning, acquisition, processing– must be considered and, of course, what type of user must be taken into account –speaker, listener, child, adult–. The problem, here, is to choose a task and a type of user representative for the definition of complexity and to properly motivate this choice. The complexity of L2 learning (Kusters, 2003) or the complexity of processing (Hawkins, 2009) are examples of measures proposed in this field.

Some researchers have attempted to apply the concept of complexity used in other disciplines in order to find useful tools to calculate linguistic complexity. Information theory, for example, offers two formalisms that might be appropriate for measuring linguistic complexity:

- *Shannon information entropy* that captures the average number of bits of information necessary to specify the state of a random variable or system described by a probability model (Bane, 2008).

- *Kolmogorov complexity* that measures the informativeness of a string as the length of the algorithm required to describe that string (Juola, 2009). This measure can be applied to measuring language complexity in such a way that the longer the description of a linguistic structure, the more complex it is (Dahl, 2004; Juola, 2009; Miestamo, 2009a).

Other than information theory, computational models (Blache, 2011), or the theory of complex systems (Andrason, 2014) are examples of areas that provide measures to quantitatively evaluate linguistic complexity.

In this paper, we propose to use a subfield of Machine Learning –*Grammatical Inference*– to measure linguistic complexity from a developmental point of view. We focus on relative complexity by considering a child learner in the process of first language acquisition. Therefore, we need a computational model for first language acquisition. This is why we have chosen grammatical inference models, since they deal with idealized learning procedures for acquiring grammars on the basis of exposure to evidence about languages (D'Ulizia et al., 2011).

The paper is organized as follows. Firstly, we present an overview of research on linguistic relative complexity. Secondly, we briefly discuss the relevance of grammatical inference models for explaining natural language acquisition. Thirdly, we present different grammatical inference algorithms that may deal with linguistic complexity. Finally, we conclude with some remarks and possible directions for future work.

2   Relative Complexity

Even though complexity is a central notion in linguistics, until recently, it has not been widely researched in the area (Sinnemäki, 2011). During the twentieth century, linguistic complexity was supposed to be invariant. Linguists, from very different theoretical schools, have agreed that all natural languages must be equally complex. However, the validity of this claim has rarely been subjected to systematic cross-linguistic investigation.

In the last fifteen years, the interest on linguistic complexity has led researchers to challenge the equi-complexity dogma by addressing the study of complexity from different points of views. In general, recent work on language complexity takes an *absolute* perspective of the concept while the *relative* complexity approach –even though considered as conceptually coherent– has hardly begun to be developed.

In general, researchers agree that it is more feasible to approach complexity from an objective or theory-oriented viewpoint than from a subjective or user-related viewpoint. To approach complexity from the relative point of view constraints the researcher to face many problems:

- What does complex mean?: More difficult, more costly, more problematic, more challenging?

- Different situations of language use (speaking, hearing, L1 acquisition, L2 learning) differ as to what is difficult and what is easy.

- Some linguistic phenomena can be difficult for a certain group of language users while facilitating the task of another group, so we have to answer the question 'complex to whom?'

- A user-based approach would require focusing on one user-type over the others or defining an idealized user-type. How do we decide which type of language use (and user) is primary?

According to Miestamo (2006), there will always be some conflict between definitions of complexity based on different types of users, and no general user-type-neutral definition is possible. This is problematic for a relative approach to complexity. Absolute definitions of complexity avoid these problems.

Among the relative complexity metrics that have been proposed, we can refer to the following ones: L2 acquisition complexity (Trudgill, 2001a); redundancy-induced complexity (Trudgill, 1999; McWhorter, 2001); irregularity-induced complexity (Trudgill, 2001b; McWhorter, 2012); incomplete dependency hypothesis (Gibson, 1998); dependency locality theory (DLT) (Gibson, 2000); structural depth (Ferreira, 1991; Abney and Johnson, 1991; Schuler, 2009); time of acquisition and degree of acquisition, etc.

Studies that have adopted a relative complexity approach have showed some preferences for L2 learners (Kusters, 2003). This is, from the following three different questions that could be answered, researchers have preferably chosen the first one:

1. Second-language learning. Do some language take longer for the adult learner to learn than others?

2. Language use. Are some languages more difficult to use than others?

3. Language acquisition: Do some languages take longer for the child to acquire than others?

However, as pointed out by Miestamo (2006), if we aim to reach a general definition of relative complexity, the primary relevance of L2 learners is not obvious. In fact, they could be considered the least important of the four possible groups that may be considered –speakers, hearers, L1 learners, L2 learners.

Taking into account that some of the ideas that backup the equi-complexity dogma are based on the process of language acquisition –learning a first language is something every child does successfully in every society, in every language, independently of the type of education and intelligence level; all children acquire language in the same way, regardless of the language they learn; children progress through the same stages in language acquisition regardless the language–, we think that studies on developmental complexity may check differences among languages by considering child first language acquisition. Due to the problems that methods for studying language acquisition (observational and experimental) may set out to the study of linguistic complexity, we defend that computational modeling of the process of language acquisition may be considered an important complementary tool that -by avoiding practical problems of analyzing authentic learner productions data– will make possible to consider children (or their simulation) as suitable candidates for evaluating the complexity of languages.

3 Grammatical Inference Relevance for Natural Language Acquisition

Within the field of Machine Learning (Olivas et al., 2009) –that focus on the development of techniques that allow computers to learn–, *Grammatical Inference* (GI) deals with the learning of grammars and languages from data (de la Higuera, 2010). This subfield of machine learning was born in the 1960s and since then has attracted the attention of researchers working on different fields (formal languages, automata theory, computational linguistics, information theory, pattern recognition, and many others).

The relevance of GI models for measuring linguistic complexity from a developmental point of view is based on the fact that the computational models developed in this area can be useful for studying first language acquisition. In fact, the initial theoretical foundations of GI were given by E.M.Gold (1967), who tried to formalize the process of natural language acquisition.

According to Pearl and Goldwater (2016), language acquisition is a problem of induction: the child learner is faced with a set of specific linguistic examples and must infer some abstract linguistic knowledge that allows the child to generalize beyond the observed data, i.e., to both understand and generate new examples. Likewise, GI is a task where the goal is to learn or infer a grammar (or some device that can generate, recognize or describe strings) for a language and from all sorts of information about this language. GI consists, therefore, of finding the grammar or automaton for a language of which we are given an indirect presentation through strings, sequences, trees, terms or graphs (de la Higuera, 2010).

GI can, therefore, provide computational models for natural language acquisition. The use of formal or computational tools to give a description of the machinery necessary to acquire a language has been recognized as an important strategy within the field of language acquisition (Frank, 2011). In general, it is recognized that computational models can shed new light on language acquisition processes (Wintner, 2010). Even though, using computational tools for studying language is as old as the onset of Artificial Intelligence, over the last twenty-five years the progress in machine learning techniques has resulted in the emergence of a wider range of computational models that are much more powerful and robust than their predecessors (Alishahi, 2011).

Using computational tools, and therefore GI algorithms, for studying natural language acquisition offers many methodological advantages. Following Alishahi (2011) and Pearl (2010), we can highlight the following ones:

- *Explicit assumptions*. When implementing a computational model, every assumption of the input data and the learning mechanism has to be specified.

- *Controlled input*. Computational models offers the possibility to manipulate the language acquisition process and see the results of that manipulation. The researcher has full control over all the input data.

- *Observable behavior*. The impact of every factor in the input or the learning process can be directly studied in the output of the model. The performance of two different mechanisms on the same data set can be compared against each other.

- *Testable predictions*. Novel situations or combinations of data can be simulated and their effect on the model can be investigated.

Besides the enumerated advantages, one of the main benefits of computational models of language acquisition for determining relative linguistic complexity is the type of questions these formalisms could answer. According to Pearl (2010), language acquisition research is concerned with three different questions: *what* children know, *when* they know it, and *how* they learn it. While theoretical research deals with the knowledge that children acquire and experimental work provides information regarding the age at which the child acquires particular linguistic knowledge, computational modeling can explain how the child learns a language. Computational models, therefore, can be used to explain the *process* of natural language acquisition, because models are meant to be simulations of the child's acquisition mechanism.

Being tools for explaining the *process* of natural language acquisition, computational models in general, and GI algorithms in particular, are potential good tools to deal with developmental linguistic complexity.

4 Grammatical Inference Algorithms and Linguistic Complexity

Even though it would be possible to use different techniques from the field of machine learning to study linguistic complexity, we consider that GI models offer some advantages over other tools.

The first advantage is their motivation. As we have said, Gold (1967) introduced his model of identification in the limit with the ultimate goal of explaining the learning process of natural language:

> The study of language identification described here derives its motivation from artificial intelligence. The results and the methods used also have implications in computational linguistics, in particular the construction of discovery procedures, and in psycholinguistics, in particular the study of child learning (...). I wish to construct a precise model for the intuitive notion "able to speak a language" in order to be able to investigate theoretically how it can be achieved artificially (Gold, 1967).

Secondly, GI models have advantages over grammar induction tools, since whereas in grammar induction what really matters is the data and the relationship between the data and the induced grammar, in GI the actual learning process is what is central and is being examined and measured, not just the result of the process (de la Higuera, 2010).

Thirdly, an important advantage of GI tools is that they allow us to reproduce the learning context of first language acquisition. In fact, in any GI problem we have a teacher that provides data to a learner, and a learner (or learning algorithm) that from that data must identify the underlying language. This process has some similarities with the process of language acquisition where instead of a teacher and a learner, we have an adult and a child. In general, all the models in GI simulate learners who are developing monolingual L1 learning from monolingual data. However, modeling can be extended to other scenarios when the appropriate input data are available.

Importantly, GI models are grounded theoretically and empirically, as required in any computational model for language acquisition (Pearl, 2010). Theoretical grounding includes a description of the knowledge learners have and how it is represented. In GI models, the learner –this is, the machine– has no previously knowledge about the language. It has just the capacity –algorithm– to learn, but no linguistic structure previously storaged in order to facilitate the process. The machine represents, therefore, the child that has to acquire a language by just being exposed to this language. Empirical grounding includes using realistic data as input, measuring the model's learning behavior against children's learning behavior, and incorporating psychologically plausible algorithms into the model. In GI, the learner is exposed to language. The learner -like the child- can received positive and negative data as well as corrections. The model counts the needed number of interactions for the machine to achieve a good level of performance in a specific domain of the language. This could be seen as equivalent to calculate the child's cost/difficulty to acquire a language. There are different ways to present results, depending on what the model is testing. Useful measures are *recall*, *precision* and *F-score*.

By taking into account the above advantages, we claim that GI can provide a good tool for measuring linguistic complexity. We claim that models in this research area are potentially suitable for measuring the developmental complexity of languages, this is, the complexity understood in terms of cost and/or difficulty in language acquisition.

In what follows, we briefly outline the functioning of two novel models in the field of GI, in order to show their potential usefulness in the study of linguistic complexity.

4.1 Angluin and Becerra-Bonache's Model

Angluin and Becerra-Bonache (2010; 2011) introduced a novel model in GI inspired by studies on children's language acquisition. While the main part of studies in GI reduce the learning problem to the acquisition of the syntax, and omit any semantic information during the learning process, Angluin and Becerra-Bonache (2010; 2011) proposed a GI model that takes into account semantics during the language learning process.

In this model, the teacher and the learner interact in a sequence of situations by producing sentences that denote an object in each situation. These interactions are developed in the following way: First, a situation is randomly generated and it is presented to the teacher and the learner; then, the learner tries to produce a sentence that designs one of the objects in this situation; after that, the teacher produces a random sentence that designs one of the objects in this situation and, finally, the learner analyzes the teacher's sentence and updates its current grammar for the language as appropriate.

Given any situation, the learner's goal is to produce correct sentences that denote one object in this situation. Semantics is formalized by using first order logic. In the model, a *situation* is composed of some objects and some of their properties and relations and it is represented as a finite set of ground atoms over some constants and predicates symbols. A *meaning* is a finite sequence of variable atoms, this is an expression formed by applying a predicate symbol to the correct number of variables as arguments. It is assumed that each utterance in the target language is assigned a unique meaning. An *utterance* is a finite sequence of words over a finite alphabet W of words. An utterance is *denoting* in a situation, if it uniquely picks out the objects it refers to in a situation. The *linguistic competence* of the teacher is represented by a finite state transducer. This transducer is used by the teacher for comprehension and production of utterances. Initially, the teacher has the meaning transducer for the target language, but the learner has no language-specific knowledge (i.e., the learner has not access to this transducer and it does not have any information about the target language). Regarding the *learning task*, the goal of the learner is to learn a grammar for the language that will enable to produce all and only the denoting utterances for any given situation. Although the learner's representation is referred as a grammar, it does not take the form of a classical grammar from formal languages. The learner's grammar has three main components: 1) Weighted co-occurrence graph; 2) general forms; 3) decision trees. Detailed information about the model can be found in Angluin and Becerra-Bonache (2010).

To evaluate the model it was used a simplification of the Feldman's *Miniature Language Acquisition task* (Stolcke et al., 1994) that consists on learning a sublanguage from sentences-picture pairs that involve geometric figures. The model was tested with limited sublanguages of ten different natural languages: English, German, Greek, Hebrew, Hungarian, Mandarin, Russia, Spanish, Swedish, Turkish.

In the experiments, each situation had two objects and one binary relation between them (above/below, to the left to/to the right to). Every object had three attributes: *form, color* and *size*. The attribute of shape had six possible values (circle, square, triangle, star, ellipse, hexagon), that of color had six possible values (red, orange, yellow, green, blue, purple), and that of size three possible values (big, medium, small). Thus, there were 108 different objects and 23,328 different situations. The total number of possible meanings was 113,064.

Two different measures were used to evaluate the performance of the learner: *correctness* and *completeness*. The *correctness* is the sum of the probabilities of the learner's sentences that are in the set of sentences that denote correctly one object. The *completeness* is the fraction of sentences that denote correctly one object and appear in the set of learner sentences. A learner achieved a level p of performance if correctness and completeness were at least p (this is a more stringent measure of performance than the F-score). In the experiments, teacher and learner interacted until the learner achieves a level $p = 0.99$. Table 1 shows the number of interactions that were necessary to achieve this level of performance in all the languages taken into account. Each entry is the median of 10 trials. The learner was evaluated after receiving 100 sentences from the teacher.

The results distinguished two different groups: 1) Greek and Russian that need at least 3.400 interactions with the teacher; and 2) the rest of languages that need at most 1.000 interactions.

In essence, the model developed by Angluin and Becerra-Bonache (2010; 2011) calculates the number of interactions that are necessary to achieve a good level of performance in a given language by using a unique algorithm to learn any of the languages analyzed. The model shows that not all the languages need the same number of linguistic interactions to reach the same level of performance. Even though we can think that these differences may be due to computational reasons (i.e., the size of the target machines), it has been shown in Angluin and Becerra-Bonache (2016) that these differences are because of linguistic reasons. For example, Mandarin has an alphabet (i.e., number of words) of half of the size of that for Greek, while its transducer has similar size to the Greek one, but Mandarin required fewer interactions to reach a high level of performance. Hence, this example shows that the differences in the results obtained

Level	0.60	0.70	0.80	0.90	0.95	0.99
English	200	200	300	400	500	700
German	200	300	300	400	550	800
Greek	400	500	700	1500	2200	3400
Hebrew	200	300	400	500	650	900
Hungarian	200	300	350	450	550	750
Mandarin	200	200	300	400	500	700
Russian	450	500	850	1750	2350	3700
Spanish	200	300	350	500	600	1000
Swedish	200	300	300	400	600	1000
Turkish	200	200	300	400	550	800

Table 1: Number of interactions that the learner needs to reach different levels of performance. Extracted from Angluin and Becerra-Bonache (2010) .

are due to linguistic rather than computational reasons, providing some evidence of the different level of linguistic complexity of the analyzed natural languages.

Therefore, this GI model may be a potential adequate tool to measure the linguistic complexity in *relative* terms. In fact, the unique algorithm used in the model could be equivalent to the innate capacity that allows humans to acquire a language. Moreover, the learner –this is, the machine– has no previously knowledge about the language. The machine represents, therefore, the child that has to acquire a language by just being exposed to this language. To count the needed number of interactions for the machine to achieve a good level of performance in a specific domain of the language may be equivalent to calculate the child's cost/difficulty to acquire a language. Finally, to show that with the same algorithm not every language requires the same number of interactions may be interpreted (in terms of complexity) as an evidence to defend that the difficulty/cost to acquire different languages is not the same and, therefore, languages differ in relative complexity.

4.2 Models based on Inductive Logic Programming Techniques

Another interesting model in GI that may be adequate to calculate linguistic complexity is the one introduced in Becerra-Bonache et. al (2015) and improved in Becerra-Bonache et al. (2016).

Inspired by Angluin and Becerra-Bonache (2010; 2011), Becerra-Bonache et al. (2015) developed a new system based on Inductive Logic Programming techniques. This system learns from pairs consisting of a *sentence* and the *context* in which this sentence has been produced. A *sentence* is represented as a sequence of words (n-grams) and for the context they use a first-order logic based representation. In contrast to other approaches, a *context* is a description of what the learner can see in the world, and not a set of candidate meanings for that utterance; the system constructs all candidate meanings itself. The model assumes that sentences are relevant, i.e., they never refer to something outside the context. The meaning of an n-gram is defined as whatever is in common among all contexts where the n-gram can be used. The algorithm incrementally learns the meaning of specific n-grams by using Inductive Logic Programming techniques. Becerra-Bonache et al. (2015) experimentally demonstrate that the proposed model can explain the gradual learning of simple concepts and language structure. The system was also tested with a toy dataset based on the Feldman's task (it contains simple noun phrases that referred only to the color, shape, size and relative position of simple objects). Experiments with three different languages (English, Dutch and Spanish) showed that the system learns a language model that can easily be used to understand, generate and translate utterances.

An improvement of the model introduced in Becerra-Bonache et al. (2015) is presented in Becerra-Bonache et al. (2016). In this paper, a system that deals with more realistic contexts (provided in the form of images) and work in noisy environments is introduced. The system learns from pairs (S,I) where S is a sentence telling something about a part of an image I. After a basic preprocessing step, each image I is transformed into a scene Sc, by using a first-order logic based representation. Therefore, the input of the learner is a dataset made up of pairs (S,Sc) where S is a sentence related to a particular scene Sc. The input pairs have similar properties to those of the inputs received by children (Fazly et al., 2010): a) *alignment ambiguity*: it is not explicitly indicated in the input which words refer to which meaning; b) *referential uncertainty*: the description of a context may contain elements that are not in the corresponding sentence; c) *noise*: a sentence may refer to things that are not present in the context. The main improvements with respect to the work presented in Becerra-Bonache et al. (2015) are the following: 1) the system can better learn the meaning of words; 2) it can learn from noisy environments; 3) it can generate relevant sentences for a given scene, rather than just any sentence. Moreover, a series of experiments based on a more realistic dataset, called *Abstract Scenes Dataset* (Zitnick and Parikh, 2013), were conducted; this dataset contains clip-art pictures of children playing outdoors and sentences that describe these images. The goal of those experiments were to study the ability of the model to generate relevant sentences for a given scene and to learn the meaning of words.

We claim that those models may be used in the research on linguistic complexity. They are models that focused on the learning process. Moreover, they do not require any prior language-specific knowledge and learn incrementally. Therefore, they present features to, somehow, ensure that the model is actually about acquisition, rather than simply about what behavior a computational algorithm is capable of producing. They use realistic data and psychologically plausible algorithms that include features like gradual learning, robustness to noise in the data, and learning incrementally.

5 Conclusions

In this paper, we have proposed to use GI algorithms to measure the relative complexity of natural languages by considering the process of children first language acquisition. GI algorithms allow us to calculate the *cost* –in terms of the number of interactions– to reach a good level of performance in a given language. Therefore, GI offers the possibility to measure the *difficulty* of acquiring different natural languages.

The adequacy of GI models for calculating linguistic complexity is based on the fact that algorithms proposed in this area are computational models of language acquisition that use real data in the learning process. As any computational simulation, GI allows the researcher to perform some manipulations that could be not possible to carry out with children. Therefore, GI may provide data to calculate linguistic complexity that would be difficult to be obtained by observing the process of language acquisition through experimental research. Unlike psycholinguistic experiments with real children, GI models can avoid the problem of the influence of external (and non linguistic) factors that can conditioning the process of language acquisition. GI algorithms allow to reproduce the same context and features for the learning of any language. By analyzing the language acquisition process in different children in order to get data on linguistic complexity differences, we could not assure that every child have the same capacity, motivation, inputs, etc. If, on the contrary, we analyze the same speaker/child acquiring different languages, we could not assure that the acquisition of one language is not conditioned by the acquisition of the other language (even in bilingual acquisition processes). All these problems can be avoided by machine learning, since the computational simulation allows to reproduce exactly the same state/environment/requirements for the acquisition of any language.

As pointed out by Pearl (2010), the main disadvantage of modeling is that we can never be absolutely sure our model is really showing how acquisition works in children's minds. In fact, the reader could object that GI do not reproduce the process of natural language acquisition. We claim that, in order to defend the usefulness of GI models in the study of linguistic complexity, it not necessary to defend an identity between the processes of inferring a grammar and acquiring a natural language. We just say that an analogy can be established between those two processes. Moreover, in the case that not even the analogy is tenable, we still claiming that machine learning techniques can offer to linguistic complexity studies efficient computational resources that can measure complexity differences among languages adequately through objective and controlled means.

In the literature on linguistic complexity, it is common to read that there is no reason to believe that all languages are equally complex. However, no definite method has been proposed up to now to measure the relative complexity of languages. If measures and techniques from different disciplines have been used to calculate absolute complexity, why not to resort to machine learning to find useful tools for calculating developmental complexity.

We are working on the development of objective and meaningful methods, based on GI, to calculate linguistic complexity. GI models can be seen as an alternative to the methods that have been used so far. They present the following advantages: their *interdisciplinarity*, they combine ideas from linguistics with computational models; their *motivation*, they are based on how humans acquire language; their *results*, they provide quantifiable experimental results; and their ability to perform *cross-linguistic analysis*.

Acknowledgements

This research has been supported by the Ministerio de Economía y Competitividad under the project number FFI2015-69978-P (MINECO/FEDER) of the Programa Estatal de Fomento de la Investigación Científica y Técnica de Excelencia, Subprograma Estatal de Generación de Conocimiento.

References

S. Abney and M. Johnson. 1991. Memory requirements and local ambiguities of parsing strategies. *Journal of Psycholinguistic Research*, 20(3):233–250.

A. Alishahi. 2011. *Computational Modeling of Human Language Acquisition*. Morgan and Claypool Publishers, Toronto.

A. Andrason. 2014. Language complexity: An insight from complex-system theory. *International Journal of Language and Linguistics*, 2(2):74–89.

D. Angluin and L. Becerra-Bonache. 2010. A model of semantics and corrections in language learning. Technical report, Yale University.

D. Angluin and L. Becerra-Bonache. 2011. Effects of meaning-preserving corrections on language learning. In *Proceedings of the 15th International Conference on Computational Natural Language Learning, CoNLL 2011*, pages 97–105. Portland.

D. Angluin and L. Becerra-Bonache. 2016. A model of language learning with semantics and meaning preserving corrections. *Artificial Intelligence*, 242:23–51.

M. Bane. 2008. Quantifying and measuring morphological complexity. In Ch. Chang and H. Haynie, editors, *Proceedings of the 26th West Coast Conference on Formal Linguistics*, pages 69–76. Cascadilla Proceedings Project, Somerville.

L. Becerra-Bonache, H. Blockeel, M. Galván, and F. Jacquenet. 2015. A first-order-logic based model for grounded language learning. In *Advances in Intelligent Data Analysis XIV - 14th International Symposium, IDA 2015, Saint Etienne, France, October 22-24, 2015, Proceedings*, pages 49–60.

L. Becerra-Bonache, H. Blockeel, M. Galván, and F. Jacquenet. 2016. Relational grounded language learning. In *ECAI 2016 - 22nd European Conference on Artificial Intelligence, 29 August-2 September 2016, The Hague, The Netherlands*, pages 1764–1765.

P. Blache. 2011. A computational model for linguistic complexity. In G. Bel-Enguix, V. Dahl, and M.D. Jiménez-López, editors, *Biology, Computation and Linguistics. New Interdisciplinary Paradigms*, pages 155–167. IOS Press, Amsterdam.

D. Crystal. 1997. *The Cambridge Encyclopedia of Language*. Cambridge University Press, Cambridge.

O. Dahl. 2004. *The Growth and Maintenance of Linguistic Complexity*. John Benjamins, Amsterdam.

C. de la Higuera. 2010. *Grammatical Inference: Learning Automata and Grammars*. Cambridge University Press, Cambridge.

A. D'Ulizia, F. Ferri, and P. Grifoni. 2011. A survey of grammatical inference methods for natural language learning. *Artificial Intelligence Review*, 36(1):1–27.

B. Edmonds. 1999. *Syntactic Measures of Complexity*. Ph.D. thesis, University of Manchester.

A. Fazly, A. Alishahi, and S. Stevenson. 2010. A probabilistic computational model of cross-situational word learning. *Cognitive Science*, 34(6):1017–1064.

F. Ferreira. 1991. Effects of length and syntactic complexity on initiation times for prepared utterances. *Journal of Memory and Language*, 30(2):210–233.

M. C. Frank. 2011. Computational models of early language acquisition. unpublished manuscript.

E. Gibson. 1998. Linguistic complexity: Locality of syntactic dependencies. *Cognition*, 68(1):1–76.

E. Gibson. 2000. The dependency locality theory: A distance-based theory of linguistic complexity. In A. Marantz, Y. Miyashita, and W. O'Neil, editors, *Image, language, brain: Papers from the first mind articulation project symposium*, pages 95–126. MIT Press, New York.

E.M. Gold. 1967. Language identification in the limit. *Information and Control*, 10:447–474.

J. Hawkins. 2009. An efficiency theory of complexity and related phenomena. In G. Sampson, D. Gil, and P. Trudgill, editors, *Language Complexity as an Evolving Variable*, pages 252–268. Oxford University Press, Oxford.

P. Juola. 2009. Assessing linguistic complexity. In M. Miestamo, K. Sinnemäki, and F. Karlsson, editors, *Language Complexity: Typology, Contact, Change*, pages 89–108. John Benjamins, Amsterdam.

W. Kusters. 2003. *Linguistic Complexity: The Influence of Social Change on Verbal Inflection*. LOT, Utrecht.

J. McWhorter. 2001. The world's simplest grammars are creole grammars. *Linguistic Typology*, 6:125–166.

J. McWhorter. 2012. *Linguistic simplicity and complexity: Why do languages undress?* Mouton de Gruyter, Berlin.

M. Miestamo, K. Sinnemäki, and F. Karlsson. 2008. *Language Complexity: Typology, Contact, Change*. John Benjamins, Amsterdam.

M. Miestamo. 2006. On the feasibility of complexity metrics. In K. Krista and M.M Sepper, editors, *Finest Linguistics. Proceedings of the Annual Finish and Estonian Conference of Linguistics*, pages 11–26. Tallinna Ülikooli Kirjastus, Tallinn.

M. Miestamo. 2009a. Grammatical complexity in a cross-linguistic perspective. In M. Miestamo, K. Sinnemäki, and F. Karlsson, editors, *Language Complexity: Typology, Contact, Change*, pages 23–42. John Benjamins, Amsterdam.

M. Miestamo. 2009b. Implicational hierarchies and grammatical complexity. In G. Sampson, D. Gil, and P. Trudgill, editors, *Language Complexity as an Evolving Variable*, pages 80–97. Oxford University Press, Oxford.

M. Mitchell. 2009. *Complexity: A Guided Tour*. Oxford University Press, New York.

F.J. Newmeyer and L.B. Preston. 2014. *Measuring Grammatical Complexity*. Oxford University Press, Oxford.

E. Olivas, J.D.M. Guerrero, M.M. Sober, J.R.M. Benedito, and A.J.S. Lopez. 2009. *Handbook Of Research On Machine Learning Applications and Trends: Algorithms, Methods and Techniques - 2 Volumes*. Information Science Reference. IGI Publishing, Hershey, PA.

G. Pallotti. 2015. A simple view of linguistic complexity. *Second Language Research*, 31:117–134.

L. Pearl and S. Goldwater. 2016. Statistical learning, inductive bias, and Bayesian inference in language acquisition. In J. Lidz, W. Snyder, and J. Pater, editors, *Oxford Handbook of Developmental Linguistics*. Oxford University Press, Oxford.

L. Pearl. 2010. Using computational modeling in language acquisition research. In E. Blom and S. Unsworth, editors, *Experimental Methods in Language Acquisition Research*, pages 163–184. John Benjamins, Amsterdam.

G. Sampson, D. Gil, and P. Trudgill. 2009. *Language Complexity as an Evolving Variable*. Oxford University Press, Oxford.

W. Schuler. 2009. Positive results for parsing with a bounded stack using a model-based right-corner transform. In *Proceedings of Human Language Technologies: The 2009 Annual Conference of the North American Chapter of the Association for Computational Linguistics*, NAACL '09, pages 344–352, Stroudsburg, PA, USA. Association for Computational Linguistics.

K. Sinnemäki. 2011. *Language Universals and Linguistic Complexity. Three Case Studies in Core Argument Making*. Ph.D. thesis, University of Helsinki.

A. Stolcke, J.A. Feldman, G. Lakoff, and S. Weber. 1994. Miniature language acquisition: A touchstone for cognitive science. *Cognitive Science*, 8:686–693.

P. Trudgill. 1999. Language contact and the function of linguistic gender. *Poznan Studies in Contemporary Linguistics*, 35:133–152.

P. Trudgill. 2001a. Contact and simplification: historical baggage and directionality in linguistic change. *Linguistic Typology*, 5(2/3):371–374.

P. Trudgill. 2001b. Linguistic and social typology: The Austronesian migrations and phoneme inventories. *Linguistic Typology*, 8:305–320.

S. Wintner. 2010. Computational models of language acquisition. In A. Gelbukh, editor, *CICLing 2010*, volume LNCS 6008, pages 86–99. Springer, Berlin.

C.L. Zitnick and D. Parikh. 2013. ringing semantics into focus using visual abstraction. In *Proceedings of the International Conference on Computer Vision and Pattern Recognition*, pages 3009–3016. Portland.

Towards a Distributional Model of Semantic Complexity

Emmanuele Chersoni
Aix-Marseille University
emmanuelechersoni@gmail.com

Philippe Blache
Aix-Marseille University
philippe.blache@univ-amu.fr

Alessandro Lenci
University of Pisa
alessandro.lenci@unipi.it

Abstract

In this paper, we introduce for the first time a Distributional Model for computing semantic complexity, inspired by the general principles of the Memory, Unification and Control framework (Hagoort, 2013; Hagoort, 2016). We argue that sentence comprehension is an incremental process driven by the goal of constructing a coherent representation of the event represented by the sentence. The composition cost of a sentence depends on the *semantic coherence* of the event being constructed and on the *activation degree* of the linguistic constructions. We also report the results of a first evaluation of the model on the Bicknell dataset (Bicknell et al., 2010).

1 Introduction

The differences in semantic processing between *typical* and *atypical* sentences have recently attracted a lot of attention in experimental linguistics. Consider the following examples:

(1)   a.   *The musician plays the flute in the theater.*
      b.   *The gardener plays the castanets in the cave.*
      c.   * *The nominative plays the global map in the pot.*

Since the early work of Chomsky (1957) and the introduction of the notion of acceptability, linguistic theory has mostly focused on the contrast between (1c) and the former two. The last sentence violates the combinatorial constraints of the lexical items, and that is the reason why, although (1c) is syntactically well-formed, we are not able to build any coherent representation for the situation it expresses. Investigations on event-related potentials (ERP)[1] brought extensive evidence that sentences like (1a) and (1b), despite being both semantically acceptable, have a different cognitive status: sentences such as (1b), including possible but unexpected combinations of lexemes, evoke stronger N400 components[2] in the ERP waveform than sentences with non-novel combinations, like (1a)(Baggio and Hagoort, 2011).

Although there are different interpretations of the N400 effect,[3] there is general agreement among researchers that it is a brain signature of *semantic complexity*, that can be reinforced at the syntactic level (the *syntactic boost* effect; see (Hagoort, 2003)): novel and unexpected combinations are more complex and require larger cognitive efforts for processing. An open question is what are the factors determining the semantic complexity of sentence comprehension. Baggio et al. (2012) claim that the real issue about compositionality and open-ended productivity is the *balance between storage and computation*. Productivity entails that not everything can be stored. However, the N400 effect suggests that there is a large amount of stored knowledge in semantic memory about event contingencies and concept combinations.

[1] An event-related potential is an electrophysiological response of the brain to a stimulus.

[2] The N400 is a negative-going deflection that peaks around 400 milliseconds after presentation of the stimulus.

[3] See, for example, Kutas and Federmaier (2000) and Van Berkum et al. (2005) for the 'feature pre-activation hypothesis'; and Baggio et al. (2012) for an interpretation of the N400 amplitude as a consequence of the cost of semantic unification. In a connectionist framework, McClelland (1994) and, more recently, Rabovsky and McRae (2014) have advanced the hypothesis that N400 amplitudes correlate with implicit prediction error in the semantic memory.

Proceedings of the Workshop on Computational Linguistics for Linguistic Complexity,
pages 12–22, Osaka, Japan, December 11-17 2016.

This knowledge is triggered by words during processing and affects the expectations on the upcoming input. Consequently, combinations that are new with respect to the already-stored knowledge require more cognitive efforts to be unified in the semantic memory. Such effect has been shown at the discourse level by the *Dependency Locality Theory* (Gibson, 2000), proving that the introduction of new discourse referents is a complexity parameter.

Hagoort (2013; 2016) has proposed **Memory, Unification and Control** (MUC) as a general model for sentence comprehension that aims at accounting for such balance between storage and computation. The Memory component of the model refers to the linguistic knowledge that is stored in long-term memory. This includes *unification-ready structures* corresponding to **constructions** (Goldberg, 2006) represented by sets of **constraints** pertaining to the various levels of linguistic representation (phonology, syntax, and semantics) for that construction. Each constraint specifies how a given construction can combine with other constructions at a particular level of linguistic representation, as well as the result of such unification.[4] The Unification component refers to the assembly of pieces stored in memory into larger structures, with contributions from context. Unification is a constraint-based process, which attempts to solve the constraints defining the constructions. Unification operations take place in parallel at all the representation levels. Therefore, syntax is not the only combinatorial component (cf. also Jackendoff (2002)): constructions are combined into larger structures also at the semantic and phonological levels.

In this paper, we present a computational model of semantic complexity in sentence processing, which is strongly inspired by MUC. Our model integrates various insights from current research in distributional semantics and recent psycholinguistic findings, which highlight the key role of knowledge about event structure and participants stored in semantic memory and activated during language processing (McRae et al., 1998; McRae et al., 2005; McRae and Matsuki, 2009; Bicknell et al., 2010; Matsuki et al., 2011). Moreover, recent experiments in EEG showed that the activation of the so-called literal' word meanings is only carried out when necessary (Rommers et al., 2013). Following such findings, some recent theoretical proposals argued that words do not really have meaning, they are rather *cues* to meaning: sentence comprehenders use them to make inferences about the event or the situation that the speaker wants to convey (Elman, 2009; Elman, 2011; Kuperberg and Jaeger, 2015; Kuperberg, 2016). In particular, our model relies on the following assumptions:

- long-term semantic memory stores **Generalized Event Knowledge (GEK)**. GEK includes people's knowledge of typical participants and settings for events (McRae and Matsuki, 2009);

- at least a (substantial) part of GEK derives from our linguistic experience and can be modeled with distributional information extracted from large parsed corpora. In this paper, we only focus on this distributional subset of GEK, which we refer to as GEK_D;

- during sentence processing, lexical items (and constructions in general) activate portions of GEK_D, which are then unified to form a coherent representation of the event expressed by the sentence.

The aim of this research is to propose a novel distributional semantic framework to model online sentence comprehension. Our two-fold goal is i.) to build an incremental distributional representation of a sentence, and ii.) to associate a **compositional cost** to such a representation to model the complexity of semantic processing. In particular, we argue that semantic complexity depends on two factors: a.) the availability and salience of "ready-to-use" event information already stored in GEK_D and cued by lexical items, and b.) the cost of unifying activated GEK_D into a coherent semantic representation, with the latter depending on the mutual semantic congruence of the events participants. We thus predict that sentences containing highly familiar lexical combinations like (1a) (*musician* is in fact a familiar subject of *play*) are easier to process than sentences expressing novel ones like (1b). Moreover, the complexity of novel combinations depends on how easily they fit with stored event knowledge.

---

[4]From a neurolinguistic perspective, Pulvermuller et al. (2013) recently proposed a model encoding such set of constraints at the brain level. The activation of a construction is carried out by means of *discrete combinatorial neuronal assemblies* (DCNAs), which encode the combinatorial links between the different objects of the construction itself.

In the following sections, we will present a global distributional semantic complexity score combining event activation and unification costs. As a first evaluation of our framework, we will use the semantic complexity score in a difficulty estimation task on the Bicknell dataset (Bicknell et al., 2010).

2   Related work

Some of the previous works applying Distributional Semantic Models (henceforth DSMs) to sentence processing focused on the problem of computing a *semantic surprisal* index for the words of the sentence, on the basis of what Hale (2001) has proposed for syntax, and defined as the negative logarithm of the probability of a word given its previous linguistic context. The higher the surprisal of a word, the lower its predictability, and high surprisal values have been shown to correlate with an increase in processing difficulty (Frank et al., 2013; Smith and Levy, 2013). Mitchell et al. (2010) proposed a model to compute surprisal, based on the product of a trigram language model and of a semantic component, based in turn on the weighted dot product of the semantic vector of a target word and of a history vector, representing its prior context. The authors interpolated their model with the output of an incremental parser and they evaluated it on the task of predicting word reading times in a test set extracted from the Dundee Corpus (Kennedy et al., 2003). Their results showed that the semantic component improves the predictions, compared to models based only on syntactic information.

Building on the work of Mitchell et al. (2010) and Mitchell (2011), Sayeed et al. (2015) tested a similar model on a multimodal language corpus (the AMI Meeting corpus; see Carletta (2007)), being able to predict spoken word pronunciation duration.

A totally different perspective was adopted by Lenci (2011): starting from the method for thematic fit estimations that was introduced in Baroni and Lenci (2010), the author presented a compositional distributional model for reproducing the expectation update on the filler of the patient slot of a verb, depending on how the agent slot had been saturated (for example, if the agent of the verb *to check* is *journalist*, likely patients will be things that journalists typically check, such as *source, spelling* etc.). Lenci tried to model explicitly the process through which we modify our predictions on upcoming linguistic input on the basis of our event knowledge: the saturation of an argument slot imposes new semantic constraints on the other positions yet to be filled, with the consequence that entities typically co-occurring with the agent become more plausible for the situation described by the sentence.

Coming to related works in experimental psychology, Pynte et al. (2008; 2009) measured vector proximity between the content words of an eye-tracking corpus by means of Latent Semantic Analysis (Landauer et al., 1998) to show how inspection times of a target word are affected by its semantic relatedness with the adjacent words in the same sentence.

In a more recent contribution, Johns and Jones (2015) presented a DSM that assumes the storage and retrieval of linguistic experiences as the fundamental operations of sentence processing, following a long tradition of exemplar theories of memory starting with Hintzman (1986; 1988). Each sentence in their model is encoded as a vector obtained by summing its word random vectors with permutations to account for the word position in the sentence (see Sahlgren et al. (2008)). Vectors that are similar to the one of the currently processed sentence (the so-called *memory traces*) are activated and then are summed into an *expectation vector*. Finally, the expectation vector is used to make predictions about forthcoming words and to construct sentence meaning.

3   An incremental model of sentence comprehension

We model the comprehension of a sentence as an incremental process driven by the goal of constructing a coherent representation of the event the speaker intends to communicate with the sentence. We assume there is a data structure called **situation model** (SM) (Zwaan and Radvansky, 1998) that is incrementally updated in working memory during language comprehension. Given a sentence s being processed,[5] SM contains a representation of the event e_s described by s, which is compositionally built from GEK_D retrieved from long-term memory, and activated by the words in s. Similarly to MUC, our model is

---

[5]Although in this paper we focus on sentence processing, our model can equally apply at the sub-sentential level, such as phrases or chunks, as well as at the discourse level.

formed by a **memory component** containing lexical information, and a **unification component** dealing with the compositional construction of the sentence semantic representation.

4   The memory component: the representation of lexical knowledge

We assume the lexicon to be a repository of constructions (the latter including words along with more complex structures) stored in long-term memory. Each construction Cxn is defined by a form and a content. The latter consists of a set of pairs $\langle e_1, \sigma_1 \rangle, \ldots, \langle e_n, \sigma_n \rangle$, such that e_i is an event stored in GEK_D and σ_i is an **activation score**, expressing the salience of the event with respect to a construction and the strength with which the event is activated (cued) by the construction. At the moment, we assume that the activation score of the event e activated by Cxn is the conditional probability of the event given the construction, $P(e|Cxn)$.

We represent events in GEK with feature structures specifying their participants and roles, much like frames in Frame Semantics. More specifically, we represent the events in GEK_D, the distributional subset of GEK,[6] as feature structures containing information directly extracted from parsed sentences in corpora: attributes are **syntactic dependencies** (e.g. NSUBJ, NMOD-IN, etc.),[7] and values are **distributional vectors** of dependent lexemes.[8] The latter can be conceived as "out-of-context" distributional vector encoding of lexical items. Any type of distributional representation can be used to this purpose (e.g., explicit vectors, low-dimensionality dense embeddings, etc.). The following is a representation of an event $e \in GEK$, extracted from the sentence *The student reads the book.*:

(2) $[_{EVENT}$ NSUBJ:$\overrightarrow{student}$ HEAD:$\overrightarrow{read}$ DOBJ:$\overrightarrow{book}]$

Unlike previous syntax-based DSMs, we extract from corpora **syntactic joint contexts**, besides single dependencies (Chersoni et al., 2016). A syntactic joint context includes the whole set of dependencies of a given lexical head, which we assume as a surface representation of an event. Each event in GEK may be cued by several lexical items, as part of their semantic content, albeit with different strength depending on their statistical distribution. For instance, the event in (2) is cued by the noun *student*, the verb *read*, and the noun *book*.

We assume GEK to be hierarchically structured, according to various levels of event schematicity. In fact, all events in GEK can be *underspecified*. Without any need to add in GEK any specific structure, underspecification makes it possible to virtually generate **schematic events**, obtained by abstracting over one or more of its valued-attributes:

(3)   a. $[_{EVENT}$ NSUBJ:$\overrightarrow{student}$ HEAD:$\overrightarrow{read}]$
        b. $[_{EVENT}$ NSUBJ:$\overrightarrow{student}$ DOBJ:$\overrightarrow{book}]$

The feature structure in (3a) is a representation of a schematic event of a student reading, without any specification of the object, while (3b) represents an undespecified event involving a student acting on a book, which could be instantiated by specific events of reading, writing, buying, etc.

5   The unification component: constructing event representations

We assume that sentence comprehension always occurs within an existing SM and results into an update of this SM. The current SM acts as a constraint on the interpretation of the upcoming constructions, and it gets updated after the interpretation of every new construction. Sentence comprehension consists in recovering (reconstructing) the event e that the sentence is most likely to describe. The event e is the event that best satisfies all the **constraints** set by the constructions in the sentence and in the active SM. Let $w_1, w_2, \ldots, w_n$ be an input linguistic sequence (e.g., a sentence or a discourse) we have to interpret.

---

[6] In this paper we assume that $GEK = GEK_D$. Therefore, we henceforth omit the subscript for simplicity.

[7] We represent syntactic dependencies according to the Universal Dependencies annotation scheme (http://universaldependencies.org/).

[8] At this stage, we stay at the syntactic level, without entering into the mapping problem between syntactic and semantic arguments as described in (Dowty, 1991). All arguments in the event description correspond to syntactic roles, having in mind they could be used as a very rough approximation of semantic roles.

Let SM_i be the semantic representation built for the linguistic input until $w_1, \ldots, w_i$, and let e_i be the event representation in SM_i. When we process w_{i+1}:

i.) the GEK associated with w_{i+1} in the lexicon, $GEK_{w_{i+1}}$, is recovered;

ii.) $GEK_{w_{i+1}}$ is **integrated** with SM_i to produce SM_{i+1}, containing the new event e_{i+1}.

We model semantic composition as an **event construction and update function** F, whose aim is to build a coherent *SM* by integrating the GEK cued by the linguistic elements that are being composed:

$$F(SM_i, GEK_{w_{n+1}}) = SM_{i+1} \tag{1}$$

The composition function is responsible for two distinct processes:

1. F **unifies** two event feature structures into a new event. Given an event $e_i \in SM_i$ and $e_j \in GEK_{w_{n+1}}$, F produces a new event $e_k \in SM_{i+1}$:

$$F(e_i, e_j) = e_k = e_i \sqcup e_j \tag{2}$$

The unification function produces an output event if the attribute-values features of the input events are **compatible**, otherwise it fails. The following is an example of successful unification:

(4) $\quad [_{EVENT}\ \text{NSUBJ}{:}\overrightarrow{student}\ \text{DOBJ}{:}\overrightarrow{thesis}] \sqcup [_{EVENT}\ \text{NSUBJ}{:}\overrightarrow{student}\ \text{HEAD}{:}\overrightarrow{read}] = [_{EVENT}$
$\text{NSUBJ}{:}\overrightarrow{student}\ \text{HEAD}{:}\overrightarrow{read}\ \text{DOBJ}{:}\overrightarrow{thesis}]$

In this example, the event of a student acting on a thesis and the event of a student reading are unified into a new event of a student reading a thesis.

2. F **weights** the unified event e_k with a pair of scores $\langle \theta, \sigma \rangle$:

- θ is a score measuring the degree of **semantic coherence** of the unified event e_k. We assume that the semantic coherence (or internal unity) of an event depends on the **mutual typicality** of its components. Consider for instance the following sentences:

    (5)   a.   The student reads a book.
            b.   The surfer reads a papyrus.

    The event represented in (5a) has a high degree of internal coherence because all its components are mutually very typical: *student* is a typical subject for the verb *read* and *book* has a strong typicality both as an object of *read* and as an object related to *student*. Conversely, the components in the event expressed by (5b) have a low level of mutual typicality, thereby resulting into an event with much lower internal coherence. We model this idea of mutual typicality by extending the notion of **thematic fit**, which is normally used to measure the congruence of a predicate with an argument. In our case, instead, thematic fit is a general measure of the semantic typicality or congruence among the components of an event. In turn, we measure the thematic fit with vector cosine in the following way:

    Given $s_i{:}a$ and $s_j{:}b$, such as s_i and s_j are two event attributes (e.g., NSUBJ, HEAD, etc.), the thematic fit of $s_i{:}a$ with respect to $s_j{:}b$, $\theta(s_i{:}a, s_j{:}b)$, is the cosine between the vector of a and the prototype vector built out of the k most salient values $c_1, \ldots, c_k$, such that $s_i{:}c_z$, for $1 \leq z \leq k$, co-occurs with $s_j{:}b$ in the same event structures.

    For instance, the thematic fit of *student* as a subject of *read* is given by the cosine between the vector of *student* and the prototype vector built out of the k most salient subjects of *read*. Similarly, we also measure the typicality of *book* as an object related to *student* (i.e., the object of events involving student as subject) as the cosine between the vector of *book* and the prototype vector built out of the k most salient objects related to *student*. Then we define the score θ of an event e as follows:

$$\theta_e = \prod_{a,b \in e} \theta(s_i{:}a, s_j{:}b) \tag{3}$$

Therefore, the semantic coherence of an event is given by the product of the mutual thematic fit between its components. The higher is the mutual typicality between the elements of an event, the higher is its internal semantic coherence.

- σ weights the **salience** of the unified event e_k by combining the weights of e_i and e_j into a new weight assigned to e_k. In this paper, we combine the σ weights with the logistic function:

$$F(\sigma_i, \sigma_j) = \sigma_k = \frac{1}{1 + e^{-(\sigma_i + \sigma_j)}} \tag{4}$$

The score σ of the unified event thus measures the strength with which it is activated (cued) by the composed linguistic expressions. This entails that events that are cued by more linguistic constructions in a sentence should incrementally increase their salience.

To sum up, we conceive composition as event unification. Unified events are weighted along two dimensions: internal semantic coherence (θ), and degree of activation by linguistic expressions (σ). These two dimensions also determine the **composition cost** of the unification process. We argue that the semantic complexity of a sentence s is inversely related to the sum of θ and σ:

$$SemComp_s = \frac{1}{\theta_s + \sigma_s} \tag{5}$$

The less internally coherent is the event represented by the sentence and the less strong is its activation by the lexical items, the more the unification is cognitively expensive and the sentence semantically complex. This is consistent with the MUC model of sentence comprehension: the harder is to build an integrated semantic representation through unification, the harder the processing effort, as reflected by a larger N400 amplitude.

6 Evaluation

As a first test for our framework, we measure the semantic complexity of the sentences in the Bicknell dataset (Bicknell et al., 2010). The Bicknell dataset was prepared to verify the hypothesis that the typicality of a verb direct object depends on the subject argument. For this purpose, the authors selected 50 verbs, each paired with two agent nouns that altered the scenario evoked by the subject-verb combination. Plausible patients for each agent-verb pair were obtained by means of production norms, in order to generate triples where the patient was *congruent* with the agent and with the verb. For each congruent triple, they also generated an *incongruent* triple, by combining each verb-congruent patient pair with the other agent noun, in order to have items describing atypical situations.

The final dataset included 100 pairs subject-verb-object triples, that were used to build the sentences for a self-paced reading and for an ERP experiment.[9] To give an example, experimental subjects were presented with sentence pairs such as:

(6)   a.   The journalist checked the spelling of his latest report. (*congruent condition*)

         b.   The mechanic checked the spelling of his latest report. (*incongruent condition*)

The sentences of each pair contain the same verb and the same object, differing for the subject. Given the subject, the object is a preferred argument of the verb in the congruent condition, whereas it is an implausible filler in the incongruent condition. Bicknell et al. (2010) reported that the congruent condition produced shorter reading times and smaller N400 signatures. Their conclusion was that verb argument expectations are dynamically updated during sentence processing, by integrating some kind of general

---

[9] Actually, Bicknell et al. (2010) used only a subset of 64 pairs, after removing the items that were potentially problematic for their experiments. In the present study, we use the original dataset.

knowledge about events and their typical participants. Lenci (2011) evaluated his model on the ability to assign a higher thematic fit score to the congruent triples than to the incongruent ones. We interpret Bicknell's experimental data as suggesting that congruent sentences are less semantically complex than incongruent sentences. Consistently, we predict that our model will assign a higher semantic complexity score to incongruent sentences than to congruent ones.

6.1 Modeling the GEK

Following the procedure described in Chersoni et al. (2016), we extracted from parsed corpora the syntactic joint contexts for all the words of the Bicknell triples. For our extraction, we used a concatenation of four different corpora: the British National Corpus (BNC; Leech (1992)); the Reuters Corpus vol.1 (RCV1; Lewis et al. (2004)); the ukWaC and the Wackypedia Corpus (Baroni et al., 2009).

For each sentence, we generated a joint context by extracting the verb and its direct dependencies. Our dependency relations of interest are subject (NSUBJ), direct object (DOBJ), indirect object (IOBJ) and a generic prepositional complement relation (PREPCOMP), on which we mapped the complements introduced by a preposition. We discarded all the modifiers and we just keep the nominal heads. Here is an example of extracted syntactic joint context: *athlete-n-nsubj___win-v-head___medal-n-dobj___at-p+olympics-n-prepcomp*. For each joint context, we also generated all its dependency subsets to obtain the underspecified schematic events. In total, we have extracted 4,204,940 syntactic joint contexts (including schematic events).

The collection of syntactic joint contexts were used to define the feature structures of the events in GEK, and cued by the target words of the Bicknell dataset. As described in section 4, each verb and noun occurring in these event structures was represented with a distributional vector in a syntax-based DSM using as contexts the dependencies extracted from the above corpora (e.g., `enemy-n:obj`).[10]

6.2 Computing the semantic complexity scores for the test sentences

The sentences in the original Bicknell dataset were first turned into S(subject)-V(erb)-O(bject) triples (e.g. NSUBJ:*journalist* HEAD:*check* DOBJ:*spelling*). For each test sentence s we computed σ_s and θ_s in the following way:

σ_s We take the activation strength of the joint context formed by the test triple given S (i.e., σ_S), V (i.e., σ_V) and O (i.e., σ_O). For instance, σ_S is the activation strength of the joint context NSUBJ:*journalist* HEAD:*check* DOBJ:*spelling*, given *journalist*. Then σ_s is obtained by applying equation (4) to the sum of σ_S, σ_V and σ_O.

θ_s This score represents the semantic coherence of the event represented by s and is obtained by measuring the mutual typicality of its components. Following equation (3), we compute θ_s as the product of the thematic fit of S given V, $\theta_{S,V}$, O given V, $\theta_{O,V}$, and the thematic fit of O given S, $\theta_{O,S}$. In particular, $\theta_{S,V}$ is the cosine between the vector of S and the centroid vector built out of the k most salient subjects of V (e.g., the cosine between the vector of *journalist* and the centroid vector of the most salient subjects of *check*), $\theta_{O,V}$ is the cosine between the vector of O and the centroid vector built out of the k most salient direct objects of V (e.g., the cosine between the vector of *spelling* and the centroid vector of the most salient objects of *check*), and $\theta_{O,S}$ is the cosine between the vector of O and the centroid vector built out of the k most salient direct objects occurring in events whose subject is S (e.g., the cosine between the vector of *spelling* and the prototype vector of the most salient objects of events whose subject is *journalist*). Following Baroni and Lenci (2010), we measured argument salience with LMI (Evert, 2005) and we fixed $k = 20$.

The final semantic complexity score $SemComp_s$ is the inverse of the sum of the σ and θ scores (see equation (5)). Notice that if the event corresponding to the sentence is not stored in GEK, its activation score is 0, and therefore the σ_s component will be null. In this case, the only relevant factor for semantic complexity is the event coherence measured by θ_s. This is consistent with the model we presented in

---

[10]We also use inverse dependencies (see Baroni and Lenci (2010)) in order to represent the relation of a target noun with its verb head: for example, given the sentence *The dog runs.*, the context of the target *dog-n* for this sentence will be *run-v:sbj-1*.

section 1 and based on the assumption that sentence processing is the result of a balance between retrieval of stored information and the building of new events through unification. If s describes a familiar event already stored in long-term memory as modelled with GEK, the complexity of s depends on how strong such event is cued by the lexical items in s and by the mutual typicality of its components. On the other hand, if the sentence describes a new event, its complexity only depends on the internal coherence of the event produced through unification.

7 Results and conclusions

For 16 pairs of triples of the Bicknell dataset we were not able to compute thematic fit scores, so we had to discard them.[11] Therefore, we are left with 84 pairs of triples (168 triples in total): in each triple, the patient is either typical (congruent) or atypical (incongruent) with respect to the agent.

First of all, the SemComp scores assigned to sentences in the congruent condition are significantly lower than the scores assigned to sentences in the incongruent conditions, according to the Wilcoxon test (W = 4791, p-value < 0.001). Our semantic complexity score is therefore able to model the higher processing difficulty of the incongruent sentences, as shown in the EEG experiments by Bicknell et al. (2010). We also evaluated the model accuracy, as the percentage of congruent sentences to which the model assigns a semantic complexity lower than score assigned to the incongruent sentence in the same pair. The model performance is compared with the random accuracy baseline, as in Lenci (2011).

Model	Hits	Accuracy	Significance
$\sigma_s + \theta_s$	62	73.8%	$p < .05$
θ_s	59	70.2%	$p < .05$
Baseline	42	50%	

Table 1: Number of hits and accuracy with or without σ scores. p-values computed with the χ^2 test.

Since the σ component is an element of novelty with respect to thematic fit-only models, we decided to test the algorithm also without it, that is to say to assign the complexity score only on the basis of the event semantic coherence. Although the difference is not huge, it is noteworthy that the σ component improves the accuracy score, supporting our hypothesis that semantic complexity depends both on retrieval and on unification costs.

Our model achieves exactly the same accuracy as the Expectation Composition and Update Model (ECU) in Lenci (2011) when evaluated on the same 84 triples (73.8%). However, it should be pointed out that ECU was tailored on the structure the Distributional Memory tensor (Baroni and Lenci, 2010) and on the Bicknell dataset. Indeed, the ranking function for the typical fillers of a slot depends on the availability in the tensor of syntactic relations (in this case, the OBJ and the VERB relation) that can be used as simultaneous constraints on a candidate. In other words, given a patient p, an agent AG and verb v, p has to have a high association score both in the triple $\{p, \text{OBJ}, v\}$ and in the triple $\{AG, \text{VERB}, p\}$. These relations work well for representing constraints on the agent and on the patient slot, but it is not clear how ECU could estimate expectations on other slots, say the instrument and/or the location one. Moreover, it does not take into account the Memory component.

Our results are obtained with a much more general model of semantic complexity that can be applied to any type of syntactic structure (the set of syntactic relations that we consider in the extraction of the joint contexts is a parameter) and is based on a less *ad hoc* and more sophisticated distributional representation of GEK. Concerning the σ component, we should also mention that a joint context for the full event was retrieved for only 22 of the 168 triples. As expected, an implementation of the memory component based only on textual corpora suffer from data sparsity, and the future developments of this model will have to take this factor into account. The introduction of a robust generalization component, which could generate new joint contexts by making inferences on new potential event participants, could help to mitigate such problem.

---

[11] We discarded from the syntax-based DSM words with a frequency below 100 in the training corpus. Consequently, for some triples one or more words did not have any vector representation in the DSM, so that we could not compute the thematic fit scores that are required by our model.

The semantic complexity model we have proposed in this paper is strongly inspired by the general cognitive principles of the MUC architecture. In particular, we rely on two components to assign semantic complexity scores: i) a memory component, consisting of a distributional subset of GEK, such that the more an event is strongly activated by linguistic cues, the easier will be its retrieval from the semantic memory; ii) a unification component, consisting of a composition and update function which unifies the GEK activated by linguistic cues into new structures. The more the unified components are mutually typical, the more semantically coherent will be the event. Our assumption is that linguistic constructions that are strongly activated by the previous context and with high values of semantic coherence are easier to process. In the future, we plan to extend our experimentations to a wider range of psycholinguistic datasets, in order to see how the model can deal with a larger number of complexity sources and linguistic structures.

Hopefully, future extensions of this model will also present a more global notion of complexity and will integrate information coming from different linguistic domains. It would be interesting, for example, to combine the predictions of our model of semantic complexity with constraint-based frameworks for the estimation of syntactic difficulty, such as Blache's Property Grammars (Blache, 2011; Blache, 2013), and to see how they correlate with experimental data.

There are many other aspects in language processing that, at the moment, our model leaves aside. Future extensions, in our view, should also account for the role played by attention,[12] since several linguistic devices (prosodic cues, non-canonical syntactic structures etc.) can be used to signal informationally relevant parts of the message to the listeners/readers, helping them in the allocation of processing resources and thus influencing complexity (Hagoort, 2016). At the best of our knowledge, such issues have still to be convincingly addressed by current models.

8 Acknowledgements

This work has been carried out thanks to the support of the A*MIDEX grant (n ANR-11-IDEX-0001-02) funded by the French Government "Investissements d'Avenir" program.

References

Giosuè Baggio and Peter Hagoort. 2011. The balance between memory and unification in semantics: A dynamic account of the N400. *Language and Cognitive Processes*, volume 26(9): 1338-1367.

Giosuè Baggio, Michiel van Lambalgen, and Peter Hagoort. 2012. The processing consequences of compositionality. *The Oxford Handbook of Compositionality*, Oxford University Press, Oxford, 1-23.

Marco Baroni, Silvia Bernardini, Adriano Ferraresi, and Eros Zanchetta. 2009. The WaCky wide web: a collection of very large linguistically processed web-crawled corpora. *Language Resources and Evaluation*, volume 43(3): 209-226.

Marco Baroni and Alessandro Lenci. 2010. Distributional memory: A general framework for corpus-based semantics. *Computational Linguistics*, volume 36(4): 673-721.

Klinton Bicknell, Jeffrey L Elman, Mary Hare, Ken McRae and Marta Kutas. 2010. Effects of event knowledge in processing verbal arguments. *Journal of Memory and Language*, volume 63(4): 489-505.

Philippe Blache. 2011. Evaluating Language Complexity in context: new parameters for a constraint-based model. *Proceedings of CSLP-2011*.

Philippe Blache. 2013. Chunks et activation: un modèle de facilitation du traitement linguistique. *Proceedings of TALN-2013*.

Jean Carletta. 2007. Unleashing the killer corpus: experiences in creating the multi-everything AMI Meeting Corpus. *Language Resources and Evaluation*, volume 41(2): 181-190.

---

[12]We thank one of our anonymous reviewers for pointing this out. On a related topic, we would like to refer the readers to Zarcone et al. (2016) for a systematic overview on the use of the notions of salience and attention in surprisal-based models of language processing.

Emmanuele Chersoni, Enrico Santus, Alessandro Lenci, Philippe Blache, and Chu-Ren Huang. 2016. Representing verbs with rich contexts: an evaluation on verb similarity. *Proceedings of EMNLP*.

Noam Chomsky. 1957. Syntactic Structures. Mouton & Co.

David Dowty. 1991. Thematic proto-roles and argument selection. Language, 67(3):547-619.

Jeffrey L Elman. 2009. On the meaning of words and dinosaur bones: Lexical knowledge without a lexicon. *Cognitive Science*, volume 33(4): 547-582.

Jeffrey L Elman. 2011. Lexical knowledge without a lexicon? *The Mental Lexicon*, volume 6(1): 1-34.

Jeffrey L Elman. 2014. Systematicity in the lexicon: on having your cake and eating it too. *The Architecture of Cognition: Rethinking Fodor and Pylyshyn's Systematicity Challenge*, edited by Paco Calvo and John Symons, The MIT Press, Cambridge, MA.

Stefan Evert. 2005. The statistics of word cooccurrences: word pairs and collocations.

Stefan L Frank, Leun J Otten, Giulia Galli, and Gabriella Vigliocco. 2013. Word surprisal predicts N400 amplitude during reading. *Proceedings of ACL*: 878-883.

Ted Gibson. 2000. The Dependency Locality Theory: a Distance-Dased Theory of Linguistic Complexity. *Image, Language, Brain*, edited by Alec Marantz, Yasushi Miyashita and Wayne O'Neil, MIT Press.

Adele E Goldberg. 2006. *Constructions at Work: The Nature of Generalization in Language*, Oxford, Oxford University Press.

Peter Hagoort. 2003. Interplay between syntax and semantics during sentence comprehension: ERP effects of combining syntactic and semantic violations. *Journal of Cognitive Neuroscience*, volume 15(6).

Peter Hagoort. 2013. MUC (memory, unification, control) and beyond *Frontiers in Psychology*, volume 4: 1-13.

Peter Hagoort. 2016. MUC (Memory, Unification, Control): A Model on the Neurobiology of Language Beyond Single Word Processing In G. Hickok and S. Small (eds.), *Neurobiology of Language*, Amsterdam, Elsevier: 339-347.

John Hale. 2001. A probabilistic Earley parser as a psycholinguistic model. *Proceedings of NAACL-HLT*: 1-8.

Douglas L Hintzman. 1986. 'Schema abstraction' in a multiple-trace memory model. *Psychological Review*, volume 93(4): 411-428.

Douglas L Hintzman. 1988. Judgements of frequency and recognition memory in a multiple-trace memory model. *Psychological Review*, volume 95(4): 528-551.

Ray Jackendoff. 2002. Foundations of Language: Brain, Meaning, Grammar, Evolution. Cambridge, Cambridge University Press.

Alan Kennedy, Robin Hill, and Joel Pynte. 2003. The Dundee Corpus. *Proceedings of the 12th European Conference on Eye Movement*.

Gina R Kuperberg and Florian T Jaeger. 2015. What do we mean by prediction in language comprehension? *Language, Cognition and Neuroscience*, volume 31(1): 32-59.

Gina R Kuperberg. 2016. Separate streams or probabilistic inference? What the N400 can tell us about the comprehension of events. *Language, Cognition and Neuroscience*, volume 31(5): 602-616.

Marta Kutas and Kara D Federmaier. 2000. Electrophysiology reveals semantic memory use in language comprehension. *Trends in Cognitive Sciences*, volume 4(12): 463-470.

Brendan T Johns and Michael Jones. 2015. Generating structure from experience: a retrieval-based model of language processing. *Canadian Journal of Experimental Psychology*, volume 69(2).

Thomas K Landauer, Peter W Foltz, and Darrell Laham. 1998. An introduction to latent semantic analysis. *Discourse processes*, volume 25(2-3): 259-284.

Geoffrey Leech. 1992. 100 million words of English: the British National Corpus (BNC). *Language research*, volume 28(1): 1-13.

Alessandro Lenci. 2011. Composing and updating verb argument expectations: a distributional semantic model. *Proceedings of the 2nd Workshop on Cognitive Modeling and Computational Linguistics*: 58-66.

David D Lewis, Yiming Yang, Tony G Rose, and Fan Li. 2004. Rcv 1: A new benchmark collection for text categorization research. *The journal of Machine Learning research*, volume 5: 361-397.

Kazunaga Matsuki, Tracy Chow, Mary Hare, Jeffrey L Elman, Christoph Scheepers, and Ken McRae. 2011. Event-based plausibility immediately influences on-line language comprehension. *Journal of Experimental Psychology: Learning, Memory, and Cognition*, volume 37(4): 913-934.

James L McClelland. 1994. The interaction of nature and nurture in development: A parallel distributed processing perspective. *International perspectives on psychological science*, volume 1: 57-88.

Ken McRae, Michael J Spivey-Knowlton and Michael K Tanenhaus. 1998. Modeling the influence of thematic fit (and other constraints) in on-line sentence comprehension. *Journal of Memory and Language*, volume 38(3): 283-312.

Ken McRae, Mary Hare, Jeffrey L Elman, and Todd Ferretti. 2005. A basis for generating expectancies for verbs from nouns. *Memory and Cognition*, volume 33(7): 1174-1184.

Ken McRae and Kazunaga Matsuki. 2009. People use their knowledge of common events to understand language, and do so as quickly as possible. *Language and linguistics compass*, volume 3(6): 1417-1429.

Laura A Michaelis. 2013. Sign-Based Construction Grammar. *The Oxford Handbook of Construction Grammar*, edited by Thomas Hoffmann and Graeme Trousdale, Oxford University Press, Oxford: 133-152.

Jeff Mitchell, Mirella Lapata, Vera Demberg and Frank Keller. 2010. Syntactic and semantic factors in processing difficulty: An integrated measure. *Proceedings of ACL*: 196-206.

Jeff Mitchell. 2011. Composition in distributional models of semantics. PhD Thesis, The University of Edinburgh.

Friedemann Pulvermuller, Bert Cappelle and Yury Shtyrov. 2013. Brain basis of meaning, words, constructions, and grammar. *The Oxford Handbook of Construction Grammar*, edited by Thomas Hoffmann and Graeme Trousdale, Oxford University Press.

Joel Pynte, Boris New, and Alan Kennedy. 2008. On-line contextual influences during reading normal text: A multiple-regression analysis. *Vision research*, volume 48(21): 2172-2183.

Joel Pynte, Boris New, and Alan Kennedy. 2009. On-line contextual influences during reading normal text: The role of nouns, verbs and adjectives. *Vision research*, volume 49(5): 544-552.

Milena Rabovsky and Ken McRae. 2014. Simulating the N400 ERP component as semantic network error: insights from a feature-based connectionist attractor model of word meaning. *Cognition*, volume 132(1): 68-89.

Joost Rommers, Ton Dijkstra and Marcel Bastiaansen. 2013 Context-dependent Semantic Processing in the Human Brain: Evidence from Idiom Comprehension. *Journal of Cognitive Neuroscience*, 25(5):762-776.

Ivan A Sag. 2012. Sign-Based Construction Grammar: An Informal Synopsis. *Sign-Based Construction Grammar*, edited by Hans C Boas and Ivan A Sag, CSLI Publications, Stanford, CA: 61-197.

Magnus Sahlgren, Anders Holst, and Pentti Kanerva. 2008. Permutations as a mean to encode order in word space. *Proceedings of the 30th Conference of the Cognitive Science Society*: 1300-1305.

Asad Sayeed, Stefan Fischer and Vera Demberg. 2015. Vector-space calculation of semantic surprisal for predicting word pronunciation duration. *Proceedings of ACL*: 763-773.

Nathaniel J Smith and Roger Levy. 2013. The effect of word predictability on reading time is logarithmic. *Cognition*, volume 128(3): 302-319.

Jos JA Van Berkum, Colin M Brown, Pienie Zwitserlood, Valesca Kooijman, and Peter Hagoort. 2005. Anticipating upcoming words in discourse: evidence from ERPs and reading times. *Journal of Experimental Psychology: Learning, Memory, and Cognition*, volume 31(3): 443-467.

Alessandra Zarcone, Marten Van Schijndel, Jorrig Vogels and Vera Demberg. 2016. Salience and attention in surprisal-based accounts of language processing. *Frontiers in Psychology*, volume 7.

Rolf A Zwaan and Gabriel A Radvansky. 1998. Situation models in language comprehension. *Psychological Bulletin*, volume 123(2): 162-185.

CoCoGen - Complexity Contour Generator: Automatic Assessment of Linguistic Complexity Using a Sliding-Window Technique

Marcus Ströbel
Department of English Linguistics
RWTH Aachen University
stroebel@anglistik.rwth-aachen.de

Elma Kerz
Department of English Linguistics
RWTH Aachen University
kerz@anglistik.rwth-aachen.de

Daniel Wiechmann
Institute for Language Logic and Computation
University of Amsterdam
d.wiechmann@uva.nl

Stella Neumann
Department of English Linguistics
RWTH Aachen University
neumann@anglistik.rwth-aachen.de

Abstract

We present a novel approach to the automatic assessment of text complexity based on a sliding-window technique that tracks the distribution of complexity within a text. Such distribution is captured by what we term *complexity contours* derived from a series of measurements for a given linguistic complexity measure. This approach is implemented in an automatic computational tool, *CoCoGen – Complexity Contour Generator*, which in its current version supports 32 indices of linguistic complexity. The goal of the paper is twofold: (1) to introduce the design of our computational tool based on a sliding-window technique and (2) to showcase this approach in the area of second language (L2) learning, i.e. more specifically, in the area of L2 writing.

1   Introduction

Linguistic complexity has attracted a lot of attention in many research areas, including text readability, first and second language learning, discourse processing and translation studies. Advances in natural language processing have paved the way for the development of computational tools designed to automatically assess the linguistic complexity of spoken and written language samples. There are a variety of computational tools available which measure a large number of indices of linguistic complexity. Such tools afford speed, flexibility and reliability and permit the direct comparison of numerous indices of linguistic complexity. *Coh-Metrix* is a well-known computational tool that measures cohesion and linguistic complexity at various levels of language, discourse and conceptual analysis (McNamara, Graesser, McCarthy & Cai, 2014). Considerable gains have been made from the use of *Coh-Metrix*. In particular, an important contribution has been made to the identification of reliable and valid measures or proxies of linguistic complexity and their relation to text readability (Crossley, Greenfield, & McNamara, 2008), writing quality (Crossley & McNamara, 2012) and speaking proficiency (Crossley, Clevinger, & Kim, 2014). *Coh-Metrix* measures are also shown to serve as proxy for more complex features of language processing and comprehension (cf. McNamara et al. 2014). More recently, a number of tools have been developed that feature a large number of classic and recently proposed indices of syntactic complexity (*Syntactic Complexity Analyzer*, Lu, 2010; *TAASSC*, Kyle,

Proceedings of the Workshop on Computational Slinguistics for Linguistic Complexity,
pages 23–31, Osaka, Japan, December 11-17 2016.

2016) and lexical sophistication (*Lexical Complexity Analyzer*, Lu 2012; *TAALES*, Kyle & Crossley, 2015). These tools provide comprehensive assessments of text complexity at a global level. They provide as output for each measure a single score that represents the complexity of a text, i.e. a summary statistics. We present a novel approach to the assessment of linguistic complexity that enables tracking the progression of complexity within a text. In contrast to a global assessment of text complexity based on summary statistics, the approach presented here provides a series of measurements for a given complexity dimension and in this way allows for a local assessment of within-text complexity. The goal of the paper is twofold: (1) to introduce the design of our computational tool which implements such an approach by using a sliding-window technique and (2) to showcase this approach in the area of second language (L2) learning.

2 Automatic Assessment of Linguistic Complexity Using a Sliding-Window Technique

The present paper introduces a computational tool – *Complexity Contour Generator (CoCoGen)* – designed to automatically track the changes in linguistic complexity within a target text. *CoCoGen* uses a sliding-window technique to generate a series of measurements for a given complexity dimension allowing for a local assessment of complexity within a text. A sliding window can be conceived of as a window with a certain size that is moved across a text. The window size (*ws*) is defined by the number of sentences it contains. The window is moved across a text sentence-by-sentence, computing one value per window for a given complexity measure. For a text comprising n sentences, there are $w = n{-}ws{+}1$ windows. Given the constraint that there has to be at least one window, a text has to comprise at least as many sentences at the *ws* is wide ($n \geq ws$). Figure 1 illustrates how sliding windows of two exemplary *ws* (2 and 3) are mapped to sentences within a text.

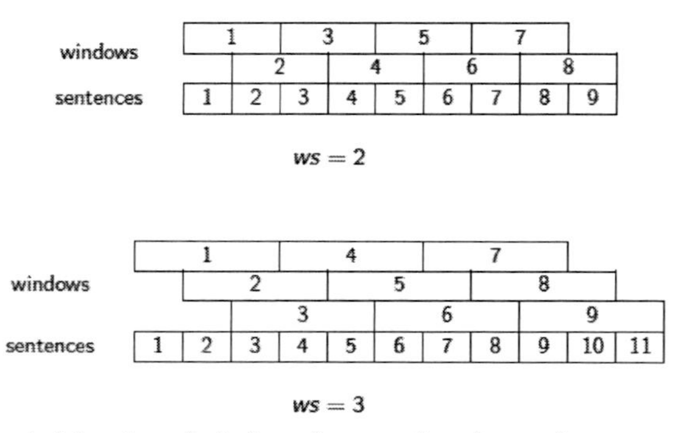

Figure 1: Mapping of windows for ws = 2 and ws = 3 to sentences

The series of measurements obtained by the sliding-window technique represents the distribution of linguistic complexity within a text for a given measure and is referred here to as a *complexity contour*. The shape of a complexity contour is affected by the *ws*, a user-definable parameter. Setting the *ws* parameter to n will yield a single value representing the average global complexity of the text. To track the progression of complexity within a text there has to be a sufficient number of windows. As a rule of thumb, there should be at least ten times as many sentences as the window is wide to have at least ten completely distinct (i.e. non-overlapping) windows. Figure 2 illustrates the smoothed curve produced by *CoCoGen*'s sliding window approach for a sequence of 50 random numbers between 0 and 10 presents complexity contours for *ws* of 5 and 10 compared to raw data.

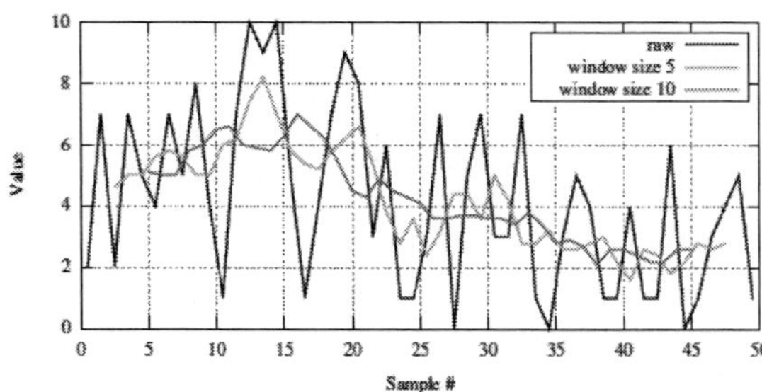

Figure 2: Sliding windows for window sizes 5 and 10 compared to raw data

In what follows, we address how a value for a window is obtained and how the comparison of texts of different sizes is afforded by a text-time scaling technique. There are different methods of obtaining a value for a window: One method is similar to using simple moving averages with a length equal to the *ws* over a set of measurements for all sentences in a text. This way the value is computed once per sentence and can be cached and reused in other windows that include that particular sentence. In addition, the values obtained for individual sentences can be cached for recalculating the window values for different *ws*. Another method is to apply the measure function directly to the contents of a window rather than a single sentence. As the number of windows can never exceed the number of sentences, compared to the first method, fewer calls to a measure function are needed, however, the number of the calls is greater. Furthermore, with this method it is not possible to reuse the values for different *ws*. Another disadvantage is that the *ws* may directly influence the resulting values for simple counting measures like word counts. The method implemented in CoCoGen is a compromise between the two methods discussed above: the measure function is called for each sentence, but it returns a fraction rather than a fixed value. The denominators and numerators of those fractions are then added to form the denominator and numerator of the resulting value. For complexity measures based on ratios, the result is the same as when the measure function is directly applied to the contents of a window. For counting measures, a fixed denominator of 1 is used, resulting in the arithmetic mean of the results for the sentences in the window. The idea behind this method is to obtain values for windows that do not depend on the *ws* chosen, allowing comparison of results for different window sizes.

$$(1) \qquad window_n = \frac{num_n + num_{n+1} + \ldots + num_{n+ws}}{den_n + den_{n+1} + \ldots + den_{n+ws}}$$

A scaling technique is implemented in the tool to allow comparing complexity contours across texts. As texts tend to vary in length given in number of sentences, the number of available windows will differ across texts. The scaling algorithm fits the number of windows w_T for a text T into a user-defined number of windows w_{scaled}. It is recommended to adjust the number of scaled windows to be at most as high as the largest number of windows in a text. In case the number of scaled windows is exceeded, the scaling algorithm will still work by linearly interpolating the missing information. However, the interpolated information will not contain actual data and thus won't be of much use. For that reason, the program issues a warning message if the number of scaled windows is higher than the window count for one of the input text files.

In its current version, *CoCoGen* supports 32 measures of linguistic complexity mainly derived from language learning research (Table 1 provides an overview, cf. Ströbel 2014 for details). Importantly, *CoCoGen* was designed with extensibility in mind, so that additional complexity measures can easily be added. It uses an abstract MEASURE class for the implementation of complexity measures.

Prior to the computation of complexity measures, *CoCoGen* pushes raw English text input through an annotation pipeline. While several open-source natural language analysis toolkits are available, CoCoGen uses several annotators from one of the most used toolkits, *Stanford CoreNLP* (Manning et al. 2014): tokenizer, sentence splitter, POS tagger, lemmatizer, named entity recognizer and syntactic parser.

Table 1: Overview of complexity measures currently implemented in CoCoGen

Measure	Label	Formula
Kolmogorov Deflate	KOLMOGOROV	Ehret & Szmrecsanyi 2011
Lexical Density	LEX.DEN	N_{lex}/N
Number of different words / sample	LEX.DIV.NDW	$N_{w\ diff}$
Number of diff. words / sample (cor.)	LEX.DIV.CNDW	$N_{w\ diff}/N_w$
Type-Token Ratio	LEX.DIV.TTR	T/N
Corrected Type-Token Ratio	LEX.DIV.CTTR	$T/\sqrt{2N}$
Root Type-Token Ratio	LEX.DIV.RTTR	$T/\sqrt{N}$
Sequences Academic Formula List	LEX.SOPH.AFL	$Seq_{N\ AWL}$
Lexical Sophistication (ANC)	LEX.SOPH.ANC	N_{slex_ANC}/N_{lex}
Lexical Sophistication (BNC)	LEX.SOPH.BNC	N_{slex_BNC}/N_{lex}
Words on New Academic Word List	LEX.NAWL	$W_{N\ AWL}$
Words not on General Service List	LEX.NGSL	$W_{N\ GSL}$
Morphological Kolmogorov Deflate	MORPH.KOLMOGOROV	Ehret & Szmrecsanyi 2011
Mean Length of Words (characters)	SYN.MLWC	N_{char}/N_w
Mean Length of Words (syllables)	SYN.MLWS	N_{syl}/N_w
Noun Phrase Postmodification (words)	SYN.NPPOSTMODW	$N_{NP\ Pre}$
Noun Phrase Premodification (words)	SYN.NPPREMODW	$N_{NP\ Post}$
Clauses per Sentence	SYN.CS	N_C/N_S
Clauses per T-Unit	SYN.CT	N_C/N_T
Complex Nominals per Clause	SYN.CNC	N_{CN}/C
Complex Nominals per T-Unit	SYN.CNS	N_{CN}/N_T
Complex T-Units per T-Unit	SYN.CTT	N_{CT}/N_T
Coordinate Phrases per Clause	SYN.CPC	N_{CP}/N_C
Coordinate Phrases per T-Unit	SYN.CPT	N_{CP}/N_T
Dependent Clauses per Clause	SYN.DCC	N_{DC}/N_C
Dependent Clauses per T-Unit	SYN.DCT	N_{DC}/N_T
Syntactic Kolmogorov Deflate	SYN.KOLMOGOROV	Ehret & Szmrecsanyi 2011
Mean Length Clause	SYN.MLC	N_W/N_C
Mean Length Sentence	SYN.MLS	N_W/N_S
Mean Length T-Unit	SYN.MLT	N_W/N_T
T-Units per Sentence	SYN.TS	N_T/N_S
Verb Phrases per T-Unit	SYN.VPT	N_{VP}/N_T

3 Application Domain: Second Language Learning

Linguistic complexity has received considerable attention in the assessment of second language (L2) performance and proficiency (cf., e.g., Ortega, 2003, 2012; Larsen-Freeman, 2006; Housen et al., 2012). It is assumed that with an increasing level of proficiency L2 writing becomes more complex and sophisticated, i.e. consisting of more advanced structures and vocabulary (Wolfe-Quinterno, Inagaki & Kim, 1998). For this reason, measures of linguistic complexity have been seen as basic descriptors of L2 performance and as indicators of L2 proficiency. While there is still much controversy as to how linguistic complexity should be defined, operationalized and measured (cf., Larsen-Freeman, 2009; Housen et al., 2012; Connor-Linton & Polio, 2014), there is a general consensus that it is a multidimensional construct affected by a number of dimensions at various levels of linguistic description (e.g. Bulté & Housen, 2014).

As mentioned in the introduction, L2 learning research has benefited tremendously from the development of computational tools designed to automatically assess linguistic complexity of texts based on a wide range of indices. More specifically, the development of such tools has made an important contribution to the identification of reliable and valid measures of linguistic complexity and their relation to L2 written and spoken performance and proficiency. A number of studies have demonstrated that automatically computed indices of linguistic complexity can successfully predict human judgments of L2 text quality (e.g. McNamara, Crossley & McCarthy, 2009) and L2 speaking proficiency (e.g. Kyle & Crossley, 2015) and can be used to discriminate between L1 and L2 texts (e.g. Crossley & McNamara 2009). More recently, a number of computational tools have been developed featuring a wide range of classic indices, fine-grained indices as well as indices informed by recent insights from language learning and processing research. One such tool is *TAALES* (Kyle & Crossley, 2015) that supports 104 classic and new indices of lexical sophistication, covering indices of frequency, range, academic language and psycholinguistic word information. Another tool is *TAASSC* (Kyle 2016) that covers 372 classical and fine-grained indices of syntactic complexity. *CRAT* (Crossley, Kyle, Davenport & McNamara, 2016) is another recently developed tool that includes over 700 indices related to lexical sophistication, cohesion and source text/summary text overlap. The coverage of such a large number of indices allows for an extensive and comprehensive assessment of text complexity and enables the identification of the most predictive and reliable indices of L2 performance and proficiency.

The sliding-window approach implemented in *CoCoGen* adds a new perspective on the assessment of text complexity. We showcase how this approach can be put to use in the area of L2 learning. The focus here is on the advanced stages of L2 English learning which in recent years have received growing attention, primarily grounded in what has come to be known as learner corpus research (cf. Granger, Gilquin & Meunier, 2015). This line of research has provided valuable insights into how and to what extent advanced L2 learners' performance deviate from target-like behavior. The vast majority of previous studies conducted in this line of research have made L1-L2 comparisons using L2 data from corpora such as the *ICLE* (cf. Granger, Dagneaux, Meunier & Paquot, 2009) and L1 data from comparable corpora such as the *LOCNESS* (cf. https://www.uclouvain.be/en-cecl-locness.html). These corpora include writing of a general argumentative, creative or literary nature and consist of relatively short texts (e.g. average text length: *ICLE* = 617 words). These texts do not represent academic writing in a narrow sense (cf. Callies & Zaytseva, 2013), a register characterized by its compressed style (cf., Biber & Gray, 2010) as well as its own phraseology/formulaic language (e.g., Ellis et al., 2008). The mastery of this register constitutes a learning target in both L1 and L2 learning (cf., Biber et al., 2011, 2013; Hyland & Tse, 2007). Correspondingly, advanced L2 learners' performance is best evaluated against an expert writer baseline (cf., Bolton, Nelson & Hung, 2002; Römer, 2009; Kerz & Wiechmann, 2015 for discussions).

The L2 learner data used in our paper come from a corpus of 110 academic research papers on a linguistic topic written by 2nd and 3rd year students enrolled in the bachelor programmes of the English Department at the RWTH Aachen University (N ~ 486,000 words, average text length = 4,500 words). All students are L1 speakers of German and meet the criteria for advanced learner status of English based on their institutional status (undergraduates with 7-9 years of formal instruction of English before entering university) (cf. Callies, 2009:116f.). The expert corpus consists of 110 research articles on linguistic topics published in peer-reviewed journals (N ~867,000 words, average text length = 7,880 words).

We are interested in whether and to what extent the progression of complexity within L2 texts deviates from the expert-writer target. We address this question for each of the 32 complexity measures currently implemented in *CoCoGen* (cf. Table 1). We used a supervised machine learning classifier to distinguish L2 texts from expert texts based on the measurements computed by the tool. The guiding idea is that in cases where the classifier cannot distinguish between learner and expert texts, L2 performance is target-like. Conversely, in cases where the classifier can distinguish between learner and expert texts, L2 performance deviates from target-like behavior. We also want to know whether there is any advantage of using complexity contours in the classification task, rather than using summary statistics. If this is the case, we would expect classification accuracy to be higher for a classifier fed with complexity contour information compared to one fed with summary statistics information.

The complexity of 220 texts in our corpora was automatically assessed using *CoCoGen*. Figure 2 below provides a visual representation of complexity contours of a single text – a randomly selected text from our expert corpus – for two selected complexity measures: SYN.CNS and LEX.SOPH.BNC. The two plots show the progression of complexity over 100 scaled windows, indicating that for both measures complexity is not uniformly distributed.

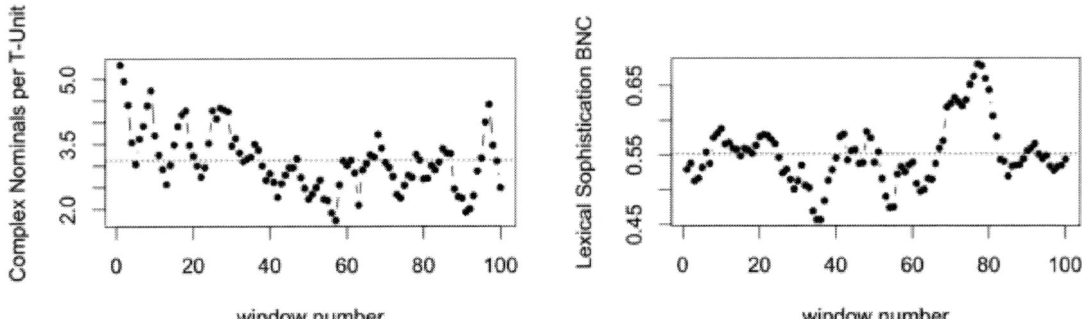

Figure 2: Visual representation of complexity contours for two selected measures in a single expert text

Figure 3 below illustrates the distribution of complexity for a single measure – SYN.MLS – in the two corpora. The thick solid lines describe the distributions of mean complexity using text-time scaling for both learners (blue) and experts (red). The shaded areas represent the corresponding interquartile ranges for both groups.

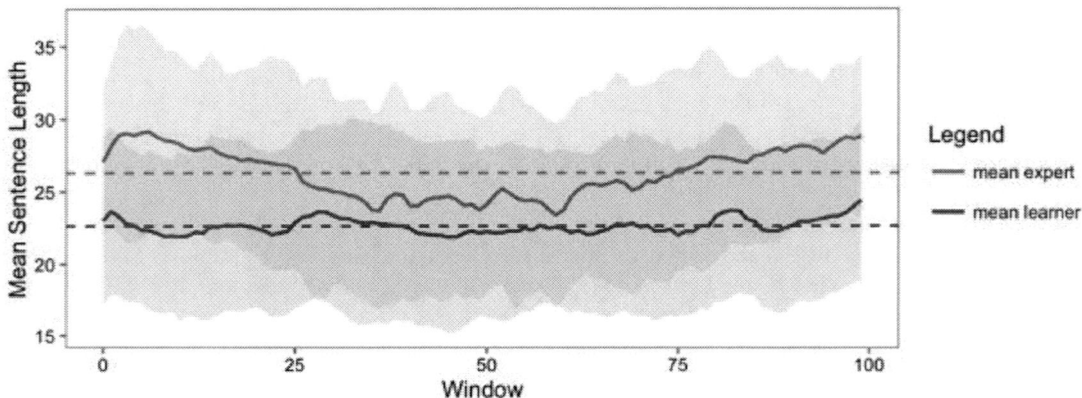

Figure 3: Distribution of complexity for a single measure in the learner and the expert corpus

For our classification task, we used a simple and transparent supervised machine learning technique: For each complexity measure, we identified the *empirical threshold complexity value*, i.e. the value that discriminates most strongly between L2 learner and expert texts in our data. This value served as the decision boundary for discriminating between the two groups. For the summary statistics-based approach, the description of text complexity of our corpus yielded 220 point estimates of text complexity – one score for each of the 110 learner and 110 expert texts. Each midpoint between any two values of the rank-ordered vector of complexity scores was used to divide the data into two groups. The optimal empirical threshold complexity value was found by maximizing the rand index (RI, Rand, 1971) and was validated using 10-fold cross-validation. For the sliding window approach, the empirical threshold values were determined for each window separately and the classification was determined by majority vote.[1]

Figure 5 visualizes the type of information available to the contour-based and summary statistics-based classification. The plot presents all measurements obtained for the LEX.DIV.CTTR complexity measure. Red dots represent expert texts, whereas blue dots represent L2 learner texts. The black vertical line separates the data used for the contour-based classification (left) from the data used for the summary statistics-based classification (right). The horizontal lines mark the empirical threshold complexity,

---

[1] Classification can also be informed by the accumulated deviation of the observed values from the threshold. We opted against this option here in the interest of transparency. However, the inclusion of this information – as well as information concerning weights of vector positions (feature weighting) – can only improve the performance of the contour-based approach advocated here.

which were used by the classifier to predict the class of a text (L2 learner/expert). In case of the summary statistics-based approach, this is a single value. In the contour-based approach, a threshold value was determined for each of the ten scaled windows. It is important to note that the thresholds found for each of the windows follow a nonlinear curve, which cannot be adequately captured by a single value.

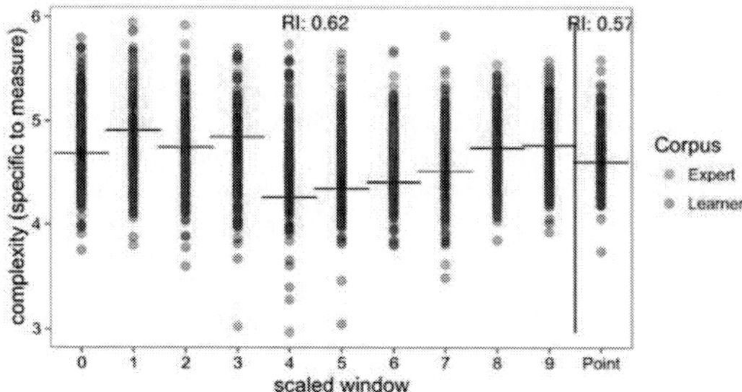

Figure 4: Measurements of complexity and empirical threshold values for LEX.DIV.CTTR for ten non-overlapping windows

Table 2 presents the Accuracy (RI), Recall, Precision, and F-measure (harmonic mean) for all measures for the summary-statistics-based and contour-based classification.

Table 2: Results of summary statistics-based (SSB) and contour-based (CB) classification

Measure	Accuracy SSB	Accuracy CB	Recall SSB	Recall CB	Precision SSB	Precision CB	F SSB	F CB
KOLMOGOROV	0.6	0.62	0.59	0.62	0.59	0.65	0.59	0.63
LEX.DEN	0.64	0.66	0.63	0.65	0.64	0.67	0.64	0.66
LEX.DIV.CNDW	0.54	0.58	0.54	0.58	0.55	0.62	0.55	0.6
LEX.DIV.CTTR	0.58	0.62	0.58	0.61	0.62	0.7	0.6	0.65
LEX.DIV.NDW	0.6	0.64	0.59	0.63	0.6	0.66	0.59	0.64
LEX.DIV.RTTR	0.58	0.62	0.57	0.61	0.59	0.68	0.58	0.64
LEX.DIV.TTR	0.54	0.58	0.54	0.58	0.55	0.62	0.54	0.6
LEX.SOPH.AFL	0.51	0.57	0.51	0.56	0.58	0.68	0.54	0.61
LEX.SOPH.ANC	0.57	0.62	0.56	0.61	0.58	0.65	0.57	0.63
LEX.SOPH.BNC	0.6	0.65	0.6	0.64	0.6	0.67	0.6	0.65
LEX.NAWL	0.54	0.59	0.54	0.58	0.54	0.69	0.54	0.63
LEX.NGSL	0.6	0.62	0.59	0.61	0.62	0.64	0.61	0.63
MORPH.KOLMOGOROV	0.57	0.62	0.57	0.62	0.57	0.65	0.57	0.63
SYN.MLWC	0.54	0.6	0.53	0.59	0.67	0.66	0.59	0.62
SYN.MLWS	0.55	0.6	0.54	0.59	0.64	0.67	0.58	0.63
SYN.NPPOSTMODW	0.56	0.6	0.56	0.59	0.59	0.65	0.57	0.62
SYN.NPPREMODW	0.57	0.6	0.56	0.6	0.62	0.65	0.59	0.62
SYN.CS	0.5	0.58	0.5	0.57	0.53	0.61	0.52	0.59
SYN.CT	0.5	0.57	0.5	0.57	0.56	0.65	0.53	0.6
SYN.CNC	0.62	0.63	0.62	0.63	0.62	0.65	0.62	0.64
SYN.CNS	0.6	0.63	0.59	0.62	0.62	0.67	0.6	0.64
SYN.CTT	0.51	0.57	0.51	0.57	0.63	0.67	0.56	0.61
SYN.CPC	0.52	0.57	0.52	0.57	0.56	0.67	0.54	0.61
SYN.CPT	0.52	0.57	0.52	0.57	0.54	0.61	0.53	0.59
SYN.DCC	0.51	0.57	0.5	0.57	0.58	0.63	0.54	0.6
SYN.DCT	0.5	0.57	0.5	0.57	0.53	0.63	0.52	0.6
SYN.KOLMOGOROV	0.59	0.63	0.58	0.62	0.59	0.65	0.59	0.64
SYN.MLC	0.63	0.63	0.63	0.63	0.64	0.64	0.63	0.64
SYN.MLS	0.59	0.63	0.59	0.63	0.59	0.65	0.59	0.64
SYN.MLT	0.58	0.62	0.57	0.61	0.64	0.67	0.61	0.64

| Syn.TS | 0.53 | 0.57 | 0.52 | 0.57 | 0.63 | 0.66 | 0.57 | 0.61 |
| Syn.VPT | 0.5 | 0.57 | 0.5 | 0.57 | 0.52 | 0.62 | 0.51 | 0.59 |

We found that the contour-based classifier outperformed the summary statistics-based classifier for all measures of complexity. The contour-based classifier also identified a larger number of complexity measures that discriminate between L2 learner and expert texts: In the global, summary statistics-based classification more than a third of the measures received a predictive accuracy (RI score) < 0.55, which is not significantly different from chance ($p_{\text{binomial test}} > 0.05$). In response to our first research question, these findings indicate that for all measures investigated in this study L2 learners' performance deviates from that of the expert-target (classification accuracy ≥ 0.57, $p_{\text{binomial test}} = 0.025$). The top three measures are all measures of lexical sophistication. In response to our second research question, we found that using complexity contours information in the classification task provides a more accurate picture of differences between learner and expert texts. While these results look promising, further work is needed to include a larger set of complexity measures proposed in the relevant literature and to investigate how the contour-based approach can contribute to the identification of the most reliable and valid complexity measures that serve as proxies of L2 performance and proficiency.

Most importantly, however, the contour-based approach opens up new interesting research questions. One possible research question concerns the identification of "gold standards" for the within-text distribution of complexity for different text type (register/genre) and to what extent compliance to such standards is related to perceived text quality. A related question is whether human ratings of text quality are affected by the "global" complexity of a text captured in terms of summary statistics, or by the "local" complexity of specific passages, captured in terms of complexity contours: For example, do human raters judge a text quality primarily based on an early partition (anchoring effects), do they judge it based on properties of a late partition (recency effects)? Another question is whether there is evidence for "local compensatory effects", i.e. whether a high level of complexity at one level of linguistic analysis (e.g. syntax) is compensated for by a low level of complexity at another level (e.g. lexicon).

4   Conclusion

We introduced *CoCoGen* (*Complexity Contour Generator*), a tool designed to automatically track the progression of linguistic complexity within a text. *CoCoGen* uses a sliding-window technique to generate a series of measurements (complexity contours) for a given complexity dimension, providing a novel approach to the automatic assessment of text complexity. For the purposes of the present study, we decided to showcase this approach in the area of L2 learning. In future work we intend to apply this approach to other research areas, in particular, readability research and discourse processing.

Reference

Biber, Douglas and Bethany Gray. 2010. Challenging stereotypes about academic writing: Complexity, elaboration,explicitness. *Journal of English for Academic Purposes,* 9(1):2–20.

Biber, Douglas, Bethany Gray, and Kornwepa Poonpon. 2011. Should we use characteristics of conversation to measure grammatical complexity in L2 writing development? *TESOL Quarterly,* 45(1):5–35.

Biber, Douglas and Kornwepa Poonpon, 2013. Pay attention to the phrasal structures: Going beyond t-units-a response to WeiWei yang. *TESOL Quarterly,* 47(1):192–201.

Bolton, Kingsley, Gerald Nelson, and Joseph Hung. 2002. A corpus-based study of connectors in student writing: Research from the International Corpus of English in Hong Kong (ICE-HK). *International Journal of Corpus Linguistics,* 7(2): 165-182.

Bulté, Bram, and Alex Housen. 2014. Conceptualizing and measuring short-term changes in L2 writing complexity. *Journal of Second Language Writing,* 26: 42–65.

Callies, Marcus. 2009. *Information Highlighting in Advanced Learner English.* John Benjamins Publishing.

Callies, Marcus and Ekatarina Zaytseva. 2013. The Corpus of Academic Learner English (CALE): A new resource for the assessment of writing proficiency in the academic register. *Dutch Journal of Applied Linguistics,* 2(1): 126-132.

Connor-Linton, Jeff and Charlene Polio. 2014. Comparing perspectives on L2 writing: Multiple analyses of a common corpus. *Journal of Second Language Writing*, 26:1-9.

Crossley, Scott A., Zhiqiang Cai, and Danielle S. McNamara. 2012. Syntagmatic, Paradigmatic, and Automatic N-gram Approaches to Assessing Essay Quality. In G. M. Youngblood and P. M. McCarthy (Eds.), *Proceedings of the Twenty-Fifth International Florida Artificial Intelligence Research Society Conference*, Palo Alto, California, pp. 214–219. The AAAI Press.

Crossley, Scott. A. and Danielle S. McNamara. 2009. Computational Assessment of Lexical Differences in L1 and L2 writing. *Journal of Second Language Writing*, 18(2):119–135.

Crossley, Scott. A. and Danielle S. McNamara. 2014. Does writing development equal writing quality? A computational investigation of syntactic complexity in L2 learners. *Journal of Second Language Writing*, 26:66–79.

Ehret, Katharina and Benedikt Szmrecsanyi. 2011. *An information-theoretic approach to assess linguistic complexity. Complexity and isolation*. Berlin: de Gruyter.

Ellis, Nick. C., R.I.T.A Simpson-Vlach, and Carson Maynard. 2008. Formulaic language in native and second language speakers: Psycholinguistics, corpus linguistics, and TESOL. *TESOL Quarterly*, 42(3): 375–396.

Granger, Sylviane, Estelle Dagneaux, Fanny Meunier, and Magali Paquot. 2009. *The international corpus of learner English*. Presses universitaires de Louvain.

Granger, Sylviane, Gaëtanelle Gilquin, and Fanny Meunier (Eds.). 2015. *The Cambridge Handbook of Learner Corpus Research*. Cambridge University Press.

Hyland, Ken and Polly Tse. 2007. Is there an "academic vocabulary"? *TESOL Quarterly*, 41(2):235–253.

Kerz, Elma and Daniel Wiechmann. 2015. Second language construction learning: investigating domain specific adaptation in advanced L2 production. *Language and Cognition*, 1–33.

Kyle, Kristopher. 2016. *Measuring syntactic development in L2 writing: Fine grained indices of syntactic complexity and usage-based indices of syntactic sophistication* (Doctoral Dissertation).

Kyle, Kristopher and Scott A. Crossley. 2014. Automatically assessing lexical sophistication: Indices, tools, findings, and application. *TESOL Quarterly*, 49(4):757–786.

Larsen-Freeman, Diane. 2006. The emergence of complexity, fluency, and accuracy in the oral and written production of five Chinese learners of English. *Applied Linguistics*, 27(4):590–619.

Larsen-Freeman, Diane. 2009. Adjusting expectations: The study of complexity, accuracy, and fluency in second language acquisition. *Applied Linguistics*. 30(4):579–589.

Lu, Xiaofei. 2010. Automatic analysis of syntactic complexity in second language writing. *International Journal of Corpus Linguistics*, 15(4):474–496.

Lu, Xiaofei. 2012. The relationship of lexical richness to the quality of ESL learners' oral narratives. *The Modern Language Journal*, 96(2):190–208.

Manning, Christopher D., Prabhakar Raghavan, and Hinrich Schutze. 2008. *Introduction to Information Retrieval*. Cambridge University Press.

McNamara, Danielle S., Arthur C. Graesser, Philip M. McCarthy, and Zhiqiang Cai. 2014. *Automated Evaluation of Text and Discourse with Coh-Metrix*. Cambridge University Press.

Ortega, Lourdes. 2003. Syntactic complexity measures and their relationship to L2 proficiency: A research synthesis of college-level L2 writing. *Applied Linguistics*, 24(4):492–518.

Römer, Ute. 2009. English in academia: Does nativeness matter? *International Journal of English Studies*, 20(2):89–100.

Ströbel, Marcus. 2014. *Tracking complexity of l2 academic texts: A sliding-window approach*. Master's thesis. RWTH Aachen University.

Team, R Core. 2013. *R: A Language and Environment for Statistical Computing*.R Foundation for Statistical Computing. Vienna, Austria.

Wolfe-Quintero, Kate, Shunji Inagaki, and Hae-Young Kim. 1998. Second Language Development in Writing: Measures of Fluency, Accuracy, & Complexity. No. 17. University of Hawaii Press, 1998.

Addressing surprisal deficiencies in reading time models

Marten van Schijndel
van-schijndel.1@osu.edu

William Schuler
schuler.77@osu.edu

Department of Linguistics, The Ohio State University

Abstract

This study demonstrates a weakness in how n-gram and PCFG surprisal are used to predict reading times in eye-tracking data. In particular, the information conveyed by words skipped during saccades is not usually included in the surprisal measures. This study shows that correcting the surprisal calculation improves n-gram surprisal and that upcoming n-grams affect reading times, replicating previous findings of how lexical frequencies affect reading times. In contrast, the predictivity of PCFG surprisal does not benefit from the surprisal correction despite the fact that lexical sequences skipped by saccades are processed by readers, as demonstrated by the corrected n-gram measure. These results raise questions about the formulation of information-theoretic measures of syntactic processing such as PCFG surprisal and entropy reduction when applied to reading times.

1   Introduction

Rare words and constructions produce longer reading times than their more frequent counterparts. Such effects can be captured by n-grams and by probabilistic context-free grammar (PCFG) surprisal. Surprisal theory predicts reading times will be directly proportional to the amount of information which must be processed, as calculated by a generative model, but the surprisal measures commonly used in eye-tracking studies omit probability estimates for words skipped in saccades. Therefore, the generative model assumed by those studies does not account for the information contributed by the skipped words even though those words must be processed by readers.[1] This deficiency can be addressed by summing surprisal measures over the saccade region (see Figure 1), and the resulting cumulative n-grams have been shown to be more predictive of reading times than the usual non-cumulative n-grams (van Schijndel and Schuler, 2015). However PCFG surprisal, which has a similar deficiency when non-cumulatively modeling reading times, has not previously been found to be predictive when accumulated over saccade regions.

This paper uses a reading time corpus to investigate two accumulation techniques (pre- and post-saccade) and finds that both forms of accumulation improve the fit of n-gram surprisal to reading times. However, even though accumulated n-grams demonstrate that the lexical sequence of the saccade region is processed, PCFG surprisal does not seem to be improved by either accumulation technique. The results of this work call into question the usual formulation of PCFG surprisal as a reading time predictor and suggest future directions for investigation of the influence of upcoming material on reading times.

[1]The present work merely accounts for the processing load introduced by the words initially skipped by a progressive saccade. This correction is consistent with any process by which those words could be processed: predictive processing, parafoveal processing, or subsequent regression. Since all of those methods would contribute load during the associated duration (e.g,. first pass time), reading time predictivity should improve if the complexity metrics account for the additional load.

Proceedings of the Workshop on Computational Linguistics for Linguistic Complexity,
pages 32–37, Osaka, Japan, December 11-17 2016.

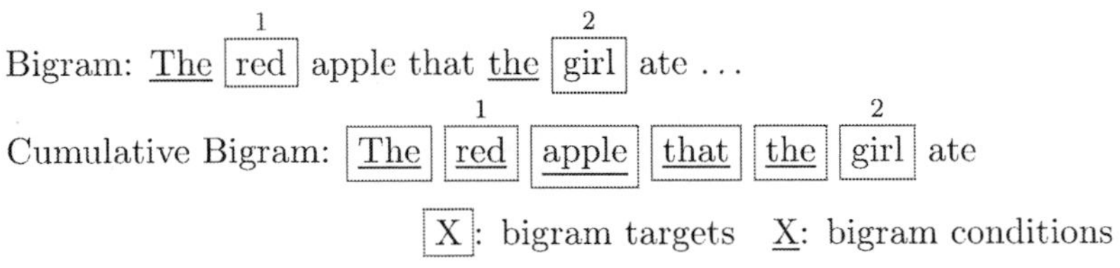

$$\text{Bigram: } \underline{\text{The}} \boxed{\text{red}}^{1} \text{ apple that } \underline{\text{the}} \boxed{\text{girl}}^{2} \text{ ate} \ldots$$

$$\text{Cumulative Bigram: } \boxed{\text{The}} \boxed{\text{red}}^{1} \boxed{\text{apple}} \boxed{\text{that}} \boxed{\text{the}} \boxed{\text{girl}}^{2} \text{ ate}$$

$$\boxed{\text{X}}\text{: bigram targets} \quad \underline{\text{X}}\text{: bigram conditions}$$

Figure 1: Eye movements jump between non-adjacent fixation regions (1, 2), while traditional n-gram measures are conditioned on the preceding adjacent context, which is never generated by the typical surprisal models used in eye-tracking studies. Cumulative n-grams sum the n-gram measures over the entire skipped region in order to better capture the information that readers need to process.

2 Data

This work makes use of the University College London (UCL) eye-tracking corpus (Frank et al., 2013). Previous reading time studies have often used the Dundee corpus (Kennedy et al., 2003), which only has data from 10 subjects. In contrast, the UCL corpus has reading time data from 43 subjects who read sentences drawn from a series of self-published online novels. The sentences in the corpus were presented as isolated sentences and in a random order.

The present work uses half of the corpus (every other sentence) for exploratory analyses, while the rest of the corpus is set aside for significance testing. The corpus was parsed using the van Schijndel et al. (2013) left-corner parser, which outputs a wide variety of incremental complexity metrics computed during parsing (such as PCFG surprisal). 5-gram back-off n-gram probabilities were computed for each word using the KenLM toolkit (Heafield et al., 2013) trained on Gigaword 4.0 (Graff and Cieri, 2003). Models were fit to Box-Cox transformed first-pass reading times for all experiments in this paper ($\lambda \approx 0.02$; Box and Cox, 1964).[2] Fixation data was excluded from analysis if the fixation occurred on the first or last word of a sentence or line or if it followed an unusually long saccade, defined here and in previous work (Demberg and Keller, 2008) as a saccade over more than 4 words (2.5% of the UCL corpus).

3 Experiments

3.1 Cumulative n-gram surprisal

N-gram surprisal is conditioned on the preceding context (see Equation 1). As stated in the introduction, however, direct use of this factor in a reading time model ignores the fact that some or all of the preceding context may not be generated if the associated lexical targets were not previously fixated by readers (see Figure 1). The lack of a generated condition results in a probability model that does not reflect the influence of words skipped during saccades. This deficiency can be corrected by accumulating n-gram surprisal over the entire saccade region (see Equation 2).

$$n\text{-gram}(w, i) = -\log \mathrm{P}(w_i \mid w_{i-n} \ldots w_{i-1}) \tag{1}$$

$$\text{cumu-}n\text{-gram}(w, f_{t-1}, f_t) = \sum_{i=f_{t-1}+1}^{f_t} -\log \mathrm{P}(w_i \mid w_{i-n} \ldots w_{i-1}) \tag{2}$$

where w is a vector of input tokens, f_{t-1} is the index of the previous fixation, f_t is the index of the current fixation.

The linear mixed model[3] that was used in this experiment included item, subject, and sentence

---

[2] The Box-Cox transform helps make the distribution of reading times more normal.

[3] A linear mixed model is a linear regression technique that separately estimates the variance for generalizable (fixed) population-level factors (e.g., human sensitivity to word length) and for non-generalizable (random) factors (e.g., each subject's individual sensitivity to word length).

ID-crossed-with-subject random intercepts[4] as well as by-subject random slopes and fixed effects for the following predictors: sentence position (sentpos), word length (wlen), region length (rlen),[5] whether the previous word was fixated (prevfix), 5-grams and cumulative 5-grams. Likelihood ratio tests were used to compare the mixed model with and without fixed effects for the 5-gram measures (see Table 1). In line with previous findings on the Dundee corpus (van Schijndel and Schuler, 2015), cumulative 5-grams provide a significant improvement over basic n-grams ($p < 0.001$), but unlike previous work, basic n-grams do not improve over cumulative n-grams on this corpus ($p > 0.05$). The benefit of cumulative n-grams suggests that the lexical processing of words skipped during a saccade has a time cost similar to directly fixated words.

3.2   Cumulative PCFG surprisal

Probabilistic context-free grammar (PCFG) surprisal is similar to n-gram surprisal in that it is also conditioned on preceding context, but PCFG surprisal is conditioned on hierarchic structure rather than on linear lexical sequences (see Equation 3). PCFG surprisal, therefore, suffers from the same deficiency as non-cumulative n-gram surprisal when modeling reading times: the condition context is never generated by the model.

$$\text{PCFG}(w, i) = -\log \text{P}(T_i = w_i \mid T_1 \ldots T_{i-1} = w_1 \ldots w_{i-1}) \tag{3}$$

$$\text{cumu-PCFG}(w, f_{t-1}, f_t) = \sum_{i=f_{t-1}+1}^{f_t} -\log \text{P}(T_i = w_i \mid T_1 \ldots T_{i-1} = w_1 \ldots w_{i-1}) \tag{4}$$

where w is a vector of input tokens, f_{t-1} is the index of the previous fixation, f_t is the index of the current fixation, T is a random variable over syntactic trees and T_i is a terminal symbol in a tree.

This experiment tested both PCFG surprisal predictors as fixed effects over the baseline from the previous section (now including cumulative n-gram surprisal as a fixed and by-subject random effect). Accumulated PCFG surprisal (see Equation 4) did not improve reading time fit ($p > 0.05$), unlike n-gram surprisal, which replicates a previous result using the Dundee corpus (van Schijndel and Schuler, 2015). In fact, not even basic PCFG surprisal was predictive ($p > 0.05$) over this baseline model in the UCL corpus, whereas it was predictive over this baseline in the Dundee corpus. Posthoc testing on the exploratory data partition revealed that PCFG surprisal becomes predictive on the UCL corpus when the n-gram predictors are removed from the baseline ($p < 0.001$), which could indicate that PCFG surprisal may simply help predict reading times when the n-gram model is too weak. Alternatively, since UCL sentences were chosen for their brevity during corpus construction, there just may not be enough syntactic complexity in the corpus to provide an advantage to PCFG surprisal over the n-gram measures, which would explain why PCFG surprisal is still predictive for Dundee reading times where there is greater syntactic complexity.

However, since cumulative n-gram surprisal is a better predictor of reading times than basic n-gram surprisal, it is conceivable that some other cumulative PCFG surprisal feature could still show up as predictive of UCL reading times even when basic PCFG surprisal fails to be predictive on this corpus. The next experiment formulates a new calculation of cumulative surprisal to explore this possibility.

3.3   Cumulative successor surprisal

In addition to past context, reading times can be influenced by the upcoming words that follow a fixation. Such effects have been observed for orthographic and lexical influences and are called successor effects (Kliegl et al., 2006). This section explores whether such successor effects

---

[4]A random intercept was added for sentence ID-crossed-with-subject in order to account for the problem of repeatedly drawing trials from the same sentential context.

[5]Region length measures the number of words in the associated first pass region.

Model	N-gram vs Cumu-N-gram		
	β	Log-Likelihood	AIC
Baseline		-12702	25476
Base+Basic	0.035	-12689^*	25451
Base+Cumulative	0.055	-12683^*	25440
Base+Both		-12683^*	25442

Baseline random slopes: sentpos, wlen, rlen, prevfix, 5-gram, cumu-5-gram
Baseline fixed effects: sentpos, wlen, rlen, prevfix

Table 1: Goodness of fit of n-gram models to reading times in the UCL corpus. Significance testing was performed between each model and the models in the section above it. Significance for the Base+Both model applies to improvement over its Base+Basic model. * p $< .001$

Model	Future-N-grams vs Future-PCFG		
	β	Log-Likelihood	AIC
Baseline		-12276	24642
Base+Future-N-grams	0.034	-12259^*	24610
Base+Future-PCFG	0.025	-12266^*	24624
Base+Both		-12259^*	24612

Baseline random slopes: sentpos, wlen, rlen, prevfix, cumu-5-gram, future-5-grams, future-PCFG
Baseline fixed effects: sentpos, wlen, rlen, prevfix, cumu-5-gram

Table 2: Goodness of fit of future n-grams and future surprisal to reading times. Significance testing was performed between each model and the models in the section above it. Significance for the Base+Both model applies to improvement over the Base+Future-PCFG model. * p < 0.001

will generalize to something as latent as the syntactic structure underlying upcoming lexical material. That is, instead of accumulating the surprisal condition over the region prior to and including each fixated target, this section attempts to accumulate upcoming syntactic structure over the region following each fixated target. Using the example in Figure 1, part of the time spent at fixation 1 might be caused by the complexity of the upcoming material: 'apple', 'that', etc. Therefore, this work compares the predictivity of future cumulative n-gram surprisal (see Equation 5) and future cumulative PCFG surprisal (see Equation 6) over the n-gram baseline from Section 3.2 on the UCL corpus (see Table 2).

$$\text{future-}n\text{-gram}(w, f_t, f_{t+1}) = \sum_{i=f_t+1}^{f_{t+1}} -\log \text{P}(w_i \mid w_{i-n} \ldots w_{i-1}) \tag{5}$$

$$\text{future-PCFG}(w, f_t, f_{t+1}) = \sum_{i=f_t+1}^{f_{t+1}} -\log \text{P}(T_i = w_i \mid T_1 \ldots T_{i-1} = w_1 \ldots w_{i-1}) \tag{6}$$

where again w is a vector of input tokens, f_t is the index of the current fixation, f_{t+1} is the index of the next fixation, T is a random variable over syntactic trees and T_i is a terminal symbol in a tree.

Future cumulative PCFG surprisal ceases to be predictive when future-n-grams are in the model, though future-n-grams are predictive over future PCFG surprisal (p < 0.001). Therefore, while future PCFG surprisal appears to be a significant predictor of reading times on its own (p < 0.001), it seems largely eclipsed by the upcoming lexical information. Further, the present study replicated this result on the Dundee corpus (Kennedy et al., 2003) where, although non-cumulative PCFG surprisal is predictive over the n-gram baseline on that corpus, future-PCFG surprisal is still not predictive ($p > 0.05$). Together, these findings suggest that PCFG surprisal does not accumulate, despite evidence that skipped lexical items are processed with some time cost.

3.4 Limitations of successor n-grams

Angele et al. (2015) demonstrated that the predictivity of successor effects cannot be exclusively driven by parafoveal preview; instead, the influence of successor effects may arise from sequence prediction, which could happen, for example, if the parser operates over super-lexical chunks (Hale, 2014). This section investigates the extent of n-gram successor predictivity on the UCL corpus. On the exploration partition, four cumulative 5-gram successor predictors are tested which utilize look-ahead for 1-word, 2-words, 3-words, or 4-words.[6] Each future n-gram variant is evaluated based on how it improves over the baseline in Section 3.2. Although there are 3- and 4-word saccades in the data, 2-word future n-grams provide the best fit to the data even on the held-out data partition (p < 0.001). In contrast, Angele et al. (2015) previously found that successor effects were mainly driven by the word following the target fixation, which suggests that the successor effect observed by Angele et al. may only account for a subset of the successor influences on reading times. It's possible that parafoveal preview, which was not possible in the masked condition of the Angele et al. (2015) study, accounts for the additional look-ahead observed in this work (e.g., parafoveal look-ahead could help with the word following the target, and the predictive effect observed by Angele et al. could help with the next word), but additional investigation of this hypothesis is left for future work.

4 Discussion

This work has confirmed previous findings that cumulative n-grams provide a better model of reading times than the typical non-cumulative reading times (van Schijndel and Schuler, 2015). In addition, this work has confirmed previous findings that upcoming lexical items can affect reading times in an n-gram successor effect (Kliegl et al., 2007; Angele et al., 2015), presumably ruling out incompatible expectations before directly fixating on that material or so that such material can be skipped via saccade. The fact that cumulative n-gram models strongly predict reading times suggests PCFG surprisal should be similarly affected, but this work has failed to find such an effect either before or at each given target word. The improved reading time fit for accumulated n-gram surprisal suggests that the material skipped during a saccade is processed with a reading time cost. Therefore, although PCFG surprisal has previously been found to predict reading times over an n-gram baseline (Boston et al., 2008; Demberg and Keller, 2008), the lack of accumulation raises questions about PCFG surprisal as a predictor of the reading time influence of syntactic processing.

Finally, the existence of n-gram successor effects raises questions about other information-theoretic measures such as entropy reduction (Hale, 2006). Entropy reduction measures the change in uncertainty at each new word. In practice, the entropy of an observation is often approximated by estimating uncertainty about the next word in a sequence given the preceding observations, but this measurement does not make much sense if the following two words are already being integrated along with the target observation (i.e. there is very little to no uncertainty about the next word in the sequence). Thus, the frontier of processing must be determined for a well-motivated measure of entropy reduction.

In conclusion, the results of this study provide greater insight into how lexical sequence information is processed during reading, providing stronger baseline measures against which to test

---

[6]Each future n-gram variant is a forward 5-gram measure that accumulates over the given number of successor words. Each only includes material up to the following fixation, so 4-word future n-grams compute future cumulative n-gram probabilities up to four words ahead, but if the upcoming saccade is only two words long, then 4-word future n-grams will only compute future n-gram probability for the upcoming two words.

higher level theories of sentence processing in the future.

Acknowledgements

This work was supported by the National Science Foundation Graduate Research Fellowship under Grant No. DGE-1343012.

References

Bernhard Angele, Elizabeth R. Schotter, Timothy J. Slattery, Tara L. Tenenbaum, Klinton Bicknell, and Keith Rayner. 2015. Do successor effects in reading reflect lexical parafoveal processing? evidence from corpus-based and experimental eye movement data. *Journal of Memory and Language*, 79–80:76–96.

Marisa Ferrara Boston, John T. Hale, Reinhold Kliegl, Umesh Patil, and Shravan Vasishth. 2008. Parsing costs as predictors of reading difficulty: An evaluation using the Potsdam Sentence Corpus. *Journal of Eye Movement Research*, 2(1):1–12.

G. E. P. Box and D. R. Cox. 1964. An analysis of transformations. *Journal of the Royal Statistical Society, B*, 26:211–234.

Vera Demberg and Frank Keller. 2008. Data from eye-tracking corpora as evidence for theories of syntactic processing complexity. *Cognition*, 109(2):193–210.

Stefan L. Frank, Irene Fernandez Monsalve, Robin L. Thompson, and Gabriella Vigliocco. 2013. Reading time data for evaluating broad-coverage models of English sentence processing. *Behavior Research Methods*, 45:1182–1190.

David Graff and Christopher Cieri, 2003. *English Gigaword LDC2003T05*.

John Hale. 2006. Uncertainty about the rest of the sentence. *Cognitive Science*, 30(4):609–642.

John Hale, 2014. *Automaton theories of human sentence comprehension*, chapter 8. CSLI lecture notes. CSLI Publications/Center for the Study of Language & Information.

Kenneth Heafield, Ivan Pouzyrevsky, Jonathan H. Clark, and Philipp Koehn. 2013. Scalable modified Kneser-Ney language model estimation. In *Proceedings of the 51st Annual Meeting of the Association for Computational Linguistics*, pages 690–696, Sofia, Bulgaria, August.

Alan Kennedy, James Pynte, and Robin Hill. 2003. The Dundee corpus. In *Proceedings of the 12th European conference on eye movement*.

R. Kliegl, A. Nuthmann, and R. Engbert. 2006. Tracking the mind during reading: the influence of past, present, and future words on fixation durations. *Journal of Experimental Psychology: General*, 135:12–35.

R. Kliegl, S. Risse, and J. Laubrock. 2007. Preview benefit and parafoveal-on-foveal effects from word n + 2. *Journal of Experimental Psychology: Human Perception and Performance*, 33(5):1250–1255.

Marten van Schijndel and William Schuler. 2015. Hierarchic syntax improves reading time prediction. In *Proceedings of NAACL-HLT 2015*. Association for Computational Linguistics.

Marten van Schijndel, Andy Exley, and William Schuler. 2013. A model of language processing as hierarchic sequential prediction. *Topics in Cognitive Science*, 5(3):522–540.

Towards grounding computational linguistic approaches to readability: Modeling reader-text interaction for easy and difficult texts

Sowmya Vajjala
Iowa State University, USA
`sowmya@iastate.edu`

Detmar Meurers
LEAD Graduate School and Research Network
University of Tübingen, Germany
`dm@sfs.uni-tuebingen.de`

Alexander Eitel
University of Freiburg, Germany
`alexander.eitel@psychologie.uni-freiburg.de`

Katharina Scheiter
LEAD Graduate School and Research Network
Leibniz-Institut für Wissensmedien (IWM), Tübingen, Germany
`k.scheiter@iwm-tuebingen.de`

Abstract

Computational approaches to readability assessment are generally built and evaluated using gold standard corpora labeled by publishers or teachers rather than being grounded in observations about human performance. Considering that both the reading process and the outcome can be observed, there is an empirical wealth that could be used to ground computational analysis of text readability. This will also support explicit readability models connecting text complexity and the reader's language proficiency to the reading process and outcomes.

This paper takes a step in this direction by reporting on an experiment to study how the relation between text complexity and reader's language proficiency affects the reading process and performance outcomes of readers after reading We modeled the reading process using three eye tracking variables: fixation count, average fixation count, and second pass reading duration. Our models for these variables explained 78.9%, 74% and 67.4% variance, respectively. Performance outcome was modeled through recall and comprehension questions, and these models explained 58.9% and 27.6% of the variance, respectively. While the online models give us a better understanding of the cognitive correlates of reading with text complexity and language proficiency, modeling of the offline measures can be particularly relevant for incorporating user aspects into readability models.

1 Introduction

Automatic Readability Assessment (ARA) has been an active area of research in computational linguistics over the past two decades, resulting in a wide range of supervised machine learning models that used both theory driven and data driven features (Petersen, 2007; Feng, 2010; Vajjala and Meurers, 2014b; Jiang et al., 2015, for example). Though the purpose of ARA is to predict text complexity, the eventual goal is ensure that the predictions reflect the comprehension difficulties in the reader. However, so far, ARA models primarily used training corpora that were based on judgements of teachers and other language experts, and not based on the actual reading performance of students, as was also recently criticized by education researchers (Valencia et al., 2014; Williamson et al., 2014; Cunningham and Mesmer, 2014). While this can be considered a shortcoming, obtaining large amounts of data on the actual reading performance of target population is difficult and time consuming. One way to tackle this is to develop a hybrid ARA model, which separately models text complexity and user's language comprehension ability and link them through another model. In this paper, we describe one approach to integrate reader and text characteristics into a single model for automatic readability assessment.

Eye-tracking was employed as a method to understand various NLP problems such as annotation task difficulty (Tomanek et al., 2010; Joshi et al., 2013; Joshi et al., 2014; Barrett and Søgaard, 2015),

Proceedings of the Workshop on Computational Linguistics for Linguistic Complexity,
pages 38–48, Osaka, Japan, December 11-17 2016.

translation difficulty (Mishra et al., 2013), and studying reader eye movements using standard corpora (Martínez-Gómez et al., 2012; Matthies and Søgaard, 2013). Cognitive psychologists have for a long time studied eye-movement patterns of readers to understand the cognitive processes in reading and comprehension, and what causes reading difficulty (Just and Carpenter, 1980; Rayner, 1998; Clifton Jr et al., 2007). Studying the eye movements of readers during reading considering both text and reader factors will give us a better understanding about the online link (during reading) between text complexity and reader proficiency. Asking readers to answer questions about the text will give us an understanding about the offline link (after reading) between text complexity and reader proficiency. Finally, having a means to combine readability models with a model of readers' language proficiency will provide us a solution to create efficient content recommendation system for readers, considering reader characteristics into account.

On this background, we report on an experiment that studies the relation between text complexity and reader proficiency during and after reading. To our knowledge, this is the first reported study to combine online and and offline measures in one experiment, and develop models for more than one form of questions. In sum, the contributions of this paper are:

1. We explored modeling the cognitive correlates of text complexity and reader proficiency by studying the eye movements of readers using three eye-tracking measures: fixation count, average fixation count, and second pass reading durations.

2. We modeled how readers will respond to two types of questions (recall and comprehension) after reading the texts of varying reading difficulty, based on their language proficiency. We believe that this model paves way for the development of better text recommendation systems for readers based on their proficiency and the readability of the text itself.

The paper is organized as follows: Section 2 surveys existing literature on the topic and puts our research in context. Section 3 explains the experimental procedure, Section 4 explains the data analysis methods and variables studied, Section 5 describes the results and Section 6 summarizes the main conclusions of this paper.

2 Related Work

The effect of text complexity on a reader's comprehension was studied in cognitive psychology literature in the 70s and 80s, for various reader groups such as high school students (Evans, 1972), elderly readers (Walmsley et al., 1981) and primary school students (Green and Olsen, 1988; Smith, 1988). The primary conclusion from this research so far has been that carefully written simplified versions of texts resulted in better comprehension. Britton and Gülgöz (1991) showed that rewriting a text based on Kintsch's reading comprehension model (Kintsch and van Dijk, 1978) resulted in better free recall of the text.

Apart from this above mentioned research on complex texts and their revised versions, studying eye movement patterns was shown to be useful in understanding the cognitive processes involved in reading and comprehension (e.g., Just and Carpenter, 1980; Rayner, 1998; Clifton et al., 2007). Eye tracking, though time and cost consuming, provides a more natural way to study the reading processes and allows us to study the processes like re-reading of the text by readers. Eye movements in reading research are typically studied in terms of fixations, saccades and regressions. Fixations refer to the relatively stationary positions of the eye at specific areas of text and saccades refer to the rapid eye movements between fixations. Regressions refer to the cases where the reader revisits and fixates on parts that were already read. Reader's comprehension difficulties were shown to manifest in longer fixations, shorter saccades and more regressions in previous research (cf. Rayner (1998) for a review).

Text readability and its effects on reading comprehension have not been explored much from the perspective of reader proficiency and reading performance, to our knowledge. Two studies that are closely related to the current research are Rayner et al. (2006) and Crossley et al. (2014). Rayner et al. (2006) explicitly studied how text's difficulty level affects eye movement measures in reading and concluded that the text difficulty rating correlated strongly with average fixation duration, number of fixations and total time. Readers' performance with comprehension questions did not have a significant correlation with text difficulty in their experiment. More recently, Crossley et al. (2014) used a moving window self-paced reading task to study the effect of text simplification on text comprehension and reading time of second language learners of English. The moving window shows a sentence step by step, without showing the full text, and with no means to do re-reading. Comprehension was assessed by means of yes/no questions and the subjects also participated in an English proficiency test. Their results showed that while text complexity affected the reading time, this effect was no longer significant upon including the subject's English reading proficiency as a covariate. In terms of comprehension, while text complexity was significant, the effect of text complexity on comprehension was less for highly proficient readers compared to low proficiency readers. Our study differs from Rayner et al. (2006) in terms of materials and analysis methods. While they used a collection on unrelated text passages for their study, we use same texts written in two versions for the experiments. Our study differs from Crossley et al. (2014) in terms of the experimental methods. While they did a self-paced reading time study with a moving window approach, we used eye-tracking, which allows us to observe more reading variables. Finally, our study differs from both the studies in terms of additional eye-tracking and reader performance variables studied.

3   Experiment

Participants: 48 non-native English speakers studying in a German university participated in this study. Their English proficiency was evaluated using a standardized online c-test (Taylor, 1953) used at the University for placement testing, and the average score of the participants was 72.6 (range: $[21, 112]$) where a score of 100+ is considered highly proficient. The participants came from different L1 backgrounds. We collected this information but it was not used in the analyses reported here.

Texts: Four texts, each written in two versions (advanced and beginner), taken from onestopenglish.com, were used in this study. Texts from the same source were used in related research (Crossley et al., 2014). Since the participants read the text from an eye-tracker, we restricted the length of texts used to 300-350 words in both versions. They read a practice text and answered questions before starting the actual experiment. Eight recall questions and six comprehension questions per text were created, which had the same answer in both versions of a text. While the recall questions primarily dealt with the factual information in the text and had short answers spanning a few words, comprehension questions were yes/no questions that needed drawing inferences. All the authors worked together to create the questions, and the final list of questions was created after a discussion to reach consensus about the questions and answers to the questions.[1] The responses of participants were manually evaluated by a graduate student, by comparing them with the gold standard answers.

Table 1 shows some statistics about the texts used, along with additional information about the complexity of the texts based on automated approaches.

Text_Version	Num. Sentences	NumWords	Flesch-Kincaid	VM	Surprisal
1_Difficult	12	296	14.75	5.2	207.5
1_Easy	15	298	10.09	3.9	147.2
2_Difficult	11	286	11.00	4.2	193.2
2_Easy	14	234	6.30	3.1	112.3
3_Difficult	11	248	11.10	4.1	165.4
3_Easy	13	230	7.74	3.0	124.6
4_Difficult	12	312	13.70	5.4	181.9
4_Easy	14	306	11.08	4.8	144.4

Table 1: Number of words in the texts used for the experiment

---

[1]The texts in both versions, c-test and the questions asked can be accessed in the Appendix of Vajjala (2015).

Flesch-Kincaid Grade Level (Kincaid et al., 1975) is a standard readability formula. VM refers to the readability score assigned by the model of Vajjala and Meurers (2014a), which is a regression model based on several lexical and syntactic features, and outputs a score between 1–6, with higher values indicating more difficult texts. Surprisal is a psycholinguistic measure of expected cognitive load during sentence processing, based on information theory. We took the average total surprisal for all sentences from Roark parser (Roark et al., 2009) as a measure of surprisal for each text. Though we modeled different notions of complexity, we only report about the models with the binary complexity from onestopenglish.com in this paper.

Procedure: We employed Latin square design for the experiment, making sure each participant read all four texts, alternating between easy and difficult versions. No participant read the same text in two versions. They answered questions on paper after each text and the eye-tracker was re-calibrated for their next reading. Participants were randomly assigned to one of the four experimental conditions, which differed in the order of texts read. We conducted the experiment using iViewX^{TM} Hi-speed eye-tracker from Senso Motoric Instruments (SMI) and collected the reading data through SMI BeGaze[2] software with Reading package.

4 Analysis Methods

4.1 Modeling

We modeled our experimental data using Generalized Additive Mixed Models (GAMMs, Wood (2006)) and in a cross validation setup. GAMMs are a combination of Generalized Additive Models (GAM) and mixed effects models. Whereas GAM allows us to model complex non-linear interactions between variables by modeling the response variable as a function a smoothed version of predictor variables, GAMM adds an additional layer of modeling convenience to GAM by allowing us to delineate between variables with fixed effects and random effects as in a mixed effects model. In these models, fixed effects refer to the independent variables considered in the experiment design and random effect variables are used to model the variation due to sampling choices. In our experiment, texts and participants can be considered random variables, since we cannot sample all possible texts or humans in a single experiment. Following previous research which used GAMMs for linguistic studies (Wieling et al., 2014; Nixon et al., 2015), we constructed our GAMM models as implemented in the mgcv[3] (Wood, 2011) package in R.

4.2 Experimental Variables

Dependent Variables: We report on three eye-tracking variables and two reader performance measures as our dependent variables:[4]

Three eye-tracking measures – average fixation count (average number of times a reader fixates on a word) and average fixation duration (average duration of such fixations in milliseconds), and average second pass reading time (in milliseconds) – were analyzed to study study how the relation between text complexity and reader proficiency affects online processing of these texts. Previous research in cognitive psychology has shown that a reader's comprehension difficulties are reflected in eye-movements through increased (Rayner, 1998) and longer (Just and Carpenter, 1980; Rayner, 1998) fixations. Both these measures are also known to correlate with text difficulty in the experiment described by Rayner et al. (2006).

Two reader performance outcome measures – number of correct answers for recall and comprehension questions – were used as dependent variables related to offline measures. Each text had eight recall and six comprehension questions, which are the maximum scores the participants can get per text respectively.

---

[2]http://www.smivision.com/en/gaze-and-eye-tracking-systems/products/begaze-analysis-software.html
[3]https://cran.r-project.org/web/packages/mgcv/
[4]We studied other eye-tracking variables as well. More details can be found in Vajjala (2015, ch. 4).

Independent (fixed effect) Variables: We considered the binary text complexity (categorical: elementary and advanced as easy and difficult respectively) and the reader's English proficiency (numeric) as two primary independent variables. Additionally, hypothesizing that there could be some effect of reading texts one after another, we also considered the order in which the participant read a given text (which depends on the experimental condition) as another independent variable.

Random Effects Variables: The two likely random effect factors that can cause a systematic variation in model construction in this experiment are participants and texts. Thus, we considered both of them as random effect variables.

5   Results

For each dependent variable, multiple GAMM models were constructed with different random effect structures, interaction components, and smoothing functions. Model performance was compared in terms of variance explained (R^2) and statistical significance of the differences were compared using the itsadug[5] (van Rij et al., 2016) package in R. We report the results with only the best performing model for each variable below.

Online measures – Fixation count: The best performing model for fixation count explained 78.9% of the variance and included a three way interaction between text difficulty, reader proficiency and text order, modeled with a tensor product smooth function and with log-transformed fixation counts. While the interaction between proficiency and text complexity was not by itself a significant factor in this model, the three way interaction between proficiency, complexity and text order was significant. The model summary, showing the parametric coefficients and the significant smooth terms can be seen in Table 2.

Parametric Coefficients

Variable	Estimate	Std. Err.	t	p-value
Intercept	2.478	0.0481	51.51	< 0.001
Difficulty-Easy	-0.178	0.023	-7.61	$*< 0.001$

Significant Smooth Terms

Variable	RE?	DF	F	p-value
te(Proficiency, Order): Difficult	No	8.095	4.273	$*< 0.001$
te(Proficiency, Order): Easy	No	4.544	7.549	$*< 0.001$
participant	Yes	41.86	11.020	$*< 0.001$
text	Yes	2.154	3.015	$*0.007$

Variance Explained (R^2 adj): 78.9%

Table 2: Best Performing Model for Fixation Count (* indicates statistically significant)

The negative co-efficient for difficulty in Table 2 shows that the fixation count decreases as one goes from difficult to easy texts. It also shows that the random variations due to the individual differences among participants and texts are both significant factors. This reiterates the usefulness of considering random effects and going beyond linear models, in understanding the relation between eye-tracking variables, reader proficiency, and text complexity. A visualization of the three way interaction between proficiency, text complexity and text order is presented in Figure 1.

We can observe from the figure that low proficiency readers make higher number of fixations (darker color indicates lower values) when they read difficult texts compared to easy texts. However, the number of fixations also increase depending when they read a text. The fixation counts are clearly lower for the texts they read in the early parts of the experiment. However, this effect (and that of text complexity) is less pronounced in more proficient readers. Thus, we can conclude that fixation count is affected by changes in both reader proficiency and text complexity.

---

[5]https://cran.r-project.org/web/packages/itsadug/

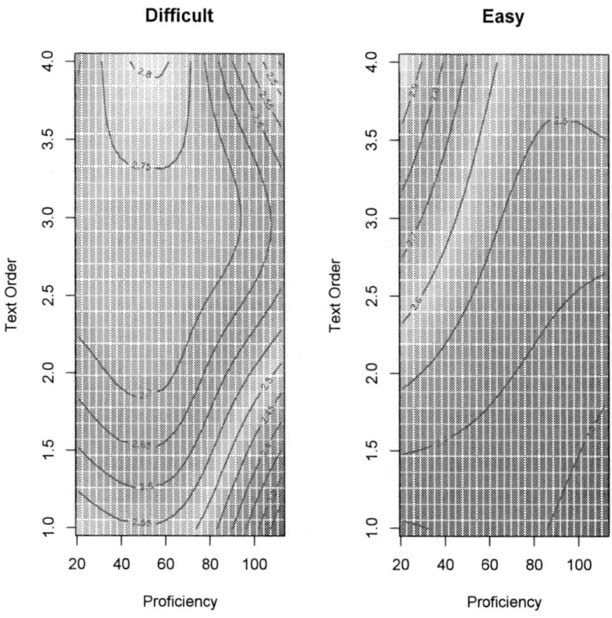

Figure 1: Interaction between Text difficulty, Reader Proficiency and Text Order for fixation count

Online measures – Average Fixation Duration (AFD): The best model for AFD explained 74% of the variance and uses the default thin plate regression spline smoothing without performing any transformations on the AFD. Table 3.

Parametric Coefficients

Variable	Estimate	Std. Err.	t	p-value
Intercept	146.863	10.1432	14.479	< 0.001
Diff-Easy	0.323	4.0968	0.079	0.937
TextOrder	9.0981	2.1122	4.307	$*<0.001$

Significant Smooth Terms

Variable	RE?	DF	F	p-value
Proficiency	No	2.031	3.121	*0.044
Participant	Yes	39.64	7.43	$< *0.001$
Text	Yes	2.63	5.80	$< *0.001$

Variance Explained (R^2 adj): 74%

Table 3: Summary of the GAMM model for Average Fixation Duration

Only proficiency ($p < 0.05$) and text order ($p < 0.001$) had a significant effect for AFD, with higher proficiencies resulting in lower fixation durations. The relationship between proficiency and AFD was non-linear and both the random effects were significant ($p < 0.001$). None of the interactions were significant. These results lead us to a conclusion that AFD is not affected by text complexity, but is affected by a reader's proficiency, in our experimental data.

Online measures – Second pass reading duration: The best performing model for second pass duration explained 67.4% of the variance and included a three way interaction between text difficulty, reader proficiency and text order, modeled with a tensor product smooth function and with log-transformed fixation counts. Table 4 summarizes the coefficients of the GAMM model. As can be observed from the model summary in Table 4, text difficulty, text order, the three way interaction between proficiency, text order and difficulty, and both the random effects – all were significant predictors for this model.

Parametric Coefficients

Variable	Estimate	Std. Error	t value	p-value
Intercept	6.11	0.09	70.43	< 0.001
Difficulty-Easy	-0.296	0.046	-6.395	$*< 0.001$
TextOrder	0.521	0.026	19.878	$* < 0.001$

Significant Smooth Terms

Variable	is Random Effect?	Est. deg. of freedom	F	p-value
te(Proficiency,TextOrder):Difficult	No	7.785	22.296	$*< 0.001$
te(Proficiency,TextOrder):Easy	No	5.32	29.646	$*< 0.001$
Participant	Yes	38.43	5.456	$*< 0.001$

Variance Explained (R^2 adj): 67.4%

Table 4: Best Performing Model for Second Pass Duration

Offline measures – Recall: The best performing model involved a three way interaction, as in fixation count and second pass reading duration, and with tensor smooths. Table 5 shows the model summary in terms of its coefficients and smooth terms. As we can see in the parametric coefficients, positive co-efficient for difficulty variable indicates that the performance of participants with recall questions increased as one moved from difficult to easy texts, which means they scored higher for easy texts. There is also a significant interaction between proficiency, text order and text difficulty, and both the random effects were significant. This leads us to a conclusion that the participants' responses to recall questions depends on both text difficulty and reader proficiency, along with other factors.

Parametric Coefficients

Variable	Estimate	Std. Error	t value	p-value
Intercept	3.006	0.321	9.347	< 0.001
Difficulty-Easy	0.679	0.192	3.527	$*< 0.001$
TextOrder	0.467	0.089	5.202	$*< 0.001$

Significant Smooth Terms

Variable	is Random Effect?	Est. deg. of freedom	F	p-value
s(Proficiency)	No	0.9887	51.29	$*< 0.001$
te(Proficiency,TextOrder):Difficulty-Difficult	No	5.78	3.194	$*0.006$
Participant	Yes	29.272	1.806	$*< 0.001$
Text	Yes	2.009	3.817	$*0.0014$

Variance Explained (R^2 adj): 58.9%

Table 5: Best Performing Model for Recall

Offline measures – Comprehension: The best model for comprehension scores explained only 27.6% of variance compared to other variables, with only proficiency being a significant predictor, apart from the random variation due to texts used. Table 6 shows the model summary for comprehension scores. It is interesting to note that text complexity did not affect reader's comprehension of a text. Thus, though we hypothesized that comprehension scores are affected by text complexity, it seems to depend only on the language proficiency of the participant and not on the reading level of the text, as was also shown by Crossley et al. (2014). However, the low performance of this model compared to others described above needs further study, in order to understand what affects readers' performance on such yes/no comprehension questions.

The experiments discussed above demonstrate that the eye-tracking measures we studied seem to be affected by text complexity, proficiency and their interaction. We also observed that one of the outcome variables, recall, seem to be influenced by both text complexity and readers' language proficiency while only the latter affected the comprehension scores.

Parametric Coefficients

Variable	Estimate	Std. Err.	t	p-value
Intercept	3.951	0.279	14.12	< 0.001
Diff:Easy	0.039	0.154	0.255	0.799
TextOrder	0.108	0.077	1.401	0.163

Significant Smooth Terms

Variable	RE?	DF	F	p-value
Proficiency	No	1.313	10.051	< 0.001
Text	Yes	2.39	4.351	0.001

Variance Explained (R^2 adj): 27.6%

Table 6: Summary of the GAMM model for Comprehension Scores

Relation between online and offline measures: Given this background, we briefly explored whether the effect of text complexity and proficiency on online processing can be used to explain the differences in the learning outcomes of the participants. We used mediation analysis as a means to address this question. Mediation analysis is the process of studying the relationship between the dependent and independent variables by means of a third "mediator" variable. In mediation models, it is generally hypothesized that the independent variable influences the mediator, which in turn influences the dependent variable. It is usually used to understand the underlying mechanism behind a known relationship. We performed this analysis using the mediation package in R (Tingley et al., 2014)[6] considering the eye-tracking measures as mediator variables and the recall and comprehension scores as the dependent variables, and text complexity and language proficiency as the independent variables respectively. To perform the mediation analyses, we need to ensure that the relationship between the mediator and the dependent variable is statistically significant in the first place. Among the three eye-tracking measures we explored, only average fixation duration showed a significant correlation with recall and comprehension. So, we performed the mediation analysis only with this as the mediator variable. There was no significant mediation effect of average fixation duration on either recall or comprehension performance of the participants. Thus, we can conclude that eye-tracking is not mediating the participant differences in the recall and comprehension scores.

6 Conclusion

In this paper, we described an approach to model the relation between text complexity and the reader's language proficiency. Our approach has two parts: modeling the cognitive correlates of text complexity using eye tracking, and a modeling for performance outcomes of the reader by asking them to answer questions about the texts they read. These experiments were motivated by the ultimate goal of recommending appropriate texts to readers considering both text complexity and reader proficiency as influencing factors. In terms of the cognitive correlates, while fixation count and second pass duration were affected by both text complexity and reader proficiency, average fixation duration was affected by reader proficiency alone. For performance measures, while the recall model explained 58.9% variance and had both text complexity and reader proficiency as significant predictors, the comprehension model model was affected by proficiency alone, and explained only 27.6% of the variance.

The results from the our analyses support the conclusion that the eye-movement patterns of the readers are sensitive to the complexity of the text they are reading, as was seen by increased fixation counts and second pass reading time with increased text complexity. Average fixation duration was affected by language proficiency but not text complexity. In terms of the outcome measures, on one hand, the performance of recall and comprehension models leaves scope for a lot of improvement to be used in real life application scenarios. But, it also reiterates the importance of considering differences between question types during modeling. Further, our comprehension questions here primarily consisted of Yes/No

---

[6]`http://cran.r-project.org/web/packages/mediation/`

questions that relied on short pieces of information. Modeling responses to other questions that require detailed responses, and that address different levels of comprehension (Day and Park, 2005) may help us build better models in future.

The approach described in this experiment used human encoded text complexity labels and an automated proficiency test. Replacing human created labels with an automated readability assessment model prediction will make the offline measures models applicable to new texts, making it useful for text recommendation based on reader language proficiency and text complexity. Thus, the approach can provide a means to personalize text recommendations considering both reading level and reader characteristics into account, without requiring any search logs per user. This approach can also avoid the problem of creating huge amounts of user based reading data to train readability assessment models by keeping the text complexity model separate from the user proficiency model, but combining them together into a ensemble model.

The current paper demonstrates a simple way of combining a model of text complexity and a simple model of reader proficiency to predict the recall and comprehension of a given reader and a given text. However, text complexity is much richer than a single number, as the wide range of linguistic features considered in Vajjala (2015) illustrate, and future modeling of the link between text complexity and reader proficiency arguably should consider incorporating different aspects of language form and content (vocabulary, syntax, discourse coherence, etc.) into the model. Similarly, future modeling of users should integrate more aspects of language proficiency (e.g., complexity, accuracy, fluency), and cognitive individual differences (e.g., working memory capacity) to build a richer proficiency profile for the user. Consequently, a comprehensive combined model of text complexity and reader proficiency will need to consider all these aspects and their potential interaction.

Acknowledgments

We would like to thank the three anonymous reviewers for their comments and Harald Baayen for patiently answering our questions about interpreting GAMM results. This research was funded by the LEAD Graduate School & Research Network [GSC1028], a project of the Excellence Initiative of the German federal and state governments, and received support through grants ANR-11-LABX-0036 (BLRI) and ANR-11-IDEX-0001-02 (A*MIDEX).

References

Maria Barrett and Anders Søgaard. 2015. Reading behavior predicts syntactic categories. *CoNLL 2015*, page 345.

Bruce K. Britton and Sami Gülgöz. 1991. Using kintsch's computational model to improve instructional text: Effects of repairing inference calls on recall and cognitive structures. *Journal of Educational Psychology*, 83:329–345.

Charles Clifton Jr, Adrian Staub, and Keith Rayner, 2007. *Eye movement research: A window on mind and brain*, chapter Eye movements in reading words and sentences, pages 341–372. Oxford:Elsevier Ltd.

Scott A. Crossley, Hae Sung Yang, and Danielle S. McNamara. 2014. What's so simple about simplified texts? a computational and psycholinguistic investigation of text comprehension and text processing. *Reading in a Foreign Language*, 26(1):92–113.

James W. Cunningham and Heidi Anne Mesmer. 2014. Quantitative measurement of text difficulty: What's the use? *The Elementary School Journal*, 115(2):pp. 255–269.

Richard R. Day and Jeong-Suk Park. 2005. Developing reading comprehension questions. *Reading in a Foreign Language*, 17(1):60–73.

Ronald V. Evans. 1972. The effect of transformational simplification on the reading comprehension of selected high school students. In *Journal of Literacy Research*.

Lijun Feng. 2010. *Automatic Readability Assessment*. Ph.D. thesis, City University of New York (CUNY).

Georgia M. Green and Margaret S. Olsen, 1988. *Linguistic Complexity and Text Comprehension: Readability Issues Reconsidered*, chapter 5. Preferences for and Comprehension of Original and Readability Adapted Materials, pages 115–140. Lawrence Erlbaum Associates.

Zhiwei Jiang, Gang Sun, Qing Gu, Tao Bai, and Daoxu Chen. 2015. A graph-based readability assessment method using word coupling. In *Proceedings of the 2015 Conference on Empirical Methods in Natural Language Processing*, pages 411–420, Lisbon, Portugal, September. Association for Computational Linguistics.

Salil Joshi, Diptesh Kanojia, and Pushpak Bhattacharyya. 2013. More than meets the eye: Study of human cognition in sense annotation. In *HLT-NAACL*, pages 733–738.

Aditya Joshi, Abhijit Mishra, Nivvedan Senthamilselvan, and Pushpak Bhattacharyya. 2014. Measuring sentiment annotation complexity of text. In *ACL (2)*, pages 36–41.

M.A. Just and P.A. Carpenter. 1980. A theory of reading: From eye fixations to comprehension. *Psychological Review*, 87:329–355.

J. P. Kincaid, R. P. Jr. Fishburne, R. L. Rogers, and B. S Chissom. 1975. Derivation of new readability formulas (Automated Readability Index, Fog Count and Flesch Reading Ease formula) for Navy enlisted personnel. Research Branch Report 8-75, Naval Technical Training Command, Millington, TN.

Walter Kintsch and Teun A van Dijk. 1978. Toward a model of text comprehension and productions. *Pschological Review*, 85(5):363–394, September.

Pascual Martínez-Gómez, Tadayoshi Hara, and Akiko N Aizawa. 2012. Recognizing personal characteristics of readers using eye-movements and text features. In *COLING*, pages 1747–1762.

Franz Matthies and Anders Søgaard. 2013. With blinkers on: Robust prediction of eye movements across readers. In *EMNLP*, pages 803–807.

Abhijit Mishra, Pushpak Bhattacharyya, Michael Carl, and IBC CRITT. 2013. Automatically predicting sentence translation difficulty. In *ACL (2)*, pages 346–351.

Jessie S Nixon, Jacolien van Rij, Peggy Mok, Harald Baayen, and Yiya Chen. 2015. Eye movements reflect acoustic cue informativity and statistical noise. *Experimental Linguistics*, page 50.

Sarah E. Petersen. 2007. *Natural Language Processing Tools for Reading Level Assessment and Text Simplification for Bilingual Education*. Ph.D. thesis, University of Washington.

Keith Rayner, Kathryn H. Chace, Timothy J. Slattery, and Jane Ashby. 2006. Eye movements as reflections of comprehension processes in reading. *Scientific Studies of Reading*, 10(3):241–255.

K. Rayner. 1998. Eye movements in reading and information processing: 20 years of research. *Psychological Bulletin*, 124:372–422.

Brian Roark, Asaf Bachrach, Carlos Cardenas, and Christophe Pallier. 2009. Deriving lexical and syntactic expectation-based measures for psycholinguistic modeling via incremental top-down parsing. In *Proceedings of the 2009 Conference on Empirical Methods in Natural Language Processing (EMNLP)*, pages 324–333. Association for Computational Linguistics.

Carlota S. Smith, 1988. *Linguistic Complexity and Text Comprehension: Readability Issues Reconsidered*, chapter Chapter 10: Factors of Linguistic Complexity and Performance, pages 247–279. Lawrence Erlbaum Associates.

W.L. Taylor. 1953. Cloze procedure: A new tool for measuring readability. *Journalism Quarterly*, 30:415–433.

Dustin Tingley, Teppei Yamamoto, Kentaro Hirose, Luke Keele, and Kosuke Imai. 2014. mediation: R package for causal mediation analysis. *Journal of Statistical Software*, 59(5):1–38.

Katrin Tomanek, Udo Hahn, Steffen Lohmann, and Jürgen Ziegler. 2010. A cognitive cost model of annotations based on eye-tracking data. In *Proceedings of the 48th Annual Meeting of the Association for Computational Linguistics*, pages 1158–1167. Association for Computational Linguistics.

Sowmya Vajjala and Detmar Meurers. 2014a. Exploring measures of "readability" for spoken language: Analyzing linguistic features of subtitles to identify age-specific tv programs. In *Proceedings of the Third Workshop on Predicting and Improving Text Readability for Target Reader Populations*, pages 21–29, Gothenburg, Sweden. ACL.

Sowmya Vajjala and Detmar Meurers. 2014b. Readability assessment for text simplification: From analyzing documents to identifying sentential simplifications. *International Journal of Applied Linguistics, Special Issue on Current Research in Readability and Text Simplification*, 165(2):142–222.

Sowmya Vajjala. 2015. *Analyzing Text Complexity and Text Simplification: Connecting Linguistics, Processing and Educational Applications*. Ph.D. thesis, University of Tübingen.

Sheila W. Valencia, Karen K. Wixson, and P. David Pearson. 2014. Putting text complexity in context: Refocusing on comprehension of complex text. *The Elementary School Journal*, 115(2):pp. 270–289.

Jacolien van Rij, Martijn Wieling, R. Harald Baayen, and Hedderik van Rijn. 2016. itsadug: Interpreting time series and autocorrelated data using gamms. R package version 2.0.

Sean A. Walmsley, Kathleen M. Scott, and Richard Lehrer. 1981. Effects of document simplification on the reading comprehension of the elderly. In *Journal of Literacy Research*.

Martijn Wieling, Simonetta Montemagni, John Nerbonne, and R Harald Baayen. 2014. Lexical differences between tuscan dialects and standard italian: Accounting for geographic and sociodemographic variation using generalized additive mixed modeling. *Language*, 90(3):669–692.

Gary L. Williamson, Jill Fitzgerald, and A. Jackson Stenner. 2014. Student reading growth illuminates the common core text-complexity standard: Raising both bars. *The Elementary School Journal*, 115(2):pp. 230–254.

S.N Wood. 2006. *Generalized Additive Models: An Introduction with R*. Chapman and Hall/CRC.

S. N. Wood. 2011. Fast stable restricted maximum likelihood and marginal likelihood estimation of semiparametric generalized linear models. *Journal of the Royal Statistical Society (B)*, 73(1):3–36.

Memory access during incremental sentence processing causes reading time latency

Cory Shain[1]
shain.3@osu.edu

Marten van Schijndel[1]
van-schijndel.1@osu.edu

Richard Futrell[2]
futrell@mit.edu

Edward Gibson[2]
egibson@mit.edu

William Schuler[1]
schuler.77@osu.edu

[1]Dept of Linguistics
The Ohio State University

[2]Dept of Brain and Cognitive Sciences
Massachusetts Institute of Technology

Abstract

Studies on the role of memory as a predictor of reading time latencies (1) differ in their predictions about when memory effects should occur in processing and (2) have had mixed results, with strong positive effects emerging from isolated constructed stimuli and weak or even negative effects emerging from naturally-occurring stimuli. Our study addresses these concerns by comparing several implementations of prominent sentence processing theories on an exploratory corpus and evaluating the most successful of these on a confirmatory corpus, using a new self-paced reading corpus of seemingly natural narratives constructed to contain an unusually high proportion of memory-intensive constructions. We show highly significant and complementary broad-coverage latency effects both for predictors based on the Dependency Locality Theory and for predictors based on a left-corner parsing model of sentence processing. Our results indicate that memory access during sentence processing does take time, but suggest that stimuli requiring many memory access events may be necessary in order to observe the effect.

1 Introduction

Any incremental model of sentence processing where an abstract meaning representation is built up word-by-word must involve storage and retrieval of information about previously encountered material from some memory store. The retrieval operations have been hypothesized to be associated with increased processing time (Gibson, 2000; Lewis and Vasishth, 2005; Wu et al., 2010), and this prediction has been borne out in experiments using constructed stimuli (Gibson, 2000; Grodner and Gibson, 2005; Boston et al., 2011; von der Malsburg et al., 2015). However, memory-based latency effects have been null or even negative in broad-coverage reading time experiments using naturally-occurring text data that included baseline controls for n-gram and probabilistic phrase-structure grammar (PCFG) surprisal (Demberg and Keller, 2008; van Schijndel et al., 2013b).

The failure of experimental latency effects to generalize to naturally-occurring data raises doubts about their existence. The effects observed in constructed stimuli could be due to (1) information theoretic phenomena (e.g., surprisal) that such experiments rarely control for, (2) limited syntactic domain (e.g., relative clauses), or (3) 'oddball' effects – i.e. effects related to the semantic strangeness and decontextualized nature of the input, rather than due to difficulty retrieving information from working memory. On the other hand, the lack of positive latency effects in studies using naturally-occurring input could be (1) because of the small number of subjects – ten – in the Dundee corpus (Kennedy et al., 2003) used by e.g. Demberg and Keller (2008) and van Schijndel et al. (2013b) or (2) because naturally-occurring newswire texts might contain too low a proportion of memory-intensive constructions to reveal a generalized memory effect.

In addition to the problem of conflicting results between constructed vs. naturally-occurring stimuli, research on the role of memory in sentence processing must also contend with the open question of where and what kinds of memory effects are predicted during sentence processing. One of the first and most

Proceedings of the Workshop on Computational Linguistics for Linguistic Complexity,
pages 49–58, Osaka, Japan, December 11-17 2016.

well-known memory-based theories of sentence processing is the Dependency Locality Theory (DLT) (Gibson, 2000), which predicts processing difficulty proportional to the number of discourse referents intervening between the current word and any dependencies it shares with words in its preceding context. Lewis and Vasishth (2005), on the other hand, predict difficulty as a function of memory decay during the retrieval operations of an incremental left-corner parser. Note that both of these accounts are locality-based (difficulty is predicted to increase with distance), modeling the notion that decay over time may make it more difficult (and hence time-consuming) to recall items from working memory. However, it is conceivable that processing difficulty may have less to do with locality than simply with whether or not a memory access or recall event has occurred, a hypothesis explored by van Schijndel and Schuler (2013) with mixed results.

The present work seeks to answer these questions by evaluating many plausible implementations of prominent theories of sentence processing as predictors of reading times on the new Natural Stories corpus (Futrell, Gibson, Tily, Vishnevetsky, Piantadosi, & Fedorenko, in prep). The Natural Stories corpus is constructed in order to embed an unusually-high proportion of rare words and memory-intensive constructions in narratives designed to resemble naturally-occurring text. It therefore occupies an intermediary position – which we will refer to as 'constructed-natural' – between isolated constructed stimuli and naturally-occurring text that might help overcome the limitations of both. We evaluate against a strong baseline model that includes controls for n-gram and PCFG surprisal. We find clear evidence for (1) a locality effect when constructing dependencies to preceding words and (2) a locality-independent 'reinstatement' effect whenever derivation fragments must be recalled from working memory during the operation of a left-corner parser. We show that both of these effects contribute independently to model fit. Our findings therefore support the existence of memory-based processing difficulty and shed light on the specific role of memory in sentence processing.

2   Related Work

Previous studies have explored the influence of memory on reading times using constructed stimuli. For example, Grodner and Gibson (2005) showed memory-related effects in self-paced reading of individual sentences constructed to contain difficult center-embeddings. Other studies have used the (constructed) Potsdam eye-tracking corpus (Kliegl et al., 2004) to investigate the predictivity of ACT-R memory influences on reading times (e.g., Boston et al., 2011; von der Malsburg et al., 2015).[1] As mentioned above, effects found in studies using constructed stimuli presented in isolation might face confounds due to 'oddball' effects or lack of extra-sentential context.

Other work has explored memory and processing using naturally-occurring stimuli (generally, newswire texts). Demberg and Keller (2008) examined the influence of the DLT on reading times using the Dundee eye-tracking corpus (Kennedy et al., 2003). They found some evidence of DLT influences on specific content words, but the effect was weak enough that it was not significant until the analysis was constrained to just nouns and verbs. Even then, the effect is not significant under multiple comparison correction. Other studies have also used the Dundee corpus to test the predicted memory effects of left-corner models of sentence processing (van Schijndel and Schuler, 2013; van Schijndel et al., 2013b), but these studies found a negative correlation between reading times and predicted left-corner memory operations, which is the opposite of what most theories of sentence processing predict. We posit that the weakness of the DLT and the unusual left-corner influence on the Dundee corpus may be caused by the limited number of subjects or by the limited number of complex dependencies in the corpus.

The Natural Stories corpus used in this study is constructed in order to tax working memory resources in the processing of otherwise natural-seeming narratives, so it plausibly mitigates concerns related to oddball effects and lack of context on the one hand and syntactically 'easy' constructions on the other. In this respect, the most similar corpus to ours of which we are aware is Bachrach et al. (2009), which like Natural Stories was constructed to read naturally but included a higher degree of syntactic complexity than is usual in naturally-occurring text. However, compared to Natural Stories, Bachrach et al. (2009)

---

[1] The present work does not directly test the predictions of ACT-R, but some of the predictors used in this study – especially the distance-weighted left-corner predictors discussed below – make similar predictions to ACT-R.

has substantially fewer subjects (23 vs. 181) and words (3540 vs. 10257). Wu et al. (2010) used the Bachrach et al. (2009) corpus to investigate the correlation between changes in embedding depth and reading times and found a positive effect on latency.[2]

3 Background

This work explores two related models of the relationship between memory and sentence processing: (1) the Dependency Locality Theory, in which memory is predicted to be used to construct syntactic dependencies to words in the preceding context with a cost proportional to the length of the dependency (or dependencies) being constructed, and (2) left-corner theories of sentence processing, such as Lewis and Vasishth (2005) and Schuler et al. (2010), in which certain parser operations require disjoint incomplete signs (referring to discourse referents) to be recalled from working memory. We outline these broader frameworks, along with a number of possible implementations of each, in the remainder of this section.

3.1 Dependency Locality Theory

The Dependency Locality Theory (DLT; Gibson, 2000) predicts a cost for integrating a word into an incomplete parse proportional to the number of discourse referents that intervene in any syntactic dependencies the word shares with words in its preceding context. For simplicity, Gibson (2000) implements this calculation in terms of abstract 'energy units' (EU) and considers all and only nouns (excluding pronouns) and finite verbs to count as discourse referents. Integration cost is the sum of the 'discourse cost' of the word itself (1 for nouns and finite verbs, 0 otherwise) and the distance of any dependencies to preceding words, measured in number of intervening discourse referents. The cost of long-distance dependencies is assessed at the gap site, producing e.g. subject-/object-relative asymmetries (the relative clause verb intervenes in its own dependency for object gaps but does not for subject gaps).

As pointed out by Gibson (2000), this implementation might benefit from modification in light of other cognitive considerations. In this study, we implemented three such modifications related to verb weights (DLT-V), coordination (DLT-C), and preceding modifier dependencies (DLT-M):

- **DLT-V**: *Verbs are more expensive.* Non-finite verbs receive a cost of 1 (instead of 0) and finite verbs receive a cost of 2 (instead of 1).

- **DLT-C**: *Coordination is less expensive.* Dependencies out of coordinate structures skip preceding conjuncts in the calculation of distance, and dependencies with intervening coordinate structures assign that structure a weight equal to that of its heaviest conjunct.

- **DLT-M**: *Exclude modifier dependencies.* Dependencies to preceding modifiers are ignored.

DLT-V is motivated by the possibility that finite verbs might be more costly to integrate than nouns (since they contain additional information about tense/aspect) and that non-finite verbs might have a non-zero discourse cost. DLT-C is motivated by the fact that coordination can generate very long dependencies that are not particularly difficult to process, suggesting that each sub-referent of a conjunction may be integrated into a conjoined set which is finally integrated at the end of the conjunction. DLT-M is designed to avoid excessive 'double-counting' of material intervening in long modifier dependencies.

These modifications can be applied in any combination, yielding eight distinct implementations of the DLT. Henceforth, we indicate that a modification was applied by suffixing its letter to 'DLT' (e.g., DLT-CM is DLT with the coordination and modifier modifications only). For an illustration of these implementations at work on an example sentence, see Figure 1.

Differences between the four variants illustrated in Figure 1 are especially apparent at the verbs *caught* and *fled* (although note also that *stealing* – a non-finite verb – only has a cost under DLT-V). There are two dependencies between *caught* and preceding words, dependency *a* to the head *and* of its conjoined

---

[2]While the Wu et al. (2010) embedding depth predictor is derived from automatic parses of their corpus, the present work used hand-corrected syntactic annotations to calculate the left-corner operations required to incrementally construct syntactic structures. Wu et al. (2010) also largely focused on the influence of frequency effects which the present work simply adopts as control predictors.

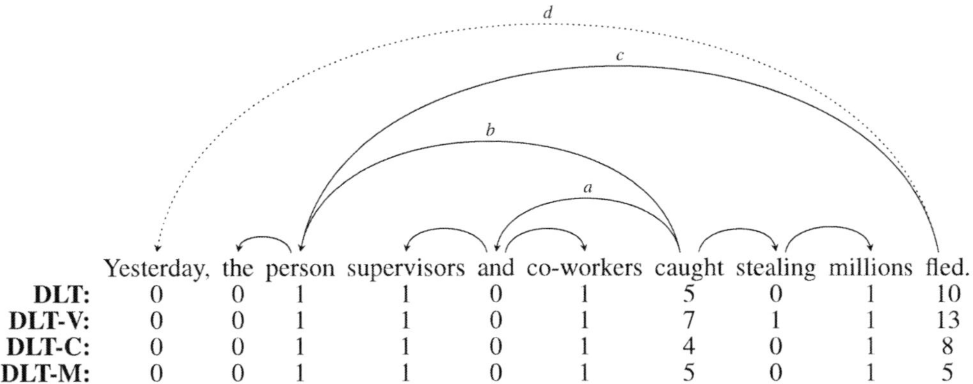

	Yesterday,	the	person	supervisors	and	co-workers	caught	stealing	millions	fled.
DLT:	0	0	1	1	0	1	5	0	1	10
DLT-V:	0	0	1	1	0	1	7	1	1	13
DLT-C:	0	0	1	1	0	1	4	0	1	8
DLT-M:	0	0	1	1	0	1	5	0	1	5

Figure 1: Integration cost calculations for implementations of DLT on an example sentence. For example, at *caught* there is an object gap and therefore dependencies back to *person* (2 nouns and 1 verb intervene) and *supervisors* (1 noun intervenes) = 4 total cost-accumulating interveners. As a finite verb, *caught* gets a cost of 1+4 = 5. Note that this figure increases if verbs become more expensive (DLT-V) and decreases if coordinates become less expensive (DLT-C). Note also that the cost of *fled* is much lower in DLT-M, since the dotted dependency to *Yesterday* is ignored.

subject, and dependency *b* to *person*, the modificand of the relative clause. Dependency *a* spans the intervening word *co-workers*. Dependency *b* is an object relative dependency. Since the gap site follows *caught*, *caught* is included as an intervener in the dependency, which therefore spans *supervisors and co-workers caught*. The DLT integration cost of *caught* is the sum of the discourse cost of *caught* itself and the costs of dependencies *a* and *b*.

These costs vary by implementation. For DLT, *caught* (a finite verb) has a discourse cost of 1, dependency *a* has a cost of 1 for its single intervening noun *co-workers*, and dependency *b* has a cost of 3 for *supervisors*, *co-workers*, and *caught*, for a total integration cost of $1 + 1 + 3 = 5$. For DLT-V, *caught* is worth 2 EU as a finite verb rather than 1. This increases both its discourse cost and its cost as an intervener in dependency *b*, thus increasing the integration cost of *caught* by 2 (from 5 to 7). For DLT-C, the cost of the conjoined noun phrase *supervisors and co-workers* is reduced from 2 to 1 (the weight of its heaviest conjunct) as an intervener in dependency *b*. This reduces the integration cost of *caught* by 1 (from 5 to 4). DLT-M does not affect the cost of *caught*, which has no dependencies to preceding modifiers.

Similar considerations govern the variation in integration cost of *fled*, which has dependencies *c* (to *person*) and *d* (to *Yesterday*). For DLT, the integration cost of *fled* is 4 (for dependency *c*) + 5 (for dependency *d*) + 1 (discourse cost of *fled*) = 10. This increases to 13 for DLT-V because the finite verb *caught*, which intervenes in both dependencies *c* and *d*, is upweighted from 1 to 2, along with *fled* itself. Because the cost of *supervisors and co-workers*, which also intervenes in both *c* and *d*, decreases from 2 to 1 for DLT-C, the DLT-C integration cost of *fled* is reduced by 2 (from 10 to 8). DLT-M ignores the preceding modifier dependency *d*, resulting in an integration cost of 4 (dependency *a*) + 1 (discourse cost of *fled*) = 5.

3.2 Left-corner parsing

Many sentence processing models (Johnson-Laird, 1983; Abney and Johnson, 1991; Gibson, 1991; Resnik, 1992; Stabler, 1994; Lewis and Vasishth, 2005) are defined in terms of left-corner parsing operations (Aho and Ullman, 1972; van Schijndel et al., 2013a), which assemble local dependencies between signs using a minimal store of incomplete derivation fragments. Left-corner parsers account for sequences of words $x_1 \ldots x_T$ as stacked-up derivation fragments a/b, each consisting of a top sign a

lacking a bottom sign b yet to come. When a left-corner parser consumes a word, it makes decisions to fork off and/or join up these derivation fragments. When the current word x_t satisfies the missing bottom sign b of a derivation fragment a/b, the parser replaces a/b in the memory store with a, indicating a completed prediction. Because this does not increase the number of derivation fragments in the memory store, we call this a no-fork (–F) operation:

$$\frac{a/b \quad x_t}{a} \, b \rightarrow x_t. \tag{–F}$$

When the current word x_t does not satisfy the missing sign of a derivation fragment, then x_t is added to the memory store as part of a new derivation fragment c. As this increases the number of stored derivation fragments, we call this a yes-fork operation (+F):[3]

$$\frac{a/b \quad x_t}{a/b \quad c} \, b \xrightarrow{+} c \, ... \, ; \quad c \rightarrow x_t. \tag{+F}$$

The other class of parser operations is join operations. In these operations, the parser decides whether to connect two previously disjoint derivation fragments. When the sign c satisfies the missing sign of the fragment a/b while predicting b', we rewrite the memory store with a single fragment a/b'. This reduces the number of derivation fragments in the memory store, so we call it a yes-join (+J) operation:

$$\frac{a/b \quad c}{a/b'} \, b \rightarrow c \, b'. \tag{+J}$$

Conversely, when memory contains a fragment a/b and a sign c, but c does not satisfy a/b, we make the appropriate left-corner predictions from c while keeping it as a separate memory item (no-join, –J):

$$\frac{a/b \quad c}{a/b \quad a'/b'} \, b \xrightarrow{+} a' \, ... \, ; \quad a' \rightarrow c \, b'. \tag{–J}$$

These two binary decisions have four possible outcomes in total: the parser can fork only (which increases the number of derivation fragments by one), join only (which decreases the number of derivation fragments by one), both fork and join (which keeps the number of derivation fragments the same), or neither fork nor join (which also preserves the number of derivation fragments). The experiments described in this paper also use a variant of a left-corner parser (van Schijndel et al., 2013b) which introduces additional derivation fragments to carry referents involved in non-local dependencies such as filler-gap constructions (see Figure 2).

As in the case of the DLT, there are a number of ways in which the memory predictions of this left-corner parsing model could be implemented. In this study, we consider three families of predictors:

- **EMBD:** *End of embedded region.* Flag integration operations where disjoint derivation fragments are merged in working memory. EMBD includes –F+J operations that reduce the stack as well as the closure of long-distance dependency carriers for gapping and heavy-shift.

- **NoF:** *'No fork' (–F) operation.* Flag parser operations that recall and transition the top sign of a derivation fragment once the bottom sign has been completed, including –F+J operations (integrations) as well as –F–J operations, in which the current derivation fragment is given a new top sign but is not integrated with another fragment. NoF models the notion that memory is required to access and update the top sign of the attentionally-focused fragment, and is not sensitive to carrier fragments.

- **REINST:** *Reinstatement operation.* Flag if either a long-distance dependency has terminated or if a –F operation has taken place (i.e. the union of EMBD and REINST flags).

---

[3] Here $b \xrightarrow{+} c$ ... indicates one or more grammar rule applications yielding a category c followed by zero or more other categories.

a)

	$t=1$	$t=2$	$t=3$	$t=4$	$t=5$	$t=6$	$t=7$	$t=8$	$t=9$
	S/S	S/S	S/S	S/S	S/S	S/S	S/S	S/S	S/VP
		NP/N	NP/RC	NP/RC	NP/RC	NP/VPgap	NP/Sgap	NP/NP	
				NP/NPconj	NP/NP				

Yesterday, the person supervisors and coworkers caught stealing millions fled.

b)

	$t=1$	$t=2$	$t=3$	$t=4$	$t=5$	$t=6$	$t=7$	$t=8$	$t=9$
	S/S	S/S	S/S	S/S	S/S	S/S	S/S	S/S	S/VP
		NP/N	NP/RC$_p$	NP/RC$_p$	NP/RC$_p$	NP/RC$_p$	NP/RC$_p$	NP/NP	
			RC/RC	RC/RC	RC/RC	RC/VPgap	RC/Sgap		
				NP/NPconj	NP/NP				

Yesterday, the person supervisors and coworkers caught stealing millions fled.

c)

Yesterday, the person supervisors and coworkers caught stealing millions fled.

Depth:	0	1	2	3	4	4	3	3	2	1
EMBD:	0	0	0	0	0	1	0	1	1	1
NoF:	0	0	1	0	0	1	0	0	1	1
REINST:	0	0	1	0	0	1	0	1	1	1

Figure 2: (a) Partial analyses of the sentence *Yesterday, the person supervisors and coworkers caught stealing millions fled,* in a left-corner parser, showing stacked-up derivation fragments (vertical axis) over time (horizontal axis). (b) Partial analyses of the same sentence using additional derivation fragments to carry referents involved in non-local dependencies (in this case, for a referent p of *the person*). (c) Calculation of predictors EMBD ('end of embedding', sensitive to carrier fragments), NoF ('no fork', ignores carrier fragments) and REINST ('reinstatement', union of EMBD and NoF) over the example sentence. Tokens are flagged when stack depth reduces (e.g., *millions*). NoF and REINST (but not EMBD) also flag when the awaited sign is encountered without joining, as is the case for *person* just before forking off the relative clause. Note that NoF does not flag *stealing*, the end of a carrier fragment, while EMBD and REINST do.

For each of these three families, we consider both boolean and distance-weighted variants. In the case of EMBD, the distance-weighted predictor EMBD-LEN is the length of the embedded region being integrated. In the case of NoF, the distance-weighted predictor NoF-LEN is the distance since the last no-fork operation at that depth level, modeling decay since the last time that the top sign of the attentionally-focused derivation fragment was recalled from working memory. The distance-weighted version of REINST (REINST-LEN) is the max of these two measures. REINST-LEN is essentially an implementation of the ACT-R retrieval cost of Lewis and Vasishth (2005), Boston et al. (2011), and von der Malsburg et al. (2015). To maintain comparability with the DLT, we implement three types of distance in each family: number of words, number of DLT discourse referents, and number of DLT-V (verb-reweighted) discourse referents. We therefore consider twelve distinct implementations of left-corner memory cost.

4 Experimental setup

4.1 The Natural Stories corpus

The Natural Stories corpus (Futrell, Gibson, Tily, Vishnevetsky, Piantadosi, & Fedorenko, in prep) is a set of 10 texts written to sound fluent while containing many low-frequency and marked syntactic constructions, especially subject- and object-extracted relative clauses, clefts, topicalized structures, extraposed relative clauses, sentential subjects, sentential complements, local structural ambiguity, and idioms. Self-paced reading time data was collected over these texts from 181 native English speakers.

One reason that previous corpus studies might have failed to find locality and integration effects is that the texts might not have included the low-frequency constructions where such effects emerge. Naturalistic texts, such as the newspaper columns forming the Dundee corpus, are produced and edited to be understood, so they will not frequently contain the kinds of low-frequency, hard-to-process events that bring out differences between processing models. The Natural Stories corpus is designed to exercise such models using constructions which are known to be difficult, providing an opportunity for memory effects to emerge where they have been obscured otherwise. The Natural Stories corpus contains 848,207 reading events. To control for edge effects, we filtered out all tokens occurring at sentence start and end, leaving 768,023 events. These were then divided into an exploratory corpus of 255,554 events and a confirmatory corpus of 512,469 events.[4]

4.2 Memory predictor implementations

The 8 DLT predictors and 12 left-corner predictors discussed in §3 were implemented over gold-standard trees in the Generalized Categorial Grammar (GCG) framework of Nguyen et al. (2012). Source trees for the entire corpus were hand-corrected by a single expert annotator from an automatic reannotation from gold-standard Penn Treebank style representations, which are distributed with the Natural Stories corpus. The GCG framework was chosen because it contains an implicit representation of syntactic dependencies and because it can be used to calculate incremental representations of the memory store of a left-corner parser. This allowed us to compute all predictors under consideration from source trees.

To control for memory-independent information theoretic effects, for each word in the corpus we also computed 5-gram forward probabilities from the Gigaword 4.0 corpus (Graff and Cieri, 2003) using the KenLM toolkit (Heafield et al., 2013) and PCFG surprisal using the van Schijndel et al. (2013a) parser.

It is an open question as to when during processing the effects in question will occur. For example, while readers may slow down when they encounter the final word of a center-embedding region, it is also possible that they would not slow down until the following word, when the need for integration is confirmed. In addition, self-paced reading (SPR) data are known to sometimes produce later effects (Kaiser, 2014; Jegerski, 2014). We therefore calculate variants of each of these 20 predictors in four spillover positions, yielding 80 possible main effects.

4.3 Statistical evaluation

Each of our 80 predictors was evaluated via likelihood ratio test of two linear mixed-effects (LME) models fitted to the exploratory dataset: a baseline model with the main fixed effect omitted, and a test model with the main fixed effect included. All models included sentence position, word length, 5-gram forward surprisal, and total PCFG surprisal as fixed effects, along with by-subject random slopes for each of these, a by-subject random slope for the main effect, and random intercepts for each subject and word. To control for sentence-level confounds, we additionally included a by-subject random slope and random intercept for sentence ID. To facilitate convergence and maintain comparability between predictors, all predictors were centered and z-transformed prior to fitting.

The likelihood ratio test assumes normally-distributed data, so we used the Box and Cox (1964) transform ($\lambda \approx -0.63$) to assure that the data match these assumptions as closely as possible.[5] Significant improvement to model fit for a given main effect indicates that it predicts reading times independently of all controls. The most significantly predictive effects on the exploratory corpus were selected for evaluation on the confirmatory corpus (see § 4.1 for discussion of the exploratory/confirmatory partition).

5 Results

Exploratory results revealed highly significant effects for a number of predictors. The 13 most significant of these were on the word following the target (spillover-1 (S1) position). This might suggest that listeners wait for confirmation of their syntactic analysis before attempting to retrieve items from working

---

[4]Code to reproduce this experiment is distributed through the ModelBlocks and NaturalStories repositories on Github.com.

[5]The Box and Cox (1964) transformation is $y' = \frac{y^{\lambda}-1}{\lambda}$. We selected $\lambda \approx -0.63$ via likelihood maximization.

		Exploratory corpus				Confirmatory corpus			
		β	β-ms	t-value	p-value	β	β-ms	t-value	p-value
Best	**NoF-S1**	1.23e-4	1.29	6.66	1.45e-10	1.46e-4	1.54	8.15	2.33e-14
	DLT-CM-S1	1.11e-4	1.16	5.85	1.42e-8	9.63e-5	1.10	6.48	4.87e-10
Canon	**REINST-S1**	1.17e-4	1.23	6.33	1.60e-9	1.35e-4	1.43	8.01	5.77e-14
	DLT-S1	8.04e-5	0.846	4.51	1.03e-05	6.04e-05	0.634	4.50	1.11e-05

Table 1: Evaluation results. **Upper:** Best left-corner (NoF-S1) and DLT (DLT-CM) predictors. **Lower:** Canonical DLT and left-corner (REINST) predictors. **Left:** Results on exploratory corpus. **Right:** results on confirmatory corpus. Column β contains the LME effect estimate per SD of the independent variable, which is valid over Box and Cox (1964)-transformed reading times. Column β-ms is a back-transformation of β into milliseconds using the equation $\beta\text{-ms} = (\lambda \bar{y}' + \lambda\beta + 1)^{1/\lambda} - (\lambda \bar{y}' + 1)^{1/\lambda}$, where $\bar{y}'$ is the mean of the transformed reading times (1.55 in our data). Because Box and Cox (1964) introduces non-linearity, β-ms is only valid at the back-transformed mean, holding all other effects at their means.

memory. It could also be an artifact of the aforementioned tendency for effects to be delayed in self-paced reading (SPR) experiments. The most significant DLT predictor was DLT-CM-S1 (the DLT with coordination and modifier modifications in S1 position), and the most significant left-corner predictor was NoF-S1 (the no-fork boolean predictor in S1 position). These predictors were therefore selected for confirmatory evaluation, along with S1 'canonical' predictors for each family (unmodified DLT and boolean REINST). These four predictors (and no others) were then evaluated on the confirmatory corpus, with results given in Table 1. The confirmatory results indicate that all four effects generalize robustly to new data, with all achieving p-values well below the Bonferroni-corrected significance threshold of $p = 0.0125$ for four comparisons. The left-corner predictors have a higher order of significance than the DLT predictors and larger effect estimates. Because the main effects are z-transformed, β values are per standard deviation. Over our entire data set, noF = 1 is 2.51 SD greater than noF = 0,[6] so a recall event is predicted to produce a delay approximately 2.5 times larger than β (3.88ms in β-ms). DLT-CM ranges between 0 and 13.19 SD (DLT-CM = 12) in our data, with 92% of events $\leq$ 1.1 SD (DLT-CM = 1) and 99% $\leq$ 4.4 SD (DLT-CM = 4). The effective predictions for noF-S1 are therefore larger than those for most instances of DLT-CM-S1 > 0, but at extreme values DLT-CM predicts larger effects.

6 Discussion

The principal contribution of this work is to give the first strong evidence of memory effects in broad-coverage sentence processing. The constructed-natural Natural Stories corpus used here reduces the likelihood of confounds due to lack of context or oddball sentences to which studies using constructed stimuli are vulnerable, as well as the likelihood of confounds due to lack of memory-intensive syntax or small numbers of subjects to which studies using naturalistic stimuli are vulnerable. Our rigorous baseline model, which includes controls for n-gram and PCFG surprisal, helps ensure that the observed effects are not due to other plausible sources of processing difficulty. Despite these controls, our evaluation results are highly significant.

In order to evaluate whether our DLT and boolean left-corner predictors could both be driven by a single effect, we ran a four-way LME comparison of models on the exploratory corpus (1) with both DLT-CM-S1 and NoF-S1 ablated, (2) with one or the other of the effects ablated, and (3) with neither ablated. Both effects significantly improved over the baseline on their own, and the joint model significantly improved over both effects individually, indicating that neither effect is reducible to the other.[7]

Our distance-weighted left-corner predictors (especially REINST-LEN) are very similar to the ACT-R retrieval predictors of e.g. Lewis and Vasishth (2005), Boston et al. (2011), and von der Malsburg et al. (2015). Many of our distance-weighted left-corner predictors showed positive effects on the exploratory

---

[6]This is because memory recalls are predicted for a small proportion ($\approx$20%) of all events.

[7]DLT-CM-S1 over baseline: $p = 7.24e-12$; NoF-S1 over baseline: $p = 7.93e-10$; both over NoF-S1: $p = 6.33e-13$; both over DLT-CM-S1: $p = 6.87e-11$. Note that in order to achieve convergence in all models, we removed controls for sentence ID from the model specification.

corpus in spillover-1 position (e.g., NoF-LEN-S1, $\beta = 5.98\mathrm{e}\text{-}05$, $p = 9.43\mathrm{e}\text{-}4$). However, these effects were substantially weaker than those of the effects selected for confirmatory evaluation. The strength of the DLT predictors in comparison to the left-corner predictors on our exploratory data suggests that our DLT effect is not simply capturing the effects of decay in left-corner parsing, further supporting the independence of the DLT effect from effects related to left-corner parsing.

Given this, we now consider some important differences in the predictions of both frameworks. First, the left-corner effects predict processing difficulty exclusively on the basis of syntactic tree configurations, while the DLT effects predict difficulty on the basis of a combination of syntax and semantics, namely (1) asymmetries in referential status between nouns/verbs and other words, and (2) word-to-word dependencies. Also, the DLT computes memory costs as soon as both words in the dependency arc are encountered, while the distance-weighted left-corner predictors compute memory costs at the right edges of subtrees in the incremental parse. They therefore not only compute cost differently but predict the cost to be incurred at different words.

The DLT also differs in important ways from our distance-weighted left-corner predictors (like REINST-LEN). The distance-weighted left-corner predictors track recency of activation of derivation fragments by measuring the distance to the most recent word in a fragment. This distance is a function of the size of the attentionally-focused derivation fragment rather than that of the fragment being recalled from memory. By computing total dependency length, the DLT can also index the complexity (in nouns and verbs) of the stored derivation fragment, depending on the location of its head. More complex derivations might be more difficult to retrieve, a possibility which none of the left-corner predictors are designed to account for.

By contrast, the boolean left-corner predictors like NoF-S1 capture phrase-structural information that is absent from the DLT, flagging moments in processing at which derivation fragments stored in memory are predicted to be accessed (which do not necessarily correspond to endpoints of word-to-word dependencies). The fact that NoF-S1 is much more successful on our data than its distance-weighted counterparts suggests that memory-related processing difficulty may be more a function of whether a memory access event has occurred than of recency of activation. Finally, the fact that NoF-S1 is slightly more successful than REINST-S1 – which is identical to NoF-S1 except that it also flags the ends of long-distance dependency carriers – shows that sensitivity to long-distance dependencies does not improve our left-corner predictor. It is therefore possible that the storage and retrieval of incomplete derivation fragments differ mechanistically from the resolution of long distance dependencies.

Acknowledgements

This work was supported by grants from the National Science Foundation: Graduate Research Fellowship Program Award DGE-1343012 to MvS; Doctoral Dissertation Research Improvement Award 1551543 to RF; Linguistics Program Award 1534318 to EG.

References

Steven P. Abney and Mark Johnson. 1991. Memory requirements and local ambiguities of parsing strategies. *J. Psycholinguistic Research*, 20(3):233–250.

Alfred V. Aho and Jeffery D. Ullman. 1972. *The Theory of Parsing, Translation and Compiling, Vol. 1: Parsing.* Prentice-Hall, Englewood Cliffs, New Jersey.

Asaf Bachrach, Brian Roark, Alex Marantz, Susan Whitfield-Gabrieli, Carlos Cardenas, and John D.E. Gabrieli. 2009. Incremental prediction in naturalistic language processing: An fMRI study.

Marisa Ferrara Boston, John T. Hale, Shravan Vasishth, and Reinhold Kliegl. 2011. Parallel processing and sentence comprehension difficulty. *Language and Cognitive Processes*, 26(3):301–349.

G. E. P. Box and D. R. Cox. 1964. An analysis of transformations. *Journal of the Royal Statistical Society, B*, 26:211–234.

Vera Demberg and Frank Keller. 2008. Data from eye-tracking corpora as evidence for theories of syntactic processing complexity. *Cognition*, 109(2):193–210.

Edward Gibson. 1991. *A computational theory of human linguistic processing: Memory limitations and processing breakdown*. Ph.D. thesis, Carnegie Mellon.

Edward Gibson. 2000. The dependency locality theory: A distance-based theory of linguistic complexity. In *Image, language, brain: Papers from the first mind articulation project symposium*, pages 95–126, Cambridge, MA. MIT Press.

David Graff and Christopher Cieri, 2003. *English Gigaword LDC2003T05*.

Daniel J. Grodner and Edward Gibson. 2005. Consequences of the serial nature of linguistic input. *Cognitive Science*, 29:261–291.

Kenneth Heafield, Ivan Pouzyrevsky, Jonathan H. Clark, and Philipp Koehn. 2013. Scalable modified Kneser-Ney language model estimation. In *Proceedings of the 51st Annual Meeting of the Association for Computational Linguistics*, pages 690–696, Sofia, Bulgaria, August.

Jill Jegerski. 2014. Self-paced reading. In Jill Jegerski and Bill VanPatten, editors, *Research methods in second language psycholinguistics*, pages 20–49. Routledge, New York.

Philip N. Johnson-Laird. 1983. *Mental models: Towards a cognitive science of language, inference, and consciousness*. Harvard University Press, Cambridge, MA, USA.

Elsi Kaiser. 2014. Experimental paradigms in psycholinguistics. In Robert J. Podesva and Devyani Sharma, editors, *Research methods in linguistics*, pages 135–168. Cambridge University Press, Cambridge.

Alan Kennedy, James Pynte, and Robin Hill. 2003. The Dundee corpus. In *Proceedings of the 12th European conference on eye movement*.

R. Kliegl, E. Grabner, M. Rolfs, and R. Engbert. 2004. Length, frequency, and predictability effects of words on eye movements in reading. *European Journal of Cognitive Psychology*, 16(1):262–284.

Richard L. Lewis and Shravan Vasishth. 2005. An activation-based model of sentence processing as skilled memory retrieval. *Cognitive Science*, 29(3):375–419.

Luan Nguyen, Marten van Schijndel, and William Schuler. 2012. Accurate unbounded dependency recovery using generalized categorial grammars. In *Proceedings of the 24th International Conference on Computational Linguistics (COLING '12)*, pages 2125–2140, Mumbai, India.

Philip Resnik. 1992. Left-corner parsing and psychological plausibility. In *Proceedings of COLING*, pages 191–197, Nantes, France.

William Schuler, Samir AbdelRahman, Tim Miller, and Lane Schwartz. 2010. Broad-coverage incremental parsing using human-like memory constraints. *Computational Linguistics*, 36(1):1–30.

Edward Stabler. 1994. The finite connectivity of linguistic structure. In *Perspectives on Sentence Processing*, pages 303–336. Lawrence Erlbaum.

Marten van Schijndel and William Schuler. 2013. An analysis of frequency- and memory-based processing costs. In *Proceedings of NAACL-HLT 2013*. Association for Computational Linguistics.

Marten van Schijndel, Andy Exley, and William Schuler. 2013a. A model of language processing as hierarchic sequential prediction. *Topics in Cognitive Science*, 5(3):522–540.

Marten van Schijndel, Luan Nguyen, and William Schuler. 2013b. An analysis of memory-based processing costs using incremental deep syntactic dependency parsing. In *Proc. of CMCL 2013*. Association for Computational Linguistics.

Titus von der Malsburg, Reinhold Kliegl, and Shravan Vasishth. 2015. Determinants of scanpath regularity in reading. *Cognitive Science*.

Stephen Wu, Asaf Bachrach, Carlos Cardenas, and William Schuler. 2010. Complexity metrics in an incremental right-corner parser. In *Proceedings of the 48th Annual Meeting of the Association for Computational Linguistics (ACL'10)*, pages 1189–1198.

Reducing lexical complexity as a tool to increase text accessibility for children with dyslexia

Núria Gala
Aix Marseille Université
LIF-CNRS UMR 7279
163, Av. de Luminy 13288 Marseille
nuria.gala@univ-amu.fr

Johannes Ziegler
Aix Marseille Université
LPC-CNRS UMR 7290
3, place Victor Hugo 13331 Marseille
johannes.ziegler@univ-amu.fr

Abstract

Lexical complexity plays a central role in readability, particularly for dyslexic children and poor readers because of their slow and laborious decoding and word recognition skills. Although some features to aid readability may be common to many languages (e.g., the majority of 'easy' words are of low frequency), we believe that lexical complexity is mainly language-specific. In this paper, we define lexical complexity for French and we present a pilot study on the effects of text simplification in dyslexic children. The participants were asked to read out loud original and manually simplified versions of a standardized French text corpus and to answer comprehension questions after reading each text. The analysis of the results shows that the simplifications performed were beneficial in terms of reading speed and they reduced the number of reading errors (mainly lexical ones) without a loss in comprehension. Although the number of participants in this study was rather small (N=10), the results are promising and contribute to the development of applications in computational linguistics.

1   Introduction

It is a fact that lexical complexity must have an effect on the readability and understandability of text for people with dyslexia (Hyönä J., Olson R. K., 1995). Yet, many of the existing tools have only focused on the visual presentation of text, such as the use of specific dyslexia fonts or increased letter spacing (Zorzi, M., Barbiero, C., Facoetti, A., Lonciari, I., Carrozzi, M., Montico, M. and Ziegler, J. C., 2012). Here, we investigate the use of text simplification as a tool for improving text readability and comprehension.

It should be noted that comprehension problems in dyslexic children are typically a consequence of their problems in basic decoding and word recognition skills. In other words, children with dyslexia have typically no comprehension problems in spoken language. However, when it comes to reading a text, their decoding is so slow and strenuous that it takes up all their cognitive resources. They rarely get to the end of a text in a given time, and therefore fail to understand what they read. Long, complex and irregular words are particularly difficult for them. For example, it has been shown that reading times of children with dyslexia grow linearly with each additional letter (Spinelli, D., De Luca, M., Di Filippo, G., Mancini, M., Martelli, M. and Zoccolotti, P., 2005) (Ziegler, J. C., Perry, C., Ma-Wyatt, A., Ladner, D. and Schulte-Korne, G., 2003). Because children with dyslexia fail to establish the automatic procedures necessary for fluent reading, they tend to read less and less. Indeed, a dyslexic child reads in one year what a normal reader reads in two days (Cunningham, A. E. and Stanovich, K. E., 1998) -a vicious circle for a dyslexic child because becoming a fluent reader requires extensive training and exposure to written text (Ziegler, J. C., Perry, C. and Zorzi, M., 2014)

In this paper, we report an experiment comparing the reading performance of dyslexic children and poor readers on original and simplified corpora. To the best of our knowledge, this is the first time that such an experiment is undertaken for French readers. Our aim was to reduce the linguistic complexity of ten standardized texts that had been developped to measure reading speed. The idea was to identify the words and the structures that were likely to hamper readability in children with reading deficits. Our hypothesis was that simplified texts would not only improve reading speed but also text comprehension.

Proceedings of the Workshop on Computational Linguistics for Linguistic Complexity,
pages 59–66, Osaka, Japan, December 11-17 2016.

A lexical analysis of the reading errors enabled us to identify what kind of lexical complexity was particularly harmful for dyslexic readers and define what kind of features should be taken into account in order to facilitate readability.

2 Experimental Study

2.1 Procedure and participants

We tested the effects of text simplification by contrasting the reading performance of dyslexic children on original and manually simplified texts and their comprehension by using multiple choice questions at the end of each text. The children were recorded while reading aloud. They read ten texts, five original and five simplified in a counter-balanced order. Each text was read in a session with their speech therapists. The texts were presented on a A4 sheet printed in 14 pt Arial font. The experiment took place between december 2014 and march 2015.

After each text, each child had to answer the three multiple-choice comprehension questions without looking at the texts (the questions were the same for the original and the simplified versions of the text). Three possible answers were provided in a randomized order : the correct one, a plausible one taking into account the context, and a senseless one. Two trained speech therapists collected the reading times and comprehension scores, annotated the reading errors, and proposed a global analysis of the different errors (cf. 3.1) (Brunel, A. and Combes, M., 2015).

Ten children aged between 8 and 12 attending regular school took part in the present study (7 male, 3 female). The average age of the participants was 10 years and 4 months. The children had been formally diagnosed with dyslexia through a national reference center for the diagnosis of learning disabilities. Their reading age [1] corresponds to 7 years and 6 months, which meant that they had an average reading delay of 2 years and 8 months.

2.2 Data set

The corpora used to test text simplification is a collection of ten equivalent standardized texts (IReST, International Reading Speed Texts [2]). The samples were designed for different languages keeping the same difficulty and linguistic characteristics to assess reading performances in different situations (low vision patients, normal subjects under different conditions, developmental dyslexia, etc.). The French collection consists on nine descriptive texts and a short story (more narrative style).

The texts were analyzed using TreeTagger (Schmid, H., 1994), a morphological analyzer which performs lemmatization and part-of-speech tagging. The distribution in terms of part-of-speech categories is roughly the same in original and simplified texts, although simplified ones have more nouns and less verbs and adjectives. Table 1 shows the average number of tokens per text and per sentence, the average number of sentences per text, the distribution of main content words and the total number of lemmas :

	IReST originals	IReST simplified
Average number tokens/text	131.4	124.2
Average number tokens/sent	8,8	9,1
Average number sent/text	15,9	14,5
Average NOUNs	39.54%	39.70%
Average VERBs	31.07%	31.87%
Average ADJs	11.68%	9.48%
Total lemmas	779	728

TABLE 1 – IReST corpora features before and after manual simplifications.

2.3 Simplifications

Each corpus was manually simplified at three linguistic levels (lexical, syntactic, discursive). It is worth mentioning that, in previous work, text simplifications are commonly considered as lexical and

---

1. We used standardized reading tests to assess the reading level of each child, i.e. lAlouette (Lefavrais, 1967) and PM47 (Raven, 1976) and a small battery of tests to assess general cognitive abilities.

2. http ://www.vision-research.eu

syntactic (Carroll, J. and Minnen, G. and Pearce, D. and Devlin, S. and Tait, J., 1999), little attention is generally paid to discourse simplification with a few exceptions. In this study, we decided to perform three kinds of linguistic transformations because we made the hypothesis that all of them would have an effect on the reading performance. However, at the time being, only the lexical simplifications have been analyzed in detail (cf. section 3.2).

The manual simplifications were made according to a set of criteria. Because of the absence of previous research on this topic, the criteria were defined by three annotators following the recommendations for readers with dyslexia (Ecalle and Magnan, 2006) for French and (Rello, L., 2014) for Spanish.

Lexical simplifications. At the lexical level, priority was given to high-frequency words, short words and regular words (high grapheme-phoneme consistency). Content words were replaced by a synonym [3]. The lexical difficulty of a word was determined on the basis of two available resources : Manulex (Lété et al., 2004) [4], a grade-level lexical database from French elementary school readers, and FLELex (François et al., 2014) [5], a graded lexicon for French as a foreign language reporting frequencies of words across different levels.

If the word in the original text had a simpler synonym (an equivalent in a lower level) the word was replaced. For instance, the word *consommer* ('to consume') has a frequency rate of 3.55 in Manulex, it was replaced by *manger* ('to eat') that has 30.13. In most of the cases, a word with a higher frequency is also a shorter word : *elle l'enveloppe dans ses fils collants pour le garder et le **consommer** plus tard >* *... pour le garder et le **manger** plus tard* ('she wraps it in her sticky net to keep it and eat it later').

Adjectives or adverbs were deleted if there was an agreement among the three annotators, i.e. if it was considered that the information provided by the word was not relevant to the comprehension of the sentence. To give an example, *inoffensives* ('harmless') was removed in *Il y a des mouches inoffensives qui ne piquent pas* ('there are harmless flies that do not sting').

In French, lexical replacements often entail morphological or syntactic modifications of the sentence, in these cases the words or the phrases were also modified to keep the grammaticality of the sentence (e.g. determiner and noun agreement) and the same content (meaning). Example, respectively with number and gender agreement : *une partie des plantes meurt* and *quelques plantes meurent* ('some plants die'), or *la sécheresse* ('drought') and *au temps sec* ('dry wheather').

Syntactic simplifications. Structural simplifications imply a modification on the order of the constituents or a modification of the sentence structure (grouping, deletion, splitting (Brouwers, L. and Bernhard, D. and Ligozat, A.-L. and François, T., 2014)). In French, the canonical order of a sentence is SVO, we thus changed the sentences where this order was not respected (for stylistic reasons) : *ensuite poussent des buissons* was transformed into *ensuite des buissons poussent* ('then the bushes grow'). The other syntactic reformulations undertaken on the IReST corpora are the following : passive voice to active voice, and present participle to present tense (new sentence through ponctuation or coordinate conjunction).

Discursive simplifications. As for transformations dealing with the coherence and the cohesion of the text, given that the texts were short, we only took into account the phenomena of anaphora resolution, i.e. expliciting the antecedent of a pronoun (the entity which it refers to). Although a sentence where the pronouns have been replaced by the antecedents may be stylistically poorer, we made the hypothesis that it is easier to understand. For instance : *leurs traces de passage* ('their traces') was replaced by *les traces des souris* ('the mice traces').

The table 2 gives an idea of the transformations performed in terms of quantity. As clearly showed, the majority of simplifications were lexical :

---

3. The following reference resources were used : the database `www.synonymes.com` and the *Trésor de la Langue Française informatisé* (TLFi) `http://atilf.atilf.fr/tlf.htm`.
4. `http://www.manulex.com`
5. `http://cental.uclouvain.be/flelex/`

Lexical Simplifications		85.91%
Direct replacements	57.04%	
Removals	13.38%	
Replacements with morphological changes	4.93%	
Replacements with syntactical changes	10.56%	
Syntactic Simplifications		9.86%
Reformulations	7.75%	
Constituent order	2.11%	
Discursive Simplifications		4.23%
Total		100 %

TABLE 2 – Linguistic transformations on the IReST French corpora.

3 Results

Two different analyses were performed : one for quantitatively measuring the reading times, the number of errors and the comprehension scores. The second one took specifically into account the lexicon : the nature of the words incorrectly read.

3.1 Behavioral data analysis

Reading Times. The significance of the results was assessed with a pairwise t-test (Student)[6]. The results are shown on table 3 :

Variables	Original texts	Simplified texts	T value	Significance
Reading times (sec)	159.94	134.70	-3.528	0.006**
Reading speed (words per minute)	64.85	**71.10**	4.105	0.003**

TABLE 3 – Significance of the results obtained.

From this table it can be seen that the overall reading times of simplified texts were significantly shorter than the reading times of original texts. While this result can be attributed to the fact that simplified texts were slightly shorter than original texts, it should be emphasized that **reading speed (words per minute), which is independent of the length of a text, was significantly greater in simplified texts than in original texts**.

Number of errors. The total number of errors included :

— (A) the total number of skipped words, repeated words (words read twice), interchanged words, line breaks, repeated lines (line read twice)
— (B) the total number of words incorrectly read for lexical reasons (the word read is a pseudo-word or a different word)
— (C) the total number of words incorrectly read for grammatical reasons (the word read has the same grammatical category (part-of-speech) but varies on number, gender, tense, mode, person)

First of all, it should be noted that **participants made fewer errors in simplified texts than in original ones** (5,5% *vs* 7,7%)[7]. The table 4 shows the distribution of all the errors :

Type of error	Original texts		Simplified texts	
(A) reading	40	10.05%	36	13.64%
(B) lexical	182	45.73%	112	**42.42%**
(C) grammatical	176	44.22%	116	**43.94%**
	398	100,00%	264	100,00%

TABLE 4 – Distribution of the types of errors in original and simplfied texts.

It can be noted that lexical and grammatical errors occurred equally often[8].

Comprehension scores

---

6. ** significant results with $p < 0.01$
7. This difference was significant in a t-test (t = 2,3, $p < 0.05$)
8. A more detailed analysis of these errors is proposed on section 3.2.

The results of the comprehension questionnaire are better for simplified than for original texts (marginal gain [9]) as shown on table 5 :

Variable	Original texts	Simplified texts	T value	Significance
Comprehension score	2.08	2.30	1.819	0.10+

TABLE 5 – Significance of the results obtained.

These results entail that **dyslexic children read the simplified version of the corpus without a significant loss of comprehension. If anything, they showed a marginal increase in comprehension scores for simplified texts**.

3.2 Lexical analysis

As we were interested in the lexicon of the corpus, an analysis of the content words (i.e. nouns, verbs, adjectives, adverbs) incorrectly read was undertaken in order to better target the reading pitfalls. From our study, we identified 404 occurrences that were incorrectly read, corresponding to 213 different lemmas (to be precise, there were 235 tokens (22 were inflected variants), i.e. *arbre* and *arbres*, or *restaient*, *restent*, *rester*). 404 wrong read words corresponds to 26.81 % of the content words of the corpora, which means that more than **one word out of four is incorrectly read**.

It is worth mentioning that we did not count monosyllabic grammatical words as determiners, pronouns or prepositions, although an important number or errors occurred also on those tokens, i.e. *le* read *la* ('the'), *ces* read *des* ('these'), *pour* read *par* ('for'). We make the hypothesis that the readers concentrate their efforts on decoding content words, and not grammatical ones, because they are those that carry the semantic information and are thus important for text comprehension. Besides, as grammatical words are usually very short and frequent in French, they have a higher number of orthographic neighbours and people with dyslexia tend to confuse short similar words.

We distinguished the words that were replaced by a pseudo-word (29.46%) and those replaced by other existing words on French vocabulary (70.37%). These figures can be compared with those obtained by Rello and collaborators (Rello, L. and Baeza-Yates, R. and Saggion, H. and Pedler, J., 2012). Non-word errors are pronunciations that do not result in an existing word, real-word errors are pronunciations that result in an incorrect but existing word. Non-word errors appear to be higher in English (83%) and in Spanish (79%), but not in French where real-word errors were clearly a majority [10] :

Category	English	Spanish	French
Real-word errors	17%	21%	**70.54%**
Non-word errors	**83%**	**79%**	29.46%

TABLE 6 – Error typology compared accross languages.

The overall error typology that we propose is shown on table 7 :

Type of lexical replacement			Original word	English translations
Pseudo-word	119	**29.46%**	*grenouille > *greniole*	frog, *
Grammatical variant	135	**33.42 %**	*oubliaient > oublient*	forgot, forget
Lexical replacement	84	**20.79%**	*attendent > attaquent*	wait, attack
Morphological variant	43	10.64%	*construction > construire*	build, to build
Orthographical neighbour	23	5.69%	*jaunes > jeunes*	yellow, young
Total	404	100%		

TABLE 7 – Error typology.

Grammatical variants concern variations on gender and number for nouns, and for person, tense and mode for verbs. Lexical remplacements are words read as if they were other words with orthographical similarities (*lieu > île*, *en fait > enfin*, *commun > connu*, etc.). Morphological variants are words of

---

9. $p < 0.1$
10. This finding will deserve more attention in future work.

the same morphological family (*baisse > basse, malchanceux > malchance*). As for orthographical neighbours, we specifically distinguish word pairs where the difference is only of one letter (*raisins > raisons, bon > don*).

Concerning word length for all the mentionned features, 36.88% of the words read were replaced by words of strictly the same length (*forment > formant, catégorie > *calégorie*), 14.11% were replaced by longer ones (*utile > utilisé, suffisant > suffisamment*), **49.01%** were replaced by shorter ones (*nourriture > nature, finie > fine, empilées > empli*). The average length of the 404 words incorrectly read is 7.65 characters (the shortest has three characters, *bon*, and the longest 16, *particulièrement*).

The average number of orthographical neighbours is 3.24, with eight tokens having more than ten neighbours : *bon, bois, basse, foule, fine, fils, garde, sont* ('good, wood, low, crowd, thin, thread, keeps, are').

As far as the grammatical categories are concerned, **the majority of the errors were on verbs**. They concerned grammatical variants of person, tense (past *imparfait* > present) and mode (present > present participle). The distribution on part-of-speech tags errors is shown on table 8 :

Part-of-speech tags of tokens incorrectly read		
VERB	196	**48.51** %
NOUN	115	28.47%
ADJECTIVE	48	11.88%
ADVERB	25	6.19%
Other categories (determiners excluded)	20	4.95%

TABLE 8 – Part-of-speech distribution of the tokens in the corpora.

We analyzed the syllabe structure of the 404 tokens. The average number of syllables is 2.09, the distribution is shown on table 9 :

Number of syllabs		
1 syllab	72	30,64%
2 syllabs	96	40,85%
3 syllabs	47	20,00%
4 syllabs	15	6,38%
5 syllabs	5	2,13%
	235	100,00%

TABLE 9 – Syllabs distribution of the tokens in the corpora.

In French, it is stated that the more frequent (and easier) structure is CV and V. In our results, 58,69% of the words contain this common structure, while **41,31%** present a more complex structure (CVC, CVCC, CYC [11], etc.), as shown on table 10 :

Syllable structure		
CV	230	47,03%
V	57	11,66%
CVC	107	21,88%
CVCC, CCVC, CYVC	47	9,61%
CYV, CCV, VCC, CVY	34	6,95%
VC, YV	10	2,04%
VCCC, CCYV, CCVCC	4	0,82%
	489	100,00%

TABLE 10 – Syllable structure.

We finally analyzed the consistency of grapheme-to-phoneme correspondences which is particularly irregular in French (silent letters, nasal vowels, etc.) [12]. As mentioned above, the average length of the words incorrectly read is 7.65 and their average in number of phonemes is 4.95. This means that the

---

11. C is a consonant, V is a vowel, Y is a semi-vowel, i.e. [j] in *essayait* [e-se-je], [w] in *doivent* [dwav]
12. This is not the case for other languages, e.g. the Spanish writing system has consistent grapheme-to-phoneme correspondences.

average difference between the number of letters and the number of real phonemes is 2.71. Only four tokens were regular (same number of phonemes than letters : *existe, mortel, partir, plus* ('exists, mortal, leave, plus')). The highest difference is 6 in *apparaissent, épargneaient* ('appear, saved') with 12 letters and 6 phonemes each, and *mangeaient* ('ate') with 10 letters and 4 phonemes. **All the words incorrectly read were thus irregular as far as grapheme-to-phoneme consistency is concerned.**

4 Discussion : determining where complexity is

According to the literature, complexity for children with dyslexia should be found on long and less frequent words. More precisely, from the analysis of the reading errors obtained on our first pilot-study, the errors mainly occur on verbs and nouns with complex syllable structure, i.e. irregular grapheme-to-phoneme correspondences, words with many orthographic neighbours or many morphological family members which are more frequent. Visual similarity is a source of error, specially for the following pairs [13] :

Letter alternation	Example	English translations
p/tt	*guêpe > guette*	wasp, watch
b/d	*bon > don, bien > dans*	good, gift / fine, in
d/q	*attendent > attaquent*	wait, attack
t/l	*ramifications > *ramificalons*	branching, *
q/g	*quand > grand*	when, big
g/j	*augmente > *anjmente*	increases, *
m/n	*commun > connu*	common, known
r/l	*grâce > glace*	grace, ice
l/i	*lieu > île, plus > puis*	place, island / plus, after
u/n	*déguiser > *dénise*	dress up, *
e/a	*vivent > vivant*	live, living
e/o	*veulent > *voulent*	want, *

TABLE 11 – Graphical alternations.

In all the replacements we can observe visual similarities. As shown in table 12 ,**the word that is actually read tends to be in most of the cases shorter and more frequent** [14] than the original one :

Type of replacement	Example	English translations	Frequencies
Similar lexical items	*meurt > mur*	dies, wall	9.89 - **179.63**
	toiles > étoiles	canvas/web, stars	16.77 - **121.99**
	poison > poisson	poison, fish	16.64 - **230.20**
Orthographical neighbours	*minuit > minute*	midnight, minute	35.57 - **57.70**
	branches > blanches	branches, white	**98.03** - 44.76
	raisins > raisons	grape, reason	9.86 - **22.87**
Morphological variants	*banquets > banque*	banquets, bank	0.21 - **19.54**
	construction > construire	build, to build	31.61 - **68.73**
	piqûres > piques	pitting, endpin	**5.03** - 0.93
Grammatical variants	*animaux > animal*	animals, animal	**415.56** - 333.50
	mangeaient > mangent	ate, eat	9.66 - **31.69**
	permettent > permet	they allow, he/se/it allows	29.90 - **89.65**

TABLE 12 – Lexical replacements typology with frequencies of the tokens.

To sum up, lexical complexity for dyslexic readers in French is to be found on verbs and nouns longer than seven characters, presenting letters with similar equivalents, with complex syllables and irregular phoneme-to-grapheme consistency. Lexical replacements of words incorrectly read should consider shorter and more frequent words and words with higher grapheme-to-phoneme consistency.

5 Conclusion

In this paper we have presented the results of a first pilot-study aiming at testing the effects of text simplification on children with dyslexia. From our results, reading speed is increased without a loss of

---

13. Other possible similar pairs (not found in our corpora) : t/f, u/v, a/o
14. The frequencies have been extracted from the Manulex database (column including the five levels).

comprehension. It is worth mentioning that reading errors were lower on simplified texts (in this experiment, simplified texts contained a majority of lexical simplifications). The comprehensive analyses of reading errors allow us to propose a detailed description of lexical complexity for dyslexic children. The causes of lexical complexity were mainly related to word length (words longer than seven characters), irregular spelling-to-sound correspondences and infrequent syllable structures.

The insights obtained as a result of this first pilot-study are currently being integrated into a model aiming at providing better accessibility of texts for children with dyslexia. We are currently working in a new study with children in French schools to refine the features that are to be taken into account in our model. These results will be integrated into a tool that will automatically simplify texts by replacing complex lexical items with simpler ones.

Acknowledgements

We deeply thank the speech therapists Aurore Brunel and Mathilde Combes for collecting the reading data and providing a first analysis of the data. We also thank Luz Rello for her valuable insights on parts of the results.

References

Brouwers, L. and Bernhard, D. and Ligozat, A.-L. and François, T. (2014). Syntactic French Simplification for French. In *Proceedings of the 3rd Workshop on Predicting and Improving Text Readability for Target Reader Populations (PITR) at EACL 2014*, page 4756, Gothenburg, Sweden.

Brunel, A. and Combes, M. (2015). Simplification de textes pour faciliter leur lisibilité et leur compréhension. Mémoire de fin d'études en vue de l'obtention du certificat de capacité d'orthophonie. Master's thesis, Aix Marseille Univ.

Carroll, J. and Minnen, G. and Pearce, D. and Devlin, S. and Tait, J. (1999). Simplifying Text for Language Impaired readers. In *Proceedings of European Association of Computational Linguistics*, pages 269–270.

Cunningham, A. E. and Stanovich, K. E. (1998). What reading does for the mind. *Am Educator*, 22 :8–15.

Ecalle, J. and Magnan, A. (2006). Des difficultés en lecture à la dyslexie : problèmes d'évaluation et de diagnostic. *Glossa*, 97 :4–19.

François, T., Gala, N., Watrin, P., and Fairon, C. (2014). FLELex : a graded lexical resource for French foreign learners. In *Proceedings of International conference on Language Resources and Evaluation (LREC 2014)*, Reykjavik.

Hyönä J., Olson R. K. (1995). Eye fixation patterns among dyslexic and normal readers : effects of word length and word frequency. *Journal of Experimental Psychology : Learning, Memory, and Cognition*, 21(6) :1430–40.

Lefavrais, P. (1967). Test de l'alouette.

Lété, B., Sprenger-Charolles, L., and Colé, P. (2004). Manulex : A grade-level lexical database from French elementary-school readers. *Behavior Research Methods, Instruments and Computers*, 36 :156–166.

Raven, J. C. (1976). Pm47 : Standard progressive matrices : Sets a, b, c, d and e.

Rello, L. (2014). *DysWebxia. A Text Accessibility Model for People with Dyslexia*. PhD thesis, Universitat Pompeu Fabra, Barcelone.

Rello, L. and Baeza-Yates, R. and Saggion, H. and Pedler, J. (2012). A First Approach to the Creation of a Spanish Corpus of Dyslexic Texts. In *LREC Workshop Natural Language Processing for Improving Textual Accessibility (NLP4ITA)*, pages 22–26, Istanbul, Turkey.

Schmid, H. (1994). Probabilistic part-of-speech tagging using decision trees. In *International Conference on new methods in language processing*, Manchester, UK.

Spinelli, D., De Luca, M., Di Filippo, G., Mancini, M., Martelli, M. and Zoccolotti, P. (2005). Length effect in word naming in reading : role of reading experience and reading deficit in italian readers. *Developmental Neuropsycholy*, 27(2) :217–235.

Ziegler, J. C., Perry, C. and Zorzi, M. (2014). Modeling reading development through phonological decoding and self-teaching : Implications for dyslexia. *Philosophical Transactions of the Royal Society B*.

Ziegler, J. C., Perry, C., Ma-Wyatt, A., Ladner, D. and Schulte-Korne, G. (2003). Developmental dyslexia in different languages : Language-specific or universal ? *Journal of Experimental Child Psychology*, 86(3) :169–193.

Zorzi, M., Barbiero, C., Facoetti, A., Lonciari, I., Carrozzi, M., Montico, M. and Ziegler, J. C. (2012). Extra-large letter spacing improves reading in dyslexia. *Proceedings of the National Academy of Sciences*, 109(28) :11455–11459.

Syntactic and Lexical Complexity in Italian Noncanonical Structures

Rodolfo Delmonte
Università Ca' Foscari
Ca' Bembo, Dorsoduro 1745, 30123 - VENEZIA
E-mail: delmont@unive.it - website: project.cgm.unive.it

Abstract

In this paper we will be dealing with different levels of complexity in the processing of Italian, a Romance language inheriting many properties from Latin which make it an almost free word order language[1]. The paper is concerned with syntactic complexity as measurable on the basis of the cognitive parser that incrementally builds up a syntactic representation to be used by the semantic component. The theory behind will be LFG and parsing preferences will be used to justify one choice both from a principled and a processing point of view. LFG is a transformationless theory in which there is no deep structure separate from surface syntactic structure. This is partially in accordance with constructional theories in which noncanonical structures containing non-argument functions FOCUS/TOPIC are treated as multifunctional constituents. Complexity is computed on a processing basis following suggestions made by Blache and demonstrated by Kluender and Chesi.

1   Introduction

In this paper we will be addressing what the CFP of the workshop has defined as "whether, and to what extent, linguistic phenomena hampering human processing correlate with difficulties in the automatic processing of language". This will be done by presenting work done in the past on the topic of noncanonical and difficult to parser syntactic structures that may create ambiguity at phonological level, and how to solve it. In that case, the goal was creating an automatic system for text-to-speech, i.e. a TTS system. This will be completed by showing results of an experiment done with statistical data-driven dependency parsers - and a rule-based one - analysing a highly noncanonical text type – children stories or fables. I will show the evaluation done both on the Italian text and the corresponding English translation.

Current approaches to deep syntactic-semantic natural language modeling are strongly statistically based and have achieved near 90% accuracy in some cases. The problem with statistical modeling is that they are strictly bound to training material. Achieving generality requires mixing diverse domains in the training data. In such cases, accuracy varies a lot depending on the language. In particular, more canonical languages achieve 85% accuracy on average – this includes English in non-projective structures and 90% accuracy on projective ones[2]. Less canonical languages, like Italian for instance, are below that threshold and average 82/83% accuracy[3].

The question is that syntactic processing is just one step towards natural language understanding, and the hope to cover sentence level semantics in the near future is not very close. In addition, if we consider Italian, the results are strongly flawed by the fact that dependency parsers are not equipped for lexically unexpressed categories as the Null Subject, which in Italian constitute some 60% of all Subject cases. Languages containing Null Subjects also include Chinese where the recognition rate for this language of such Subject positions by current state-of-art statistical parsers averages 50%

---

[1]Parameters usually referred to when defining "free" word order languages like Latin include: lack of articles, Null Subjects, lack of expletives, freely omitting the complementizer, intensive case marking, etc. to quote the most important ones. Italian only has some of them and the resulting constructions for a simple declarative clause may include all possible permutations at constituent level, but not at word level as Latin for instance would do.

[2] Experiments with different domains for test and training are reported in Surdenau et al. 2008 where in particular the conplete task with WSJ(Marcus et al. 1993) averages 86% F measure, when Brown(Francis & Kucera 1967) is used it drops to 76%. Average performance for 5 different domains when training and test domain diverge show a significant drop whenever we move from WSJ 89% to biomedical domain GENIA 66.6%, to dialogue domain of SwitchBoard 69% and to Brown 80%.

[3]This value has been reported in a mail thread by Giuseppe Attardi experimenting with Universal Dependencies treebanks and the newly released SyntaNet, "the world's most accurate parser", as it is publicized on the web.

Proceedings of the Workshop on Computational Linguistics for Linguistic Complexity,
pages 67–78, Osaka, Japan, December 11-17 2016.

accuracy. Semantic processing is thus highly flawed by the grammatically incomplete structures produced by data-driven dependency parsers.

An important factor that determines levels of complexity in linguistic data are presence of non-canonical structures which in some languages and some domains are almost negligible, as for instance English in the corpus constituted by WSJ news – see below. But when we move to the BROWN corpus the presence of such structures is important and determines a decrease in accuracy and a drop in performance that can range from 6 to 8 points (See McClosky et al. 2010, Hara et al. 2010, Gildea 2001). Italian on the contrary is very rich on such non-canonical structures including discontinuities of all sorts, but as before some genre or domain has more than others.

The paper is organized into two main sections, the following one, section 2 devoted to performance related cases of complexity where we take the stance to use LFG theory and Parsing Strategies to explain ambiguity in the data. We will then present results of a study carried out on non-canonical Italian sentences as they have been treated by most well-known parsers of Italian. In this section we will then show results from an experiment with current best statistical data-driven dependency parsers of Italian when presented with a highly non-canonical text.

2   Different types of complexities: Performance and Parsing Strategies

As the call for paper clarifies, the notion of complexity is highly polysemous and may be related to a number of different issues. In the past, we have been approaching language complexity by way of structural ambiguity and parsing preferences, in a number of papers dealing with some of the issues mentioned above that we will present shortly below. In particular, in the paper published in Delmonte, 1984 we discuss issues related to so-called "Syntactic Closure" where performance and theoretical issues are strongly interrelated. Similar problems have been discussed in the paper published in Delmonte, 1985 which poses questions linking phonology and parsing, again performance related issued.

In our approach we have always indicated LFG (Lexical-Functional Grammar)(Bresnan, 1982) as the theoretical and practical backbone of our research activity, which has inspired also heavily the way in which our computational work has been carried out. This is due to the choice of LFG to support a psycholinguistic approach in which performance played an important role and to call for a processor as a fundamental component of the overall theory(ibid. xxii-xxiv). LFG is a transformationless theory which is based on the lexicon and the existence of lexical rules to account for main NP movements. Long-distance dependencies are accounted for by properties of the f-structure. In a paper appearing in 1989, Kaplan & Zaenen introduce the notion of "uncertainty" in functional assignment. A displaced f-structure, receiving one of the non-argumental pragmatically related functions, FOCUS or TOPIC, will be made dependent or will fuse with the missing function in a following or preceding f-structure that requires it. Requirements are dictated by grammatical principles of Completeness and Uniqueness. Lately, long-distance dependencies in LFG and processing related theories have been pragmatically based in a paper by Y.Falk(2009) and we will return to this position in the final section.

2.1 Syntactic Closure and Parsing Strategies

The problem of Syntactic Closure (hence SC) will be here discussed inside a Theory of Performance or a Linguistic Realization Theory(hence LRT) which in turn is represented in LFG. Consider the two examples (ibid. 103, same numbering):

(1) Tino ha detto che Bruno è morto ieri. / Tino said that Bruno died yesterday.
(2) Tino ha detto che Bruno è partito ieri. / Tino said that Bruno left yesterday.

A competence theory will give both sentences an ambiguous structural description, on the basis of the fact that the adverbial "ieri/yesterday" can be attached both in the embedded and in the main clause, and will make available two structural representations. The theory of SC (hence TSC) which operates inside LRT has to explain why there is a preference for a particular analysis, i.e. attaching the adjunct lower, inside the embedded clause and not in the clause governed by the main verb DIRE/SAY. In LFG Adjuncts are not argument-like structures and cannot be subcategorized in the lexicon. There can only be semantic restrictions for compatibility and appropriateness.

Syntactic ambiguity can disappear in case TENSE in the embedded clause is no longer "compatible" with tense features contained in the Temporal Adjunct, as for instance in the following examples (ibid. p.104, same numbering):

(3) Giovanni ha detto che non tornerà più ieri. / John said he will never come back yesterday
(4) Ho trovato le scarpe che più desidero ieri. / I have found the shoes I like more yesterday

However, there may be still another class of examples, this time lexically biased, where tense is compatible but attachment will preferentially go up to the main clause (ibid. p.105, there (8) and (9)):

(5) Finalmente ho terminato il lavoro che mi rendeva schiavo ieri. / At the end I finished the work which made me slave yesterday.
(6) C'è che ho lasciato la persona che amavo ieri. / It happened that I left the person I loved yesterday.
(7) Sai, ho trovato il regalo che speravo ieri. / You know what, I found the present I hoped yesterday.

In these examples, the strong form of the verb attracts attachment, the weak form doesn't. The three verbs are lexically represented as follows according to LFG:

TERMINARE   <(SUBJ), (OBJ), (ADJ)>
AMARE   <(SUBJ), (OBJ)>
SPERARE   <(SUBJ), (XCOMP)>

The attachment attraction is induced by the force of alternative lexical entries for the same verb, and this in turn is determined by frequency of usage and a stability in the underlying structure that justify these findings on SC also in sentences isolated from context (p.105). As said above, semantic appropriateness depends on the knowledge of the world the speaker will have available in order to decide which sequence of predicate, argument sand adjuncts to select in the context.
   The theory of sentence understanding that we purport assumes that the order of application of the rules in a rule-based parser is determined by two principles obeying certain parameters. The two principles are Lexical Preference (LP) and Final Arguments (FAs); the former has as default parameter the strength of alternate categories in the choice of syntactic rules called Syntactic Preference(Delmonte, 2000). The latter principle, FAs, is bound to the hypotheses developed by the parsing process, and the parameter is called Invoked Attachment (IA). The "closure" property of syntactic phrases in turn is governed by lexical elements and their underlying lexical form, as indicated by Ford et al., (1981, 747). The default principle to prioritize alternate categories in the execution of phrase structure rules is the strength of those categories (ibid. 749). In the two sentences (our numbering, p.111, there 18, 19):

(8) La 1 donna 2 ha 3 sistemato 4 il 5 vestito 6 su 7 quell' 8 attaccapanni 9 . 10 / The woman has hanged the dress on that peg.
(9) La 1 donna 2 ha 3 chiesto 4 il 5 vestito 6 su 7 quell' 8 attaccapanni 9 . 10
/ The woman has asked the dress on that peg.

As the parser reaches position (4) it has to build the OBJect and then complete the VP. To do that, it will call for lexical information, which have the following strong forms:

SISTEMARE   <(SUBJ), (OBJ), (PCOMP)>
CHIEDERE   <(SUBJ), (OBJ)>

After choosing to build an OBJect, at position 6, in one case, - with the verb SISTEMARE/HANG - the LP principle will hamper taking the PP to be analysed as ADJunct of the noun DRESS and so consumed locally inside the OBJect NP. The parser will require the PP to be interpreted as PCOMP and as such be left for the upper VP level. This will also be promoted by the other principle, FAs, which says that: the final argument in the lexical form of a given predicate is a syntactic phrase that must be coherent with it - NP/OBJ, PP/PCOMP - and cannot be followed by other constituents coherent with the same form. On the contrary, the LP will allow the PP to be consumed locally in the OBJect NP. In one case the theory speaks of LATE CLOSURE, where the PP is prevented from being consumed inside the NP headed by DRESS. The PP in this case has been given low priority by the presence of alternate options, i.e. the presence of a PCOMP in the strong form of the main governing verb SISTEMARE/HANG.

2.2 Functional vs Syntactic Reversibility in Question Parsing and Semantic Roles

In Delmonte(1985) we were basically concerned with a recognition grammar to supply information to a text-to-speech system for the synthesis of Italian which is shown to have to rely heavily upon lexical information, in order to instantiate appropriate grammatical relations and assign Semantic Roles. Italian is an almost free word order language which nonetheless adopts fairly analysable strategies for major constituents which strongly affect the functioning of the phonological component. Two basic claims have been made: i. difficulties in associating grammatical functions to constituent structure can be overcome only if Lexical Theory is adopted as a general theoretical framework, and translated into adequate computational formalisms like ATN or CHART; ii. decisions made at previous point affect Focus structure construal rules, which are higher level phonological rules that individuate intonation centre, contribute to build up adequate Intonational Groups and assign pauses to adequate sites, all being very sensitive to syntactic and semantic information. In the paper, I then concentrate on Subject/Object function association to c-structure in Italian, and its relation to ATN formalism, in particular HOLD mechanism and FLAGging. This is done by analysing wh- structures, both direct questions and relative clauses which eventually constitute non-canonical structures in which Subject Inversion is almost obligatory.

We define reversible structures at syntactic and functional level as the ones that allow their arguments to assume both SUBJect and OBJect functions as in the examples below (ibid. 137, number 1,2):

(12)a The secretary has been killed by the director.
   b. The book has been read by John.

While 12a. allows reversing the two core functions, the b. example doesn't. It is clear that non-reversible passive structures contain additional grammatical cues to speed up comprehension, which are only available from lexical entries in which selectional restrictions are listed. These features are then used to constrain assignment of semantic roles. From a purely processing point of view, passive structures are the canonical case of NP requiring reinterpretation when verb morphology is accessed. Thus, the NP SUBJect computed so far, will receive reversed Semantic Role associated to the OBJect in the lexical entry of the verb – in LFG by means of lexical rules.

As said above, Italian is a language that allows Null Subjects: SUBJects in Italian have specific properties:

- it can appear in preverbal – the canonical position - or postverbal position as a case of Subject Inversion;

- be unexpressed as a case of obviative or extrasentential pronominal in tensed clauses;

- be stranded or extraposed, i.e. moved out of its matrix clause and placed after heavy Complements (phrases or sentences)

It is also necessary to clarify that lexical properties are paramount also in English, where not always NP1 appearing in preverbal position entertains SUBJect function, nor NP2 can be always interpreted as OBJect as the following examples clearly show (ibid. 137, numbers 3-7)[4]:

(13)a. Computers have been given no consideration whatsoever by linguists in Italy
   b. Her father Mary hates.

---

[4] where we have cases of fronted NP2 detectable only by having access to NPs inherent semantic features. Thus, in a.,it is OBJect2 which has been passivized and not NP2; in b. we have a topicalized sentence with fronted NP2; in c. SELL is used in ergative structural configuration, in which NP2 is raised to Subject; the same applies to d., a case in which Subject NP would be always omitted (subjectless impersonal structures are frequently used in technical and scientific English); also e. is a subjectless structure, in which "tough predicate" appears and Object NP2 is raised to Subject position.

c. The latest book by Calvino sells well.
d. The logical operator .NOT. applies to the parenthesized statement.
e. Geneva is easy to reach in Italy.

And now briefly, NP2 need not always be interpreted as Object of its clause, as shown below (ibid. 137, numbers 8'10)[5]:

(14)a. There came the magician with his magic rod.
    b. But the real murderer is the landlord.
    c. Mary gave John a beautiful present.
    d. In the corner stood an old boxer.

Now, STRUCTURAL reversibility involves the possibility to use the same constituent order and to freely alternate the instantiation of grammatical functions, while the underlying Semantic Roles change. The result is that with Structural reversibility only one interpretation will result. Even though Semantic Roles can be associated interchangeably to either preverbal or postverbal NP without violating selectional restrictions or semantic compatibility conditions, it is the final constituent order and structure that decides on the interpretation. In this sense, non-reversible passives only allow a single well-formed mapping.

Coming to wh- structures we can see the difference existing between Italian and English: the following example is only allowed in Italian where in fact it is obligatory (ibid.138, number 13):

(15)a. *This is the cheese that ate the mouse that ate the cat that chased the dog.
    b. Questo è il formaggio che ha mangiato il topo che ha mangiato il gatto che inseguì il cane.
    c. Questo è il formaggio che ha mangiato il topo che ha mangiato il gatto che il cane inseguì.
    d. This is the cheese that the mouse ate that the cat ate that the dog chased.

This example shows a case of non-reversible functional structure: postverbal positions are available structurally but not functionally in English which semantically will only allow SUBJect interpretation for MOUSE, CAT, DOG but require preverbal positioning. Italian makes available postverbal position by means of SUBJect Inversion and thus the correct interpretation is triggered by the lexicon. These sentence contain double non-canonical structures – relatives and inversion - and require more computation than canonical ones. The canonical version would have the relative pronoun for CHEESE interpreted in OBJect position, then a preverbal SUBJect position for the DOG.

In STRUCTURAL reversibility constituent order is crucial and characterizes configurational languages with fixed word order. On the contrary, with FUNCTIONAL reversibility ,constituent order is irrelevant, and what really matters is a lexically informed and constrained mapping. In configurational languages, grammatical functions can be associated in a reliable way to fixed or canonical constituent orders - examples 13. 14. above are both structurally and lexically marked. In Italian no such order exists because both preverbal and postverbal constituent positions constitute an unmarked case for SUBJect/OBJect functional assignment.

As a result, a parser of Italian is unable to produce reasonable predictions on the underlying grammatical relations in lack of morphological and lexical cues: it will have to rely on lexical and extralinguistic information. To better exemplify this, we will discuss wh- constructions which in English are more easily computable but in Italian are usually difficult to parse. The following example is very instructive (taken from Ritchie, 1980, his 120):

(16)a. Dove ha sepolto il tesoro che ha rubato l'uomo di cui parlavi?
    b. Where did the man who you mentioned bury the treasure which he stole?
    c. *Dov'è che l'uomo che hai menzionato ha sepolto il tesoro che ha rubato?

---

[5]where a. is a presentation sentence with a dummy pronoun "there" and the Subject NP is in postverbal position; b. is a predication sentence in which something is predicated about the NP Subject "the landlord" in postverbal position; in c. the postverbal NP is OBject2 of ditransitive Verbs constructions, which has undergone dative shift; and in d. we have a case of locative inversion.

In a. the NP SUBJect "l'uomo" has been displaced beyond two bounding nodes - in Italian NP and S' count as such (Rizzi, 1980): it binds two SUBJect positions and also the NP OBJect position inside the lower relative clause headed by "cui". On the contrary, the Null Subject position in front of "parlavi" is assigned obviative or disjoint reference, to an external antecedent. The only correct version for the English example reported in b. is a. On the contrary c. which tries to translate literally the same order is ungrammatical. The same happens with yes-no questions like this one (ibid.139, number 15):

(17)a. Ha finito i compiti tua sorella?
    b. Has your sister finished her homework?

where postverbal position is again reserved for NP Object and the NP Subject "tua sorella" has been stranded or "extraposed". Simple wh- questions have the same problem, i.e. they lack structural cues to help detecting functional assignment, as in examples below (ibid. 139, numbers 16,17):

(18)a. Quale pesce ha pescato la segretaria?
    b. Quale segretaria ha pescato il pesce?
    c. Which fish did the secretary catch?
    d. Which secretary caught the fish?

Fully ambiguous structures are the following complex Italian wh- questions(ibid.139, numbers 19,20):

(19)a. Chi era la persona che ha incontrato Gino?
    b. Who was the person who met John?
    c. Who was the person who John met?
(20)a. Chi ha detto che avrebbe assunto il capo?
    b. Who said that he/she would have hired the chief?
    c. Who said that the chief would have hired?

Both INCONTRARE and ASSUMERE are only transitive verbs that make available two NP positions which are fully functionally reversible. On the contrary PESCARE that we saw before, is not functionally reversible. Another possibility would be the one constituted by the example below (ibid. 140, number 24):

(21)a. Chi ha detto che sta arrivando Gino?
    b. Who said that Gino is arriving?

In this case, the only functional role that can be associated to "Gino" is the one of inverted SUBJect seen that ARRIVARE is an unaccusative verb. Eventually we present a case of passive focussing, which is in many cases obligatory – as this one - in order to convey the novelty of the event:

(22)a. E' stato ucciso il presidente Kennedy! /President Kennedy has been killed.
    b. Il presidente Kennedy è stato ucciso./ President Kennedy has been killed.

Example b. is a version of an agentless passive in which the SUBJect is already Topic of discourse and the news needs only be confirmed. On the contrary, 22a presents the news out of the blue. The question here is complicated by the fact that the SUBJect is postponed in OBJect position to convey new information. In a transformation grammar, this would require movement back and forth, twice: at first to recover the grammatical function of sentential SUBJect, and then back since the same NP constituent has to be interpreted as Affected Theme and not as Agent in deep structure. Example 22a. is impossible in English, and only 22b is allowed: linguistic theories have been using Passive structures to determine their difference and specialty in the treatment of this important structure. They have all been based on English examples: Subject inverted structures in passive constructions might have induced different theoretical approaches. Similar to Italian examples are Russian Subject inverted structures, which have been considered as strictly depending on information structure distribution, due to contextual factors: Partee et al. 2011 treats these cases as Perspective Structures. Subject inversion in Russian involves Existential sentences, Locative inversion, Passive inversion but also Unergative inversion (see Glushan & Calabrese, 2014).

3   Computing Complexity

In the ATN formalism, examples 19/20 are analysed as follows: a question element is contained in a register HOLD which is used to store it temporarily until the rest of the clause is processed. Then the element is passed down to any constituent that might use it - NP SUBJect/OBJect - or in turn could be allowed to pass it down to one of its internal constituent in case of complement clauses. Eventually, CHI might be made to fill in the lower SUBJect position or even the lower OBJect position, but in this case, "il capo" should be made to climb up – or erase and substitute the contents of the register by taking the position now occupied by "little_pro", a certainly more expensive choice. In a CHART inspired parse of the same sentences, all structures would be made available and the decision to choose the most appropriate would be left for the discourse level to make. The HOLD mechanism does not seem to be particularly adequate to solve the ambiguous structures we proposed, since it usually works searching for a HOLE where to insert some linguistic material it has already found and judged to be displaced. In our case the situation is totally reversed: first come the HOLE(S) then the material to fill in. To suit the limitations imposed by Short-Term or working Memory, no more than 7 single linguistic items can be stored before they enter Long-Term Memory. This is mimicked by the working of an incremental parser that computes fully interpreted structures which in LFG should correspond to F-structures. In our previous work(2009, Chapter 3) we presented a principle-based version of the parser that takes advantage of the Minimalist Theory (hence MT) to instruct the "processor" while inputting words incrementally in the working memory. In the sections above, the theory we followed was LFG but in both cases it is now the lexicon that drives the computation: in fact, lexical information in the MT makes available features to the processor that will use Merge and Move to select appropriate items and build a complete structural representation. To justify memory restrictions, the parser takes advantage of an intermediate level of computation, called PHASE constituted by a fully realized argument structure preceded by a Verb. Reaching the verb is paramount also for LFG theory, for selection but also for grammatical function assignment. In Chesi(2016:31-32) the author proposes a complexity metrics called Feature Retrieval Cost (hence FRC) that he associates to the MT theory. In particular, the moves of an MT-inspired processor are accompanied by reading times, which seem to (partially) confirm the prediction of the theory. In turn, these predictions are computed on the basis of local and non-local features and depend strictly on the type of argument selection operated by the verb. This is what has been discussed above, with the so-called REVERSIBILITY notion applied to structure and function.

In addition, Chesi(ibid.33) following Friedmann et al. and Gibson(1998), assumes that referential properties of NPs as shown at determiner level may induce different cost measures: definite NPs being heavier to process than Proper Nouns, and these in turn heavier to process than deictic personal pronouns (you/I). This hierarchy is then partially reinforced by presence of distinct features. Reversibility however is a cost inducing factor, but as we saw above, it applies whenever strong transitive verbs are present. Eventually, linguistic elements causing main difficulties in processing are those definite NPs which cannot be distinguished by the parser on the basis of semantic selectional restrictions, and are involved in non-local (or long-distance) dependencies. The underlying idea is that higher costs are related to the integration of new referential material which needs to be coreferential with previously mentioned antecedents: this is regarded heavier but on the same level of third person pronouns, followed by easier to integrate Proper Nouns that can be identified uniquely in the world.

Following this line of reasoning, we take complexity measures to be sensible to non-canonical structures that are pragmatically motivated and are used to encode structured meaning with high informational content, related to the FOCUS/TOPIC non-argument functions in LFG. Non-canonical structures can be said to help the reader or interlocutor to better grasp the intended (pragmatically) relevant meaning in the context of use (see Birner & Ward, 2004;2006). In Levy et al.(2012) the authors "report an investigation into the online processing of non-projective dependencies in the context of prominent contemporary theories of syntactic comprehension."(ibid.3) which is totally dedicated to extraposed Relative Clauses (hence ERC) in order to show that readers develop a high level of expectancies for the presence of a possible non-projective or noncanonical modifying structure of an already computed NP head. Predictability of a certain noncanonical structure (hence NCS) highly depends on its frequency of use in given contexts. Italian noncanonical structures are relatively highly represented, as the following table shows, in our treebank called VIT(Delmonte et al., 2007), where they have been explicitly marked with the labels indicated below:

NCS/ Types	LDC	S_DIS	S_TOP	S_FOC	DiscMods	Total | % Non | % NCS | Project. | / TSSe
Counts	251	1037	2165	266	12,437	16,156 | 7% | 84.59%

Table 1: Non-projective/noncanonical structures in VIT divided up by functional types.

The final percentage is computed on the total number of constituents, amounting to 230,629.[6] If we compare these data with those made available by Mambrini & Passarotti(2013) for Latin, where the same index amounts to 6.65% - data taken from the Latin Dependency Treebank containing some 55,000 tokens-, we can see that Italian and Latin are indeed very close. The second percentage is computed by dividing up number of NCS/TotalNumber of SimpleSentences. As for tree projectivity in the Penn Treebank (here marked as PT), numbers are fairly low as can be seen in the following table.

TBs/NCS	NCS	UnxSubj	TUtt	TSSen
VIT Totals	3,719	9,800	10,200	19,099
PT Totals	7,234	2,587	55,600	99,002
VIT %	27.43%	51.31%		
PT %	13.16%	0.26%		

Table 2: NonCanonicalStructures and Unexpressed Subjects in VIT and PT.

Total number of constituents for PT amounts to 720,086. Percent of NCS are computed on the number of Total Utterances, while percentage of Unexpressed Subjects are computed on the number of Total Simple Sentences. The nonprejectivity index for PT would then amount to 0.01004%. Expectancies for an Italian speaker for presence of a NCS are thus predictable to be fairly high, due to processing difficulties raised by number of Unexpressed Subjects(UnxSubj), in particular, as discussed above. This will not apply to an English speakers because NCS are unfrequent and used only in specific contexts and situations.

4   An Experiment with Rule-Based and Statistical Dependency Parsers

In this final section we will present results of the analysis of a highly non-canonical text, the fable of "the 3 little pigs"(see Appendix 1). We have been using what are regarded best parsers of Italian today, as they have been evaluated in EVALITA (Bosco & Mazzei, 2012; see www.evalita.it) evaluation campaigns. Most of them are accessible on the web[7]. Two of the parsers are fully statistical . TextPro and DeSR – while the others are hybrid rule-based/statistical parsers – TULE and VISL. We checked the output of the four parsers and marked both labeled and dependency errors. Results are shown in the table below. In Table 3. we report errors made by each parser, divided up into two classes, Labels and Dependencies. We then indicate number of words, and words with punctuation that we use to make statistics on Error Rate of each parser. As can be easily gathered, Mean values average well over 20% error rate with a resulting accuracy of less than 80%. Another important measure we report is number of fully errorless sentences: their means is below 5 over 25, that is only one fifth of the sentences are able to provide a correct mapping to semantics. The parsers share their

---

[6] LDC = Left Dislocated Complement S_DIS = Dislocated Subject (postposed); S_TOP = Topicalized Subject (preposed); S_FOC = Focalized Subject (inverted); DisMods = Discontinuous Modifers which include PP, PbyP, PofP, VP, RelCl, AP

[7] http://beta.visl.sdu.dk/visl/it/parsing/automatic/parse.php

http://hlt-services2.fbk.eu/textpro/?page_id=56

http://tanl.di.unipi.it/it/

http://www.tule.di.unito.it/

fully correct sentences on the total number of five which are in fact the ones containing only canonical structures. All remaining sentences have one or more noncanonical structure, thus showing that statistical data-driven parsers are unfit to cope with narrative Italian text. This is partly due to their models which are unable to generalize to noncanonical structure. In addition, their algorithms are unable to use global measures of grammaticality to improve their local choices, and in many cases cannot correct the choice of labeling as OBJect an inverted or simply dislocated NP, when the SUBJect is eventually missing, thus leaving the structure without a SUBJect.

	TULE	VISL	DeSR	TextPro	Means	StanfordLP
Label	37	45	52	57	47,75	17
Deps	32	56	44	59	47,75	24
WordsNoPu	349	348	361	360	354,5	0
totalWords	386	386	387	387	386,5	395
CorrectSent	7 over 26	4 over 24	5 over 27	3 over 26	4,75	14 over 27
ErrRtNoPu	19,77%	29,02%	26,59%	32,22%	26,90%	10,38%
ErrorRate	17,88%	26,17%	24,81%	29,97%	24,71%	10,38%

Table 3: Experiment with four parsers of Italian + Stanford LP

We then used the same text in its English translation to check what Stanford Parser was able to do. Translating Italian fables into English erases most cases of noncanonical structures so that the result is a much simpler (canonical) text to parse. As can be seen, now the number of fully correct sentence is over half the whole set 14/27 and error rate has decreased dramatically to 10% yielding a 90% accuracy.

In the Appendix, we report the Italian text, where we marked with underscores all noncanonical structures, and with italics all sequences of ambiguous attachment which may cause errors. In addition, the story has 37 Null Subjects which have been correctly found only by TULE parser - but not bound to an antecedent or syntactic controller[8]. Then there are 9 long distance dependencies, relative and wh- clauses, all correctly bound again by TULE. And 9 additional so-called open adjuncts, participials and adjectival phrases which have only been marked as verb dependent, but which also need argument dependency, since they all require agreement to be checked – this being a shortcoming of dependency structure representation. None of these structures have been marked, and in fact they constitute one of the elements causing main errors, also for Stanford parser.

5   Conclusion

Computing sentence complexity has been related to the level of F-structure mapping following LFG theoretical approach, which has no relation at all with Linear/Dominance precedence or Distance sensitive computation, these latter parameters having no consideration for lexical properties of Head-Dependence or Constituent-Governor relations. To account for the processing or parsing performance related evaluation, at first we proposed to consider the working of the mental parser to be simulated by that of an incremental ATN parser. On the contrary, Blache(2011) defines a list of six constraints on the basis of which to compute linguistic complexity, which are based solely on structural criteria. Other parameters are related to frequency of words, number of phrase-level categories in a representation, ambiguity level of each POS-tagged word, or simply number of words in the structure. Dependency-structure related criteria are then used to evaluate complexity by combining Dependency and Linearity related constraint violations. The definition of a Global Difficulty Model is then based on the sum of Local complexity evaluation indices called ID (Incomplete Dependency), DLT (Dependency Locality Theory) and Depth (depth of syntactic structure). However, this approach is applied by Blache(2011) to the output of a parser, be it dependency or constituency based, be it rule or statistically based.

---

[8] LFG theory distinguishes four cases of empty categories: syntactic controlled ones – so-called long distance dependencies; lexical control, subcategorized infinitivals; structural control, open adjuncts; and anaphoric control, empty pronominals.

In a more recent paper Blache(2015) presents an approach to complexity evaluation which also encompasses a parsing phase. It is based on the idea that chunking and their fusion into "constructions" are a sufficient structural level for the default identification of meaningful parts of the sentence. This is then related to "Properties" of the relations between words which are again constituted by six constraints proposed in his previous papers. Finally, the parsing process is defined as consisting in "evaluating properties when scanning a new word in the sentence"(ibid., p.14). He then distinguishes two possible parsing styles: "shallow" (when no context is needed and linearity and co-occurrence are enough to define relations between adjacent words); and "deep" (when building different partitions of the set of words in the sentence is needed and then evaluating the properties of the current word is possible). However, this second case is no longer incrementally justified, requiring a global evaluation of the sentence. So, the new approach is called "hybrid parsing" where chunks are aggregated in "buffers" – these corresponding strictly speaking to the "registers" of our ATN parser.

Kluender(1998) demonstrates the validity of a processing approach to wh- islands in which the cost of holding an uninterpreted constituent in working memory explains the increased level of complexity, using ERPs. The approach is the constructional one where there is no constituent displacement nor movement to account for, but following also Falk(2009; but see also Goldberg, 2005), the explanation is given by the multifunctionality associated to noncanonical structural elements which in LFG theory receive the nonargument roles of FOCUS/TOPIC. Constructions being typically language dependent, may vary from English to Italian, a language this latter that allows more freedom to the position of constituents in the sentence. Following this approach, explaining the additional load of FOCUS constituents in postverbal position becomes very easy: the empty slot in SUBJect position is at first associated to little_pro (the Null Subject) and then searched in preceding discourse, for a coreferential interpretation. When the FOCUS constituent in postverbal position is reached, a new interpretation is proposed which substitutes the previous one, eliminating the presence of a Null Subject in working memory. In this way, all cases of wh- FOCUS/TOPIC resemble a case of "garden path" from a processing point of view. On the contrary, those cases of NP FOCUS structures like the ones determined by presence of an unaccusative verb, or simply a focussed passive structure, have no additional processing cost. Once the verb is processed, seen that Italian constructions allow both preverbal and postverbal SUBJect, the computation goes straightforwardly: in the case of preverbal position the NP is both SUBJect and TOPIC, whereas in the case of postverbal position, the NP is SUBJect and FOCUS in full accordance with the information theory assumption that Old comes before New(see Birner & Ward, 2004;2006).

References

Birner, B. & Ward, G. 2004. Information structure and non-canonical syntax. In Horn, L. & Ward, G. The Handbook of Pragmatics. London: Blackwell. 153-174.

Birner, B. & Ward, G. 2006. Information structure. In Aarts, B. & McMahon, A. The Handbook of English Linguistics. London: Blackwell. 291-317.

Blache P. (2011). A computational model for linguistic complexity, in Proceedings of the first International Conference on Linguistics, Biology and Computer Science.

Blache P. (2015). Hybrid Parsing for Human Language Processing, in B. Sharp, W. Lubaszewski and R. Delmonte (eds) 2015. Natural Language Processing and Cognitive Science, Libreria Editrice Cafoscarina, Venice, p.9-20.

Bosco C. and A. Mazzei. 2012. The evalita 2011 parsing task: the dependency track. In Working Notes of EVALITA 2011, Rome, Italy.

Bresnan J. (ed.), 1982. The Mental Representation of Grammatical Relations, The MIT Press, Cambridge MA.

Cristiano Chesi, Il processamento in tempo reale delle frasi complesse, in E.M.Ponti, M.Budassi(eds.), 2016. Compter Parler Soigner - Tra linguistica e intelligenza artificiale, Pavia University Press, Pavia, p. 21-38. http://archivio.paviauniversitypress.it/oa/9788869520389.pdf

Delmonte R., 1984, La Syntactic Closure nella Teoria della Performance, Quaderni Patavini di Linguistica 4, 101-131.

Delmonte R., 1985. Parsing Difficulties & Phonological Processing in Italian, Proceedings of the 2nd Conference of the European Chapter of ACL, Geneva, 136-145.

Delmonte R.(2000), Parsing Preferences and Linguistic Strategies, in LDV-Forum - Zeitschrift fuer Computerlinguistik und Sprachtechnologie - "Communicating Agents", Band 17, 1,2, (ISSN 0175-1336), pp. 56-73.

Delmonte R.(2002), Relative Clause Attachment And Anaphora: Conflicts In Grammar And Parser Architectures, in A.M. Si Sciullo(ed), Grammar and Natural Language Processing, UQAM, Montreal, pp.63-87.

Delmonte R., 2004. Parsing Arguments and Adjuncts, *Proc. Interfaces Conference, IEEE - ICEIS (the International Conference on Enterprise Information Systems)*, Pescara, 1-21.

Delmonte R., 2005, Deep & Shallow Linguistically Based Parsing, in A.M.Di Sciullo(ed), UG and External Systems, John Benjamins, Amsterdam/Philadelphia, pp.335-374.

Delmonte R. Bristot A., Tonelli S. (2007), VIT - Venice Italian Treebank: Syntactic and Quantitative Features, in K. De Smedt, Jan Hajic, Sandra Kübler(Eds.), Proc. Sixth International Workshop on Treebanks and Linguistic Theories, Nealt Proc. Series Vol.1, pp. 43-54.

Falk Y., 2009. Islands: A Mixed Analysis. In Butt and King 2009, *Proceedings of the LFG09 Conference*. Stanford, CA: CSLI Publications, 261–281.

Ford M., J.Bresnan, R.M.Kaplan, 1981. A competence-based theory of syntactic closure, in J.Bresnan (ed.), The Mental Representation of Grammatical Relations, MIT Press, 727-796.

Francis W. N. and H. Kucera. 1964. Brown Corpus. Manual of Information to accompany A Standard Corpus of Present-Day Edited American English, for use with Digital Computers. Revised 1971, Revised and Amplified 1979.

Friedmann N., A. Belletti, L. Rizzi (2009). "Relativized relatives: Types of intervention in the acquisition of A-bar dependencies". Lingua, 119.1, pp. 67–88.

Hara T., Y. Miyao, J. Tsujii, 2010. Evaluating the Impact of Re-training a Lexical Disambiguation Model on Domain Adaptation of an HPSG Parser. in H.Bunt et al.(eds.), Trends in Parsing Technologies, Text, Speech and Language Technology 43. 257-270.

Haug, Dag Trygve Truslew. 2012. From dependency structures to LFG representations. In Miriam Butt & Tracy Holloway King (eds.), Proceedings of the LFG12 conference, 271–291. CSLI Publications.

Gibson E. (1998). "Linguistic complexity: locality of syntactic dependencies". Cognition, 68.1, pp. 1–76.

Gildea D., 2001. Corpus variation and parser performance. Proceedings of Empirical Methods in Natural Language Processing (EMNLP 2001), pp. 167–202, Pittsburgh, PA, 2001.

Glushan Z. and A. Calabrese, 2014. Context Sensitive Unaccusative in Russian and Italian, Proceedings of the 31st West Coast Conference on Formal Linguistics, ed. Robert E. Santana-LaBarge, 207-217.

Goldberg, A.E., 2005. Constructions, Lexical Semantics and the Correspondence Principle: Accounting for Generalizations and Subregularities in the Realization of Arguments. In *The Syntax of Aspect*, Nomi Erteschik-Shir and Tova Rapoport (eds.). Oxford University Press.

Jinho D. Choi, Joel Tetreault, Amanda Stent, 2015. It Depends: Dependency Parser Comparison Using A Web-based Evaluation Tool, *Proceedings of the 53rd Annual Meeting of the Association for Computational Linguistics and the 7th International Joint Conference on Natural Language Processing*, pages 387–396, Beijing, China.

Kaplan R.M., J. Bresnan, 1982. Lexical-Functional Grammar: A Formal System for Grammatical Representation, in J.Bresnan(ed.), The Mental Representation of Grammatical Relations, The MIT Press, Cambridge MA, pp. 173-281, republished in M.Dalrymple, R.M.Kaplan, J.T.Maxwell, A.Zaenen, (1995), Formal Issues in Lexical-Functional Grammar, CSLI, Stanford, pp- 1-102 (numbering in the paper is referred to this version).

Kluender, R. (1998) On the distinction between strong and weak islands: a processing perspective. Syntax Semantics 29, 241–279.

Levy R., Fedorenko E., Breen M., T. Gibson, 2012. The Processing of Extraposed Structures in English, Cognition, 122(1).

Mambrini F., M.Passarotti, 2013. Non-projectivity in the Ancient Greek Dependency Treebank, Proceedings of the Second International Conference on Dependency Linguistics (DepLing 2013), 177–186, Prague.

Marcus, Mitchell P., Beatrice Santorini, and MaryAnn Marcinkiewicz, 1993. Building a large annotated corpus of English: The Penn Treebank. Computational Linguistics, 19(2):313–330.

McClosky David, Eugene Charniak, Mark Johnson, 2010. Automatic Domain Adaptation for Parsing, in Human Language Technologies: The 2010 Annual Conference of the North American Chapter of the ACL, 28–36.

Partee, Barbara et al. 2011. Russian Genitive of Negation Alternations: the role of verb semantics. *Scando Slavica* 57:2, 135-159.

Rizzi L., 1982. *Issues in Italian Syntax*, Oordrecht, Foris Pub.

Surdeanu Mihai, Richard Johansson, Adam Meyers, Lluis Marquez, Joakim Nivre, 2008. The CoNLL-2008 Shared Task on Joint Parsing of Syntactic and Semantic Dependencies, in CoNLL 2008: Proceedings of the 12th Conference on Computational Natural Language Learning, 159–177.

Wanner E., M.Maratsos(1978), An ATN Approach to Comprehension, in M.Halle, J.Bresnan, G.A.Miller(eds.), 1978. Linguistic Theory and Psychological Reality, MIT Press, 119-161.

APPENDIX 1 – The Story of the Three Little Pigs

C'erano una volta <u>tre fratelli porcellini</u> che vivevano felici nella campagna. <u>Nello stesso luogo</u> però viveva anche <u>un terribile lupo</u> che si nutriva proprio di porcellini grassi e teneri. <u>Questi allora, per proteggersi dal lupo</u>, decisero di costruirsi <u>ciascuno</u> una casetta. <u>Il maggiore, Jimmy che era saggio</u>, lavorava di buona lena e costruì *la sua casetta con* solidi mattoni *e cemento*. <u>Gli altri</u>, Timmy e Tommy, <u>pigri</u> se la sbrigarono in fretta costruendo *le loro casette con* la paglia *e con pezzetti di legno*. I due porcellini pigri passavano le loro giornate suonando e cantando una canzone che diceva: chi ha paura del lupo cattivo. Ma ecco che improvvisamente il lupo apparve alle loro spalle. <u>Aiuto, aiuto</u>, gridarono <u>i due porcellini</u> e cominciarono a correre <u>più veloci che potevano</u> verso la loro casetta per sfuggire al terribile lupo. Questo <u>intanto</u> si leccava già i baffi pensando al suo prossimo pasto così invitante e saporito. Finalmente i porcellini riuscirono a raggiungere la loro casetta e vi si chiusero dentro sbarrando la porta. Dalla finestra cominciarono a deridere il lupo cantando la solita canzoncina: chi ha paura del lupo cattivo. Il lupo stava <u>intanto</u> pensando al modo di penetrare nella casa. Esso si mise ad osservare <u>attentamente</u> la casetta e notò che non era davvero molto solida. Soffiò con forza un paio di volte e la casetta si sfasciò completamente. <u>Spaventatissimi</u> i due porcellini corsero *a perdifiato verso* la casetta del fratello. "Presto, fratellino, aprici! Abbiamo *il lupo alle* calcagna". Fecero appena in tempo ad entrare e tirare il chiavistello. Il lupo *stava già arrivando deciso* a non rinunciare al suo pranzetto. <u>Sicuro di abbattere anche la casetta di mattoni</u> il lupo si riempì *i polmoni di* aria e cominciò a soffiare *con forza alcune volte*. Non c'era niente da fare. La casa non si mosse di un solo palmo. Alla fine <u>esausto</u> il lupo si accasciò a terra. I tre porcellini si sentivano *al sicuro nella* solida casetta di mattoni. <u>Riconoscenti</u> i due porcellini oziosi promisero *al fratello che* <u>da quel giorno</u> anche essi avrebbero lavorato sodo.[9]

Once upon a time there were three little pigs who lived happily in the countryside. But in the same place lived a wicked wolf who fed precisely on plump and tender pigs. The little pigs therefore decided to build a small house each, to protect themselves from the wolf. The oldest one, Jimmy who was wise, worked hard and built his house with solid bricks and cement. The other two, Timmy and Tommy, who were lazy settled the matter hastily and built their houses with straw and pieces of wood. The lazy pigs spent their days playing and singing a song that said, "Who is afraid of the big bad wolf?" And one day, lo and behold, the wolf appeared suddenly behind their backs. "Help! Help!", shouted the pigs and started running as fast as they could to escape the terrible wolf. He was already licking his lips thinking of such an inviting and tasty meal. The little pigs eventually managed to reach their small house and shut themselves in, barring the door. They started mocking the wolf from the window singing the same song, "Who is afraid of the big bad wolf?" In the meantime the wolf was thinking a way of getting into the house. He began to observe the house very carefully and noticed it was not very solid. He huffed and puffed a couple of times and the house fell down completely. Frightened out of their wits,the two little pigs ran at breakneck speed towards their brother's house. "Fast, brother, open the door! The wolf is chasing us!" They got in just in time and pulled the bolt. Within seconds the wolf was arriving, determined not to give up his meal. Convinced that he could also blow the little brick house down, he filled his lungs with air and huffed and puffed a few times. There was nothing he could do. The house didn't move an inch. In the end he was so exhausted that he fell to the ground. The three little pigs felt safe inside the solid brick house. Grateful to their brother, the two lazy pigs promised him that from that day on they too would work hard.[i]

---

[i] This work is licensed under a Creative Commons Attribution 4.0 International Licence. Licence details: http://creativecommons.org/licenses/by/4.0/

---

[9] This is a modified version of the Italian version of the original story, which I have done to make it shorter.

Real Multi-Sense or Pseudo Multi-Sense:
An Approach to Improve Word Representation

Haoyue Shi[1], Caihua Li[1] and Junfeng Hu[1,2]*
[1] School of Electronics Engineering and Computer Science,
Peking University, Beijing, China
[2] Key Laboratory of Computational Linguistics,
Ministry of Education, Peking University, Beijing, China
`{hyshi,peterli,hujf}@pku.edu.cn`

Abstract

Previous researches have shown that learning multiple representations for polysemous words can improve the performance of word embeddings on many tasks. However, this leads to another problem. Several vectors of a word may actually point to the same meaning, namely pseudo multi-sense. In this paper, we introduce the concept of pseudo multi-sense, and then propose an algorithm to detect such cases. With the consideration of the detected pseudo multi-sense cases, we try to refine the existing word embeddings to eliminate the influence of pseudo multi-sense. Moreover, we apply our algorithm on previous released multi-sense word embeddings and tested it on artificial word similarity tasks and the analogy task. The result of the experiments shows that diminishing pseudo multi-sense can improve the quality of word representations. Thus, our method is actually an efficient way to reduce linguistic complexity.

1 Introduction

Representing meanings of words by embedding them into a high dimensional vector space, so called word embedding, is a useful technique in natural language processing. An intuitive idea is to encode one word into a single vector, which contains the semantic information of the word in corpus (Bengio et al., 2003; Collobert and Weston, 2008; Mnih and Hinton, 2007; Mikolov et al., 2010).

There is a consensus that natural languages always include lots of polysemous words. For example, when the word *star* appears together with words like *planet, satellite*, it may roughly denote a kind of celestial body; when *star* appears with words like *movie, song, drama*, it may stand for a famous person. For most cases, we human beings can easily point out which sense a word belongs to based on its context. Considering the polysemous words, some previous approaches have learned multiple embeddings for a word, discriminating different senses by their context, related syntax and topics (Reisinger and Mooney, 2010; Huang et al., 2012; Chen et al., 2014; Pina and Johansson, 2014; Neelakantan et al., 2015; Cheng and Kartsaklis, 2015; Liu et al., 2015). The authors also provided methods to disambiguate among the multiple representations. Li and Jurafsky (2015) have demonstrated that multi-sense word embeddings could be helpful to improve the performance on many NLP and NLU tasks.

However, this leads to another problem. It's much more difficult for computer than human beings to detect whether two appearances of a same word stand for the same sense. Moreover, the contexts may be totally different even if these appearances belong to the same meaning based on human judgement. Previous multi-sense word embedding approaches often tend to embed a word in such situation into more than one vector by mistake (actually, they have the same meaning and should be embedded into only one vector). Consider three different representations of word *bear* learnt by the method introduced by Neelakantan et al. (2015), which are shown by their nearest neighbors in the vector space *MSSG-50d*.

- emerald, **bears, three-toed, snake, periwinkle, ruffed, hoopoe**, distinctive, unmistakable

- **bird, wolf**, arrow, **pelican**, emerald, canyon, diamond, **buck, deer**

This work is supported by the National Natural Science Foundation of China (grant No.61472017, M1552004).

Proceedings of the Workshop on Computational Linguistics for Linguistic Complexity,
pages 79–88, Osaka, Japan, December 11-17 2016.

- pride, lady, hide, king, gift, crane, afflict, promise, reap, protect

The words clearly related to the domain *animals* are bolded. We could infer that the first two representations have the same meaning that points to the animal bear, and the third representation has different meaning. We call such different learnt representations of a word with the same meaning (e.g. the first two representations of word *bear* shown above) *pseudo multi-sense*, where we judge whether senses are pseudo multi-sense by comparing their domains.

Given the word embeddings, which have multiple vectors for each polysemous word, we introduce an algorithm based on domains and semantic relations to detect pseudo multi-sense, since word representations which stand for the same meaning would have the same hypernym and belong to the same domain. Then we try to eliminate the effect of pseudo multi-sense by training a global transition matrix which projects the original word vectors into a new vector space based on the detected pseudo multi-sense pairs, minimizing the distance between pseudo multi-sense pairs in the vector space while keeping the spatial relation of other pairs. We propose the algorithm in Section 3 and evaluate it in Section 4.

Obviously, detecting and diminishing pseudo multi-sense would make word sense representations, which can be processed by computer, closer to human thinking. We also suggest this approach can improve the performance on real world NLU tasks by evaluating the algorithm on the analogy test dataset introduced by Mikolov et al. (2013a), and also on WordSim-353 (Finkelstein et al., 2001) and SCWS (Huang et al., 2012) dataset which include human judgements on similarity between pairs of words.

2 Background and related work

2.1 Distributional word representations

Since Bengio et al. (2003) applied neural network to language model, which treats word embeddings as parameters and thus it allows us to learn the language model and word embeddings at the same time, many researchers have proposed other neural network models (Mnih and Hinton, 2007; Collobert and Weston, 2008; Mikolov et al., 2013a) to improve in both efficiency and accuracy. What's more, hierarchical softmax by Morin and Bengio (2005), noise contrastive estimation by Mnih and Kavukcuoglu (2013) and negative sampling by Mikolov et al. (2013c) make it possible to learn accurate word embeddings in a short time.

2.2 Multi-sense word embeddings

Most vector-space models (VSMs) represent a word with only one vector, which clearly fails to capture homonymy and polysemy. And thus, Huang et al. (2012) proposed a method to generate the context embeddings in the following way. Firstly, they generate single-sense word embeddings and compute out the context embeddings. Then they cluster the context embeddings, and the result are used to re-label each occurrence of each word in the corpus. Thirdly, the model they proposed is applied to the labeled corpus to generate the multi-sense embeddings. Chen et al. (2014) took external knowledge base into consideration and built a model to learn a separate vector for each sense pre-defined by WordNet (Miller, 1995). Neelakantan et al. (2015) improved multi-sense word embedding model by dropping the assumption that each word should have the same number of senses, and proposed a non-parametric model to automatically discover a varying number of senses per word type. Cheng and Kartsaklis (2015) proposed a syntax-aware approach for multi-sense word embeddings.

2.3 WordNet and WordNet domain knowledge

WordNet (Miller, 1995) is a large lexical database of English. Nouns, verbs, adjectives and adverbs are grouped into sets of cognitive synonyms, namely synsets, each expressing a distinct concept. Synsets are represented by a word, a pos tag and a label, and interlinked by means of conceptual-semantic and lexical relations (hypernymy/hyponymy). Chen et al. (2014) used WordNet to improve word embeddings.

Magnini and Cavaglia (2000) and Bentivogli et al. (2004) presented a WordNet Domains Hierarchy, which is a language-independent resourse composed of 164 domain labels. What's more, González et al. (2012) provided a graph based improvement and released a domain knowledge (Extended WordNet

Domains) base aligned to WordNet 3.0, which we use in our experiments as domain knowledge. Extended WordNet Domains contains 170 domains and the probability of each synset in WordNet 3.0 in each domain. The domains it provided include *acoustics, agriculture, volleyball, etc.*

2.4 Vector space projection

Even though bilingual data always plays an important role in the modern statistical machine translation system, it had failed to map the missing word and phrase entries between two languages until Mikolov et al. (2013b) proposed a simple but effective method to extend dictionaries and translation tables. The main idea of this novel method is to learn a linear projection between the languages using a small bilingual dictionary but making little assumption about the languages, which has proved to be able to project the vector representation of any word from the source space to the target space accurately. Our vector space projection algorithm is very similar to this.

3 Pseudo multi-sense detection and elimination by vector space projection

3.1 Domain based pseudo multi-sense detection

3.1.1 Direct domain similarity

Given a word and its context, we human beings can easily determine the domains this word belongs to. WordNet makes it convenient for users to get the domains of all synsets of a word. To determine the domain of a sense given the multi-sense word embeddings, we can intuitively define the probability that the kth sense of word w belongs to domain d as

$$P_D(w, k, d) \propto \sum_{w' \in NN(w,k)} D(p(w'), d) \tag{1}$$

where $NN(w, k)$ is the nearest neighbors of the kth sense of word w in the given word embeddings, $p(w')$ is the protocol representation of word w' (e.g. when w' is *star_s1*, $p(w')$ would be *star*), $D(p(w'), d)$ is the sum probability that domain d appears in all synsets of $p(w')$ in WordNet provided by Extended WordNet Domain. Then we can compute the domain similarity between the kth and the lth sense of word w by

$$Sim_D(w, k, l) = \frac{1}{n} |TopN(P_D, w, k, n) \cap TopN(P_D, w, l, n)| \tag{2}$$

where $TopN(P, w, k, n)$ is the set of x that $P(w, k, x)$ ranks top n in decreasing order (in our experiments, $n = 5$).

3.1.2 Semantic hierarchical similarity

However, in the knowledge base we applied, the domain knowledge is sometimes not enough for dectecting pseudo multi-sense, especially for some abstract words. For example, it's hard to specify which domain the word *extract* belongs to. What's more, based on González et al. (2012), the Extended WordNet Domain cannot reach the precision of 100%. So we tend to apply semantic hierarchy, particularly hypernymy relations, to help improve our pseudo multi-sense detecting as supplement, since hypernymy somehow contains some domain information. With WordNet, we can also get the semantic relations (e.g. hypernymy, hyponymy, synonymy) of synsets. With the consideration of the DAG structure of semantic relations, for hypernyms of a specific word, the nearer the hypernym, the more information it contains. So we penalize the *far hypernyms*, like *whole, entity, thing*, which cover a large amount of words as their hyponyms. Similar to the definition of $P_D(w, k, t)$, we can define the probability that the kth sense of word w has the hypernym h, where h is a synset in WordNet, as

$$P_H(w, k, h) \propto \frac{1}{d(w, h)} \sum_{w' \in NN(w,k)} H(p(w'), h) \cdot \frac{1}{d(p(w'), h)} \tag{3}$$

where $d(w, h) = \min_{sw \in Synsets(w)} dis(sw, h)$, $dis(x, y)$ is the distance between two synsets x and y in WordNet, $H(p(w'), h)$ is the frequency that the synset h appears as a hypernym of a synset of $p(w')$ in WordNet. In particular, if h is not a hypernym of w in WordNet, $P_H(w, k, h) = 0$.

We then compute the semantic hierarchical similarity between the kth and the lth sense of word w by

$$Sim_H(w, k, l) = \frac{1}{n}|TopN(P_H, w, k, n) \cap TopN(P_H, w, l, n)| \tag{4}$$

With the definition of domain similarity and semantic hierarchical similarity, we can compute the similarity between the kth and the lth sense of word w by

$$Sim(w, k, l) = Sim_D(w, k, l) + Sim_H(w, k, l) \tag{5}$$

When $Sim(w, k, l) > \lambda$, where λ is a hyper-parameter ($\lambda = 1$ in our experiments), we consider the kth and the lth sense of word w have the same meaning. In other words, we are able to detect pseudo multi-sense pair (w_k, w_l) based on $Sim(w, k, l)$, which is called pseudo multi-sense detection.

3.2 Pseudo multi-sense elimination

Having the existing word embeddings, assume that we have a detected pseudo multi-sense group $G = \{w_{k_1}, w_{k_2}, ..., w_{k_n}\}$, in which $w_{k_1}, w_{k_2}, ..., w_{k_n}$ are senses of word w, taking the same meaning. Thus, we can find a representative vector for the group. Let $v_s(w, k_i)$ be the corresponding vectors of w_{k_i}, and $v_r(G)$ be the representative vector for the group G. Such vector $v_r(G)$ can be randomly chosen from $\{v_s(w, k_1), v_s(w, k_2), ..., v_s(w, k_n)\}$, or simply the mean vector of them. Other methods to compute $v_r(G)$ are also worth trying if reasonable.

Inspired by Mikolov et al. (2013b), we assume there is a transition matrix, by which for all pseudo multi-sense group G, $\forall w_{k_i} \in G$, $v_{w_{k_i}}$ can be projected to $v_r(G)$. The experiments shown in Section 4 supported our assumption. In other words, we suggest that there exists a global matrix Φ, for any given pseudo multi-sense group $G = \{w_{k_1}, w_{k_2}, ..., w_{k_n}\}$ and its representative vector $v_r(G)$, we have

$$v_r(G) = \Phi * v_s(w, k_i), \forall w_{k_i} \in G, \forall G \tag{6}$$

Stochastic gradient descent (SGD) is a stochastic approximation of the gradient descent optimization method for minimizing an objective function written as a sum of differentiable functions by iteration. In order to obtain a consistent Φ for the projection of all pseudo multi-sense group, we can learn an approximate Φ with SGD for optimization. Then we use the obtained Φ to project existing word embeddings, and thus we can get a new vector space in which pseudo multi-sense has been eliminated compared to the original space.

4 Experiments

We evaluate our pseudo multi-sense detecting and eliminating method both qualitatively and quantitatively. We apply our method to the released word embeddings by Huang et al. (2012) and Neelakantan et al. (2015), which were both trained on the same Wikipedia corpus, and display the performance of our method based on the nearest neighbor task, word similarity tasks and the analogy task. In the following parts, MSSG and NP-MSSG are word embeddings released by Neelakantan et al. (2015); 50d and 300d are the dimensions of the vector space. The vector space released by Huang et al. (2012) are 50-dimensional.

4.1 Nearest Neighbors

As we hypothesized, previous multi-sense word embedding methods would produce a lot of pseudo multi-sense examples. For the convenience of view, we only focus on the semantic relation in the qualitative evaluation part. We extracted the most probable hypernym for each sense of some sample words by Eq(4), using the synset semantic relations provided by WordNet (Miller, 1995). If different representations of one word have the same hypernym, we consider them as pseudo multi-sense.

In Table 1, we show the nearest neighbors for each sense of each sample word with multiple word embeddings and our result of pseudo multi-sense detecting. For most of the representations, according to their nearest neighbors, we got reasonable hypernyms. However, there are also some unexpected cases

STAR

Huang et al.	princess, series, cast, serial, midway, sparkle, 1940s, leo, closet, co-star	01
	silver, boy, cat, version, adventures, stars, emerald, destroyer, terrace, planet	02
	energy, disk, wheel, disadvantage, block, puff, radius, diamond, chord	03
	version, bronze, standard, colors, ring, emblem, silver, wear, shoulder, red	01
	workshop, shop, paper, merchandise, plain, corporation, stock, likeness	03
	guard, baseball, starter, tennis, basketball, brazil, class, world, morocco, ncaa	01
	appearance, entertainer, pat, alumnus, freelance, brother, session, receiver	01
	fictional, ongoing, manga, super, japanese, silver, interactive, asian, fiction	01
	die, express, ride, opera, spanish, musical, hour, disaster, sun, blue	01
	galaxy, spiral, variable, guide, magnitude, companion, satellite, crater	02
MSSG-50d	blue, dragon, acbl, diamond, purple, legion, arrow, mercury, eagle, cross	01
	fan, legend, show, moesha, heroes, guest-star, flicka, lassie, tv-movie	01
	stars, sun, constellation, galaxy, eridani, pegasi, supergiant, ceti, starburst	02

01: person.n.01   02: celestial_body.n.01   03: whole.n.02

ROCK

Huang et al.	blur, indulgence, pop, noise, bands, lacuna, reformed, wave, genre, taster	01
	energy, silver, cat, song, cd, planet, dawn, hero, video, terrace	02
	metal, classic, legendary, dubbed, american, hard, belgian, short-lived, debut, da	01
	soft, shifting, disappear, fill, crystalline, false, pitch, expanse, heat, pile	03
	vinyl, concert, limited, box, summer, double, dance, enhanced, gold, inch	04
	hop, well-known, folk, occasional, jazz, music, concert, array, hard, pop	01
	morris, miami, wood, ghost, silver, pearl, chase, corner, oak, thousand	03
	hard, pop, cm, jazz, hip, hop, r&b, gutter, wave, subculture	01
	hard, hip, short-lived, classic, jazz, raw, metal, ep	01
	jazz, rally, star, roll, live, entertainer, appearance, session, pop, cover	01
MSSG-50d	metal, rippling, dense, swirling, chirping, blues, punk, psychedelia, bands, pop	01
	sand, rocks, butte, ash, sandy, little, cedar, rocky, sugarloaf, spring-fed	03
	hip, alternative, indie, progressive, hop, reggae, roll, rock/metal, post-hardcore	01

01: popular_music.n.01   02: person.n.01   03: material.n.01   04: whole.n.02

NET

Huang et al.	reduction, amount, increases, stamina, zero, worksheet, improvements, sum	01
	raw, atomic, destination, brave, orbit, generalize, clock, ca, exhale, fresh	02
	monthly, minimum, retail, banking, dividend, investor, tax, consumer, flat, dollar	03
	cash, annual, bribe, yen, generate, yen, liabilities, stocks, lifetime	03
	limousine, panic, alarm, cotton, racket, rush, 9th, buffalo, corps, recovered	04
	palm, stalk, blanket, challah, qibla, putting, recess, curtain, tighten, lean	04
	indent, text, poser, instruction, libraries, mosaic, campaigns, graphics, imperative	04
	freight, processing, volume, needs, passenger, junction, electrical, ferry, shipping	04
	contribution, bonus, compensation, bribe, yen, liabilities, stocks, yen, profit	03
	1909, quarterback, columbus, bills, bath, elite, 1903, tigers, affiliated, eagles	04
MSSG-50d	droplet, pile, wellbore, squeeze, amount, volume, steady, turn, moves, balance	04
	boards, run, ball, spot, sideline, at-bat, clock, stretch, running, phils	04
	revenue, trillion, assets, profit, billion, pre-tax, liabilities, index, us$, fdi	03

01: whole.n.02   02: seize.v.01   03: income.n.01   04: artifact.n.01

Table 1: Nearest neighbors (by cosine similarity) of sample words and the result of pseudo multi-sense detecting. Column 1 shows the existing word embeddings we use to detect pseudo multi-sense. In Column 2, each row shows the nearest neighbors of one sense in the vector space (Column 1). In Column 3, we present a meaning label for each sense, following the standard of WordNet synset description. We argue that "senses" with the same label actually have the same meaning, namely pseudo multi-sense.

from the result based on the word vectors released by Huang et al. (2012), while no such cases are found in the vectors released by Neelakantan et al. (2015). For example, we got [whole.n.02] as the hypernym of the three sample words (which seems too general since *whole* can be the hypernym of nearly all entities), and [person.n.01] as a hypernym of *ROCK* (which seems not very reasonable according to the nearest neighbors). By intuition, we suggest that is because of the quality of the word embeddings. Possibly, the level of confidence to extract domains and hypernyms for each sense could be a metric for evaluating the quality of word embeddings. From this point of view, the word embeddings released by Neelakantan et al. (2015) are also with higher quality.

4.2 Word Similarity

Now we focus on applying a qualitative evaluation to our method. For each word in the embedded vector space, we first determine the pseudo multi-sense with Eq(5). Then we try to minimize the distance between vectors which belong to the same pseudo multi-sense group, since we argue that they actually represent for the same meaning in the vector space, by training such a matrix Φ, which projects all vectors to a new vector space and eliminate the distance between pseudo multi-sense vectors. We train the matrix Φ by minimizing the following formula.

$$L = \sum_{(x,x_r)} ||\Phi x - x_r||^2 \tag{7}$$

where x is a vector which belongs to a pseudo multi-sense group and x_r is the representative vector of the corresponding group. In our experiments, we tried both random sampling and computing mean vector for getting such representative vector.

4.2.1 Similarity Metrics

The similarity here is a metric between words to evaluate the performance of word embeddings, which will be used to compare with human judgements, differently from the similarities we introduced in Section 3, which are used to detect pseudo multi-sense.

Neelakantan et al. (2015) introduced three metrics to compute the similarity between words in multi-sense word embeddings, which are $avgSim, avgSimC$ and $localSim$, defined by the following equations.

$$avgSim(w, w') = \frac{1}{K}\frac{1}{K'} \sum_{i=1}^{K} \sum_{j=1}^{K'} s(v_s(w, i), v_s(w', j)) \tag{8}$$

where K and K' are the numbers of senses for w and w', $v_s(w, i)$ is the vector of the ith sense of word w, and $s(v_s(w, i), v_s(w', j))$ is the similarity measure between vectors $v_s(w, i)$ and $v_s(w', j)$. In our experiments, we apply cosine similarity as s.

$AvgSimC$ and $localSim$ can be computed when we have the context of the words.

$$avgSimC(w, w') = \frac{1}{K}\frac{1}{K'} \sum_{i=1}^{K} \sum_{j=1}^{K'} P(w, c, i)P(w', c', j)s(v_s(w, i), v_s(w', j)) \tag{9}$$

where $P(w, c, i)$ is the probability for word w to take the ith sense with context vector c.

$$localSim(w, w') = s(v_s(w, k), v_s(w', k')) \tag{10}$$

where $k = \text{argmax}_i P(w, c, i)$, $k' = \text{argmax}_{i'} P(w', c', i')$.

4.2.2 WordSim-353

WordSim-353 is a standard dataset for evaluating the quality of word vectors introduced by Finkelstein et al. (2001), which includes 353 pairs of nouns (without context). Each pair is presented with 13 to 16 human judgements on similarity and relatedness on a scale from 0 to 10. For example, pair (stock, market) gets the score of 8.08, while pair (stock, egg) only gains the score of 1.81.

In this dataset, since the context of words is not given, we can only compute the $avgSim$ for each pair of word to evaluate our method. The result is shown in Table 2.

4.2.3 SCWS

Stanford Contextual Word Similarity (SCWS) dataset proposed by Huang et al. (2012) is also a standard dataset to evaluate the performance of word embeddings quantitatively. It contains 2,003 pairs of words and the context they occur in.

Then as Neelakantan et al. (2015) did in their work, we also report the Spearman rank correlation between a model's output similarities and the human judgements. We also tried both random sampling and mean vector to get the representative vector for each pseudo multi-sense group. The result of our experiments are shown in Table 3.

Model	avgSim		
	original	random	mean
Huang et al. 50d	64.2	**65.1**	65.0
MSSG 50d	63.2	65.0	**65.1**
MSSG 300d	**70.9**	70.8	70.5
NP-MSSG 50d	62.4	64.0	**64.4**
NP-MSSG 300d	68.6	**69.1**	68.8

Table 2: Experimental result on WordSim-353 dataset (Spearman $\rho \times 100$). We apply both random choosing and mean vector to compute the representative vector for each group of pseudo multi-sense. Our method gains a slight improvement on all models except MSSG-300d.

Model	localSim			avgSim			avgSimC		
	original	random	mean	original	random	mean	original	random	mean
Huang et al.	26.1	**37.6**	36.9	62.8	61.4	62.9	65.7	65.9	66.1
MSSG 50d	49.2	52.4	**53.2**	64.2	64.9	64.8	66.9	67.0	67.2
MSSG 300d	57.3	62.1	**62.2**	67.2	67.3	67.2	69.3	69.1	69.4
NPMSSG50d	50.3	**55.5**	54.9	64.0	64.1	64.5	66.1	66.3	66.4
NPMSSG300d	59.8	**62.3**	62.2	67.3	67.3	67.4	69.1	68.9	69.2

Table 3: Experimental result on SCWS dataset (Spearman $\rho \times 100$). It shows that the elimination of pseudo multi-sense can significantly improves the performance of word embeddings with the metric *localSim*, while the performances of projected vectors on the metric *avgSim* and *avgSimC* are about the same as those of original vectors. In other words, the elimination of pseudo multi-sense improves the ability of representing a real sense of each sense vector locally.

4.3 Analogy

Analogy task is another method to evaluate the performance of word embeddings. In single-sense word embeddings, if the word A is similar to word B in the same sense as word C is similar to D, there should be an algebraic relationship $v(A) - v(B) = v(C) - v(D)$, where $v(A)$ is the vector of word A in the word embeddings (Mikolov et al., 2013a). Based on such relationship, we conduct the following experiment, which shows that our method is able to improve the quality of multi-sense word embeddings.

In order to compare the quality of different versions of word vectors, our experiment runs on the Semantic-Syntactic Word Relationship dataset, which contains five types of semantic questions and nine types of syntactic questions, as shown in Table 4, including 19544 such quadruples totally.

For each quadruple in the test dataset, we mark it as w_1, w_2, w_3, w_4. The relationship between w_1 and w_2 is similar to that between w_3 and w_4. In single-sense word embeddings, we just need to check whether $v(w_4)$ is the most similar vector to $v(w_1) - v(w_2) + v(w_3)$ among all the vectors, and apply the same procedure for w_1, w_2, w_3. For multi-sense word embeddings, we check whether there is a combination of senses $\{k_1, k_2, k_3, k_4\}$ so that $v_s(w_4, k_4)$ is the most similar vector to $v_s(w_1, k_1) - v(w_2, k_2) + v(w_3, k_3)$, where $v_s(w, k)$ is the vector of word w's k^{th} sense. What's more, since the equivalence of the two pairs, we also check by such procedure for $v_s(w_1, k_1), v_s(w_2, k_2), v_s(w_3, k_3)$. For every quadruple, once one of the requirements above is satisfied, we treat it as correct. We report the accuracy for each multi-sense vector space in Table 5.

Type of relationship	Word Pair 1		Word Pair 2	
Common capital city	Athens	Greece	Oslo	Norway
All capital cities	Astana	Kazakhstan	Harare	Zimbabwe
Currency	Angola	kwanza	Iran	rial
City-in-state	Chicago	Illinois	Stockton	California
Man-Woman	brother	sister	grandson	granddaughter
Adjective to adverb	apparent	apparently	rapid	rapidly
Opposite	possibly	impossibly	ethical	unethical
Comparative	great	greater	tough	tougher
Superlative	easy	easiest	lucky	luckiest
Present Participle	think	thinking	read	reading
Nationality adjective	Switzerland	Swiss	Cambodia	Cambodian
Past tense	walking	walked	swimming	swam
Plural nouns	mouse	mice	dollar	dollars
Plural verbs	work	works	speak	speaks

Table 4: Sample quadruple instances in analogy testing dataset. The relations are divided into 5 semantic types and 9 syntactic types.

Model	Semantic			Syntactic		
	original	random	mean	original	random	mean
Huang et al.	52.8	**53.5**	53.4	53.5	**56.1**	55.9
MSSG 50d	75.8	**77.5**	77.4	85.2	87.9	**88.0**
MSSG 300d	92.0	92.8	**93.1**	93.3	94.1	**94.5**
NPMSSG 50d	74.6	75.4	**75.6**	80.7	82.1	**82.3**
NPMSSG 300d	83.9	85.7	**85.9**	89.0	**90.2**	90.1

Table 5: Test result for analogy task. We also apply both random choosing and mean vector to get the representative vector for each pseudo multi-sense group. It shows that our improved vectors perform better on this task.

Overall, our detection and elimination of pseudo multi-sense on word embeddings reach higher performance on the nearest neighbor, word similarity and analogy task.

5 Conclusion and future work

In this paper, we introduced the concept of *pseudo multi-sense*, which is the word embedding models often embed one meaning to multiple senses, to describe the common problem in multi-sense word embeddings. Then we proposed a method based on both domains and semantic relations to detect such cases. What's more, we trained a global transition matrix based on the detected pseudo multi-sense from the given word embeddings, which is used to eliminate the distance between senses actually have the same meaning. The evaluation of our pseudo multi-sense eliminated vector showed that detecting and eliminating pseudo multi-sense significantly improved the ability for each vector in the word embeddings to represent for an exact meaning. We suggest that the following research directions could be considered.

- For the detection of pseudo multi-sense, taking syntactic information and other information we have or we can extract from corpus into account is a reasonable idea to improve the performance.

- Involve the pseudo multi-sense detection and elimination into the neural network structure, so that the learnt word embeddings could have higher quality than those learnt by existing methods without consideration of pseudo multi-sense.

- Though we have gained an improvement on experiments, we don't have a deep understanding about the reason that why elimination of pseudo multi-sense works well and why pseudo multi-sense cases are ubiquitous in all kinds of word embeddings. In future work, we could focus on finding a reasonable explanation of the fact.

References

Yoshua Bengio, Réjean Ducharme, Pascal Vincent, and Christian Jauvin. 2003. A neural probabilistic language model. *journal of machine learning research*, 3(Feb):1137–1155.

Luisa Bentivogli, Pamela Forner, Bernardo Magnini, and Emanuele Pianta. 2004. Revising the wordnet domains hierarchy: semantics, coverage and balancing. In *Proceedings of the Workshop on Multilingual Linguistic Ressources*, pages 101–108. Association for Computational Linguistics.

Xinxiong Chen, Zhiyuan Liu, and Maosong Sun. 2014. A unified model for word sense representation and disambiguation. In *EMNLP*, pages 1025–1035. Citeseer.

Jianpeng Cheng and Dimitri Kartsaklis. 2015. Syntax-aware multi-sense word embeddings for deep compositional models of meaning. *arXiv preprint arXiv:1508.02354*.

Ronan Collobert and Jason Weston. 2008. A unified architecture for natural language processing: Deep neural networks with multitask learning. In *Proceedings of the 25th international conference on Machine learning*, pages 160–167. ACM.

Lev Finkelstein, Evgeniy Gabrilovich, Yossi Matias, Ehud Rivlin, Zach Solan, Gadi Wolfman, and Eytan Ruppin. 2001. Placing search in context: The concept revisited. In *Proceedings of the 10th international conference on World Wide Web*, pages 406–414. ACM.

Aitor González, German Rigau, and Mauro Castillo. 2012. A graph-based method to improve wordnet domains. In *International Conference on Intelligent Text Processing and Computational Linguistics*, pages 17–28. Springer.

Eric H Huang, Richard Socher, Christopher D Manning, and Andrew Y Ng. 2012. Improving word representations via global context and multiple word prototypes. In *Proceedings of the 50th Annual Meeting of the Association for Computational Linguistics: Long Papers-Volume 1*, pages 873–882. Association for Computational Linguistics.

Jiwei Li and Dan Jurafsky. 2015. Do multi-sense embeddings improve natural language understanding? *arXiv preprint arXiv:1506.01070*.

Yang Liu, Zhiyuan Liu, Tat-Seng Chua, and Maosong Sun. 2015. Topical word embeddings. In *AAAI*, pages 2418–2424.

Bernardo Magnini and Gabriela Cavaglia. 2000. Integrating subject field codes into wordnet. In *LREC*.

Tomas Mikolov, Martin Karafiát, Lukas Burget, Jan Cernocky, and Sanjeev Khudanpur. 2010. Recurrent neural network based language model. In *Interspeech*, volume 2, page 3.

Tomas Mikolov, Kai Chen, Greg Corrado, and Jeffrey Dean. 2013a. Efficient estimation of word representations in vector space. *arXiv preprint arXiv:1301.3781*.

Tomas Mikolov, Quoc V Le, and Ilya Sutskever. 2013b. Exploiting similarities among languages for machine translation. *arXiv preprint arXiv:1309.4168*.

Tomas Mikolov, Wen-tau Yih, and Geoffrey Zweig. 2013c. Linguistic regularities in continuous space word representations. In *HLT-NAACL*, volume 13, pages 746–751.

George A Miller. 1995. Wordnet: a lexical database for english. *Communications of the ACM*, 38(11):39–41.

Andriy Mnih and Geoffrey Hinton. 2007. Three new graphical models for statistical language modelling. In *Proceedings of the 24th international conference on Machine learning*, pages 641–648. ACM.

Andriy Mnih and Koray Kavukcuoglu. 2013. Learning word embeddings efficiently with noise-contrastive estimation. In *Advances in Neural Information Processing Systems*, pages 2265–2273.

Frederic Morin and Yoshua Bengio. 2005. Hierarchical probabilistic neural network language model. In *Aistats*, volume 5, pages 246–252. Citeseer.

Arvind Neelakantan, Jeevan Shankar, Alexandre Passos, and Andrew McCallum. 2015. Efficient non-parametric estimation of multiple embeddings per word in vector space. *arXiv preprint arXiv:1504.06654*.

Luis Nieto Pina and Richard Johansson. 2014. A simple and efficient method to generate word sense representations. *arXiv preprint arXiv:1412.6045*.

Joseph Reisinger and Raymond J Mooney. 2010. Multi-prototype vector-space models of word meaning. In *Human Language Technologies: The 2010 Annual Conference of the North American Chapter of the Association for Computational Linguistics*, pages 109–117. Association for Computational Linguistics.

A Preliminary Study of Statistically Predictive Syntactic Complexity Features and Manual Simplifications in Basque

Itziar Gonzalez-Dios, María Jesús Aranzabe, Arantza Díaz de Ilarraza
IXA NLP Group
University of the Basque Country (UPV/EHU)
`itziar.gonzalezd@ehu.eus`

Abstract

In this paper, we present a comparative analysis of statistically predictive syntactic features of complexity and the treatment of these features by humans when simplifying texts. To that end, we have used a list of the most five statistically predictive features obtained automatically and the Corpus of Basque Simplified Texts (CBST) to analyse how the syntactic phenomena in these features have been manually simplified. Our aim is to go beyond the descriptions of operations found in the corpus and relate the multidisciplinary findings to understand text complexity from different points of view. We also present some issues that can be important when analysing linguistic complexity.

1 Introduction and Related Work

Linguistic complexity has gained a lot of attention in the last years from different points of view. In Natural Language Processing (NLP), for example, there are two main research lines that deal with text complexity: readability assessment (RA) and automatic text simplification (ATS). RA seeks to analyse the complexity of the texts to classify them according to a level by means of analysis of linguistic features and machine learning techniques (DuBay, 2004; Benjamin, 2012; Zamanian and Heydari, 2012). On the other hand, ATS deals with the complexity of the texts in order to give a more accessible and simple equivalent version by reducing its lexical and syntactic complexity (Shardlow, 2014; Siddharthan, 2014). In the last years, parallel corpora of original and simplified texts have also been created in order to study the phenomena considered as complex and the changes performed when simplifying (Caseli et al., 2009; Bott and Saggion, 2014; Brunato et al., 2015).

In Basque, linguistic complexity has been studied from both neurolinguistic and computational points of view. From a neurolinguistic point of view, the internal word ordering (Laka and Erdozia, 2010), the relative clauses (Carreiras et al., 2010), and the effect of phrasal length on sentence word order (Ros et al., 2015) have been analysed. From the computational point of view, text complexity has been studied for readability assessment (Gonzalez-Dios et al., 2014) or automatic text simplification (Aranzabe et al., 2012).

In this paper, from the computational point of view, we want to see if the syntactic features that are statistically predictive of readability have been considered by humans when simplifying texts and how they have been treated. To that end, we analyse the phenomena involved in the most five predictive syntactic features (the ratios of conditional, concessive, purpose, temporal and relative clauses) in the Corpus of Basque Simplified Texts (CBST) (Gonzalez-Dios, 2016) in the two simplification approaches contained (structural and intuitive). This way, we want to make a linguistic analysis of the simplified texts beyond the description of the corpus and relate them to computational and neurolinguistic studies when possible. So, we want to start understanding the grounds of linguistic complexity from a multidisciplinary point of view.

This paper is structured as follows: in Section 2 we present the resources and the methodology we have followed in this analysis and in Section 3 we show the treatment of the of the phenomena in the

Proceedings of the Workshop on Computational Linguistics for Linguistic Complexity,
pages 89–97, Osaka, Japan, December 11-17 2016.

corpus CBST. In Section 4 we show how the phenomena have been simplified and in Section 5 we expose some issues that are necessary to keep on with the analysis of text complexity. Finally, we conclude and outline the future work in Section 6.

2 Resources and Experimental Set Up

To analyse wheater the syntactic phenomena considered in the statistically predictive features have been treated by humans, we have used two resources: a list of predictive features and a corpus of simplified texts. To get the list of predictive features, we have based on the experiments carried out to assess the readability of Basque texts (Gonzalez-Dios et al., 2014). In these experiments, in addition to create a model to classify texts as simple or complex, a list with most predictive features or linguistic ratios was created using the data mining software *Weka* (Hall et al., 2009) and the rankers Chi Square Ranker and InfoGain Ranker. The features in the list are classified according to their linguistic type: global, lexical, morphological, morpho-syntactic, syntactic and pragmatic.

To train the readability assessment model and get the list of predictive features, two corpora of scientific popularisation domain were used: 1) the *Elhuyar (T-comp)* corpus, which contains 200 texts for adults which, was considered as a complex corpus and 2) the *Zernola (T-simp)* corpus, containing 200 texts for children, was considered as simple. These corpora were analysed with the framework for the automatic analysis of Basque (Aduriz and Díaz de Ilarraza, 2003), the sentence and clause boundary detector (Aranzabe et al., 2013) and the apposition detector (Gonzalez-Dios et al., 2013).

The second resource is the Corpus of Basque Simplified Texts (CBST) (Gonzalez-Dios, 2016). This corpus compiles 227 original sentences[1] of the *Elhuyar (T-comp)* corpus that have been simplified by two language experts following the structural and intuitive approaches. The structural approach was performed by a court translator that followed easy-to-read guidelines inspired by Mitkov and Štajner (2014) such as use simple and short sentences with only a finite verb in each, use high frequency words, use always the same word to refer to same concept, keep logical and chronological ordering, recover elided arguments and verbs, and resolve anaphora. She was also given a set of operations performed in a previous phase of the corpus that included operations such as substitute synonyms, split clauses or reorder clauses. The intuitive approach was performed by a teacher following her experience on teaching Basque as foreign language and her intuition. In both approaches the target audience was open.

So, to see how the phenomena contained in the most predictive syntactic features have been treated in the CBST corpus, we have followed this methodology:

1. We have extracted the syntactic features from the list of predictive features and their significance according to the two rankers (Table 1).

Ratio	Chi square	InfoGain
Conditional clauses / clauses	249.9054	0.7057
Concessive clauses / clauses	189.0847	0.5338
Purpose clauses / clauses	148.062	0.3808
Temporal clauses / clauses	143.678	0.3716
Relative clauses / clauses	77.1949	0.2398
Causal clauses / clauses	61.3733	0.1814
Modal clauses / clauses	60.4716	0.1657
Completive clauses / clauses	54.202	0.1632

Table 1: Most predictive syntactic features.

2. We have extracted automatically the clauses related to the five most predictive features (conditional clauses, concessive clauses, purpose clauses, temporal clauses and relative clauses, henceforth target clauses) from the CBST corpus.

---

[1] In total, there are 785 sentences and 13 303 words.

3. Following the annotation of the corpus, we have performed the analysis of the target clauses by tagging manually if they have been treated or not (binary classification) and how they have been simplified. In the case of the relative clauses, we have added complementary information: we have annotated if the elided element is the object or subject to be able to compare if the treatment of clauses suits to the findings by Carreiras et al. (2010).

The results of the treatment are shown in Section 3

3 Treatment of the Predictive Syntactic Features in the CBST

In the CBST there are 114 clauses (89 sentences) that contain the target clauses. In Table 2 we show the percentages of the target clauses that have been treated in both simplification approaches. In parentheses we show the raw numbers.

Clause type	Quantity	Structural approach	Intuitive approach
Conditional clauses	17	82.35 (14)	35.29 (6)
Concessive clauses	5	100.00 (5)	80.00 (4)
Purpose clauses	22	22.73 (5)	22.73 (5)
Temporal clauses	17	52.94 (9)	58.82 (10)
Relative clauses	53	79.25 (42)	52.83 (28)
Total	114	85.50 (75)	71.82 (63)

Table 2: Percentages of simplified clauses in both structural and intuitive approaches.

Looking at the results of the conditional clauses, we see that there is a big difference depending on the approach. While in the structural approach 82.35 % has been simplified, 35.29 % has been treated in the intuitive. The percentages of both approaches are closer in the case of the temporal clauses (structural: 52.94 %; intuitive: 58.82 %), but they also differ in the relative clauses (structural: 79.25 %; intuitive: 52.83 %). The treatment of the purpose clauses has been slight in both approaches, and we do not have enough data for the analysis of the concessive clauses. According to the simplification approach in general, we see that there have been more simplified target clauses in the structural approach (85.50 %) than in the intuitive (71.82 %).

In Section 4 we present how these target sentences have been manually simplified.

4 Simplification of the Target Clauses the CBST

As we also want to know how the simplification is carried out in the target clauses, we analyse the macro-operations that have been performed. Eight macro-operations[2] are defined in the annotation scheme of the CBST: delete, merge, split, transformation, insert, reordering, no_operation and other. The most found macro-operations in the target clauses are split and transformations. In the split operations sentences are divided, and in the transformation operations different changes are performed in words, phrases or clauses. Transformations can be lexical, morphological, syntactic, discursive, corrections and reformulations. The detailed description of each macro-operation and the operations involved is found in Gonzalez-Dios (2016).

In the following subsections, we present the results according to the macro-operations mainly performed. These macro-operations are split, transformation, split and transformation together in the same clause and only others (delete, insert or reordering). We illustrate the results with examples of original and simplified versions in both approaches.

4.1 Conditional Clauses

In the conditional clauses (Table 3), the most applied macro-operation has been the transformation in both approaches. The syntactic transformations that have been applied are a) the change of the syntactic connective, b) transforming a clause into a phrase, c) transforming a subordinate clause into a main

---

[2]Macro-operations are an abstraction or generalisation of different simplification operations.

clause or d) changing the finite verb with a non finite. There have also been morphological transformations like changing the verb mood from potential or conditional to present or past indicative and lexical transformations.

Approach	Treated	Split	Transformation	Split + Trans	Only others
Structural	14	28.57 (4)	42.86 (6)	14.29 (2)	14.29 (2)
Intuitive	6	0.00 (0)	66.67 (4)	33.33 (2)	0.00 (0)

Table 3: Macro-operations performed in conditional clauses.

In Table 4 we show two examples of conditional clauses. In the first sentence, a split, an insert and a change in the verb mood and tense (from hypothetic to present potential) have been performed in the structural approach while in the intuitive approach only the change in the verb mood and tense (form hypothetic to past indicative) has been carried out. In the second sentence, no operation has been performed in the structural approach but the syntactic connective has been changed (conditional to causal). There has been a reordering too.

Original	Structural	Intuitive
Bidean arrokazko planeta txikiagoren bat aurkitu izan balu, bereganatu egingo zuen (...) If it had probably found a smaller planet made out of stone, it would have appropriated it (...)	*Bidean arrokazko planeta txikiagoren bat aurki dezake; orduan, planetak bereganatu egingo du; (...)* It can find a a smaller planet made out of stone; then, it will appropiate the planet; (...)	*Bidean arrokazko planeta txikiagoren bat aurkitu izan bazuen, bereganatu egingo zuen.* If it had found a smaller planet made out of stone, it would have appropriated it (...)
gene konpontzailea mutatuta badago, ezin du bere funtzioa bete, (...) if the repairing gene is muted it cannot perform its function, (...)	*gene konpontzailea mutatuta badago, ezin du bere funtzioa bete.* if the repairing gene is muted it cannot perform its function, (...)	*ezin dute funtzio hori bete mutatuta daudelako; (...)* it cannot perform its function because they are muted; (...)

Table 4: Example of simplifications of conditional clauses.

4.2 Purpose Clauses

In the purpose clauses (Table 5) the reordering (exactly, the operation named change of the order of clauses) has also been used in the intuitive approach. The transformations that have been applied in both approaches are a) the conversion of subordinate clauses into main or coordinate clauses at syntactic level, b) lexical transformations and c) reformulations.

Approach	Treated	Split	Transformation	Split + Trans	Only others
Structural	5	20.00 (1)	40.00 (2)	40.00 (2)	0.00 (0)
Intuitive	5	0.00 (0)	20.00 (1)	20.00 (1)	60.00 (3)

Table 5: Macro-operations performed in purpose clauses.

In Table 6 we show the simplified versions of two purpose clauses. In the first clause, a split has been performed in the structural approach while no operation was performed in the intuitive (not treated). The second clause was not treated in the structural approach while the ordering of clauses was altered (reordering) in the intuitive.

Original	Structural	Intuitive
Datu horiek eta tesian ateratako ondorio guztiak baliagarriak izango dira jarraipen berezitua egiteko (...) All that data and the results of the PhD thesis will be useful to make a specialised monitoring (...)	*(...) jarraipen berezitua egingo zaie. Horretarako, datu horiek guztiak eta tesiko ondorio guztiak baliatuko dira.* (...) a specialised monitoring will be done to them. To that end, all that data and all the results of of the PhD thesis will be used.	*Datu horiek eta tesian ateratako ondorio guztiak baliagarriak izango dira jarraipen berezitua egiteko (...)* All that data and all the results of the PhD thesis will be useful to make a specialised monitoring (...)
euste-indar bera izateko, eraso-angelua handiagoa izan behar du, (...) to keep the same holding strength, the clearance angle should be bigger (...)	*euste-indar bera izateko, eraso-angelua handiagoa izan behar du, (...)* to keep the same holding strength, the clearance angle should be bigger (...)	*eraso-angeluak handiagoa izan behar du euste-indar bera izateko.* the clearance angle should be bigger to keep the same holding strength (...)

Table 6: Example of simplifications of purpose clauses.

4.3 Temporal Clauses

In the temporal clauses (Table 7), the transformation has also been the most used macro-operation. The syntactic transformations that have been carried out are similar to those found in the conditional sentences: a) the change of the syntactic connective, b) transforming a clause into a phrase, c) transforming a subordinate clause into a main clause or d) changing the finite verb with a non finite). There have also been morphological transformations (e.g. change the persons of the verb) and reformulations.

Approach	Treated	Split	Transformation	Split + Trans	Only others
Structural	9	33.33 (3)	44.44 (4)	11.11 (1)	11.11 (1)
Intuitive	10	10.00 (1)	70.00 (7)	20.00 (2)	0.00 (0)

Table 7: Macro-operations performed in temporal clauses.

In Table 8 we show an example of a temporal clause which has undergone a split and a reordering of phrases and clauses in both approaches. As we see, although the operations performed are the same, the output text is different.

Original	Structural	Intuitive
Printzipio hori gertatzen da hegazkinen hegoetan hegan egiten ari denean, (...) That principle happens in the wings of the plane when it is flying, (...)	*Hegan egiten dugu; orduan, hegazkinen hegoetan gertatzen da printzipio hori.* We fly; then, that principle happens in the wings of the aircrafts.	*Printzipio hori hegazkinen hegoetan gertatzen da; hegazkinak orduan egiten du hegan.* That principle happens in the wings of the aircrafts; the plane flies then.

Table 8: Example of simplifications of temporal clauses.

4.4 Relative Clauses

In the relative clauses (Table 9), although the transformation has been the most used macro-operation, the split has also been important above all in the structural approach. The transformations that have been carried out are, as in the conditional and temporal clauses, a) the change of of the syntactic connective, b) transforming a clause into a phrase, c) transforming a subordinate clause into a main clause or d) changing the finite verb with a non finite. There have also been lexical transformations and reformulations. The other macro-operations involved are the insertion of non required phrases, the reordering of phrases and clauses and the deletion of the phrases.

Approach	Treated	Split	Transformation	Split + Trans	Only others
Structural	42	33.33 (14)	52.38 (22)	7.14 (3)	7.14 (3)
Intuitive	28	14.29 (4)	71.43 (20)	7.14 (2)	7.14 (2)

Table 9: Macro-operations performed in relative clauses.

In the sentence of Table 10 the same transformation has been performed in both approaches: the finite verb *"eusten dien"* (that keeps them) has transformed into the non-finite verb *"eusteko"* (to keep).

Original	Structural	Intuitive
hegazkin horiei airean eusten dien printzipio fisikoa (...) the physical principle that keeps these planes in the air (...)	*hegazkin horiei airean eusteko printzipio fisikoa (...)* the physical principle to keep these planes in the air (...)	*hegazkin horiei airean eusteko printzipio fisikoa (...)* the physical principle to keep these planes in the air (...)

Table 10: Example of simplifications of relative clauses.

As relative clauses have also been studied from a neurolinguistic point of view by Carreiras et al. (2010), now we compare our findings. They claim that Basque subject relative clauses are harder to process than object relative clauses. So, we want to see if the relative clauses where the subject has been elided have been mainly treated in both approaches. These results are shown in Table 11.

Approach	Subject relative clause	Object relative clause
Structural	80.95 (34/42)	81.82 (9/11)
Intuitive	69.04 (29/42)	9.09 (1/11)

Table 11: Simplification of subject and object relative clauses.

In the case of the structural approach, more than 80 % of the subject and object relative clauses have been simplified. In the intuitive approach, on the other hand, almost 70 % of the subject clauses relative clauses have been simplified while the object relative clauses have hardly been. So, we see that in the case of the intuitive approach the results are consequent to the findings by Carreiras et al. (2010). In the structural approach, however, we think that the guidelines have influenced these results.

5 Discussion

While carrying out these experiments and performing the data analysis, we have found some issues we want to point out. The aim of this analysis is to guide a future study and make a reflection of the data and resources.

The first main issue is the data scarcity problem since in some cases e.g. the concessive clauses we were not able to analyse the results. However, we think that it is important to perform preliminary studies that can raise other questions while bigger corpora are created or compiled.

After having detected contradictory results when comparing the treatment by human editors to the statistically predictive features, we decided to carry out a deeper analysis of other phenomena that are found in the sentences of our target clauses. In this analysis, we want to see e.g. if in the sentences containing purpose clauses there are other phenomena that have been simplified. For example, in Table 12, we present a sentence containing a purpose clause where the relative clause also found has been reformulated.

Original	Structural
Hegan egiteko, pisu hori guztia konpentsatzen duen indar bat behar da.	*Hegan egiteko pisu hori guztia konpentsatu behar da indar baten bidez.*
To fly, it is needed a force that compensates all that weight	To fly all that weight should be compensated by means of a force.

Table 12: A sentence where a purpose clause has not been simplified but other phenomena have been.

These are the cases we show in Table 13: in the percentage of the second column both the target clause and other phenomena have been treated, in the third column only other phenomena have been treated, in the forth column only the target clause and in the fifth column no simplification has performed. We recall that the raw numbers are shown in parentheses.

Sentences containing	Target clause and other phenomena		Other phenomena		Only target clause		No simplification	
	Str.	Int.	Str.	Int.	Str.	Int.	Str.	Int.
Conditional clauses	70.59 (12)	29.41 (5)	17.65 (3)	52.94 (9)	11.76 (2)	5.88 (1)	0.00 (0)	11.76 (2)
Purpose clauses	18.18 (4)	22.73 (5)	77.27 (17)	63.64 (14)	4.55 (1)	0.00 (0)	0.00 (0)	13.64 (3)
Temporal clauses	47.06 (8)	47.06 (8)	41.18 (7)	29.41 (5)	5.88 (7)	11.76 (2)	5.88 (7)	11.76 (2)
Relative clauses	67.92 (36)	50.94 (27)	16.98 (9)	33.96 (18)	13.21 (7)	1.89 (1)	1.89 (1)	13.21 (7)

Table 13: Applied operations in the sentences containing the target clauses.

The combination of the simplification carried out in other phenomena is not, however, homogeneous in all the cases. It is noticeable in the case of purpose clauses, but it is not so noticeable in the rest. To study how different phenomena may affect each other will be our next step. In fact, as we have 114 target clauses in 89 sentences, we find that in 28.09 % of the sentences there is more than one target clause. So, we think that other phenomena in the sentences can be important. To enlarge this analysis, based on our manual analysis, we consider that in the future we should also take into account other parameters such as the length of the target clause or its subordination depth to get to know why a clause has been simplified and not the other.

Another interesting issue is the comparison of approaches, as we have seen that depending on the approach the results vary a lot. The guidelines and the target audience human editors had in mind has influenced their simplification decisions. This has been seen in the case of conditional and relative clauses where the results differ the most. We think that the guideline 'use simple and short sentences with only a finite verb in each'[3] has been important when performing the simplification in the structural approach and according to the intuition this guideline may not be needed. Moreover, in the case of the relative clauses we have seen that it can be sufficient to treat only subject relative clauses as performed in the intuitive approach and also corroborated by the neurolinguistic studies. The ideal situation will be to based on the neurolinguistic works to write simplification guidelines and that is why we think that multidisciplinary work should be encouraged.

As conclusion of the operations performed, we want to point out that both splitting and syntactic transformations such as a) changing the syntactic connective, b) transforming a clause into a phrase, c) transforming a subordinate clause into a main clause or d) changing the finite verb with a non finite seem to be important operations together with e) lexical operations and f) reformulations. These operations should be taken into account in the Basque ATS system although some of them are not feasible or require

---

[3]This guideline or a similar ones are found in many easy-to-read guidelines or recommendations in several languages.

a deeper analysis.

We have also seen in Table 8 that the mere description of the operations is not enough to capture all the changes performed in the sentences. This should lead to a re-thinking of the annotation scheme or annotation methodology.

6 Conclusion and Future Work

In this paper, we have presented the treatment that the phenomena in the statistical predictive syntactic features have undergone in the CBST corpus with the aim of contrasting machine and human perspectives. We have seen that in the structural approach there is a tendency to treat these phenomena, while the data in the intuitive approach is more diverse. In the case of relative clauses, we have related our findings to a neurolinguistic study and we have seen that the results of the intuitive approach agree. Looking at the simplifications macro-operations, we have corroborated the importance of the split and transformation operations in both approaches.

In the future, we would like to carry out an analysis the combination of the phenomena at sentence level to see how they may affect each other and to broaden this study when the CBST corpus be enlarged. In fact, data scarcity has been a problem to draw conclusions about the results, but we want to open a way to analyse the corpora based on different approaches. We also plan to reanalyse and compare our results as new neurolinguistic study are carried out and published, since we consider that multidisciplinary approaches can be helpful to get to understand linguistic complexity.

Acknowledgements

Itziar Gonzalez-Dios's work is funded by postdoctoral grant for the new doctors by the Vice-rectory of Research of the University of the Basque Country (UPV/EHU). This research was also supported by the Basque Government (IT344-10), and the Spanish Ministry of Economy and Competitiveness, EXTRECM project (TIN2013-46616-C2-1-R).

References

Itziar Aduriz and Arantza Díaz de Ilarraza, 2003. *Inquiries into the Lexicon-syntax Relations in Basque*, chapter Morphosyntactic disambiguation ands shallow parsing in Computational Processing of Basque. University of the Basque Country.

María Jesús Aranzabe, Arantza Díaz de Ilarraza, and Itziar Gonzalez-Dios. 2012. First Approach to Automatic Text Simplification in Basque. In Luz Rello and Horacio Saggion, editors, *Proceedings of the Natural Language Processing for Improving Textual Accessibility (NLP4ITA) workshop (LREC 2012)*, pages 1–8.

María Jesús Aranzabe, Arantza Díaz de Ilarraza, and Itziar Gonzalez-Dios. 2013. Transforming Complex Sentences using Dependency Trees for Automatic Text Simplification in Basque. *Procesamiento de Lenguaje Natural*, 50:61–68.

Rebekah George Benjamin. 2012. Reconstructing Readability: Recent Developments and Recommendations in the Analysis of Text Difficulty. *Educational Psychology Review*, 24(1):63–88.

Stefan Bott and Horacio Saggion. 2014. Text Simplification Resources for Spanish. *Language Resources and Evaluation*, 48(1):93–120.

Dominique Brunato, Felice Dell'Orletta, Giulia Venturi, and Simonetta Montemagni. 2015. Design and Annotation of the First Italian Corpus for Text Simplification. In *The 9th Linguistic Annotation Workshop held in conjuncion with NAACL 2015*, pages 31–41.

Manuel Carreiras, Jon Andoni Duñabeitia, Marta Vergara, Irene de la Cruz-Pavía, and Itziar Laka. 2010. Subject Relative Clauses are not Universally Easier to Process: Evidence from Basque. *Cognition*, 115(1):79–92.

Helena M. Caseli, Tiago F. Pereira, Lucia Specia, Thiago. A. S. Pardo, Caroline. Gasperin, and Sandra Aluísio. 2009. Building a Brazilian Portuguese Parallel Corpus of Original and Simplified Texts. In *the Proceedings of CICLing*, pages 59–70.

William H. DuBay. 2004. The Principles of Readability. *Impact Information*, pages 1–76.

Itziar Gonzalez-Dios, María Jesús Aranzabe, Arantza Díaz de Ilarraza, and Ander Soraluze. 2013. Detecting Apposition for Text Simplification in Basque. In *Computational Linguistics and Intelligent Text Processing*, pages 513–524. Springer.

Itziar Gonzalez-Dios, María Jesús Aranzabe, Arantza Díaz de Ilarraza, and Haritz Salaberri. 2014. Simple or Complex? Assessing the Readability of Basque Texts. In *Proceedings of COLING 2014, the 25th International Conference on Computational Linguistics: Technical Papers*, pages 334–344, Dublin, Ireland, August. Dublin City University and Association for Computational Linguistics.

Itziar Gonzalez-Dios. 2016. *Euskarazko egitura sintaktiko konplexuen analisirako eta testuen sinplifikazio automatikorako proposamena / Readability Assessment and Automatic Text Simplification. The Analysis of Basque Complex Structures*. Ph.D. thesis, University of the Basque Country (UPV/EHU).

Mark Hall, Eibe Frank, Geoffrey Holmes, Bernhard Pfahringer, Peter Reutemann, and Ian H Witten. 2009. The WEKA Data Mining Software: an Update. *ACM SIGKDD Explorations Newsletter*, 11(1):10–18.

Itziar Laka and Kepa Erdozia. 2010. Linearization References Given "Free Word Order"; Subject Preferences Given Ergativity: a Look at Basque. In Torrego E. (ed.)., editor, *Festschrift for Professor Carlos Piera*. Oxford University Press.

Ruslan Mitkov and Sanja Štajner. 2014. The Fewer, the Better? A Contrastive Study about Ways to Simplify. In *Proceedings of the Workshop on Automatic Text Simplification - Methods and Applications in the Multilingual Society (ATS-MA 2014)*, pages 30–40, Dublin, Ireland, August. Association for Computational Linguistics and Dublin City University.

Idoia Ros, Mikel Santesteban, Kumiko Fukumura, and Itziar Laka. 2015. Aiming at Shorter Dependencies: the Role of Agreement Morphology. *Language, Cognition and Neuroscience*, 30(9):1156–1174.

Matthew Shardlow. 2014. A Survey of Automated Text Simplification. *International Journal of Advanced Computer Science and Applications (IJACSA), Special Issue on Natural Language Processing*, pages 58–70.

Advaith Siddharthan. 2014. A Survey of Research on Text Simplification. *The International Journal of Applied Linguistics*, pages 259–98.

Mostafa Zamanian and Pooneh Heydari. 2012. Readability of texts: State of the art. *Theory and Practice in Language Studies*, 2(1):43–53.

Dynamic pause assessment of keystroke logged data for the detection of complexity in translation and monolingual text production

Arndt Heilmann
RWTH Aachen
University / Aachen, Germany
`heilmann@anglistik.`
`rwth-aachen.de`

Stella Neumanm
RWTH Aachen
University / Aachen, Germany
`neumann@anglistik.`
`rwth-aachen.de`

Abstract

Pause analysis of key-stroke logged translations is a hallmark of process based translation studies. However, an exact definition of what a cognitively effortful pause during the translation process is has not been found yet (Saldanha and O'Brien, 2013). This paper investigates the design of a key-stroke and participant- dependent identification system of cognitive effort to track complexity in translation with keystroke logging (cf. also (Dragsted, 2005) (Couto-Vale, in preparation)). It is an elastic measure that takes into account idiosyncratic pause duration of translators as well as further confounds such as bi-gram frequency, letter frequency and some motor tasks involved in writing. The method is compared to a common static threshold of 1,000 ms in an analysis of cognitive effort during the translation of grammatical functions from English to German. Additionally, the results are combined with an eye-tracking analysis for further validation. The findings show, that at least for smaller data sets a dynamic pause assessment may lead to more accurate results than a generic static pause threshold of similar duration.

1   Introduction

Translation studies can be grouped into two major fields of research: Product-based translation studies and process-based translation studies. In the former, corpus based studies are currently being used for example to find out what makes translation different from original texts in a lingua-culture. Process based studies are rather interested in the emergent translation and how it comes into being. The interest in process based translation research has been growing exponentially in the past twenty years due to technological advances like affordable eye-tracking equipment and key-stroke logging programs that allow researchers to analyze the translators' behavior while translating along with the emergent product. Both methods can be used to operationalize cognitive effort during translation. Straightforwardly, reading times of stretches of the source text can for example be operationalize processing difficulties during the process of translation. For stretches of text with higher complexity longer reading times would be expected (Shreve et al., 2010). Complexity in the process of translation does not only encompass syntactic features of the source text but also typological differences between the two languages in question modulating the possibilities of rendering the lexical-semantics of the source to something equivalent in the target language. Also multiple translation possibilities for words add to the complexity of the task of translation(Schaeffer et al., 2016). This is also reflected in longer production times and thus pauses (Dragsted, 2005). However, what exactly a pause is, is subject to debate in translation process research. Typical pause measures that have been applied by scholars of translation process research, range from one (Jakobsen, 1998) to five seconds (cf. Saldanha and O'Brien (2013) for an overview). However, these

Proceedings of the Workshop on Computational Linguistics for Linguistic Complexity,
pages 98–103, Osaka, Japan, December 11-17 2016.

pause limits were chosen relatively arbitrarily and it is hard to tell if they are too high or too low to capture translation related cognitive effort (ibid., 121). Also, different translators may have different baselines of production speed and an inter-keystroke span of 1,000 ms (Jakobsen, 1998), for example, might be an indicator of increased cognitive effort for one person but not for another. More recent approaches have been modelling translator dependent baselines for identifying a minimal pause length of cognitive effort (cf. Dragsted, 2005 and Couto-Vale, in preparation) thus neutralizing a confounding factor like participant-specific baselines of pausing behavior. Dragsted manually searched for a plausible pause value for one participant. This allowed her to develop a relative measure for pause length across subjects. She divided the randomly selected participant's production speed minus the time spent on revision by the identified pause value (Dragsted, 2005). While superior too a very rigid pause identification measure, Couto-Vale, (in preparation) rightly notes that Dragsted's measure can still be improved upon. Couto-Vale's method involves a further adjustment of a minimal cognitively effortful pause based on the type of character produced. This means he employs a classification system for characters that need one or more action keys like 'shift' to be produced. He classifies characters by means of the action key combinations first and then classifies them into categories of pauses 32 ms, which is a custom threshold . The category with the highest number of pauses is multiplied by two and additional 128 ms (also arbitrarily) are added to the threshold. Inter-key spans of a character of a respective key-combination higher than this threshold are considered to be cognitively effortful. Couto-Vale, (in preparation) suggests to combine participant specific and key combination specific thresholds. This appears reasonable and useful, however, why exactly this formula should yield cognitively effortful pauses does not become clear. There is, thus, still a need for further differentiation between mere typing related inter key spans (which are essentially confounds) and cognitively effortful pauses. Among such confounding factors are not only key combinations such as those considered by Couto-Vale, (in preparation) but also frequency effects of letters and letter bigrams which should be accounted for when assessing cognitive effort during text production. Their influence on inter key spans is at the heart of this article an will be discussed further below.

2   Modeling dynamic thresholds

For the method of pause identification, we draw upon Couto-Vale's (in preparation) category based classification system. In order to identify a cognitively effortful pause, we assign a character to the subcategories of participant, case, bigram frequency and character frequency first and then combined these to a supercategory. A character like 'a', typed by participant A1 in the German word *haben* ('have') would thus be categorized by means of the ID of the participant, the type of key pressed and frequency information which then combined to a super category with the label: *'participantA1|lower-case|high bigram frequency| high character frequency'*. A script classifies characters as upper case (shift-key + character-key), lower case , space or deletions. Deletions and space characters are grouped separately from the character keys. Especially deletions behave very differently since they almost always occur with an inter-key span of below 10 ms. The reason for this is that the backspace-key was kept pressed until the mistyped word was deleted. The keystroke logger Translog-II (Carl, 2012), which was used to record the keystrokes for the data at hand, recognizes this event as multiple key presses with a minimal inter-key span. These minimal spans would have skewed the pause analysis due to a large number of very low values. For alphabetical characters, each character press is also characterized as belonging to a high frequency group of German letters or a low frequency group. Characters receiving the same classification are grouped into the same category along with their inter-key spans in milliseconds. If an inter-key span exceeded 10,000 milliseconds, it was excluded beforehand since this pause was deemed unlikely to be linked to the complexity of the input, but rather lexical decision problems or dictionary look-ups. Inter-key spans in a super category consisting of participant, case and frequency classifications were tagged as a cognitively effortful pause when they were higher than the third quartile + three times the interquartile range of that category. Such values can be considered extreme outliers (Norman and Streiner, 2007) and it is thus likely that most of the inter-key spans below this threshold are related to normal typing activity. For the frequency classifications, character frequencies below the median of the character frequency lists are classified as 'low frequency' and above as 'high frequency'. The same is done for bigram frequencies. However, keeping the frequency types apart led to super-categories with the frequency classification of low|low, low|high, high|high or high|low. Due to the very fine grained distinctions some categories did not receive many data points. This would have made it difficult to make a reliable judgement with respect to outliers. Therefore a way to combine bigram and character frequencies was devised to reduce the number of subcategories and thus attenuate this problem.

3 Assessing possible interaction effects of frequency types

The formation of a sum score could have distorted the effects frequency on processing effort of either if character frequency would be modulating the effect bigram frequency on inter-key spans (or vice versa). In order to avoid this, a possible interaction effect of both was explored. Five translations of the same text by five different translators were analyzed statistically. Their keystrokes were logged with Translog-II (Carl, 2012). The participants were allowed to use an online dictionary, though this might affect pausing behavior and may be responsible for very long pauses not related to the processing of linguistic complexity but vocabulary problems. The five participants were German students of English linguistics enrolled in their master's and the source text was an abridged popular scientific text written in English. Prior to the translation, the participants were asked to copy a short German text, in order to familiarize themselves with the keyboard. The data consists of the participants' keystrokes and the inter-key spans associated with them. Only inter-keyspans between two characters were taken into account. Pauses after mouse-events or arrow-keys were excluded. The term inter-key span will be used instead of pause in order to differentiate it from time spans signifying a possible cognitively effortful pause (cf. the KD-files of the CRITT Translation Process Database for a similar data structure (Schaeffer et al., 2016).)

The data was analyzed by means of linear mixed regression model in R using the R-package *lme4* (Bates et al., 2015). Mixed regression models allow to control against item-specific variation. We applied the R-package *lmer-test* which calculates p-values with a combination of F-tests and likelihood ratio tests through Satterthwaite approximations (Kuznetsova et al., 2015). Cognitive effort was operationalized by the inter-keyspans for preceding each character in milliseconds. This measure was log-scaled in order to approximate a normal distribution. The model was enriched with case information (upper, lower), bigram-frequency and character-frequency (interval data) sourced from the 'Wortschatz' project (UniLeipzig, 2012) (Lyon, 2012). Since no data was available for bigram frequencies for characters preceded by 'space', the mean bigram frequency was used as a proxy for these cases. Punctuation marks and spaces were excluded from the analysis as were deletions. Since no bigram information was available for word initial characters, these were assessed with the character frequency only. Both were modelled as an interaction effect. The frequencies were log-scaled and z-scored. Each source text token was given a unique ID to control against item-specific variation in the form of a random effect. Participant specific variation was factored in by modeling each participant as a random effect as well. The final model was: *Pausetime per character ~ bigram frequency * Character Frequency + Case+ (1|Unique Source Text ID)+ (1|Participant)*

The model retreived a highly significant effect for the interaction between bigram frequency and Character Frequency (b=0.08, p<0.001). Also the main effects for Character Frequency (b=-0.21, p<0.001) and bigram frequency (b=-0.17, p<0.001) were significant as was Case (b=-2.04, p<0.001). These findings for case corroborate Couto-Vale, (in preparation) suggestion to use key combination-dependent thresholds when determining pauses. However, the results obtained here may be confounded by the fact that almost every upper case letter is also located word-initially which alone leads to longer inter-key spans (Immonen and Mäkisalo, 2010) so that it is hard to differentiate between the effect of upper case letters and word-initial characters. While the estimate of both frequency types is distinctly

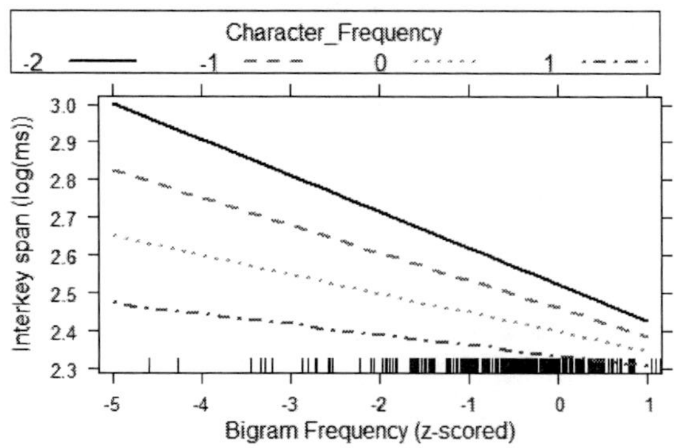

Figure 1: The interaction effect of bigram frequency and character frequency on the inter-key span. High frequency characters occuring in high frequency bigrams lead to shorter inter-key spans.

weaker than that of case, the results show that the higher the letter and bigram frequency, the smaller the inter-key spans. This is especially pronounced for high frequency letters in high frequency bigrams, as can be determined from the significant interaction between these two variables. These differences may become the decisive factor for being either correctly within a static pause threshold or erroneously above it. In order to account for this interaction effect the combined frequency category was formed by multiplying the z-scored frequencies for a character by the z-scored frequencies of a bigram it occured in at second position. The super-categories thus consisted of inter-key spans of key presses classified by *'participant|case|combined frequency'*.[1]

4   Comparison with a static threshold

To test if the dynamic method performs better than the static one, the cognitive effort during the translation of grammatical subjects from English into German was compared with the effort during the translation of other grammatical functions. The same materials and participants from section 2 were used. Additionally, the source texts were annotated with grammatical functions following the Cardiff Grammar (Fawcett, 2008) and aligned with the productions. For the analyses, cognitive effort was operationalized by the average time per pause while translating a grammatical function from an English source text to a German target text. This means, that the time associated with each identified pause for the translation of a grammatical element in the source text was summed up and then divided by the number of identified pauses. The minimum threshold to identify a pause for the static method was set to 1,000 ms which is an often used customary threshold (Carl and Kay, 2011), (Jakobsen, 1998). The minimum threshold for the dynamic method of pause identification was calculated in the way described above i.e. by means of category- dependent outlier identification. Inter-key spans of > 20 seconds were excluded, since they were likely to be caused by dictionary look-ups and not linguistic complexity. The participants and materials were the same as in Section 2. Eye-tracking data in form of the total reading time for the grammatical functions was used to triangulate the findings. Again linear mixed models were employed. For the pause-related models we controlled for the length of the translation of a grammatical function by counting the number of typed and deleted characters ('TT item length'). For the reading related model the length (in characters) of the grammatical functions of the source text was controlled for ('ST item length'). participant and

---

[1]In order to classify a key as high or low frequency, the median frequency of the combined frequency category was used as the decisive criterion as before

item-specific variation were modeled as random effects: *Operationalization of 'Cognitive Effort'* *~ Grammatical Functions + Item Length (count data)+ (1|Participant)+(1|Unique Source Text ID)*

The dynamic measure of the average time spend in pause found significantly higher average pause time for the translation of conjunctions (b=1611.69, p< 0.05) and the translations of main verbs (b=1213.79, p< 0.05). compared to that of grammatical subjects.[2] The static measure, however, did not find significant effects for the translation of coordinating conjunctions (b=1286.64, p= 0.15) or main verbs (b=1213.79, p= 0.06). The eye-tracking data corroborates the results of the dynamic but not the static method of pause identification since the results for the measure of Total Reading Time for the variables Coordinators (b=-0.42, p<0.05) and Main Verb (b=-0.52, p<0.0001) are significant here, too[3]. Still, the static measurement found marginally significant results for the translations of main verbs and it is possible that with more datapoints, the static measure would have found similar results to that of the dynamic measurement. Another interesting observation is that the estimates for Coordinators and Main Verbs in the reading time measure are negative and not positive as in the pause measures. Usually, longer reading times are associated with higher processing effort in monolingual reading. However this relationship of reading time to cognitive effort does not necessarily hold true for translation since it is a very complex task. It is more likely that the translation of these grammatical functions requires excessive target text monitoring and local decision making that is not bound to the source text any more - once the necessary information is acquired. This case highlights the need to look at both eye-tracking data and keystroke logging data to draw conclusions about cognitive effort in translation.

5 Conclusion

This paper shows that additionally to participant-specific and key-combination dependent thresholds, it is worthwhile to also include frequency information for letters and bigrams in the target language to identify cognitive effort in translation, since they have a significant interaction effect on inter-key spans.

While the static threshold did not show the significant results of the eye-tracking data and the dynamic pause measure, it is very possible, that with more data points the static threshold would have found similar results. Using static thresholds with larger amounts of data might thus still be a useful approach to identify cognitive effort in translation if time and resources are scarce. For smaller data sets a dynamic pause measure seems to be a more appropriate solution to identify cognitive effort and linguistic complexity along with it.

Acknowledgments

This study was carried out as part of the TRICKLET project, supported by the German Research Foundation (DFG) under grant project number NE 1822/2-1)

References

Douglas Bates, Martin Mächler, Ben Bolker, and Steve Walker. 2015. Fitting linear mixed-effects models using lme4. *Journal of Statistical Software*, 67(1):1–48.

Michael Carl and Martin Kay. 2011. Gazing and typing activities during translation: A comparative study of translation units of professional and student translators. *Meta*, 56(4):952–975.

---

[2]Further variable levels and control variables (non significant): **Static Avg. Pause Time:** Adjunct; b=624.77; p=0.37 Auxiliary; b=-96.62; p=0.94 Complement; b=287.89; p=0.64; TT Item Length; b=9.66; p=0.2; **Dynamic Avg. Pause Time:** Adjunct; b=560.51; p=0.37 Auxiliary; b=218.14; p=0.85 Complement; b=69.41; p=0.9; TT Item Length; b=8.2; p=0.21; **Total Reading Time** Adjunct; b=-0.15; p=0.28 Auxiliary; b=-0.34; p=0.14 Complement; b=0.02; p=0.86

[3]The control variable ST Item Length was also significant with (b=0.03; p= <0.001

Michael Carl. 2012. Translog - II: A program for recording user activity Data for empirical reading and writing Research. In *Proceedings of the Eight International Conference on Language Resources and Evaluation, European Language Resources Association (ELRA)*.

Barbara Dragsted. 2005. Segmentation in translation: Differences across levels of expertise and difficulty. *Target*, 17(1):49–70.

Robin Fawcett. 2008. *Invitation to systemic functional linguistics through the Cardiff grammar: an extension and simplification of Halliday's systemic functional grammar*. Equinox textbooks and surveys in linguistics. Equinox.

Sini Immonen and Jukka Mäkisalo. 2010. Pauses reflecting the processing of syntactic units in monolingual Text Production and translation. *Hermes Journal of Language and Communication Studies*, 44:45 – 61.

Arnt Lykke Jakobsen. 1998. Logging time delay in translation, LSP texts and the translation process. pages 73 – 101.

Alexandra Kuznetsova, Per Bruun Brockhoff, and Rune Haubo Bojesen Christensen. 2015. Tests in Linear Mixed Effects Models. Available at: https://CRAN.R-project.org/package=lmerTest.

James Lyon. 2012. German letter frequencies. Available at: http://practicalcryptography.com/cryptanalysis/letter-frequencies-various-languages/german-letter-frequencies.

Geoffery Norman and David Streiner. 2007. *Biostatistics: The Bare Essentials*. B.C. Decker.

Gabriela Saldanha and Sharon O'Brien. 2013. *Research Methodologies in Translation Studies*. St. Jerome.

Moritz Schaeffer, Barbara Dragsted, Kristian Tangsgaard Hvelplund, Laura Winther Balling, and Michael Carl. 2016. Word translation entropy: Evidence of early target language activation during reading for translation. In Michael Carl, Srinivas Bangalore, and Moritz Schaeffer, editors, *New Directions in Empirical Translation Process Research: Exploring the CRITT TPR-DB*, pages 183–210. Springer International Publishing, Cham.

Gregory M. Shreve, Isabel Lacruz, and Erik Angelone. 2010. Cognitive effort, syntactic disruption, and visual interference in a sight translation task. In Gregory M. Shreve and Erik Angelone, editors, *Translation and Cognition*, pages 63 – 84. Benjamins.

UniLeipzig. 2012. Wortschatz. Available at: http://corpora.uni-leipzig.de.

Implicit readability ranking using the latent variable of a Bayesian Probit model

Johan Falkenjack
SICS East Swedish ICT AB
Linköping, Sweden
johan.falkenjack@liu.se

Arne Jönsson
SICS East Swedish ICT AB
Linköping, Sweden
arne.jonsson@liu.se

Abstract

Data driven approaches to readability analysis for languages other than English has been plagued by a scarcity of suitable corpora. Often, relevant corpora consist only of easy-to-read texts with no rank information or empirical readability scores, making only binary approaches, such as classification, applicable. We propose a Bayesian, latent variable, approach to get the most out of these kinds of corpora. In this paper we present results on using such a model for readability ranking. The model is evaluated on a preliminary corpus of ranked student texts with encouraging results. We also assess the model by showing that it performs readability classification on par with a state of the art classifier while at the same being transparent enough to allow more sophisticated interpretations.

1 Introduction

Modern models of readability analysis for classification often use classification algorithms such as SVM (Petersen, 2007; Feng, 2010; Falkenjack et al., 2013) which give us an assessment whether a text is easy-to-read or not. Such models have a very high accuracy, for instance, a model using 117 parameters from shallow, lexical, morphological and syntactic analyses achieves 98,9 % accuracy (Falkenjack et al., 2013). However, these models do not tell us much about whether a given text is easier to read than any other text, other than the binary classification. In order to perform a more fine grained prediction we normally need to train the models using a corpus of graded texts, for an overview of such methods see Collins-Thompson (2014).

There are attempts to grade texts without an extensive corpus of graded texts (Pitler and Nenkova, 2008; Tanaka-Ishii et al., 2010). Tanaka-Ishii et al. (2010) present an approach which predicts relative difficulty based on pairwise comparison between texts and thus models degree of readability on an ordinal scale. Probabilistic models have also been used, by for instance Martinez-Gómez and Aizawa (2013). Their model is based on a Bayesian network that comprises 22 linguistic features. The model is trained on a corpus with eye fixations as a measure of reading difficulty. The paper focuses on readability diagnosis and presents a variety of linguistic features important for readability.

In this paper we present a novel way of assessing the relative readability of texts based on the latent variable of a Bayesian Probit model trained for classification. The Probit model is a straightforward way to model the probability that a text is considered easy-to-read or not. In its traditional interpretation it belongs to the wider family of linear classification models. However, in this paper we illustrate that when using a latent variable interpretation, the Probit model lends itself particularly well to readability assessment.

The probabilistic nature of the Probit model allows us to interpret and assess the relative readability between texts. Roughly, if $P(Y_{Text_1} = 1|X_{Text_1}) > P(Y_{Text_2} = 1|X_{Text_2})$ then $Text_1$ is easier to read than $Text_2$. Meanwhile, the latent variable underlying the Probit model is even easier to interpret and might even be viewed as a semi-linear and affine measure of degree of readability in itself.

Proceedings of the Workshop on Computational Linguistics for Linguistic Complexity,
pages 104–112, Osaka, Japan, December 11-17 2016.

2 Method

We construct both a Probit model and a Support Vector Machine for classifying easy-to-read texts. However, here we focus on presenting the Probit model as the SVM is already well established in the field of readability assessment. We also present the various evaluation methods used to assess the Probit method. We begin, however, by describing our corpora.

2.1 Corpora

We use three different Swedish corpora. Two are used to train the model and evaluate the classification performance of the model. The third corpus is used to evaluate the ranking performance of the model.

2.1.1 Training and classification evaluation

The source of easy-to-read texts is LäSBarT (Mühlenbock, 2008). We also use the general text corpus SUC (Ejerhed et al., 2006). From each of these two corpora we have selected 700 texts with a similar distribution of lengths. We make the assumption that texts from SUC are not easy-to-read but in reality we expect a small portion of the SUC-texts to actually be easy-to-read. This means that the sets are not well separated making perfect classification infeasible.

This set of 1400 texts from LäSBarT and SUC are labelled according to their source corpus and split into a training set of 350 texts from each corpus and a test set of the same size.

2.1.2 Ranking evaluation

We also use 9 sets of ordered texts from the MASTER project (Kanebrant et al., 2015). This corpus consists of 30 texts split into partially overlapping sets. There are 14 samples of general fiction split in 3 partially overlapping sets of 6 texts, 8 samples from social science textbooks split in 3 partially overlapping sets of 4 texts, and 8 samples from natural science textbooks split in 3 partially overlapping sets of 4 texts.

Each set is ordered through the texts being labelled with the average performance of weak readers on reading comprehension tests based on the text, where weak readers are defined as those readers scoring below the mean on all texts they were assigned (3 for general fiction or 2 for social and natural sciences). The readers were students in the Swedish 4th grade, 6th and 8th grade corresponding to an age of 11, 13 and 15 years respectively, giving rise to the 3 sets in each genre. The number of weak students we had access to varied, but for grades 4 and 6 we had roughly 200 weak students per text each year, whereas the number of weak students for grade 8 were rarely above 30 per text.

We refer to this corpus as preliminary as the sample of students used in this paper does not correspond to all data collected by Kanebrant et al. (2015) and has not gone through rigorous post-processing. At this time however, this is the only empirically based readability ranked data in Swedish.

2.2 Feature set

We use the small set of features for readability classification presented in Falkenjack and Jönsson (2014). This feature set is the result of a genetic feature selection scheme in an attempt to eliminate parsing based features[1].

The set consist of 8 features, of which 6 are part-of-speech (in which delimiters are included) tag unigrams for adverbs (AB), interrogative/relative possessive pronouns (HS), cardinal numbers (RG), and major (MAD), minor (MID) and pairwise (PAD) delimiters. The last two features consist of OVIX, or Word variation index (Ordvariationsindex), a type-token ratio based measure normalized for use on texts with different lengths, and SweVocH, the ratio of words in the text belonging to a lexicon of "highly frequent words" in a reference corpus. The feature set was optimized specifically for use with an SVM classifier (Falkenjack and Jönsson, 2014) but we assume it will work well enough with other models as well.

---

[1] Accuracy of the small feature set on the task of classifying the SUC and LäsBart corpora is 98.5% compared to 98.9% for a 119 parameter model, that also includes parsing based features, although these high accuracies might be a result of some over-fitting due to the lack of a separate test set not used for cross-validation.

2.3 For comparison: Support Vector Machine

The Support Vector Machine (SVM) is a linear classification model that can be viewed as state-of-the-art in easy-to-read classification with high accuracies achieved even with small feature sets (Falkenjack and Jönsson, 2014). The SVM works by finding a hyperplane in feature space which optimally separates two classes. This can be extended to non-linear models using different kernel functions but in this paper we use a linear SVM. Fitting an SVM to data entails solving a Quadratic Programming problem, in this paper we use Platt's Sequential Minimal Optimization algorithm (Platt, 1998) accessed through the `kernlab` library (Karatzoglou et al., 2004) for the R statistical programming language.

2.4 Probit model

The Probit model is a well established model in statistical learning, introduced in the 1930s (Gaddum, 1933; Bliss, 1934) and used primarily for classification. It is closely related to the younger but somewhat more well known Logit model, or Logistic regression, but has some properties which makes it especially suitable to Bayesian modelling (McCulloch et al., 2000). The Probit model takes the form given in Equation 1

$$\Pr(Y = 1 \mid X) = \Phi(X^T \beta) \tag{1}$$

where Φ is the Cumulative Distribution Function for the Standard Normal Distribution (if Φ is replaced by the logistic function we get the Logit model), Y is the dependent variable, or label, and X are the covariates, or features, on which Y depend. In the readability classification case, Y is an indicator value indicating whether the text is easy-to-read or not, while X is a vector of feature values of the features covered in Section 2.2.

A particular strength of the Probit model for readability analysis is that it can be viewed as a **latent variable model**. A latent variable model is a model which assumes one or more unobserved, or latent, variables which connect observed variables. If we assume a latent variable Y^* and an error term $\epsilon \sim N(0, 1)$ then a latent variable equivalent to Equation 1 can be written as Equation 2.

$$\Pr(Y^* > 0 \mid X) \quad \text{where} \quad Y^* = X^T \beta + \varepsilon \quad \text{and} \quad Y = \begin{cases} 1 & \text{if } Y^* > 0 \\ 0 & \text{otherwise.} \end{cases} \tag{2}$$

This formulation allows us to view the Probit model as a linear regression over an unobserved, or latent, real valued variable which underlies the assigned labels in the classification problem. This is particularly useful when different classes are defined by the degree of some linear property as in the case with easy-to-read classification where the underlying property is degree of readability which now is being indirectly modelled on an interval scale.

2.5 Model estimation: Gibbs Sampling

Fitting a Probit model to data can be done in a number of ways. For the traditional Frequentist Probit model, often referred to as Probit regression, Maximum Likelihood Estimation is the preferred method. This approach is well established but yields only a point estimate of β.

In the Bayesian framework we want to estimate the full posterior distribution for the model. For the Probit model, as for many other statistical models, this problem turns out to be infeasible to solve analytically so a numerical approach is generally applied instead. A Markov Chain Monte Carlo sampler can be used to draw a sample from the posterior distribution of a Probit model. If the prior distributions over β are Normal we have conjugacy with the Normal distribution of the errors and a Gibbs sampler can be constructed using a data augmentation scheme based on the latent variable interpretation presented above (Albert and Chib, 1993).

We use a C++ implementation of such a Gibbs sampler, accessed through the R statistical programming language using the `MCMCpack` library (Martin et al., 2011).

2.5.1 Prior

As we use a Bayesian fitting method we need to supply a prior. However, we opt to use only a weak regularization prior rather than a more informative prior based on any belief about specific coefficient values.

We use 0 as prior mean for all coefficients and $100 \times I$ as prior covariance ($= 1/100 \times I$ prior precision), effectively putting an independent $N(0, 100)$ prior on each coefficient. This prior is only weakly informative but keeps the coefficients from growing towards infinity and the covariances from growing towards 1, thus avoiding over-fitting. We also standardize the covariates, which avoids introducing a bias to any specific coefficient when using equal priors.

2.5.2 Sampling scheme and MCMC diagnostics

For a Gibbs sampler of a Bayesian Probit model, the output is draws from the posterior distribution over the coefficients β. As successive draws from an MCMC sampler are not independent, we thin our sample by keeping only every 200th generated draw. We also discard the first 500 thinned draws in a burn-in phase. We first show that the sample converges to the true posterior by running 5 parallel chains, taking a sample of 5 000 draws from each chain. To illustrate that the chains converge on the same distribution we calculate the potential scale reduction factor (Gelman and Rubin, 1992) for each feature and plot the value of these as the chain gets longer (Brooks and Gelman, 1998). The so called Gelman plots in Figure 1 show values very close to 1 for all features and thus indicate that the chains have converged to the same distribution which we can assume is the true posterior. The MCMC diagnostics are performed using the CODA library (Plummer et al., 2006).

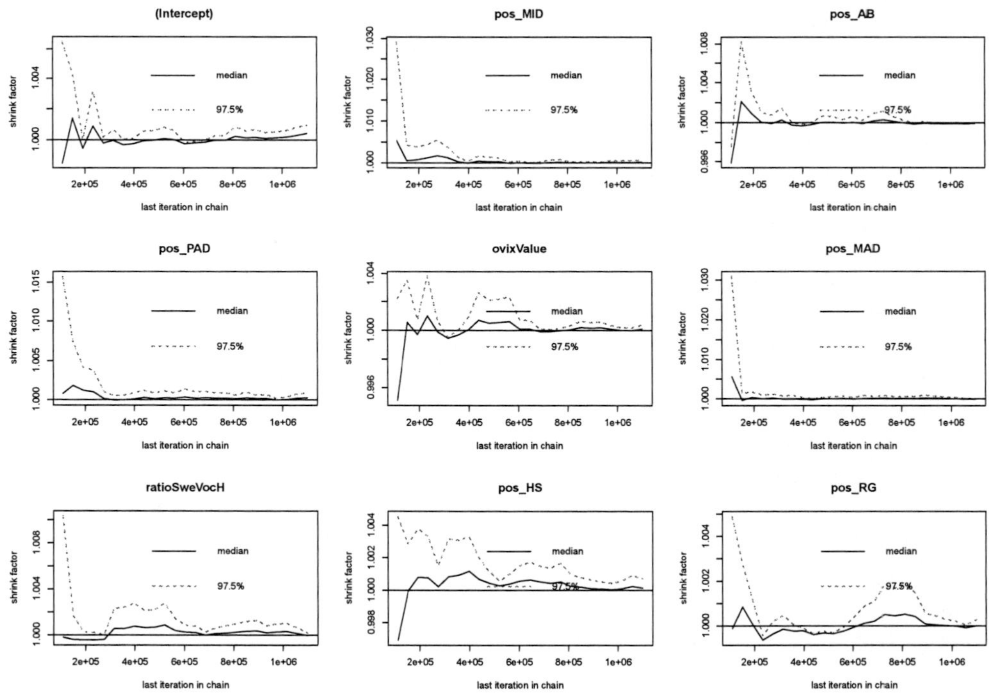

Figure 1: Gelman plots for the 8 feature coefficients and the intercept.

After illustrating that all the chains converge to the true posterior, we simulate a single longer chain, keeping a total of 100 000 draws. We compute the maximum inefficiency factor (IF) for the sample. The IF is a measure of the loss of efficiency from using a dependent rather than independent sample and is calculated for each feature (Heckman and Leamer, 2001). In this case, the maximum IF is ~ 1.02 which is acceptable.

2.6 Prediction

The fitting approach we use model the class label only as a function of the latent variable and fits the latent variable to the data. This means that besides traditional measures of classifier performance we can also inspect this latent readability value for each text.

For instance, we can plot the distributions for all true positives and all false positives and see whether true positives are generally more readable, according to the latent variable, than false positives (see Figure 3). This latent variable can also be viewed as a measure of classifier confidence and can, by definition, be converted into a probability for use in ensemble methods.

2.6.1 Posterior predictive distribution

Going one step further we should realize that we do not have a single instance of the Probit model. We do not, as is usual in Frequentist statistics, have only a Maximum Likelihood Estimate (MLE) of the "best fitting" instance.

Rather, we have 100 000 draws from the posterior distribution of the model. That is, effectively we have 100 000 instances of the Probit model. Each of these instances can be used to predict a value for a new observation, giving us 100 000 values for this observation. These values constitute a sample from the posterior predictive distribution, or PPD, for that observation.

This PPD can be used to calculate, for instance, the probability that text T_1 is easier to read than text T_2 according to the model, by simply calculating what proportion of the draws that result in $Y^*_{T_1} < Y^*_{T_2}$.

We can also inspect the posterior predictive distribution directly. The variance of which can be viewed as another measure of confidence, but rather our confidence in the model itself than the model's confidence when making a specific prediction.

2.7 Evaluation

We present results from two evaluations, one classification task using the SUC/LäSBarT dataset and one ranking evaluation on the smaller MASTER data set.

2.7.1 Classification

While this paper focuses on ranking, it should be noted that what we are actually modelling is a classifier. Thus, we should say something about how the PPD is used for classification. To be clear, within the Bayesian paradigm, the full PPD is the answer to the question "What is the degree of readability of text T?", however, we can do a lot with the PPD. Firstly, we can transform it into a probability of belonging to either class by simply computing the ratio of draws generating each class label.

A more refined way of assigning actual class labels utilizes Bayesian decision theory, which, in short, combines the PPD with a loss function. This loss function can take many forms but can be described as a way to quantify the cost of making different erroneous decisions. The task is then to find and make those decisions which minimize the expected loss.

In our case, the decision to make is what label or probability to apply to a new observation. However, as classification is not the main focus of this paper we will simply use the sign of the PPD mean value as decision rule. This also makes comparisons to the SVM reference classifier easy.

2.7.2 Latent variable ranking

To evaluate the model for ranking we use the small sets of ordered texts from the MASTER project (Kanebrant et al., 2015) covered in Section 2.1.

We compute PPD of the latent variable readability for each text and the corresponding ranking of the texts. Using these distributions and the reference readability, as defined in Section 2.1, we can compute the posterior distribution of regular Pearson correlation as well as Kendall rank correlation, also known as Kendall's τ. Kendall's τ is a correlation metric used for comparing different total orders (or with some tweaking, partial orders as well) on the same set (Kendall, 1948).

Support Vector Machine		
	Easy	Non-easy
Easy	341	17
Non-easy	9	333

Probit model, posterior mean		
	Easy	Non-easy
Easy	340	14
Non-easy	10	336

Table 1: Confusion matrices for the two classifiers.

3   Results

We present three results. First we present the estimated posterior of the Probit model, then we compare its ability to classify texts to a more conventional SVM model, and finally we give preliminary results on the Probit model's ability to also rank texts.

3.1   Fitted model

For completeness we plot the posterior densities for all coefficients in Figure 2.

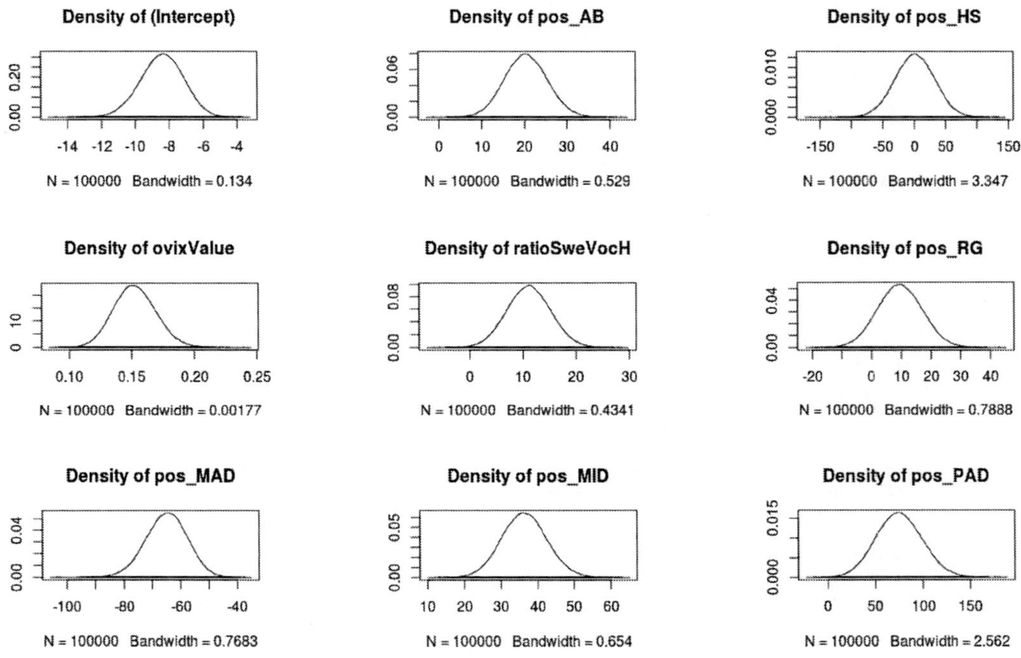

Figure 2: The posterior densities for all coefficients.

3.2   Classifier performance

Table 1 depicts the confusion matrices for the two classifiers. As can be seen the two models are comparatively good as classifiers with roughly 96.3% accuracy for the SVM and 96.6% accuracy for Probit.

Figure 3 shows kernel density estimates of the posterior predictive distributions for all texts, separated into the four false/true positive/negative categories. As we can see, the distributions for incorrectly classified texts lie closer to 0 for both false positives and false negatives than for correct classifications. Generally this can be interpreted to mean that the confidence of the classifier is lower for these examples or that their estimated degree of readability is less extreme.

However, it is also illuminating to look at a the PPDs of the first correctly and the first incorrectly classified texts.

In the first plot in Figure 4 we can see the posterior distribution of readability for a correctly classified easy-to-read text. This distribution is centred far from 0 implying a high degree of class confidence by

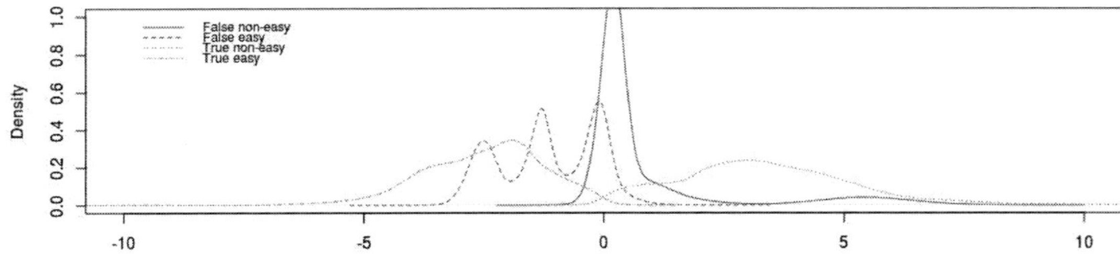

Figure 3: Total densities for false labels and true labels. Negative values correspond to easy to read texts and positive are non-easy.

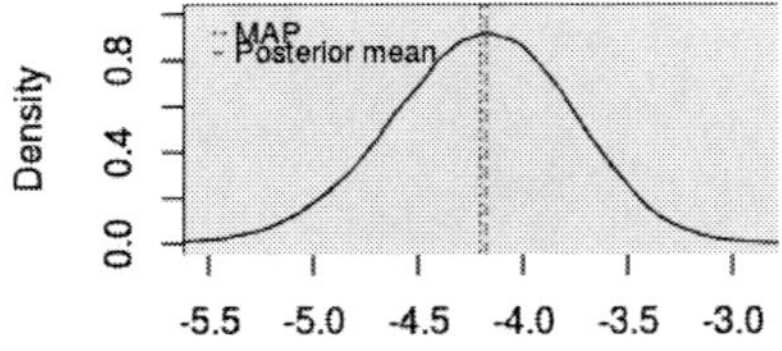
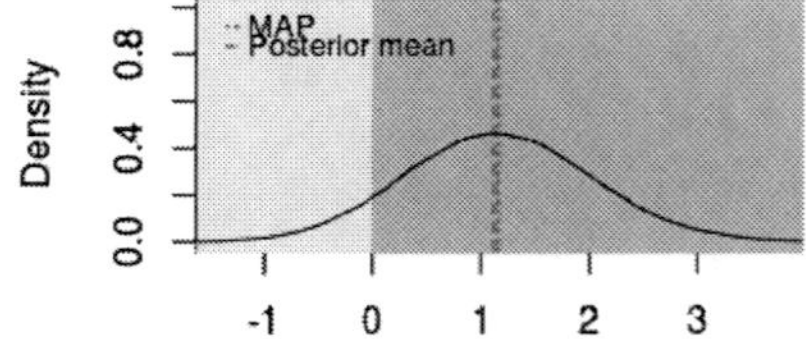

Figure 4: The posterior predictive distribution of readability values for one correctly and one erroneously classified easy-to-read text.

the model as well as a low degree of difficulty, i.e. a high degree of readability.

If we instead look at the second plot in Figure 4 we see the posterior distribution of readability for an incorrectly classified easy-to-read text. This text belongs to the easy-to-read corpus but has a posterior mean on the non-easy-to-read side of 0, i.e. it is classified as non-easy-to-read. We can see that the posterior mean lies relatively close to zero and a not insignificant part of the distribution actually lies on the correct side of 0, note also that the x-axis scales differ between the two plots, the variance of the first, "correct", PPD is smaller than that of the second, "erroneous", PPD.

3.3 Latent variable ranking

Figure 5 presents the posterior distributions of the Pearson ρ and Kendall τ correlations. The bars indicating posterior mass of Kendall τ are scaled to the height of the graphs. A large τ indicate strong rank order correlation and a large ρ indicate a strong linear correlation.

For both types of correlation, the distributions vary among different test sets but the majority of the sets show a definite correlation and some sets show a strong correlation. General fiction for grades 4 and 6, social science for grade 4 and natural science for grades 6 and 8 looks very good while social science grade 8 and natural science grade 4 still show some correlation. However, social science grade 6 and general fiction grade 8 show basically no correlation at all. It should be restated that the test sets are small and preliminary, and not investigated for any specific problems with the data, but even so, we view the fact that 5 out of the 9 test sets show strong correlations with our predicted rankings, and another 2 shows some correlation, as promising.

4   Conclusions

We have presented the Probit model, its latent variable interpretation, a Bayesian approach to fitting a Probit model to data based on this interpretation, as well as interpretations of other aspects of the model. The Bayesian approach gives us posterior distributions over all coefficients and predicted values. These express the uncertainty of the model and, though outside the scope of this paper, lend themselves to advanced approaches to decision making.

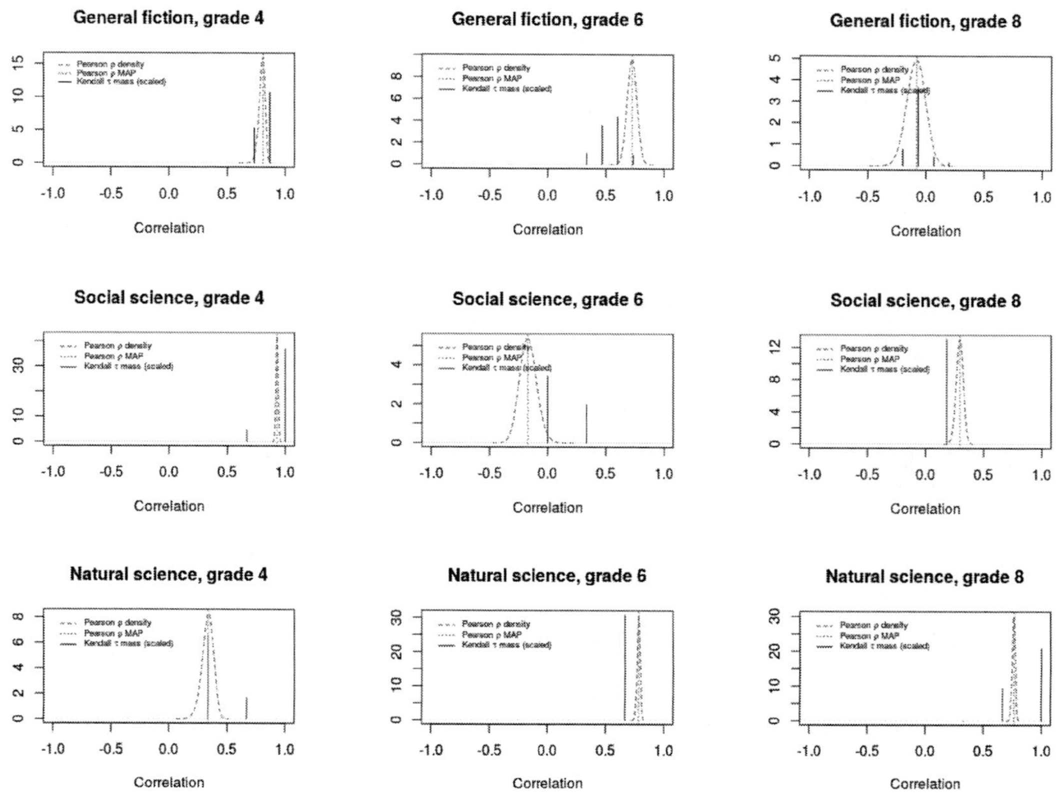

Figure 5: Posterior density of Pearson ρ and scaled mass of Kendall τ correlations.

To further assess the model we also compared its ability to classify texts to a state of the art SVM classification model. We show that for classification the Probit model performs more or less on par with a Support Vector Machine model even when using a feature set developed for SVM.

We also have the predicted values of the latent variable, readability, which we use for readability ranking; one of the main reasons for using the Probit model. The results from the evaluation of readability are promising and encourage further research.

Future work will focus on developing a fitting algorithm allowing us to utilize mix of binary classified data and a small amount of ranked data to train a hybrid of the Probit model presented in this paper and the Ordered Probit model (Becker and Kennedy, 2010). Hopefully by then a less preliminary data set of ranked documents from the MASTER project might be available for evaluation.

Acknowledgements

This research was financed by VINNOVA, Sweden's innovation agency, and The Knowledge Foundation in Sweden.

References

James H. Albert and Siddhartha Chib. 1993. Bayesian Analysis of Binary and Polychotomous Response Data. *Journal of the American Statistical Association*, 88(422):669–679.

William E. Becker and Peter E. Kennedy. 2010. A graphical exposition of the ordered probit. *Econometric Theory*, 8(1):127–131, 10.

C. I. Bliss. 1934. The method of probits. *Science*, 79(2037):38–39.

Stephen P. Brooks and Andrew Gelman. 1998. General methods for monitoring convergence of iterative simulations. *Journal of Computational and Graphical Statistics*, 7(4):434–455.

Kevyn Collins-Thompson. 2014. Computational assessment of text readability: A survey of current and future research. *ITL - International Journal of Applied Linguistics*, 165(2):97–135.

Eva Ejerhed, Gunnel Källgren, and Benny Brodda. 2006. Stockholm Umeå Corpus version 2.0.

Johan Falkenjack and Arne Jönsson. 2014. Classifying easy-to-read texts without parsing. In *Proceedings of the 3rd Workshop on Predicting and Improving Text Readability for Target Reader Populations (PITR), Gothenburg, Sweden.*

Johan Falkenjack, Katarina Heimann Mühlenbock, and Arne Jönsson. 2013. Features indicating readability in Swedish text. In *Proceedings of the 19th Nordic Conference of Computational Linguistics (NoDaLiDa-2013), Oslo, Norway*, NEALT Proceedings Series 16.

Lijun Feng. 2010. *Automatic Readability Assessment*. Ph.D. thesis, City University of New York.

John Henry Gaddum. 1933. Methods of biological assay depending on a quantal response. In *Reports on Biological Standard III.*, number 183 in Special Report Series of the Medical Research Council. Medical Research Council.

Andrew Gelman and Donald B. Rubin. 1992. Inference from iterative simulation using multiple sequences. *Statistical Science*, 7(4):457–472.

James Heckman and Edward Leamer, editors. 2001. *Handbook of Econometrics*, volume 5. Elsevier, 1 edition.

Erik Kanebrant, Katarina Heimann Mühlenbock, Sofie Johansson Kokkinakis, Arne Jönsson, Caroline Liberg, Åsa af Geijerstam, Jenny Wiksten Folkeryd, and Johan Falkenjack. 2015. T-master – a tool for assessing students' reading abilitiesstudies on automatic assessment of students' reading ability. In *Proceedings of the 7th International Conference on Computer Supported Education (CSEDU 2015), Lisbon, Portugal.*

Alexandros Karatzoglou, Alex Smola, Kurt Hornik, and Achim Zeileis. 2004. kernlab – an S4 package for kernel methods in R. *Journal of Statistical Software*, 11(9):1–20.

Maurice G. Kendall. 1948. *Rank correlation methods*. Griffin, London.

Andrew D. Martin, Kevin M. Quinn, and Jong Hee Park. 2011. MCMCpack: Markov chain monte carlo in R. *Journal of Statistical Software*, 42(9):22.

Pascual Martinez-Gómez and Akiko Aizawa. 2013. Diagnosing Causes of Reading Difficulty using Bayesian Networks. In *Proceedings of IJCNLP 2013*, pages 1383–1391, October.

Robert E. McCulloch, Nicholas G. Polson, and Peter E. Rossi. 2000. A bayesian analysis of the multinomial probit model with fully identified parameters. *Journal of Econometrics*, 99(1):173–193.

Katarina Mühlenbock. 2008. Readable, Legible or Plain Words – Presentation of an easy-to-read Swedish corpus. In Anju Saxena and Åke Viberg, editors, *Multilingualism: Proceedings of the 23rd Scandinavian Conference of Linguistics*, volume 8 of *Acta Universitatis Upsaliensis*, pages 327–329, Uppsala, Sweden. Acta Universitatis Upsaliensis.

Sarah Petersen. 2007. *Natural language processing tools for reading level assessment and text simplification for bilingual education*. Ph.D. thesis, University of Washington, Seattle, WA.

Emily Pitler and Ani Nenkova. 2008. Revisiting readability: a unified framework for predicting text quality. In *Proceedings of the Conference on Empirical Methods in Natural Language Processing (EMNLP '08).*

John C. Platt. 1998. Sequential Minimal Optimization: A Fast Algorithm for Training Support Vector Machines. Technical Report MSR-TR-98-14, Microsoft Research, April.

Martyn Plummer, Nicky Best, Kate Cowles, and Karen Vines. 2006. Coda: Convergence diagnosis and output analysis for mcmc. *R News*, 6(1):7–11.

Kumiko Tanaka-Ishii, Satoshi Tezuka, and Hiroshi Terada. 2010. Sorting Texts by Readability. *Computational Linguistics*, 36(2):203–227.

CTAP: A Web-Based Tool Supporting Automatic Complexity Analysis

Xiaobin Chen and **Detmar Meurers**
LEAD Graduate School and Research Network
Department of Linguistics
Eberhard Karls Universität Tübingen, Germany
{xiaobin.chen,detmar.meurers}@uni-tuebingen.de

Abstract

Informed by research on readability and language acquisition, computational linguists have developed sophisticated tools for the analysis of linguistic complexity. While some tools are starting to become accessible on the web, there still is a disconnect between the features that can in principle be identified based on state-of-the-art computational linguistic analysis, and the analyses a teacher, textbook writer, or second language acquisition researcher can readily obtain and visualize for their own collection of texts.

This short paper presents a web-based tool development that aims to meet this challenge. The Common Text Analysis Platform (CTAP) is designed to support fully configurable linguistic feature extraction for a wide range of complexity analyses. It features a user-friendly interface, modularized and reusable analysis component integration, and flexible corpus and feature management. Building on the Unstructured Information Management framework (UIMA), CTAP readily supports integration of state-of-the-art NLP and complexity feature extraction maintaining modularization and reusability. CTAP thereby aims at providing a common platform for complexity analysis, encouraging research collaboration and sharing of feature extraction components to jointly advance the state-of-the-art in complexity analysis in a form that readily supports real-life use by ordinary users.

1 Introduction

Linguistic complexity is a multifaceted construct used in a range of contexts, including the analysis of text readability, modeling the processing difficulty of sentences in human sentence processing, analyzing the writing of second language learners to determine their language proficiency, or for typological comparison of languages and their historical development. To analyze linguistic complexity in any of these contexts, one needs to identify the observable variedness and elaborateness (Rescher, 1998; Ellis, 2003, p. 340) of a text, which can then be interpreted in relation to the nature of the task for which a text is read or written, or the characteristics of the individuals engaged in reading or writing. In this paper, we are concerned with this first step: identifying the elaborateness and variedness of a text, sometimes referred to as absolute complexity (Kusters, 2008).

Measure of absolute complexity for the purpose of selecting reading materials or the analysis of learner language range from more holistic, qualitative perspectives to more analytic, quantitative approaches. While we here focus on the latter, reviews of both can be found in Pearson and Hiebert (2014), Collins-Thompson (2014), Benjamin (2012), Ellis and Barkhuizen (2005) and Wolfe-Quintero (1998).

The present paper describes a system that supports the extraction of quantitative linguistic features for absolute complexity analysis: the Common Text Analysis Platform (CTAP). CTAP is an ongoing project that aims at developing a user-friendly environment for automatic complexity feature extraction and visualization. Its fully modularized framework enables flexible use of NLP technologies for a broad range of analysis needs and collaborative research. In the following sections, we first sketch demands

Proceedings of the Workshop on Computational Linguistics for Linguistic Complexity,
pages 113–119, Osaka, Japan, December 11-17 2016.

that a system for complexity analysis and research should satisfy, before providing a brief description of
the CTAP modules and how they are integrated to address the demands.

2 Identifying Demands

In order to find out how complexity had been measured in L2 research, Bulté and Housen (2012) reviewed
forty empirical studies published between 1995 and 2008 and compiled an inventory of 40 complexity
measures used in these studies (pp. 30–31). Although they found that there was "no shortage of complexity measures in SLA studies", most studies used no more than 3 measures to measure complexity. This
was largely "due to the lack of adequate computational tools for automatic complexity measurement and
the labour-intensiveness of manual computation" (p. 34). The authors were optimistic that some online
complexity analyzers would come out in the near future and the situation would change.

As Bulté and Housen predicted, a number of complexity analysis tools were released in the past few
years (e.g., Xiaofei Lu's Syntactic and Lexical Complexity Analyzers[1], CohMetrix's Web interface to its
106 complexity features[2], and Kristopher Kyle's Suite of Linguistic Analysis Tools[3], etc.). While they
make it possible for researchers to measure absolute linguistic complexity easier and faster, these tools
were generally not designed for collaborative research and are limited in terms of usability and platform
compatibility, provide no or very limited flexibility in feature management, and do not envisage analysis
component reusability. As a result, they are not suitable (and generally were not intended) as basis for
collaborative research on complexity, such as joint complexity feature development.

Commercial systems such as ETS's TextEvaluator[4] and Pearson's Reading Maturity Metric[5] also implemented automatic complexity analysis for readability assessment (see Nelson et al. (2012) for a comprehensive review and assessment of such systems.) However, the commercial nature of these systems
limits the transparency of the mechanisms they employ and future research cannot be freely developed on
this basis. The Text Analysis, Crawling, and Interpretation Tool TACIT (Dehghani et al., 2016) provides
an open-source platform for text analysis. While linguistic complexity analyses could be integrated in
this framework, it so far is primarily geared towards crawling and text analysis in a social media context,
e.g., for sentiment analysis.

These complexity analysis tools overlap in terms of the complexity features offered by different systems. For example, the tools exemplified earlier contain a significant amount of lexical feature overlap
across systems. While this can be useful for cross-validating calculated results, it also duplicates analyses options without giving the user the choice of selecting the set of analyses needed to address the
specific needs. A more optimal scenario would be based on a common framework where developers of
feature extraction tools can collaborate and share analysis components, release analysis tools to be used
by researchers who focus on different aspects of the complexity problems (e.g., relative complexity for a
specific target audience).

Another issue of existing complexity analysis tools concerns (re)usability. Many of these tools are
released as standalone precompiled software packages or program source code. Precompiled packages
not only cause cross-platform compatibility problems, but also are difficult to adapt to meet the user's
specific needs. The source code option provides maximum flexibility, but are usable only to expert users
or programmers. It should be noted that a lot of complexity researchers are linguists, psychologists, or
cognitive scientists, but not necessarily computer scientists or programmers. Consequently, developing
a complexity analysis system with user-friendly interface and visualization features are on demand.

Last but not least, there is also the challenge of complexity feature proliferation over the past years.
Researchers are systematically exploring and identifying new features that contribute to our understanding of linguistic complexity. For example, CohMetrix (McNamara et al., 2014) provides 106 metrics for
measuring cohesion and coherence. Housen (2015) identified more than 200 features for measuring L2

---

[1] `http://www.personal.psu.edu/xxl13/download.html`

[2] `http://cohmetrix.com`

[3] `http://www.kristopherkyle.com`

[4] Formerly SourceRater, cf. `https://texteval-pilot.ets.org/TextEvaluator`

[5] `http://www.pearsonassessments.com/automatedlanguageassessment/products/100000021/`
`reading-maturity-metric-rmm.html#tab-details`

complexity. Vajjala (2015) accumulated another 200 features for doing readability assessment. Although features overlap across systems, the number of complexity features used and compared by researchers is large and likely to grow . Not every study needs to use all these features, nor any tool provides a full set. Researchers interested in linguistic complexity arguably would benefit from a system that readily supports them in choosing and applying complexity analyses from a large repository of features, without requiring NLP expertise.

3   System Architecture of CTAP

The CTAP system is designed to address the issues reviewed in the previous section. The goal is a system that supports complexity analysis in an easy-to-use, platform independent, flexible and extendable environment. The system consists of four major user modules—Corpus Manager, Feature Selector, Analysis Generator, and Result Visualizer—as well as a Feature Importer administrative module. Figure 1 shows the system architecture and module relationships.

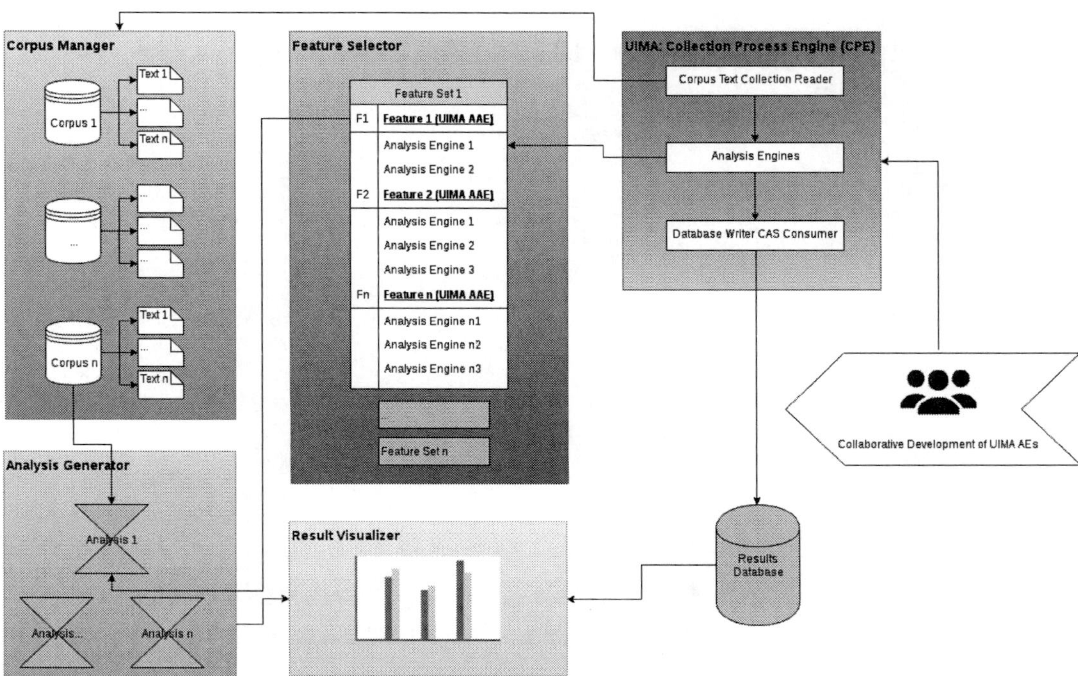

Figure 1: CTAP modules and their relationship

The Corpus Manager helps users manage the language materials that need to be analyzed. They can create corpora to hold texts, folders to group corpora and tags to label specific texts. The text labels will then be used to help filter and select target texts for analysis. They can also be used to group texts for result visualization purposes.

Other complexity analyzers usually limit users to a fixed set of features that the analyzer extracts. The Feature Selector from CTAP enables users to group their selection of the complexity features into feature sets. This flexibility is realized by utilizing the Unstructured Information Management framework (UIMA[6]) provided by the Apache Foundation. By using the UIMA framework, every complexity feature can be implemented as an Aggregate Analysis Engine (AAE) which chains up a series of primitive Analysis Engines (AEs). Each AE may be a general purpose NLP components, such as a sentence segmenter, parser, or POS tagger. It may also be one that calculates some complexity feature values based on analysis results from upstream AEs or components. This setup enables and encourages reusability of

---

[6]https://uima.apache.org

AEs or analysis components, thus making collaborative development of complexity feature extractors easier and faster.

After collecting/importing the corpora and selecting the complexity features, the users can then generate analyses in CTAP's Analysis Generator. Each analysis extracts a set of features from the designated corpus. Results of the analysis are then persisted into the system database and may be downloaded to the user's local machine for further processing. The user can also choose to explore analysis results with CTAP's Result Visualizer. The UIMA framework supports parallel computing that can easily scale out for handling big data analysis needs.

The Result Visualizer is a simple and intuitive module that plots analysis results for the user to visualize preliminary findings from the analysis. It supports basic plot manipulation and download. Figures 2–5 show screenshots of the user modules.

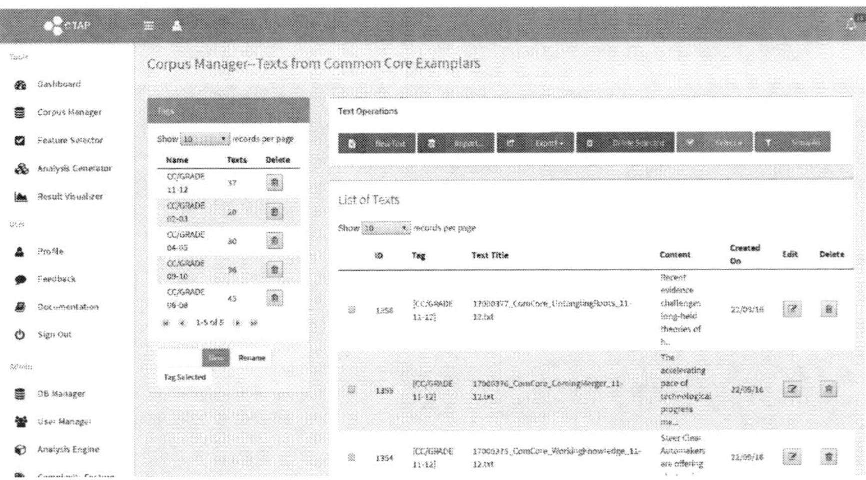

Figure 2: Corpus Manager module screen shot

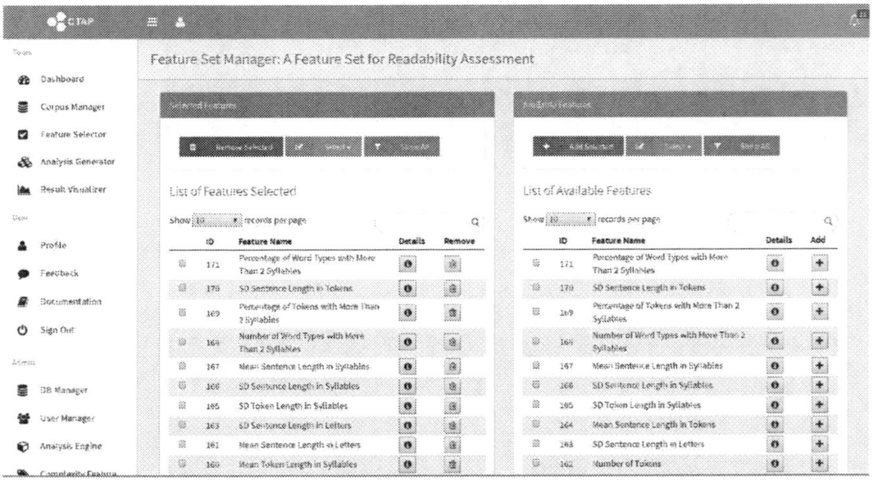

Figure 3: Feature Selector module screen shot

4   Design Features of CTAP

The target users of the CTAP system are complexity feature developers and linguists or psychologists who might not necessarily be computer science experts. As a result, the system features the following design.

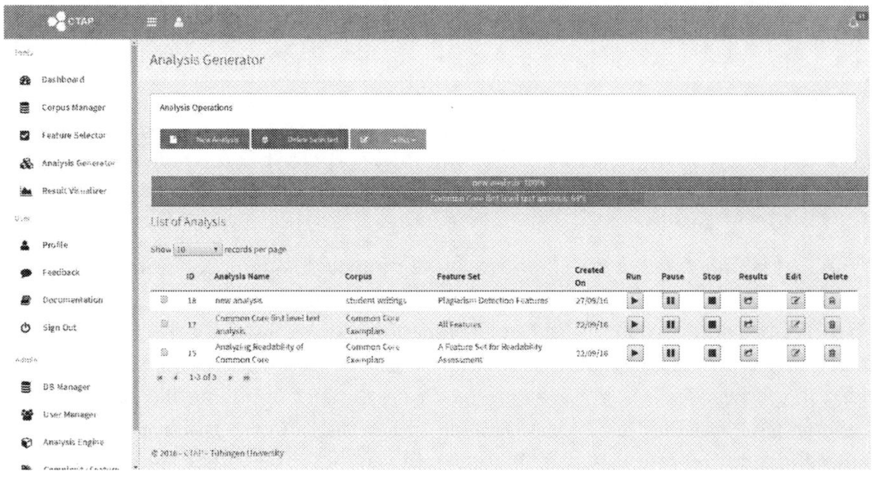

Figure 4: Analysis Generator module screen shot

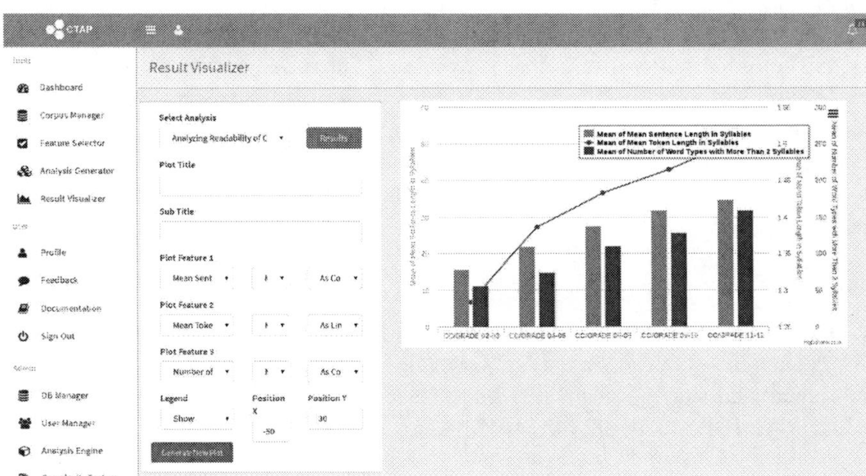

Figure 5: Result Visualizer module screen shot

Consistent, easy-to-use, friendly user interface.   The CTAP system is deployed as a Web application, which strikes a balance between usability, flexibility and cross-platform compatibility. The GUI provided on the Web makes it easy to access, user-friendly and platform neutral. The CTAP client frontend was written with Google Web Toolkit[7] (GWT), an open source and free technology that enables productive development of high-performance web applications. This avoids the necessity to compile the software for different operating systems, which has been proved to be a major frustration for small development teams or single developers who do not have enough resources to deal with platform differences.

Modularized, reusable, and collaborative development of analysis components.   The CTAP analysis back-end is written under the UIMA framework. Each analysis unit is implemented as a UIMA AE. Since a lot of the AEs are commonly required by different complexity features, modularizing analysis into smaller AEs makes it easier to reuse and share components. The AEs included into CTAP are open sourced and we encourage contribution from feature developers. A community effort will enhance complexity research to a greater extent.

---

[7]http://www.gwtproject.org

Flexible corpus and feature management. This feature is a luxury in light of the existing complexity analysis tools. However, this feature is of special value to users with lower information and communication technology competence. Users choose from the feature repository the system provides a set of features that meet their needs, the CTAP system then generates a UIMA AAE to extract the chosen feature values. It frees users from tediously editing analyzer source code, which is also often error-prone.

5 Summary and Outlook

The CTAP project is under active development at the moment. A demo version of the system has been finished (http://www.ctapweb.com), establishing the feasibility of the design, architecture, and the features described in this paper. Additional functionality, such as allowing users to add their own feature extractors and providing modules supporting machine learning to combine the collected evidence will be added in the near future. We are currently working on populating the system with complexity feature extractors implemented as UIMA AEs by either migrating existing analyzer code as well as reimplementing features reported on in other complexity studies. To validate and exemplify the approach, we plan to replicate the state-of-the-art linguistic complexity analyses for English (Vajjala and Meurers, 2014) and German (Hancke et al., 2012) using CTAP, making the components on which the analyses are based readily available.

In making the tool freely available under a standard Creative Commons by-nc-sa licence, we would also like to call for contribution from other researchers. Interested parties are encouraged to join and contribute to the project at https://github.com/ctapweb. Only by making use of joint effort and expertise can we envisage a production level system that can support joint progress in the complexity research community, while at the same time making the analyses readily available to ordinary users seeking to analyze their language material—be it to study language development or to develop books better suited to the target audience.

Acknowledgments

We would like to thank the anonymous reviewers for their comments. This research was funded by the LEAD Graduate School & Research Network [GSC1028], a project of the Excellence Initiative of the German federal and state governments, and received support through grants ANR-11-LABX-0036 (BLRI) and ANR-11-IDEX-0001-02 (A*MIDEX).

References

Rebekah George Benjamin. 2012. Reconstructing readability: recent developments and recommendations in the analysis of text difficulty. *Educational Psychology Review*, 24(1):63–88.

Bram Bulté and Alex Housen. 2012. Defining and operationalising l2 complexity. In Alex Housen, Folkert Kuiken, and Ineke Vedder, editors, *Dimensions of L2 Performance and Proficiency: Complexity, Accuracy and Fluency in SLA*, pages 21–46. John Benjamins, Amsterdam.

Kevyn Collins-Thompson. 2014. Computational assessment of text readability: A survey of past, present, and future research. *International Journal of Applied Linguistics*, 165(2):97–135.

Morteza Dehghani, Kate M. Johnson, Justin Garten, Reihane Boghrati, Joe Hoover, Vijayan Balasubramanian, Anurag Singh, Yuvarani Shankar, Linda Pulickal, Aswin Rajkumar, and Niki Jitendra Parmar. 2016. Tacit: An open-source text analysis, crawling, and interpretation tool. *Behavior Research Methods*, pages 1–10.

R. Ellis and G. P. Barkhuizen. 2005. *Analysing learner language*. Oxford University Press, Oxford.

Rod Ellis. 2003. *Task-based Language Learning and Teaching*. Oxford University Press, Oxford, UK.

Julia Hancke, Detmar Meurers, and Sowmya Vajjala. 2012. Readability classification for German using lexical, syntactic, and morphological features. In *Proceedings of the 24th International Conference on Computational Linguistics (COLING)*, pages 1063–1080, Mumbai, India.

Alex Housen. 2015. L2 complexity—a difficult(y) matter. Oral presentation given at the Measuring Linguistic Complexity: A Multidisciplinary Perspective workshop, Université catholique de Louvain, Louvain-la-Neuve.

Wouter Kusters. 2008. Complexity in linguistic theory, language learning and language change. *Language complexity: Typology, contact, change*, pages 3–22.

Danielle S. McNamara, Arthur C. Graesser, Philip M. McCarthy, and Zhiqiang Cai. 2014. *Automated Evaluation of Text and Discourse with Coh-Metrix*. Cambridge University Press, New York, NY.

J. Nelson, C. Perfetti, D. Liben, and M. Liben. 2012. Measures of text difficulty: Testing their predictive value for grade levels and student performance. Technical report, The Gates Foundation.

P. David Pearson and Elfrieda H. Hiebert. 2014. The state of the field: Qualitative analyses of text complexity. *The Elementary School Journal*, 115(2):161–183.

Nicolas Rescher. 1998. *Complexity: A philosophical overview*. Transaction Publishers, London.

Sowmya Vajjala and Detmar Meurers. 2014. Readability assessment for text simplification: From analyzing documents to identifying sentential simplifications. *International Journal of Applied Linguistics, Special Issue on Current Research in Readability and Text Simplification*, 165(2):142–222.

Sowmya Vajjala. 2015. *Analyzing Text Complexity and Text Simplification: Connecting Linguistics, Processing and Educational Applications*. Ph.D. thesis, University of Tübingen.

Kate Wolfe-Quintero, Shunji Inagaki, and Hae-Young Kim. 1998. *Second Language Development in Writing: Measures of Fluency, Accuracy & Complexity*. Second Language Teaching & Curriculum Center, University of Hawaii at Manoa, Honolulu.

Coursebook Texts as a Helping Hand for Classifying Linguistic Complexity in Language Learners' Writings

Ildikó Pilán, David Alfter, Elena Volodina
Språkbanken, University of Gothenburg, Sweden
`{ildiko.pilan,david.alfter,elena.volodina}@svenska.gu.se`

Abstract

We bring together knowledge from two different types of language learning data, texts learners read and texts they write, to improve linguistic complexity classification in the latter. Linguistic complexity in the foreign and second language learning context can be expressed in terms of proficiency levels. We show that incorporating features capturing lexical complexity information from reading passages can boost significantly the machine learning based classification of learner-written texts into proficiency levels. With an F_1 score of .8 our system rivals state-of-the-art results reported for other languages for this task. Finally, we present a freely available web-based tool for proficiency level classification and lexical complexity visualization for both learner writings and reading texts.

1 Introduction

Second or foreign (L2) language learners pass through different development stages commonly referred to as *proficiency levels*. A popular scale of such levels is the Common European Framework of Reference for Languages (CEFR) (Council of Europe, 2001). As learners advance to higher levels, the complexity of the linguistic input that they are able to comprehend (*receptive* skills) and the output that they produce (*productive* skills) increases in terms of both lexical and grammatical patterns. Although learners' receptive and productive knowledge overlap, they only do so partially, the latter being typically a subset of the former corresponding to a somewhat lower linguistic complexity overall (Barrot, 2015).

In previous work, NLP methods have been successfully applied for assessing separately receptive and productive L2 levels (see section 2). We, on the other hand, hypothesize that, since a shared linguistic content exists between what L2 learners are exposed to (*L2 input texts*, e.g. reading passages from coursebooks) and what they produce (*L2 output texts*, e.g. essays), transferring knowledge from one text type may improve the classification of linguistic complexity levels in the other. We focus on the automatic prediction of CEFR levels for L2 learner essays for a number of reasons. Essay writing is a popular means to assess learners' proficiency level and it is a rather subjective and time-consuming task. Moreover, such data is rather scarce and cumbersome to collect (Volodina et al., 2016). Our target language is Swedish since corpora for both L2 text types are available for this language.

We compare two different strategies aiming at improving L2 essay classification results without additional data of this type: (i) employing a word list based on a coursebook corpus for lexical features, (ii) *domain adaptation* experiments, i.e. training a machine learning model on L2 input texts and using it to classify the essays. We first compare the distribution of words per CEFR levels in the essays using two different word lists and find that a list based on L2 input texts correlates well with the manually assigned CEFR labels of the essays. Using this list in machine learning experiments produces a significant performance boost which exceeds our domain adaptation attempts and compares well also to previously reported results for this task. Finally, we present an online tool for assessing linguistic complexity in L2 Swedish input and output texts that performs a machine learning based CEFR level classification and a lexical complexity analysis supported by a color-enhanced visualization of words per level.

Proceedings of the Workshop on Computational Linguistics for Linguistic Complexity,
pages 120–126, Osaka, Japan, December 11-17 2016.

2 Background

Recently a number of attempts emerged at the classification of CEFR levels in input texts (also known as *L2 readability*) which include, among others, systems for French (François and Fairon, 2012), Portuguese (Branco et al., 2014), Chinese (Sung et al., 2015), Swedish (Pilán et al., 2015), and English (Xia et al., 2016). The same type of classification for learner-written texts remains somewhat less explored. Investigations include Vajjala and Lõo (2014) for Estonian and Hancke (2013) for German reporting an F_1 score of .78 and .71 respectively. The systems above are based on supervised learning methods based on rich feature sets.

Relatively few studies exist in the field of assessing the complexity and quality of L2 texts with the use of domain adaptation. Experiments relying on such methods have been explored so far for transferring essay grading models between writing tasks based on different prompts (Zesch et al., 2015; Phandi et al., 2015), and for L2 readability classification by transferring models trained on texts written for native language users to reading passages aimed at L2 learners (Xia et al., 2016).

3 Receptive and Productive L2 Swedish Corpora

Two corpora with L2 focus are currently available for Swedish: SweLL (Volodina et al., 2016), comprised of L2 output texts in the form of learner essays, and COCTAILL (Volodina et al., 2014) containing L2 coursebooks written by experts for L2 learners. The essays in the **SweLL** corpus were written by adult L2 Swedish learners (with available metadata) and they address a variety of topics. In the case of the coursebook corpus, **COCTAILL**, instead of using it in its entirety, we only include reading passages in our dataset. Other coursebook components whose linguistic annotation may be less reliable (e.g. gapped exercises) are excluded. We derive the CEFR level of the reading texts from the level of the lesson (chapter) they occurr in. It is worth mentioning that these two corpora are *independent* from each other, i.e. the essays written by the learners are not based on, or inspired by, the reading passages.

Both corpora span beginner (A1) to advanced (C1) proficiency with texts manually labeled for CEFR levels, and automatically annotated across different linguistic dimensions. These include lemmatization, part-of-speech (POS) tagging and dependency parsing using the Sparv pipeline[1] (Borin et al., 2012). Since A1 level is rather under-represented in both corpora, we exclude them from our experiments. The distribution of texts per type and CEFR level in our datasets is shown in Table 1, where A2 corresponds to elementary level, B1 to intermediate, B2 to upper intermediate and C1 to advanced level.

Writer (text type)	Unit	A2	B1	B2	C1	Total
Learner (L2 output)	**Texts**	83	75	74	88	**320**
	Tokens	18,349	29,814	32,691	60,095	**140,949**
Expert (L2 input)	**Texts**	157	258	288	115	**818**
	Tokens	37,168	79,124	101,297	71,723	**289,312**

Table 1: Overview of CEFR-level annotated Swedish datasets.

4 L2 Lexical Complexity: a Comparison of Word Lists

KELLY (Volodina and Kokkinakis, 2012) is a popular L2 Swedish word lists, compiled based on web corpora. It contains 8,425 headwords with not only frequency information, but also suggested CEFR levels based on normalized frequencies. The list has been successfully applied previously in machine learning experiment for classifying CEFR levels in L2 input texts (Pilán et al., 2015).

SVALex (Francois et al., 2016) is another Swedish word list with an L2 focus, created recently. The list contains word frequencies based on reading passages from COCTAILL (see Section 3), which, however, are not connected to suggested CEFR levels. Therefore, we propose an enhanced version of this list,

---

[1] https://spraakbanken.gu.se/sparv/

SVALex+, that includes mappings from frequency distributions to a single CEFR label following the methodology described in Alfter et al. (2016). To create the mappings, as a first step, frequency counts are normalized. Part of this consists of taking the raw frequency counts from SVALex and calculating *per-million-word* (PMW) frequency distributions for all words. These distributions are complemented with *word diversity* distributions, i.e. information about how often a word is used in different coursebooks at each level in the COCTAILL corpus. The intuition is that, if a word is used often at a certain level, but only in one book, it is less representative of a level than if it appears in several coursebooks. We then combine these two distributions into one single *normalized frequency* ($Freq^n$) value for each word by taking the average of the PMW frequency distribution and the word diversity distribution.

The second step consists of mapping these normalized frequencies to CEFR levels. Rather than mapping to the CEFR level at which a word first appears, we establish a *significant onset of use*, a threshold indicating a difference between normalized frequency distributions that is sufficiently large for a level to qualify as mapping for a word. We set this threshold to 0.4 based on initial empirical investigations with L2 teachers during which the overlap between teacher- and system-assigned levels for a small subset of words have been compared. Thus, we map each word to the lowest CEFR level L for which $Freq^n_L - Freq^n_{L-1} > 0.4$ holds, with $L - 1$ being the previous CEFR level and $Freq^n_{L-1} = 0$ if $L = $ A1.

Table 2 compares the percentage of tokens belonging to different CEFR levels based on KELLY and SVALex+ (rows) per essay CEFR level (columns).

	Essay CEFR levels									
	KELLY					SVALex+				
	A1	**A2**	**B1**	**B2**	**C1**	**A1**	**A2**	**B1**	**B2**	**C1**
A1	69.0	72.91	72.56	73.3	70.91	74.28	77.86	65.09	61.96	56.92
A2	4.08	3.96	4.18	4.31	5.22	2.54	3.6	8.01	9.31	10.67
B1	1.2	1.79	1.52	2.4	3.16	1.73	2.91	9.82	12.59	14.28
B2	.67	.68	1.17	.83	1.11	.43	.66	.86	1.07	1.86
C1	.43	.31	.31	.4	.5	.14	.17	.33	.48	.81

Table 2: Distribution of token CEFR levels (in %) per essay CEFR levels.

We can observe that the distribution of tokens per CEFR level based on KELLY remains rather unchanged: A1 and C2 level essays contain, for instance, approximately the same amount of A1-C1 tokens. SVALex+, on the other hand, correlates better with the overall CEFR level of the essays. The highlighted cells show a decrease of lower level tokens in higher level essays and an increase of higher level tokens in more advanced essays. This would suggest that using SVALex+ may improve CEFR level classification performance for learner essays. The amount of B2 and C1 tokens seems still rather limited even at higher levels which can be explained to some extent by SVALex+ containing receptive vocabulary that learners might not be able to use productively.

5 Essay Classification Experiments

5.1 Feature Set

We use the feature set that we described in Pilán et al. (2015) and Pilán et al. (2016) for modeling linguistic complexity in L2 Swedish texts. The 61 features of this set can be divided into five sub-groups: *length-based* (e.g. average sentence and token length), *lexical* (e.g. amount of tokens per CEFR level), *morphological* (e.g. past verbs to verbs ratio), *syntactic* (e.g. average dependency length) and *semantic* features (e.g. number of senses). For a more detailed description of the feature set see the cited works.

5.2 Experimental Setup

We use the sequential minimal optimization algorithm from WEKA (Hall et al., 2009) and the feature set mentioned above for all experiments. Results are obtained using 10-fold cross-validation, unless otherwise specified. Reported measures include F_1 and quadratic weighted kappa (κ^2), a distance-based scoring function taking into consideration also the degree of misclassifications. Our baselines consist of assigning the most frequent label in the dataset to each instance (MAJORITY) and cross-validated results on the learner essays using KELLY (E-KELLY) for lexical features.

Domain adaptation We compare these to two models using information from SVALex+ (E-SVALEX+ with SVALex+ instead of KELLY and E-KELLY&SVALEX+ including both lists), as well as to two simple domain adaptation setups inspired by Daumé III and Marcu (2006). In a domain adaptation scenario, data from a source domain is used to predict labels in a different, target domain. In our SOURCE-ONLY setup, a model trained on coursebook texts is applied to the essays, our target domain. In +FEATURE the CEFR levels predicted by a model trained on coursebook texts is used as an additional feature when training a classifier for the essays. For both the SOURCE-ONLY and the +FEATURE setup the KELLY list has been used.

5.3 Classification Results

The results of our experiments are presented in Table 3.

Essays (baselines)	F_1	κ^2	Essays (using SVALex+)	F_1	κ^2	Coursebooks → Essays	F_1	κ^2
MAJORITY	.120	.000	E-SVALEX+	**.808**	**.922**	SOURCE-ONLY	.438	.713
E-KELLY	.721	.886	E-KELLY&SVALEX+	**.816**	**.930**	+FEATURE	.709	.879

Table 3: Results for different classification improvement strategies.

Substituting KELLY-based features with their SVALex+ based equivalents increases classification performance substantially, from .721 to .822 in terms of F_1. This is most likely connected to the fact that word frequencies based on the general (web) corpus, KELLY, reflect less precisely learners' progression in terms of lexical complexity compared to SVALex+, which is based on texts explicitly intended for L2 learners (see Table 2). Combining both KELLY and SVALex+ achieves a slight gain, but the performance difference remains rather negligible compared to using SVALex+ alone. The high κ^2 values for the SVALex+ based models indicate that very few misclassifications occur with a distance of more than one CEFR level. By inspecting the confusion matrices we find that only two instances fall into this category for the E-SVALex+ model, and none for E-KELLY&SVALex+.

Applying a coursebook model to the essays (SOURCE-ONLY) results in a radical performance drop compared to the in-domain models, which indicates that the distribution of feature values in L2 input and output texts differ to a rather large extent. For the same reason, adding the output of a coursebook based classifier (+FEATURE) performs less accurately than the E-KELLY baseline. These results, however, do not exclude the possibility of a successful transfer between these domains. Additional domain adaptation techniques may be able to bridge the gap between the source and target domain distributions.

Our SVALex+ based models achieve state-of-the-art performance compared to CEFR level classification systems for other languages such as the German system with .71 F_1 from Hancke (2013), and the Estonian one with .78 F_1 by Vajjala and Lõo (2014). Both of these systems, however, were built using an approximately three times larger annotated in-domain corpus.

6 An Online Tool for L2 Linguistic Complexity Analysis

To put our L2 linguistic complexity analysis methods to practical use, we have made them available as a free online tool[2]. Figure 1 shows the web interface of the current version of our system.

Users can type or paste a text in a text box and indicate whether the text was written by experts as reading material ("Text readability") or by learners ("Learner essay"). The text is then automatically analyzed in several steps. First, it undergoes an automatic linguistic annotation with Sparv (e.g. POS

---

[2]https://spraakbanken.gu.se/larkalabb/texteval

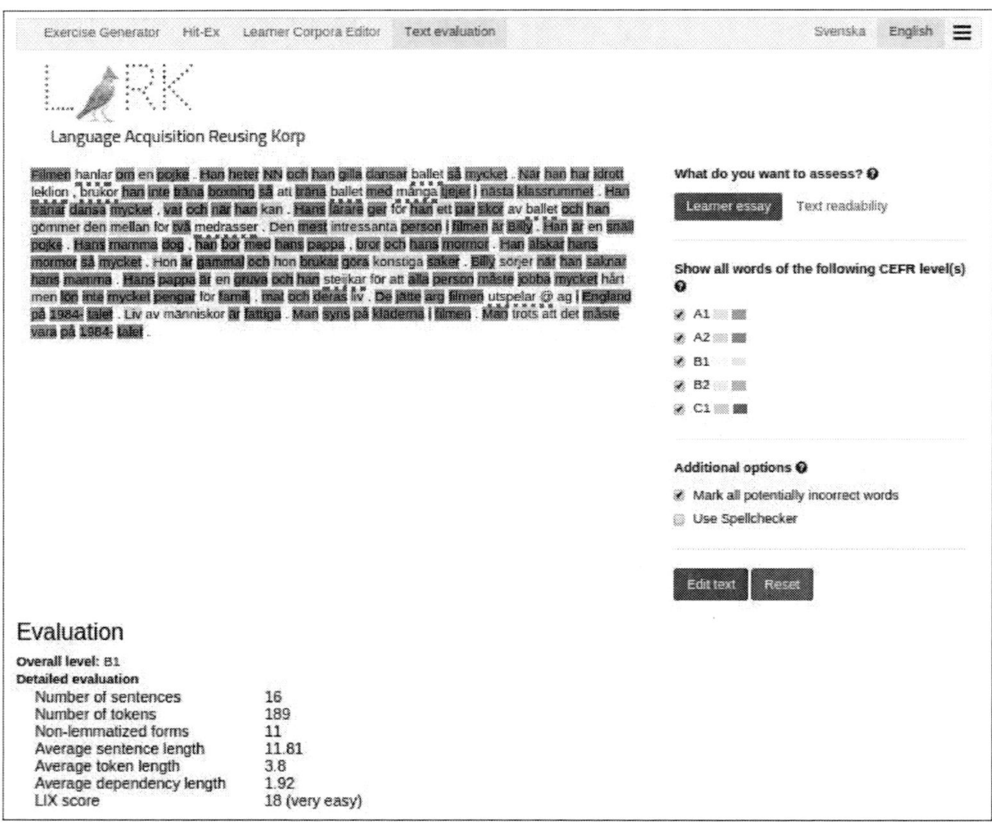

Figure 1: The interface for linguistic complexity analysis

tags, dependency relations). Then the annotated text is fed to a machine learning algorithm based on the feature set described in section 5 that assesses the overall linguistic complexity of the text provided in terms of CEFR levels[3]. Some simple statistics and values for traditional readability measures (e.g. average token length, LIX (Björnsson, 1968)) are also included in the final results at the bottom of the page.

In addition to an overall assessment, a detailed visual L2 lexical complexity analysis can be performed. Users can highlight words of different CEFR levels in their text by ticking one (or more) of the check boxes in the right-side menu. The visualization highlights receptive and productive vocabulary items within the same CEFR level with the darker and lighter shade of the same color respectively. The highlighting is based on information from two vocabulary list: SVALex+ for receptive vocabulary and a word list based on SweLL (Alfter et al., 2016), for productive vocabulary, created using the mapping approach described in Section 4 for SVALex+.

7   Conclusions

We described an exploration of different methods to improve the classification of texts produced by L2 Swedish learners into proficiency levels reflecting L2 linguistic complexity. By incorporating information from coursebooks in the form of lexical features indicating the distribution of CEFR levels per token in the texts, we created a system that reaches state-of-the-art performance reported for other languages for this task. Finally, we presented an online tool for linguistic complexity analysis of L2 texts. In the future, additional domain adaptation techniques could be tested for these text types and the effects of incorporating a learner essay based word list on the classification of L2 input texts could also be investigated.

---

[3]Currently these are in-domain models based on KELLY which we plan to update with the improved (E-SVALex+) model.

References

David Alfter, Yuri Bizzoni, Anders Agebjörn, Elena Volodina, and Ildikó Pilán. 2016. From Distributions to Labels: A Lexical Proficiency Analysis using Learner Corpora. In *Proceedings of the joint 5th NLP4CALL and 1st NLP4LA workshop, SLTC 2016*, volume No. 130. Linköping Electronic Conference Proceedings.

Jessie Barrot. 2015. Comparing the linguistic complexity in receptive and productive modes. *GEMA Online Journal of Language Studies*, 15(2):65–81.

Carl Hugo Björnsson. 1968. *Läsbarhet*. Liber.

Lars Borin, Markus Forsberg, and Johan Roxendal. 2012. Korp - the corpus infrastructure of Språkbanken. In *LREC*, pages 474–478.

António Branco, João Rodrigues, Francisco Costa, João Silva, and Rui Vaz. 2014. Rolling out text categorization for language learning assessment supported by language technology. *Computational Processing of the Portuguese Language. Springer*, pages 256–261.

Council of Europe. 2001. *Common European Framework of Reference for Languages: Learning, Teaching, Assessment*. Press Syndicate of the University of Cambridge.

Hal Daumé III and Daniel Marcu. 2006. Domain adaptation for statistical classifiers. *Journal of Artificial Intelligence Research*, pages 101–126.

Thomas Francois, Elena Volodina, Ildikó Pilán, and Anaïs Tack. 2016. SVALex: a CEFR-graded Lexical Resource for Swedish Foreign and Second Language Learners. In *Proceedings of the Tenth International Conference on Language Resources and Evaluation (LREC 2016)*, Paris, France, may.

Thomas François and Cédrick Fairon. 2012. An 'AI readability' formula for French as a foreign language. In *Proceedings of the EMNLP and CoNLL 2012*.

Mark Hall, Eibe Frank, Geoffrey Holmes, Bernhard Pfahringer, Peter Reutemann, and Ian H. Witten. 2009. The WEKA data mining software: An update. In *The SIGKDD Explorations*, volume 11, pages 10–18.

Julia Hancke. 2013. Automatic prediction of CEFR proficiency levels based on linguistic features of learner language. *Master's thesis, University of Tübingen*.

Peter Phandi, Kian Ming A. Chai, and Hwee Tou Ng. 2015. Flexible Domain Adaptation for Automated Essay Scoring Using Correlated Linear Regression. In *Proceedings of the 2015 Conference on Empirical Methods in Natural Language Processing*, pages 431–439, Lisbon, Portugal. Association for Computational Linguistics.

Ildikó Pilán, Sowmya Vajjala, and Elena Volodina. 2015. A readable read: Automatic Assessment of Language Learning Materials based on Linguistic Complexity. *In Proceedings of CICLing 2015, to appear in International Journal of Computational Linguistics and Applications*. Available at http://arxiv.org/abs/1603.08868.

Ildikó Pilán, Elena Volodina, and Torsten Zesch. 2016. Predicting proficiency levels in learner writings by transferring a linguistic complexity model from expert-written coursebooks. In *Proceedings of the 26th International Conference on Computational Linguistics (COLING)*, Osaka, Japan. Association for Computational Linguistics.

Yao-Ting Sung, Wei-Chun Lin, Scott Benjamin Dyson, Kuo-En Chang, and Yu-Chia Chen. 2015. Leveling L2 texts through readability: Combining multilevel linguistic features with the CEFR. *The Modern Language Journal*, 99(2):371–391.

Sowmya Vajjala and Kaidi Lõo. 2014. Automatic CEFR Level Prediction for Estonian Learner Text. *NEALT Proceedings Series Vol. 22*, pages 113–127.

Elena Volodina and Sofie Johansson Kokkinakis. 2012. Introducing the Swedish Kelly-list, a new lexical e-resource for Swedish. In *Proceedings of LREC*, pages 1040–1046.

Elena Volodina, Ildikó Pilán, Stian Rødven Eide, and Hannes Heidarsson. 2014. You get what you annotate: a pedagogically annotated corpus of coursebooks for Swedish as a Second Language. *NEALT Proceedings Series Vol. 22*, pages 128–144.

Elena Volodina, Ildikó Pilán, Ingegerd Enström, Lorena Llozhi, Peter Lundkvist, Gunlög Sundberg, and Monica Sandell. 2016. Swell on the rise: Swedish learner language corpus for european reference level studies. In *Proceedings of the Tenth International Conference on Language Resources and Evaluation (LREC 2016)*.

Menglin Xia, Ekaterina Kochmar, and Ted Briscoe. 2016. Text Readability Assessment for Second Language Learners. In *Proceedings of the 11th Workshop on Innovative Use of NLP for Building Educational Applications*, pages 12–22, San Diego, CA. Association for Computational Linguistics.

Torsten Zesch, Michael Wojatzki, and Dirk Scholten-Akoun. 2015. Task-Independent Features for Automated Essay Grading. In *Proceedings of the Building Educational Applications Workshop at NAACL*.

Using Ambiguity Detection to Streamline Linguistic Annotation

Wajdi Zaghouani, Abdelati Hawwari[‡], Sawsan Alqahtani[‡], Houda Bouamor,
Mahmoud Ghoneim[‡], Mona Diab[‡] and Kemal Oflazer

Carnegie Mellon University in Qatar
{wajdiz,hbouamor}@qatar.cmu.edu, ko@cs.cmu.edu

[‡]George Washington University
{abhawwari,sawsanq,ghoneim,diab}@gwu.edu

Abstract

Arabic writing is typically underspecified for short vowels and other markups, referred to as diacritics. In addition to the lexical ambiguity exhibited in most languages, the lack of diacritics in written Arabic adds another layer of ambiguity which is an artifact of the orthography. In this paper, we present the details of three annotation experimental conditions designed to study the impact of automatic ambiguity detection, on annotation speed and quality in a large scale annotation project.

1 Introduction

Written Modern Standard Arabic (MSA) poses many challenges for natural language processing (NLP). Most written Arabic text lacks short vowels and diacritics rendering a mostly consonantal orthography (Schulz, 2004). Arabic diacritization is an orthographic way to describe Arabic word pronunciation, and avoid word reading ambiguity. In Arabic, diacritics are marks that reflect the phonological, morphological and grammatical rules. The lack of diacritics leads usually to considerable lexical and morphological ambiguity. Full diacritization has been shown to improve state-of-the-art Arabic automatic systems such as automatic speech recognition (ASR) systems (Kirchhoff and Vergyri, 2005) and statistical machine translation (SMT) (Diab et al., 2007). Hence, diacritization has been receiving increased attention in several Arabic NLP applications (Zitouni et al., 2006; Shahrour et al., 2015; Abandah et al., 2015; Belinkov and Glass, 2015). Building models to assign diacritics to each letter in a word requires a large amount of annotated training corpora covering different topics and domains to overcome the sparseness problem. The currently available MSA diacritized corpora are generally limited to religious texts such as the Holy Quran, educational texts or newswire stories distributed by the Linguistic Data Consortium.

This paper presents a work carried out within a project to create an optimal diacritization scheme for Arabic orthographic representation (OptDiac) project (Zaghouani et al., 2016a; Bouamor et al., 2015). The overreaching goal of our project is to manually create a large-scale annotated corpus with the diacritics for a variety of Arabic texts. The creation of manually annotated corpora presents many challenges and issues related to the linguistic complexity of the Arabic language. In order to streamline the annotation process, we designed various annotation experimental conditions in order to answer the following questions: Can we automatically detect linguistic difficulties such as linguistic ambiguity? To what extent is there agreement between machines and human annotators when it comes to detecting ambiguity? Can the automatic detection of the ambiguity speed up the annotation process?

In the next two sections we discuss related work (Section2) and the annotation framework (Section 3). Afterwards, we present the experimental setup in Section 4. In Section 5, we present the results of the evaluation experiment and in Section 6, we analyze the annotation disagreement errors found during the evaluation.

Proceedings of the Workshop on Computational Linguistics for Linguistic Complexity,
pages 127–136, Osaka, Japan, December 11-17 2016.

2 Background and Related Work

2.1 Arabic Diacritics

The Arabic script consists of two classes of symbols: letters and diacritics. Letters comprise long vowels such as 'A', 'y', 'w' as well as consonants.[1] Diacritics on the other hand comprise short vowels, gemination markers, nunation markers, as well as other markers (such as hamza, the glottal stop which appears in conjunction with a small number of letters, elongation, dots on letters, and emphatic markers). If present, these diacritics marks help to render a more precise reading of a given word in context as observed in the ARET project (Maamouri et al., 2012). In this experiment, we are mostly addressing three types of diacritical marks: short vowels, nunation (marker for indefiniteness), and shadda (gemination).

The available Arabic text content has some percentage of these diacritics present depending on domain and genre. For instance, religious text such as the Quran is fully diacritized to minimize chances of reciting it incorrectly as discussed in (Atwell et al., 2010). The same finding applies in most children educational texts and classical poetry. However, the majority of news text and variety of other genres are sparsely diacritized: For example, around 1.5% of tokens in the United Nations Arabic corpus bear at least one diacritic (Diab et al., 2007).

2.2 Annotation Ambiguity

In general, there are several reasons that may cause disagreement in annotation decisions including human errors, lack of precision in the guidelines, and the lack of expertise and training of the annotators. This disagreement rate further increases due to the inherent natural ambiguity in the human language itself where various interpretations for a word are possible. Such linguistic ambiguity has been reported in many annotation projects involving various linguistic phenomenon, such as the coreference relations, the predicate-argument structure, the semantic roles and the L2 language errors (Versley and Tbingen, 2006; Iida et al., 2007), prosodic breaks (Jung and Kwon, 2011; Ruppenhofer et al., 2013; Rosen et al., 2013), as well as the various Arabic PropBank projects (Diab et al., 2008; Zaghouani et al., 2010; Zaghouani et al., 2012) and the Arabic TreeBank (Maamouri et al., 2010).

Poesio and Artstein (2005) classify ambiguity into explicit and implicit types. The explicit ambiguity refers to the individuals' understanding of the annotation task. On the other hand, implicit ambiguity refers to those revealed after observing and contrasting the annotation done in the same task by other annotators. Annotators are generally asked to detect and resolve ambiguous cases, which can be a difficult task to accomplish. This leads to a lower inter-annotator agreement in such tasks.

2.3 Annotation Complexity

There are many studies that evaluate the language complexity in addition to the quality of manual annotation and also allow the identification of many factors causing lower inter-annotator agreements. For example, Bayerl and Paul (2011) showed that there is a correlation between the inter-annotator agreement and the complexity of the annotation task; for instance, the larger the number of categories is, the lower the inter-annotator agreement is. Moreover, the categories prone to confusions are generally limited. This brings out two complexity issues related to the number of categories and to the existence of ambiguity between some the categories as explained in (Popescu-Belis, 2007). Furthermore, there are some annotation tasks for which the choice of a label is entirely left to the annotator, which can lead to even more complexity and lower agreement. In our project, the annotators frequently encounter complex linguistic issues such as ambiguity and the multiple possible and acceptable solutions including the free edit mode. In the next sections, we present these issues in detail.

3 Annotation Framework

The annotation pipeline in large annotation projects requires the involvement of many dedicated parties. In our project, the annotation is led by a lead annotator with a team of four native Arabic-speaking annotators from three Arab countries (Egypt, Palestine, and Tunisia) and a programmer. All the annotators

---

[1] Arabic transliteration is presented in the Buckwalter scheme (Buckwalter, 2002)

hold at least a university-level degree and they have a good knowledge of the Arabic language. The lead annotator is responsible for the entire annotation pipeline including the corpus compilation, the annotation of the gold-standard evaluation files, the guidelines, the ongoing training of the annotators, and the evaluation of the annotation quality throughout the lifespan of the project.

3.1 Guidelines

Before starting the task, we provided the annotators with detailed guidelines, describing our diacritization scheme and specifying when and where to add the diacritics required. We describe the annotation procedure and explain how to deal with borderline cases. We also include several annotated examples to illustrate the specified rules. We provide some examples of each case including the diacritization exceptions and some specific rules for: the Shadda gemination mark, the Soukoun (absence of a vowel) and the Nunation marks at the end of a word. Moreover, in some cases, the letters followed by a long Alif letter ﺍ, should not be diacritized as it is considered a deterministic diacritization as in ﻣﻴﺜﺎﻕ /miyvAqu/ 'Treaty' and not ﻣﻴﺜﺎﻕ /miyvaAqu/.[2] A summary of the most common Arabic diacritization rules is also added as a reference in the guidelines.

3.2 Annotation Tool

We designed and implemented MANDIAC, a web-based annotation tool and a work-flow management interface (Obeid et al., 2016), the tool is based on QAWI (Obeid et al., 2013) a token-based editor, used to annotate and correct spelling errors in Arabic text for the Qatar Arabic Language Bank (QALB) project.[3] The basic interface of the annotation tool is shown in Figure 1, apart from the surface controls, the interface allows annotators to select from an automatically generated diacritized words list and/or edit words manually as shown. The annotation interface allows users to undo/redo actions, and the history is kept over multiple sessions. The interface includes a timer to keep track of how long each sentence annotation has taken. We used the timer feature to measure the annotation speed later on during the evaluation experiments.

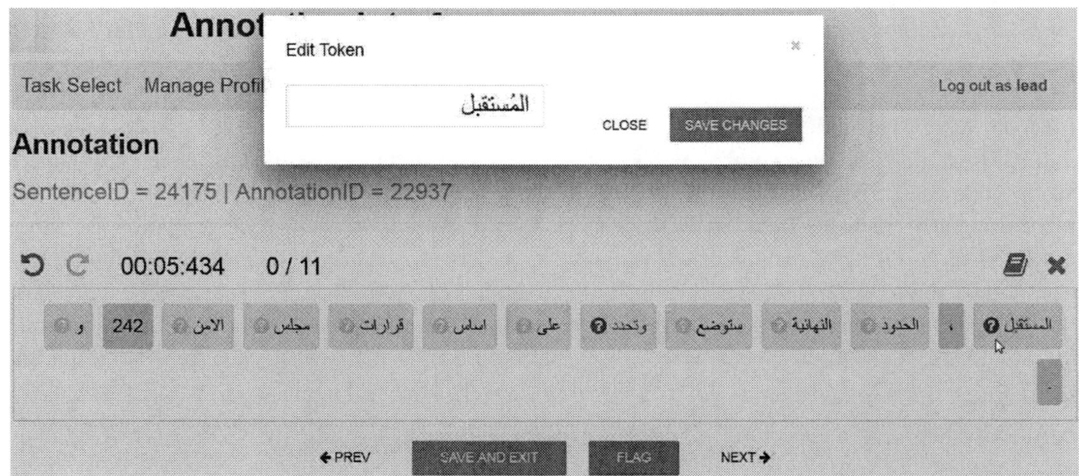

Figure 1: Editing a word marked as possibly ambiguous

---

[2] In this case the short vowel /a/ following the letter ﺙ /v/ should not be added as specified in the Arabic diacritization guidelines.

[3] The Qatar Arabic Language Bank (QALB) project is large-scale manually annotated Arabic text correction project (Zaghouani et al., 2014; Zaghouani et al., 2015; Zaghouani et al., 2016b; Mohit et al., 2014; Rozovskaya et al., 2015).

4 Experimental setup

4.1 Evaluation sets

We use the corpus of contemporary Arabic (CCA) compiled by Al-Sulaiti and Atwell (2006). It is a balanced corpus divided into the following genres: autobiography, short stories, children's stories, economics, education, health and medicine, interviews, politics, recipes, religion, sociology, science, sports, tourism and travel. The CCA corpus text genres were carefully selected by its compilers since the target users of the corpus were mostly language teachers and teachers of Arabic as a foreign language. Various metadata information are included in the corpus such as the information about the text, the author and the source. In order to use the CCA corpus, a normalization effort was done to produce a consistent XML mark-up format to be used in our annotation tool. Furthermore, we split paragraphs and sentences by period and remove repeated sentences after the initial segmentation in order to start the annotation process.

4.2 Annotation Process

The annotation consists of a single annotation pass as commonly done in many annotation projects due to time and budget constraints (Rozovskaya and Roth, 2010; Nagata et al., 2006; Izumi et al., 2004; Gamon et al.,). While performing the annotation task, the annotators do not need to add the diacritics for each word, instead, we use MADAMIRA (Pasha et al., 2014), a system for morphological analysis and disambiguation of Arabic, to provide automatically diacritized candidates. Therefore, the annotators are asked to choose the correct choice from the top three candidates suggested by MADAMIRA, when possible, if it appears in the list. MADAMIRA is able to achieve a lemmatization accuracy of 96.0% and a diacritization accuracy of 86.3%. Otherwise, if they are not satisfied with the given candidates, they can manually edit the word and add the correct diacritics. We hypothesize that such integration of an automatic analyzer in the annotation process will lead to a much faster annotation than purely manual annotation, provided that the preassigned tags are sufficiently accurate.

4.3 Ambiguity Detection

In order to classify each word as ambiguous or not, we apply several preprocessing and filtering steps on the datasets. We run MADAMIRA on the datasets to provide us with all possible morphological analyses associated with confidence scores for each word in context. MADAMIRA applies SVM and language models to derive predictions for the words morphological features and then scores each words analysis list based on how well each analysis agrees with the model predictions. The top scoring analysis is MADAMIRA's most probable reading of the word in context. We hypothesized that ambiguous words in context would have other competing high-scoring analyses within a threshold difference from the top scoring one. Based on a previous experience, we chose the threshold to be 15%, therefore, we keep the top scoring analysis and all other analyses that are within 15% difference from the top one. We further reduce this list to remove redundant and insignificant variants based on certain criteria. We remove case and mood diacritic marks, which encode inflectional properties. Additionally, we remove the diacritics of the third possessive pronouns because its diacritic marks are highly affected by the case and mood marks that we attempt to neutralize. Additionally, we filter out nouns that are exactly the same but differ only in the letter Alef normalization (ا إ أ آ |, >, <, { and A) (e.g الاِنْتِخابِيَة Al<inotixAbiy~ap and الاِنْتِخابِيَة AlAinotixAbiy~ap 'The electoral'); thus, if we have two instances differ only in Alef normalization we only keep one of them. We also remove the addition of gemination sign known as shaddah (~) to the Sun letters to assimilate the letter Lam (ل l) of a preceding definite article 'Al' in nouns (e.g. النازِي AlnAziy~ and النّازِي Aln~Aziy~ 'The Nazi' and also in الرَغْبَة Alragobap and الرَّغْبَة Alr~agobap 'The desire'). The above filtering process is performed because it decreases the possible analyses but they do not have an impact in detecting the lexical ambiguity which is our goal. We finally make sure that the remaining analyses are unique because we may end up with repeated words after removing specific diacritics marks; additionally, words that are the same orthographically but differ in other features such as lemma and part of speech tags are also removed.

If the resulting list of possible analyses contain more than one possibility, the word is marked as ambiguous; otherwise, it is believed to be not ambiguous. Words that have no analysis generated using MADAMIRA are also considered ambiguous. For each sentence, we count the number of words that are marked as ambiguous using our approach, and then calculate the percentage of ambiguity. We sort the sentences according to their ambiguity percentages in descending order so that we give annotators ranked sentences for annotation. Because we are concerned with MSA dataset only, we further filter out dialectal sentences using AIDA (Elfardy and Diab, 2012), a tool that classifies words and sentences as MSA (formal Arabic) or DA (Dialectal Arabic).

5 Evaluation

For the evaluation, we used a sample of 10K-Words from the CCA corpus representing 4 domains with approximately 2.5K-words per domain (children stories, economics,sports and politics). We have three experimental conditions for three evaluations carried over a period of six weeks.

1. **The first condition (COND1):** In the first experimental condition (COND1), four annotators were given raw undiacritized sentences and were asked to add the missing diacritics as per the guidelines. They either select one of the top three diacritization choices computed by MADAMIRA or manually edit the word.

2. **The second condition (COND2):** In the second experimental condition (COND2), we provided the raw undiacritized sentences to a first group of two annotators (Group 1) and we asked them to mark and add the required diacritics only to the words they believe are ambiguous while ignoring the rest of the non ambiguous words in the sentence.

3. **The third condition (COND3):** For the third experimental condition (COND3), we gave, to a different group of two annotators (Group 2), the same sentences assigned to Group 1 while having the sentences explicitly marked as potentially ambiguous using the MADAMIRA as explained previously (again the top three MADAMIRA choices were provided). Furthermore, in COND3, the annotators were asked to tell whether they agree or not with the ambiguity class provided for each word using the tool and also by adding the missing diacritics in case they agree that the given word is ambiguous.

The Inter-Annotator Agreement (IAA) is measured by using pairwise percent agreement averaged over all pairs of annotations (APP). The pairwise percent agreement (also called observed agreement) is computed as the percentage of times two annotators assign the same label to a unit. If a single letter in a given word has one diacritization mismatch, then the whole word is considered as disagreement. A high APP score denotes that at least two annotators agree on the annotation and therefore, the probability that the annotation is erroneous is very small.

	CCA Corpus
APP$_{COND1}$	83.10%
APP$_{COND2}$	69.09%
APP$_{COND3}$	**88.31%**

Table 1: Inter-Annotator Agreement (IAA) in terms of Average Pairwise Percent agreement (APP) recorded during the evaluation of 10K-words from the CCA dataset in three experimental conditions; higher is better.

Furthermore, in order to measure the impact on the annotation speed, we measured the mean annotation time by computing the average time required to annotate a word for a sentence and then average it over all sentences for a given experimental condition by all the annotator. The Average annotation speeds are shown in Table 2.

	Annotation Speed
Words / Minute$_{COND1}$	8.22
Words / Minute$_{COND2}$	6.59
Words / Minute$_{COND3}$	**10.09**

Table 2: Average annotated words per minute recorded during the evaluation of 10K-words from the CCA dataset in three experimental conditions

The results obtained in Table 1 and Table 2 show that in COND1 the annotators obtained a fairly good agreement of 83.10% and average speed of 8.22 words/minute ranking in the second place in terms of performance overall. COND2 obtained surprisingly has the lowest agreement of only 69.09% and also lowest time performance of only 6.59 words / minute. A follow up with the annotators revealed that the results of COND2 are due to the fact that annotators spent a lot of time thinking whether a given word is ambiguous or not so they can add the required diacritics. This leads to spending more time due to the hesitation in addition to the difficulty of the task as we will show in the next section. Finally, COND3 reveals the best overall performance with a high agreement of 88.31% and the highest rate of words per minute of 10.09. The results of COND3 can be explained by the automatic ambiguity analysis provided to the annotators which substantially reduced the hesitation in deciding if a given word is ambiguous and therefore it reduced the annotation possibilities by assisting the annotators in their decisions.

6 Error analysis

We found that a large number of the agreement errors are due to the inherent linguistic complexity of the Arabic language leading to some annotation hesitations and inconsistency between the annotators when there is an obvious ambiguity in the context. For instance, in many cases the annotators did not agree on whether to add the diacritics or not, while in other cases, the annotators disagreed on the interpretation of the word. We compiled below the list of the most important cases of disagreement observed during the error analysis.

1. **Lexical Ambiguity:** This means that a word could carry more than one acceptable reading (homonymy) such as in the case of the word (قبل qbl which has the following two lexical readings a. قَبْلَ qabola 'before' and b. قِبَلَ /qibala/ 'capability'.

2. **Morphological Ambiguity:** For this category, we observed two types of annotation disagreement: word-structure ambiguity and inflection ambiguity. The diacritization of word structure can be interpreted as a morphological task. As in the diacritization of the second letter of trilateral verbs such as in حَسِبَ يَحْسَبُ Hasiba/yaHosabu 'To think' versus حَسَبَ يَحْسِبُ /Hasaba/yaHosibu/ 'To count'. Since the Arabic language is a morphologically rich language, each inflected word could have a different way to be diacritized, especially in cases where some pronouns are attached to the verbs or the nouns as in أَحْسَنا /AaHosanA/ 'they help/do good' (3rd,Dual,Masculine) versus in أَحْسَنّا /AaHosan~A/ 'we help/do good' (1st,Plural). In another disagreement case, we found some cases of verbal voice inflection confusion between the active voice and the passive voice such as in تَعُدُّ /taEud~u/ 'she counts' versus تُعَدُّ /tuEid~u/ 'It is considered'.

3. **Part of Speech Ambiguity (POS):** This is one of the most frequent disagreement cases found during the error analysis, in fact, it is common to have many possible POS for a given word in Arabic depending on the personal interpretation of the sentence as in the case of the verb نُجِيبُ /nujiybu/ 'we+answer' versus the adjective نَجِيبٌ /najiybN/ 'outstanding'.

4. **Case Endings Ambiguity:**

In Arabic, the case endings are those attached to the ends of words to indicate the words' grammatical function. Using the case endings correctly, requires a solid knowledge of grammar. With no surprise, we found many annotation disagreement in this category. For example, the genitive ثَلاثٍ /valAvK/ 'three' was confused with the nominative ثَلاثٌ /valAvN/ 'three'.

5. **The indeclinable nouns (Diptote):** Indeclinable nouns are a type of nouns that have special case endings rules and they only have two possible case endings. When the noun is indefinite, the possible case endings are /-a/ for the genitive and /-u/ for the nominative, while the accusative has no nunation. We located several cases of Diptote errors when the noun is indefinite such as in: أَشِقَّاءَ /¿a$iq~A'a/ 'brothers' (genitive) versus أَشِقَّاءٍ 'brothers' with a wrong genitive nunation marker.

6. **Phonology ambiguity:** As the diacritization is considered an orthographic representation of the phonological phenomena, some phonological cases depend on the phonological context and some changes could happen as a result of an assimilation phenomena. For example, we noticed several cases of disagreement related to the definite article Al as it could be pronounced in two ways: the first way is known as the sun letter /Al/ where the letter /l/ is silent and a gemination diacritic sign is marked on the following letter. The second case is the moon letter /Al/, where the letter /l/ is pronounced as in the example of الدَّهِشَةُ /Ald~h$apu/ 'The+surprise' versus الدَهْشَةُ /Aldah$apu/ 'The+surprise'.

7. **Pragmatic variations:** In this type of disagreement, the annotators were confused between two possible and acceptable ways to pronounce a given word and the difference is only dictated by the regional usage as the case of the word دولي /dwly/ 'international' which could be diacriticized as دَوْليّ /dawoliy~/ or as دُوَليّ /duwaliy~/.

8. **Level of Diacritization:** We observed that frequently, the annotators did not agree on the level of diacritization to be added despite the existence of guidelines. Cases of disagreement like the following are frequently observed: لِلمُلْتَزِمات liAlmulotazimAt 'for+the+committed' (PL+Fem.) versus لِلمُلتَزمات /liAlmultazmAt/ 'for+the+committed' (PL+Fem.).

9. **Diacritization Typos:** While not frequent, several cases of extra diacritics marks were added accidentally by the annotators as in قَصَّرنا /qaS~aronA/ 'We+abridged' versus the wrong extra diacritic a in قَصَّرنا /qaaS~aronA/.

Conclusion

In this paper, we present our method to detect the ambiguous annotation cases within a Diacritization annotation project. We discussed the complex linguistic challenges inherent in Arabic linguistic annotation. The results obtained in the evaluation suggest that the automatic ambiguity detection could effectively reduce the annotation time and also increase the Inter-annotator agreement. Moreover, we believe that the higher the accuracy of MADAMIRA choices, the faster the annotation could be as as manual edits will be reduced. However, we believe that the nature of the ambiguity of the Arabic language as attested by many disagreement cases, has strongly impacted the overall agreement results. On the other hand, we believe that a better agreement could be achieved if the annotators followed the annotation guidelines consistently.

Acknowledgments

This publication is made possible by grant NPRP-6-1020-1-199 from the Qatar National Research Fund (a member of the Qatar Foundation). The statements made herein are solely the responsibility of the authors.

References

Gheith A Abandah, Alex Graves, Balkees Al-Shagoor, Alaa Arabiyat, Fuad Jamour, and Majid Al-Taee. 2015. Automatic diacritization of arabic text using recurrent neural networks. *International Journal on Document Analysis and Recognition (IJDAR)*, 18(2):183–197.

Latifa Al-Sulaiti and Eric Steven Atwell. 2006. The design of a corpus of contemporary arabic. *International Journal of Corpus Linguistics*, 11(2):135–171.

Eric Atwell, Nizar Habash, Bill Louw, Bayan Abu Shawar, Tony McEnery, Wajdi Zaghouani, and Mahmoud El-Haj. 2010. Understanding the quran: A new grand challenge for computer science and artificial intelligence. *ACM-BCS Visions of Computer Science 2010*.

Petra Saskia Bayerl and Karsten Ingmar Paul. 2011. What determines inter-coder agreement in manual annotations? a meta-analytic investigation. *Computational Linguistics*, 37(4):699–725.

Yonatan Belinkov and James Glass. 2015. Arabic diacritization with recurrent neural networks. In *Proceedings of the 2015 Conference on Empirical Methods in Natural Language Processing*, pages 2281–2285, Lisbon, Portugal.

Houda Bouamor, Wajdi Zaghouani, Mona Diab, Ossama Obeid, Kemal Oflazer, Mahmoud Ghoneim, and Abdelati Hawwari. 2015. A pilot study on arabic multi-genre corpus diacritization. In *Proceedings of the Association for Computational Linguistics Second Workshop on Arabic Natural Language Processing*, pages 80–88, Beijing, China.

Tim Buckwalter. 2002. Buckwalter Arabic morphological analyzer version 1.0. Technical Report LDC2002L49, Linguistic Data Consortium.

Mona Diab, Mahmoud Ghoneim, and Nizar Habash. 2007. Arabic diacritization in the context of statistical machine translation. In *Proceedings of Machine Translation Summit (MT-Summit)*, Copenhagen, Denmark.

Mona Diab, Aous Mansouri, Martha Palmer, Olga Babko-Malaya, Wajdi Zaghouani, Ann Bies, and Mohammed Maamouri. 2008. A pilot arabic propbank. In *Proceedings of the 7th International Conference on Language Resources and Evaluation (LREC)*.

Heba Elfardy and Mona Diab. 2012. Aida: Automatic identification and glossing of dialectal arabic. In *Proceedings of the 16th eamt conference (project papers)*, pages 83–83.

Michael Gamon, Jianfeng Gao, Chris Brockett, Alexandre Klementiev, William B. Dolan, Dmitriy Belenko, and Lucy Vanderwende. In *Third International Joint Conference on Natural Language Processing, IJCNLP, Address=Hyderabad, India, Year=2008, Pages = 449–456, Title = Using Contextual Speller Techniques and Language Modeling for ESL Error Correction*.

Ryu Iida, Mamoru Komachi, Kentaro Inui, and Yuji Matsumoto. 2007. Annotating a japanese text corpus with predicate-argument and coreference relations. In *Proceedings of the Linguistic Annotation Workshop*, LAW '07, pages 132–139, Stroudsburg, PA, USA. Association for Computational Linguistics.

Emi Izumi, Kiyotaka Uchimoto, and Hitoshi Isahara. 2004. The NICT JLE corpus exploiting the language learners' speech database for research and education. *International Journal of The Computer, the Internet and Management*, 12(2):119–125, May.

Youngim Jung and Hyuk-Chul Kwon. 2011. Consistency maintenance in prosodic labeling for reliable prediction of prosodic breaks. In *Proceedings of the 5th Linguistic Annotation Workshop*, LAW V '11, pages 38–46, Stroudsburg, PA, USA. Association for Computational Linguistics.

Katrin Kirchhoff and Dimitra Vergyri. 2005. Cross-dialectal data sharing for acoustic modeling in arabic speech recognition. *Speech Communication*, 46(1):37–51.

Mohamed Maamouri, Ann Bies, Seth Kulick, Wajdi Zaghouani, David Graff, and Michael Ciul. 2010. From speech to trees: Applying treebank annotation to arabic broadcast news. In *Proceedings of International Conference on Language Resources and Evaluation (LREC 2010)*.

Mohamed Maamouri, Wajdi Zaghouani, Violetta Cavalli-Sforza, Dave Graff, and Mike Ciul. 2012. Developing aret: an nlp-based educational tool set for arabic reading enhancement. In *Proceedings of the Seventh Workshop on Building Educational Applications Using NLP*, pages 127–135. Association for Computational Linguistics.

Behrang Mohit, Alla Rozovskaya, Nizar Habash, Wajdi Zaghouani, and Ossama Obeid. 2014. The first qalb shared task on automatic text correction for arabic. In *Proceedings of the EMNLP Workshop on Arabic Natural Language Processing*, page 39.

Ryo Nagata, Atsuo Kawai, Koichiro Morihiro, and Naoki Isu. 2006. A feedback-augmented method for detecting errors in the writing of learners of english. In *Proceedings of the 21st International Conference on Computational Linguistics and 44th Annual Meeting of the Association for Computational Linguistics*, pages 241–248, Sydney, Australia.

Ossama Obeid, Wajdi Zaghouani, Behrang Mohit, Nizar Habash, Kemal Oflazer, and Nadi Tomeh. 2013. A web-based annotation framework for large-scale text correction. In *Sixth International Joint Conference on Natural Language Processing*, page 1.

Ossama Obeid, , Houda Bouamor, Wajdi Zaghouani, Mahmoud Ghoneim, Abdelati Hawwari, Mona Diab, and Kemal Oflazer. 2016. Mandiac: A web-based annotation system for manual arabic diacritization. In *Proceedings of the International Conference on Language Resources and Evaluation (LREC-2016) Workshop on Free/Open-Source Arabic Corpora and Corpora Processing Tools (OSACT2)*.

Arfath Pasha, Mohamed Al-Badrashiny, Mona Diab, Ahmed El Kholy, Ramy Eskander, Nizar Habash, Manoj Pooleery, Owen Rambow, and Ryan Roth. 2014. Madamira: A fast, comprehensive tool for morphological analysis and disambiguation of arabic. In *Proceedings of the Ninth International Conference on Language Resources and Evaluation (LREC'14)*, Reykjavik, Iceland, May. European Language Resources Association (ELRA).

Massimo Poesio and Ron Artstein. 2005. Annotating (anaphoric) ambiguity. In *In Proceedings of the Corpus Linguistics Conference*.

Popescu-Belis, 2007. *Le role des metriques d'evaluation dans le processus de recherche en TAL*, pages 67–91. Traitement Automatique de la Langue, vol. 48, n. 1.

Alexandr Rosen, Jirka Hana, Barbora Štindlová, and Anna Feldman. 2013. Evaluating and automating the annotation of a learner corpus. *Language Resources and Evaluation*, pages 1–28, April.

Alla Rozovskaya and Dan Roth. 2010. Annotating esl errors: Challenges and rewards. In *NAACL Workshop on Innovative Use of NLP for Building Educational Applications*, Los Angeles, CA.

Alla Rozovskaya, Houda Bouamor, Nizar Habash, Wajdi Zaghouani, Ossama Obeid, and Behrang Mohit. 2015. The second qalb shared task on automatic text correction for arabic. In *Proceedings of the ACL-IJCNLP Workshop on Arabic Natural Language Processing*, page 26.

Josef Ruppenhofer, Russell Lee-Goldman, Caroline Sporleder, and Roser Morante. 2013. Beyond sentence-level semantic role labeling: linking argument structures in discourse. *Language Resources and Evaluation*, 47(3):695–721.

Eckehard Schulz. 2004. *A Student Grammar of Modern Standard Arabic*. Cambridge University Press, Cambridge, United Kingdom.

Anas Shahrour, Salam Khalifa, and Nizar Habash. 2015. Improving arabic diacritization through syntactic analysis. In *Proceedings of the 2015 Conference on Empirical Methods in Natural Language Processing*, pages 1309–1315, Lisbon, Portugal.

Yannick Versley and Universitt Tbingen. 2006. Disagreement dissected: vagueness as a source of ambiguity in nominal (co-) reference. In *In: Ambiguity in Anaphora Workshop Proceedings*, pages 83–89.

Wajdi Zaghouani, Mona Diab, Aous Mansouri, Sameer Pradhan, and Martha Palmer. 2010. The revised arabic propbank. In *Proceedings of the Association for Computational Linguistics Fourth Linguistic Annotation Workshop*, pages 222–226. Association for Computational Linguistics.

Wajdi Zaghouani, Abdelati Hawwari, and Mona Diab. 2012. A pilot propbank annotation for quranic arabic. In *Proceedings of the Fourth Workshop on Computational Linguistics for Literature co-located with the North American Association Computational Linguistics conference (NAACL-HLT 2012*, page 78.

Wajdi Zaghouani, Behrang Mohit, Nizar Habash, Ossama Obeid, Nadi Tomeh, Alla Rozovskaya, Noura Farra, Sarah Alkuhlani, and Kemal Oflazer. 2014. Large scale arabic error annotation: Guidelines and framework. In *Proceedings of the Ninth International Conference on Language Resources and Evaluation (LREC-2014), Reykjavik, Iceland, May 26-31, 2014.*, pages 2362–2369.

Wajdi Zaghouani, Nizar Habash, Houda Bouamor, Alla Rozovskaya, Behrang Mohit, Abeer Heider, and Kemal Oflazer. 2015. Correction annotation for non-native arabic texts: Guidelines and corpus. In *Proceedings of the Association for Computational Linguistics Fourth Linguistic Annotation Workshop*, pages 129–139.

Wajdi Zaghouani, Houda Bouamor, Abdelati Hawwari, Mona Diab, Ossama Obeid, Mahmoud Ghoneim, Sawsan Alqahtani, and Kemal Oflazer. 2016a. Guidelines and framework for a large scale arabic diacritized corpus. In *The Tenth International Conference on Language Resources and Evaluation (LREC 2016)*, pages 3637–3643. European Language Resources Association (ELRA).

Wajdi Zaghouani, Nizar Habash, Ossama Obeid, Behrang Mohit, Houda Bouamor, and Kemal Oflazer. 2016b. Building an arabic machine translation post-edited corpus: Guidelines and annotation. In *International Conference on Language Resources and Evaluation (LREC 2016)*.

Imed Zitouni, Jeffrey S. Sorensen, and Ruhi Sarikaya. 2006. Maximum entropy based restoration of arabic diacritics. In *Proceedings of the 21st International Conference on Computational Linguistics and 44th Annual Meeting of the Association for Computational Linguistics*, pages 577–584, Sydney, Australia.

Morphological Complexity Influences Verb–Object Order
in Swedish Sign Language

Johannes Bjerva◇♣   **Carl Börstell**♣

◇ Center for Language and Cognition, University of Groningen, The Netherlands
♣ Department of Linguistics, Stockholm University, Sweden
j.bjerva@rug.nl, calle@ling.su.se

Abstract

Computational linguistic approaches to sign languages could benefit from investigating how complexity influences structure. We investigate whether morphological complexity has an effect on the order of Verb (V) and Object (O) in Swedish Sign Language (SSL), on the basis of elicited data from five Deaf signers. We find a significant difference in the distribution of the orderings OV vs. VO, based on an analysis of morphological weight. While morphologically heavy verbs exhibit a general preference for OV, humanness seems to affect the ordering in the opposite direction, with [+human] Objects pushing towards a preference for VO.

1   Introduction

Word order is one of the most well-documented grammatical features of the (spoken) languages of the world. One specific case regarding word order is the order of a Verb V and its (direct) Object O in a simple transitive clause. In a sample of 1,519 languages of the world, 46.9% ($n = 713$) of the languages have a dominant OV order, whereas 46.4% ($n = 705$) have a dominant VO order (Dryer, 2013).[1]

For signed languages, the two observed dominant word orders are SOV and SVO, for which the latter has been generalised as a grammatical order in most sign languages. However, a number of factors are said to affect the ordering of O and V, for instance that morphologically complex verbs (e.g., those exhibiting morphological reduplication, handshape or directional object agreement, or coinciding with non-manual marking) prefer a verb-final position, hence occurring *after* its object. One reason for this ordering preference has been suggested to relate directly to the interaction between the verb and its object, since some complexity features involve types of "agreement" with the object. Thus, the idea is that the object needs to be introduced *before* verb agreement with the object is available on the verb (Napoli and Sutton-Spence, 2014). This relates directly to findings from spoken languages, for which it has been noted that the ordering of verb and controller NP affects the agreement realisation, such that verbs preceding their controller NP do not always agree with the controller (Corbett, 2006). Furthermore, among spoken languages, word order also interacts with the presence or absence of morphological marking. For instance, SOV languages generally differentiate Subject and Object on the basis of morphological marking (e.g., case), while SVO languages differentiate these argument roles by word order alone (i.e., by linear distance between the arguments) (Sinnemäki, 2010). In a study looking at young, emerging sign languages, it was argued that humanness as an animacy feature accounts for word order preferences, in that SOV is preferred unless both S and O are [+human], in which case SVO is preferred (Meir et al., in press).

For Swedish Sign Language (SSL), the dominant word order has been identified as SVO (Bergman and Wallin, 1985), which has also been corroborated by a small-scale corpus study more recently (Börstell et al., 2016). Although different types of morphological complexity (e.g., reduplication and agreement) have been suggested to influence word order in SSL (Bergman and Wallin, 1985; Bergman and Dahl,

---

[1]The remaining 101 languages in the sample allow for both orders, neither being dominant.

Proceedings of the Workshop on Computational Linguistics for Linguistic Complexity,
pages 137–141, Osaka, Japan, December 11-17 2016.

Table 1: Features of morphological complexity in SSL

Handshape	Whether an Object classifier was present in the verb's handshape (Emmorey, 2003).
Directionality	Whether an Object location was present in the verb's movement (Padden, 1988).
Reduplication	Whether the verb was reduplicated (Bergman and Dahl, 1994).
Non-manual	Whether a non-manual morpheme accompanied the verb (Crasborn, 2006).

1994), no study has explicitly addressed this issue. Thus, the aim of this study is to use statistical bootstrapping methods to establish whether morphological complexity affects the order of Object and Verb in SSL. By doing so, we seek to tease apart the different factors influencing word order patterns in SSL, and incorporate the notion of morphological complexity more explicitly as a property of signed language grammar, particularly with regard to the interaction between morphology and syntax. Uncovering the intricacies of this interaction can also be helpful for developing sign language technology, and can serve as a starting point when annotating sign language corpora. Information about the effect of complexity can be used to inform machine learning systems, e.g., by including this information as features, or by predicting a verb's complexity as an auxiliary task in a neural network (see, e.g., Plank et al. (2016) and Bjerva et al. (2016)).

2   Data and Methodology

2.1   Data and Annotations

The data consisted of video recorded descriptions of 17 transitive events (see Table 2) by five Deaf signers of SSL (4 male; aged 18–44), all using SSL as their first language. The signers were individually recorded describing the stimuli events to another signer, who was instructed to correctly identify the described event from three different options. Descriptions were annotated in the ELAN software (Wittenburg et al., 2006). In total, 145 individual transitive verbs were annotated for the categories in Table 1.

Handshape and Directionality involve morphological complexity dependent on the Object: Object classifier handshapes are selected on the basis of the Object's physical properties; Directionality involves the incorporation of referential locations in signing space, such that the verb moves between – or *agrees* with – locations established for various discourse referents (here, the Object(s)). Both of these categories entail the verb form being altered according to its Object, in a sense making the verb form *dependent* on physical and spatial properties of the Object. This has been suggested to influence the order of O and V, such that an Object-dependent Verb *follows* its Object, i.e., OV (Napoli and Sutton-Spence, 2014).

The latter two categories also involve morphological complexity, but rather independent from the Object: Reduplication involves phonological repetition, for signed language often associated with aspectual and/or pluractional morphology (Fischer and Janis, 1990; Bergman and Dahl, 1994); Non-manual concerns the addition of non-manual markers (e.g., facial expression, or so-called oral adverbs[2]) accompanying a verb. These are associated with both phonological and morphological weight, and are also found to be associated with a post-Object position (Napoli and Sutton-Spence, 2014).

Each individual verb in the data set was coded for these four categories by one of the authors of this paper. If a verb occurred with two objects (i.e., a direct and an indirect object), the verb token was counted as two items: once for each object. The annotations were binary features (yes vs. no), but for the Object-dependent categories (i.e., Handshape and Directionality) also matched to the relevant object. That is, the Handshape value yes would only be assigned for the object indexed by the handshape. Each item in the data set was also annotated for whether its Object was human or inanimate.[3] Thus, we could differentiate the four complexity features' effect on word order on the basis of the animacy of the Object in question.

Each Object was also annotated as Overt or Elliptical: that is, if the Object occurred within the same clause as its Verb, it was coded as Overt; if the Object was present in an adjoining clause, it was coded

---

[2] Adding adverbial meaning by use of grammaticalised mouth gestures.
[3] In the elicitation stimuli, no referents were [-human, +animate].

Table 2: Video clips for the clause elicitation task

Valency	Event
Monotransitive	A girl tearing a paper
	A man placing a book on a bookshelf
	A girl pulling a cart through a living room
	A man tapping a watermelon on a table
	A woman lifting a box onto a table
	A girl pulling a man by the hand
	A woman looking at a man
	A girl feeding a woman
	A woman rolling a ball on the floor
	A woman pushing a girl
	A man tapping a girl by the shoulder
	A girl brushing a woman's hair
	A man washing a plate
Ditransitive	A woman giving a shirt to a man
	A man throwing a ball to a girl
	A man showing a woman a picture
	A woman taking a pair of scissors from a girl

Table 3: Comparison between OV and VO orders per condition. Numbers indicate p-values as obtained by the bootstrap test, with p-values indicating the probability that the OV condition is not significantly more complex than the VO condition. n/a indicates a too small sample size to examine the difference in question.

Object type	All	Overt	Overt-hum	Overt-inanim
DO + IO	< 0.0005	< 0.01	< 0.05	< 0.001
DO	< 0.0005	< 0.01	> 0.05	< 0.001
IO	> 0.05	n/a	n/a	n/a

as Elliptical.[4] For the latter, the order of V and O was determined by linear order on the utterance level.

2.2 Statistical Analysis

In order to avoid making unwarranted assumptions about the distribution of the variable we investigate (verb complexity), we chose to use a non-parametric bootstrapping test (Efron and Tibshirani, 1990; Efron and Tibshirani, 1994). Instead of fitting the parameters of a distribution specified a priori to our data, we repeatedly resample from our original sample (the data) to estimate the amount of variation and thus the significance of our results. For a high-level introduction to this statistical method, we refer the reader to Calmettes et al. (2012).

In the data set used in this paper, we compare annotations of 145 verbs. We calculate the complexity of each verb as being the number of features present, divided by the maximum number of features (see Table 1). We then use bootstrap resampling to estimate the populations as divided into two groups, comparing the complexity between OV and VO items.[5] We subdivide our data into groups depending on whether or not the argument is overt, and if so whether or not this argument is [+human] or [+inanimate]. Additionally, we investigate whether the Object in question is direct (DO) or indirect (IO). This leads to a total of 12 possible comparisons between the OV and VO orders.

3 Results and Analysis

Running a bootstrap resampling test with resampling, using 10,000 iterations estimating the mean of the populations, yields differences at the p-levels reported in Table 3, with $p < 0.05$ indicating that the mean complexity of OV is significantly higher than that of VO.

---

[4]Cases of covert, implicit (i.e., semantic) Objects were excluded from the data set.

[5]We use the implementation found at `http://gcalmettes.github.io/bootstrap-tools/`.

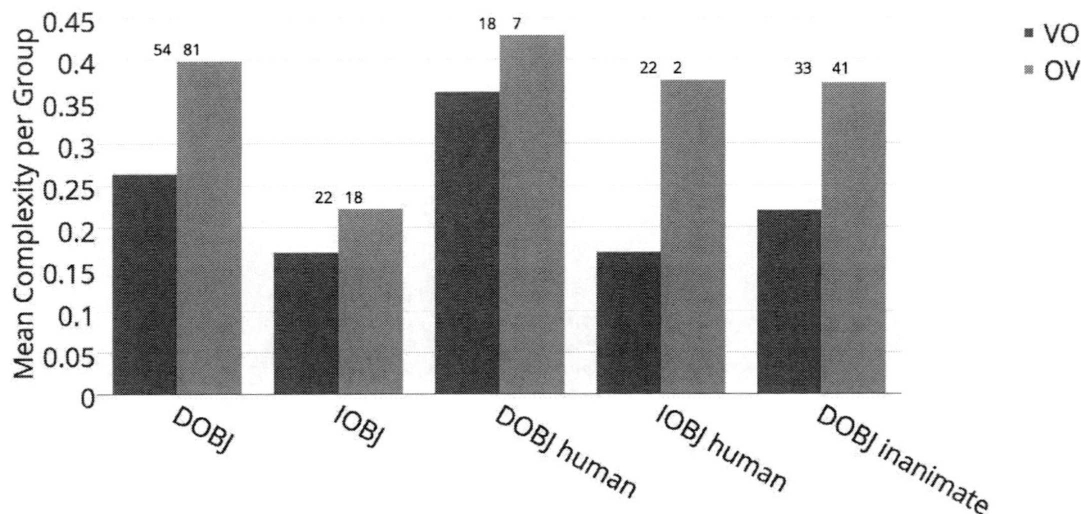

Figure 1: Mean complexity (y-axis) and number of samples (numbers above each bar) per condition. IOBJ inanimate is not plotted as the condition contains no data.

We see a division here on the basis of animacy. For all tokens (DO + IO), we see that the mean complexity in OV is significantly higher than that of VO across conditions. For the DO tokens, the same is true for all conditions but the overt-human. For the IO tokens, there is no significant difference between OV and VO based on complexity. Instead, an important aspect here is that the IO row contains several n/a cells. This is due to that fact that for the IO tokens (of which all are [+human]), the distribution of VO vs. OV is so skewed that practically all items fall into the former category, making statistical testing impossible (see Figure 1).[6] This should be taken as an indication that humanness is, in fact, associated with the VO order to a high degree, which corroborates the findings by Meir et al. (in press). Thus, while morphologically complex verbs prefer the OV order, humanness pushes towards VO.

4 Discussion and Conclusions

We have shown that morphological complexity is a relevant factor when investigating word order patterns in SSL. From a computational perspective, this suggests that machine learning approaches to SSL could benefit from using morphological complexity and animacy as features. As claimed for other sign languages (Napoli and Sutton-Spence, 2014), the incorporation of Object features (Handshape classifiers and Directionality) together with other morphological features (Reduplication and Non-manual marking) influence the ordering of V and O in SSL. Furthermore, animacy features of the Object also affect the ordering of V and O, such that [+human] Objects push towards the order VO. As argued by, e.g., Meir et al. (in press), this would be explained by disambiguation strategies in reversible sentences, observable in several emerging sign languages. That is, for sentences in which both S and O are possible Agents, the roles are disambiguated by separating S from O by putting V in between the two. In the case of non-reversible sentences, this strategy is not needed, and other preferences may play a larger role. For general linguistic theory, this relates to the notion of Differential Object Marking (Bossong, 1985; Aissen, 2003), and the preference of explicitly marking Objects that are high in the prominence hierarchy (e.g., animacy).

Acknowledgements

We thank Wendy Sandler and Irit Meir for sharing their elicitation stimuli that were used to obtain the data for this study, and the anonymous reviewers for their helpful suggestions.

---

[6]The data is elicited based on video stimuli, which makes it quite challenging to elicit data for the IO -human condition.

References

Judith Aissen. 2003. Differential Object Marking: Iconicity vs. Economy. *Natural Language & Linguistic Theory*, 21(3):435–483.

Brita Bergman and Östen Dahl. 1994. Ideophones in Sign Language? The place of reduplication in the tense-aspect system of Swedish Sign Language. In Carl Bache, Hans Basbøll, and Carl-Erik Lindberg, editors, *Tense, Aspect and Action. Empirical and Theoretical Contributions to Language Typology*, pages 397–422. Mouton de Gruyter.

Brita Bergman and Lars Wallin. 1985. Sentence structure in Swedish Sign Language. In William C. Stokoe and Virginia Volterra, editors, *Sign language research '83*, pages 217–225, Silver Spring, MD. Linstok Press.

Johannes Bjerva, Barbara Plank, and Johan Bos. 2016. Semantic Tagging with Deep Residual Networks. In *Proceedings of COLING 2016*, Osaka, Japan, December.

Carl Börstell, Mats Wirén, Johanna Mesch, and Moa Gärdenfors. 2016. Towards an annotation of syntactic structure in Swedish Sign Language. In Eleni Efthimiou, Stavroula-Evita Fotinea, Thomas Hanke, Julie Hochgesang, Jette Kristoffersen, and Johanna Mesch, editors, *Proceedings of the 7th workshop on the Representation and Processing of Sign Languages: Corpus Mining*, pages 19–24, Paris. European Language Resources Association (ELRA).

Georg Bossong. 1985. *Differentielle Objektmarkierung in den Neuiranischen Sprache*. Gunter Narr Verlag, Tübingen.

Guillaume Calmettes, Gordon B Drummond, and Sarah L Vowler. 2012. Making do with what we have: use your bootstraps. *Advances in physiology education*, 36(3):177–180.

Greville Corbett. 2006. *Agreement*. Cambridge University Press, New York, NY.

Onno Crasborn. 2006. Nonmanual Structures in Sign Language. In Keith Brown, editor, *Encyclopedia of Language & Linguistics*, number 1999, pages 668–672. Elsevier, Oxford.

Matthew S. Dryer. 2013. Order of object and verb. In Matthew S. Dryer and Martin Haspelmath, editors, *The World Atlas of Language Structures Online*. Max Planck Institute for Evolutionary Anthropology, Leipzig.

Bradley Efron and Robert Tibshirani. 1990. *Statistical data analysis in the computer age*. University of Toronto, Department of Statistics.

Bradley Efron and Robert Tibshirani. 1994. *An introduction to the bootstrap*. CRC press.

Karen Emmorey, editor. 2003. *Perspectives on classifier constructions in sign languages*. Lawrence Erlbaum Associates, Mahwah, NJ.

Susan D. Fischer and Wynne Janis. 1990. Verb sandwiches in American Sign Language. In Siegmund Prillwitz and Tomas Vollhaber, editors, *Current trends in European sign language research*, number 2, pages 279–293, Hamburg. Signum Verlag.

Irit Meir, Mark Aronoff, Carl Börstell, So-One Hwang, Deniz Ilkbasaran, Itamar Kastner, Ryan Lepic, Adi Lifshitz Ben Basat, Carol Padden, and Wendy Sandler. in press. The effect of being human and the basis of grammatical word order: Insights from novel communication systems and young sign languages. *Cognition*.

Donna Jo Napoli and Rachel Sutton-Spence. 2014. Order of the major constituents in sign languages: Implications for all language. *Frontiers in Psychology*, 5:1–18.

Carol Padden. 1988. *Interaction of morphology and syntax in American Sign Language*. Garland Publishing, Inc., New York, NY & London.

Barbara Plank, Anders Søgaard, and Yoav Goldberg. 2016. Multilingual part-of-speech tagging with bidirectional long short-term memory models and auxiliary loss. In *Proceedings of ACL 2016*.

Kaius Sinnemäki. 2010. Word order in zero-marking languages. *Studies in Language*, 34(4):869–912.

Peter Wittenburg, Hennie Brugman, Albert Russel, Alex Klassmann, and Han Sloetjes. 2006. ELAN: A professional framework for multimodality research. In *Proceedings of the 5th International Conference on Language Resources and Evaluation (LREC 2006)*, pages 1556–1559.

A Comparison Between Morphological Complexity Measures:
Typological Data vs. Language Corpora

Christian Bentz
University of Tübingen
DFG Center for Advanced Studies
Rümelinstraße 23
chris@christianbentz.de

Tatyana Ruzsics
University of Zürich
CorpusLab, URPP Language and Space,
Freiestrasse 16
tatyana.soldatova@uzh.ch

Alexander Koplenig
Instiute for German Language (IDS)
Mannheim, Germany
koplenig@ids-mannheim.de

Tanja Samardžić
University of Zürich
CorpusLab, URPP Language and Space,
Freiestrasse 16
tanja.samardzic@uzh.ch

Abstract

Language complexity is an intriguing phenomenon argued to play an important role in both language learning and processing. The need to compare languages with regard to their complexity resulted in a multitude of approaches and methods, ranging from accounts targeting specific structural features to global quantification of variation more generally. In this paper, we investigate the degree to which morphological complexity measures are mutually correlated in a sample of more than 500 languages of 101 language families. We use human expert judgements from the *World Atlas of Language Structures* (WALS), and compare them to four quantitative measures automatically calculated from language corpora. These consist of three previously defined corpus-derived measures, which are all monolingual, and one new measure based on automatic word-alignment across pairs of languages. We find strong correlations between all the measures, illustrating that both expert judgements and automated approaches converge to similar complexity ratings, and can be used interchangeably.

1 Introduction

Languages are often compared with regard to their complexity from a computational, theoretical and learning perspective. In computational linguistics, it is generally known that methods mainly developed for the English language do not necessarily transfer well to other languages. The cross-linguistic variation in the amount of information encoded at the level of a word is, for instance, recognized as one of the main challenges for multilingual syntactic parsing (formulated as *The Architectural Challenge* (Tsarfaty et al., 2013)). Complexity of this kind is also found to influence machine translation: translating from morphologically rich languages into English is easier than the other way around (Koehn, 2005). From the perspective of human learning, interesting relationships have been established between the size of populations and morphological complexity (Lupyan and Dale, 2010), as well as the proportion of second language learners and the complexity of case systems: languages with more non-native learners tend to have fewer cases (Bentz and Winter, 2013). These findings are attributed to learning pressures reducing complexity.

An important problem for comparing language complexity is the lack of a standard complexity measure applicable to a wide range of languages and research questions. Many definitions and measures have been proposed to assess linguistic and, in particular, morphological complexity (Baerman et al., 2015; Sampson et al., 2009). The respective approaches to calculating complexity, and their scope of

142

Proceedings of the Workshop on Computational Linguistics for Linguistic Complexity,
pages 142–153, Osaka, Japan, December 11-17 2016.

application, can vary considerably. While factors that need to be taken into account in assessing language complexity are rather well studied, little is known on how different measures relate to each other.

The goal of this paper is to assess the degree to which different language complexity measures are mutually correlated. We are especially interested in the relation between a measure derived from human expert judgements, and several corpus-based measures that do not involve human judgements. We quantify the relations between the measures using 519 languages of overall 101 families represented both in the *World Atlas of Language Structures* (WALS) (Dryer and Haspelmath, 2013) and in parallel corpora (Koehn, 2005; Mayer and Cysouw, 2014). Our findings suggest that the correlation between the measures is strong enough to allow their interchangeable use.

2 Related work

There is a recent rise of interest in defining and measuring linguistic complexity, reflected in three volumes on the topic (Sampson et al., 2009; Baerman et al., 2015; Miestamo et al., 2008). In this spirit, some of our data sources have already been used for quantitative comparisons of a wide range of languages. Lupyan and Dale (2010), for instance, extract indicators of morphological complexity from the WALS, and relate them to the size of speaker populations. In a similar vein, Bentz and Winter (2013) and Bentz et al. (2015) investigate the relationship between morphological complexity, lexical diversity, and the proportion of adult second language learners in speaker populations. We adopt an approach to quantifying the typological data similar to the one presented in these studies, but we adapt it to the needs of our comparison.

The idea of using parallel corpora for language complexity comparison dates back to Greenberg (1959). It was revived with the development of large parallel corpora and computational tools for their processing. Cysouw and Waelchli (2007) provide an overview of how massively parallel texts can be applied to cross-linguistic studies, and describe the potential of such corpora. Recently, massively parallel corpora have been used for studies in lexical typology (Waelchli and Cysouw, 2012), and word order typology (Östling, 2015).

Finally, a new data set specifically intended for information content comparison is under construction at Google (Sproat et al., 2014). The goal of this project is to provide maximally parallel sentences in a set of languages with detailed functional glosses. Once completed, this data set will enable more comprehensive complexity measures than those used in our paper, however, for a relatively small set of languages.

3 Measures

In this section, an overview of the measures used is given. We start with the quantification of expert judgements extracted from the WALS. Next, we move to four corpus-based approaches using type-token ratios, unigram word entropy, relative entropy of word structure, and word alignments.

3.1 Typological measure based on WALS: C_{WALS}

We choose 28 chapters/features of the *World Atlas of Language Structures* (Dryer and Haspelmath, 2013) which are relevant for describing morphology. For example, Chapter 30A "Number of Genders" gives a range of 5 values from "None" to "5 or more", which we directly map to values 1 to 5 indicating increasing complexity. Some features are binary. For instance, Chapter 67A on "The Future Tense", gives a binary distinction between whether there is a morphological marker or not. We code this as 0 and 1. In other chapters such as 70A "The Morphological Imperative" the values have to be reordered to reflect an increasing complexity of morphology. Details about the chapters, their categories, the necessary transformations, and the final values are given in Appendix 8.1.

We arrive at 28 WALS features of morphology with values ordered by increasing use of morphology to encode the feature. There are 1713 languages in WALS for which at least 1 feature value is given. There are only 10 languages for which all 28 features are available. Note, however, that our transformations result in scales of different sizes for different features. To make the values comparable, we normalize all the values to the interval [0,1]. As a normalization factor we use each feature's maximum value, so that the value of 1 across all the features corresponds to the maximum use of morphology.

Based on the obtained data set we assign a morphological complexity score to each language by averaging the values of the features:

$$C_{WALS} = \frac{\sum_{i=1}^{n} f_i}{n},\tag{1}$$

where f_i is the feature value of feature i, and n is the number of features available per language. Hence, C_{WALS} is the feature value average per language.

Table 3.1 gives C_{WALS} values for the subset of 34 languages which are represented by either 27 or 28 features.

ISO	Name	Family	No. Chapters	C_WALS
tur	Turkish	Altaic	27	0.775
evn	Evenki	Altaic	27	0.748
abk	Abkhaz	Northwest Caucasian	28	0.704
zul	Zulu	Niger-Congo	27	0.684
swh	Swahili	Niger-Congo	27	0.675
qvi	Quechua (Imbabura)	Quechuan	28	0.662
eus	Basque	Basque	28	0.647
apu	Apurina	Arawakan	27	0.573
lez	Lezgian	Nakh-Daghestanian	28	0.568
arz	Arabic (Egyptian)	Afro-Asiatic	28	0.563
hun	Hungarian	Uralic	28	0.558
heb	Hebrew (Modern)	Afro-Asiatic	27	0.529
wyb	Ngiyambaa	Pama-Nyungan	27	0.528
ckt	Chukchi	Chukotko-Kamchatkan	28	0.519
khk	Khalkha	Altaic	27	0.516
tiw	Tiwi	Tiwian	27	0.495
hix	Hixkaryana	Cariban	27	0.489
hae	Oromo (Harar)	Afro-Asiatic	27	0.487
jpn	Japanese	Japanese	27	0.474
aey	Amele	Trans-New Guinea	27	0.456
rus	Russian	Indo-European	28	0.453
ell	Greek (Modern)	Indo-European	28	0.452
spa	Spanish	Indo-European	27	0.440
deu	German	Indo-European	27	0.397
kut	Kutenai	Kutenai	28	0.357
ind	Indonesian	Austronesian	28	0.336
eng	English	Indo-European	28	0.329
hau	Hausa	Afro-Asiatic	28	0.322
plt	Malagasy	Austronesian	27	0.309
ayz	Maybrat	West Papuan	27	0.292
rap	Rapanui	Austronesian	27	0.218
mri	Maori	Austronesian	27	0.194
yor	Yoruba	Niger-Congo	28	0.178
vie	Vietnamese	Austro-Asiatic	27	0.141

Table 1: Morphological complexity values according to features represented in the WALS. This is a subset of 34 languages with 27 or 28 feature values, though not necessarily of the same features.

3.2 Corpus-based measures

Word entropy: C_H We also measure morphological complexity using *word entropy* (C_H) as described in Bentz and Alikaniotis (2016). This reflects the *average information content* of words. By trend, languages that have a wider range of word types, i.e. packing more information into word structure, rather than phrase or sentence structure, will score higher on this measure.

A "word" is here defined as a unigram, i.e. a string of alpha-numeric Unicode characters delimited by white spaces. Let T be a text that is drawn from a vocabulary of word types $\mathcal{V} = \{w_1, w_2, ..., w_V\}$ of size $V = |\mathcal{V}|$. Further assume that word type probabilities are distributed according to $p(w) = Pr(T = w)$ for $w \in \mathcal{V}$. The average information content of word types can then be calculated as (Shannon and Weaver, 1949)

$$H(T) = -\sum_{i=1}^{V} p(w_i) \log_2(p(w_i)).\tag{2}$$

A crucial step to estimate $H(T)$ is to get word type probabilities $p(w_i)$. The *maximum likelihood* or *plug-in* estimator just takes type frequencies normalized by the overall number of tokens. However, this estimator underestimates the entropy, as it does not take into account unseen types, which is especially problematic for small texts (Hausser and Strimmer, 2009). A method with a faster convergence rate is the

James-Stein shrinkage estimator (Hausser and Strimmer, 2009). Word probabilities are here estimated as

$$\hat{p_{w_i}}^{shrink} = \lambda \hat{p_{w_i}}^{target} + (1 - \lambda)\hat{p_{w_i}}^{ML},\tag{3}$$

where $\hat{p_i}^{ML}$ denotes the word probability according to the maximum likelihood account, $\lambda \in [0, 1]$ is the "shrinkage intensity", and $\hat{p_i}^{target}$ is the "shrinkage target", namely the maximum entropy case of a uniform $p_{w_i} = \frac{1}{V}$. Hausser and Strimmer (2009) illustrate that the optimal shrinkage parameter λ can be found analytically. Given this parameter, the probability $\hat{p}_{w_i}^{shrink}$ plugged into the original entropy equation yields

$$\hat{H(T)}^{shrink} = -\sum_{i=1}^{r} \hat{p_{w_i}}^{shrink} \log_2(\hat{p_{w_i}}^{shrink}).\tag{4}$$

Relative entropy of word structure: C_D C_D is taken from Koplenig et al. (2016), and inspired by earlier accounts to measure different dimensions of language complexity by making use of Lempel-Ziv compression algorithms (Juola, 1998; Juola, 2008; Montemurro and Zanette, 2011; Ehret and Szmrecsanyi, 2016).[1] Let T be a text that is drawn from an alphabet of characters (not words as above) $\mathcal{A} = \{c_1, c_2, ..., c_A\}$ of size $A = |\mathcal{A}|$. Kontoyiannis et al. (1998) illustrate that the per character entropy of T can then be estimated as

$$\hat{H}(T) = \left[\frac{1}{n}\sum_{i=1}^{n}\frac{l_i}{\log_2(i+1)}\right]^{-1},\tag{5}$$

where n is the overall number of characters in the text T, and l_i is the length of the longest substring from position i onward that has not appeared before, i.e. in T_1^{i-1}. Note that the average match length l_i is related to the redundancy and predictability in T. If match-lengths are generally long, then there is more redundancy and more predictability, if they are short, then there is less redundancy and less predictability in the text.

To estimate the amount of redundancy/predictability contributed by within-word structure, Koplenig et al. (2016) replace each word token in T by a token of the same length but with characters randomly drawn with equal probability from the alphabet $\mathcal{A}$. The entropy of the original text is then subtracted from the masked text to yield

$$\hat{D} = \hat{H}(T^{masked}) - \hat{H}(T^{original}).\tag{6}$$

The bigger $\hat{D}$, the more information is stored within words, i.e. in morphological regularities. This measure of morphological complexity is denoted C_D in the following.

Type/Token ratios: C_{TTR} We take the ratio of word types over word tokens as a simple baseline measure (Kettunen, 2014). The range of word types is expanded by productive morphological markers. Hence, higher values of C_{TTR} correspond to higher morphological complexity. Given a text T drawn from a vocabulary of word types $\mathcal{V} = \{w_1, w_2, ..., w_V\}$ of size $V = |\mathcal{V}|$ the measure is

$$C_{TTR} = \frac{V}{\sum_{i=1}^{V} fr_i},\tag{7}$$

where V is the number of types, and fr_i is the token frequency of the ith type.

---

[1] Note that Koplenig et al. (2016) do not call this a "complexity" metric, since they remain neutral about whether word internal structure is more or less difficult to grasp from the perspective of a learner.

Word alignment based measure: C_A Finally, we consider a measure based on word alignment, which, to our knowledge, has not been implemented before. Word alignment is an essential step in phrase-based statistical machine translation (Koehn et al., 2003). The intuition behind the alignment based approach is that words in morphologically richer languages tend to be translated, and therefore aligned, to several words in a morphologically poorer language. As in the case of C_H and C_{TTR} measures the term "word" is understood here in an orthographic sense.

Word alignment from a source to a target language can result in three different scenarios[2]: a single word in the source language is aligned to a single word ("OneToOne") or several words ("OneToMany") in the target language, or several words in the target language are aligned to a single word in the source language ("ManyToOne"). We illustrate these cases by an example of alignments from English to Russian in Figure 3.2:

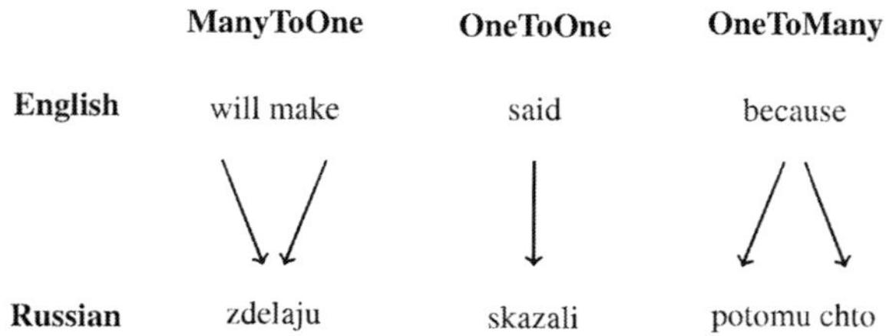

Figure 1: Example of three word alignment categories in a word-aligned English to Russian text.

When word alignments are performed from a morphologically poorer to a morphologically richer language, "ManyToOne" alignments tend to be more frequent than 'OneToMany" alignments, and the other way around. This observation can be quantified using C_A measure:

$$C_A = \frac{\#\mathsf{ManyToOne} - \#\mathsf{OneToMany}}{\#\mathsf{AllAlignments}}, \qquad (8)$$

where $\#\mathsf{ManyToOne}$ is the number of all alignments from "ManyToOne" category, $\#\mathsf{OneToMany}$ is the number of all alignments from "ManyToOne" category, $\#\mathsf{AllAlignments}$ is the number of all alignments. A single alignment can be represented by one arrow as in Figure 3.2.

A positive value of C_A indicates that the target language is packaging more information into single words than the source language, negative values correspond to the opposite case. Hence, languages can be compared using C_A values based on word alignments from a fixed source language. An inherent property of the C_A measure is that it is derived based on fully parallel bilingual texts and therefore takes into account direct realisations of how languages encode information through word alignments. The alignment measure is therefore conceptually different from the other three monolingual measures.

4   Data and methods

The corpus-based measures C_D, C_H, C_A and C_{TTR} are calculated using parallel corpora. C_D (Koplenig et al., 2016) is estimated based on the the Book of Matthew (New Testament) from the Parallel Bible Corpus (PBC) (Mayer and Cysouw, 2014). This gives a sample of 1124 so-called "doculects", i.e. indirect representations of languages (defined by ISO-639-3 codes). C_H is estimated based on a sample of parallel texts from the PBC (all books), the *Universal Declaration of Human Rights* (UDHR),[3] and the *European Parliament Corpus* (EPC) (Koehn, 2005). This amounts to 1242 doculects. C_{TTR} is calculated for 1144 doculects of the full PBC.[4]

Since the implementation of C_A requires sentence aligned bitexts with a fixed source language, it is estimated based on PBC with Hebrew being fixed as a source language. However, the complete

---

[2]Here we assume that the symmetrization heuristic (Och and Ney, 2003) is applied to alignments.

[3]http://unicode.org/udhr/

[4]Note that differences in numbers of doculects can derive from a specific book (e.g. Book of Matthew) not being translated into specific languages.

Bible only exists for around 16% of the languages covered by the PBC. In order to ensure that we use fully parallel texts to calculate the C_A measure, and that these are consistent in terms of the size and content across languages, we only use the New Testament (NT). The average size of the NT appears to be sufficient for producing stable ranking results as confirmed by convergence tests with an increasing amount of parallel verses (see Appendix 8.2).

The PBC as well as the other parallel corpora available for large scale comparative studies is usually rather short in comparison to bilingual text data used to train classical alignment models for machine translation. Therefore we use the Efmaral alignment method (Östling and Tiedemann, 2016) which proves to be the optimal solution for relatively short texts in terms of accuracy and efficiency.

In order to compare different corpus-based measures and the WALS-based measure, we merge the data sets by ISO-639-3 codes. Thus we end up with a data set of 519 languages for which all measures are available.

5   Results

In this section we first investigate how all considered measures of morphological complexity agree between each other using the full dataset and the subsets corresponding to the three biggest language families in our data: Atlantic-Congo, Austronesian, Indo-European, as well as the rest of the 101 families referred further as "Other". Then we proceed with a comparison of how corpus-based measures correlate with the WALS-based measure when we consider increasing subsets of typological features.

5.1   Pairwise correlations between complexity measures

As a result of applying each complexity measure to the data we get a ranked list of languages. Therefore we choose the non-parametric Spearman rank correlation to evaluate associations between each pair of measures.

Figure 2 gives an overview of pairwise correlations between all 5 morphological complexity measures for the full dataset of 519 languages. The density plots on the diagonal panels show the distribution of values for each measure. The lower off-diagonal panels illustrate the correlations between the measures using scatterplots. Each plot shows linear regressions fitted based on subcategorized data: Atlantic-Congo (red), Austronesian (green), Indo-European (blue) and "Other" (purple). The upper panels quantify the correlations for the overall data set (black), and by family (respective colour). Notice that the scale on the y-axis does not apply to the density plots, only to the scatterplots.

The lower off-diagonal scatterplots show that there is always a positive correlation between the different measures, and that this holds across all the four subsets of our data. For the full data set, the correlations between corpus-based measures are generally stronger (ranging from 0.756 to 0.918) than the correlations with C_{WALS} (ranging from 0.318 to 0.437). The strongest correlation is found between C_D and C_{TTR} (0.918), and the weakest between C_{WALS} and C_A (0.318). All correlations reported here are significant at the $p < 0.001$ level.[5]

5.2   Correlations with the WALS measure

Figure 3 focuses on correlations between the typological measure C_{WALS} and the corpus-based measures C_D, C_H, C_A, and C_{TTR}. The values on the left-hand side of the graph correspond to Spearman correlations for each measure calculated over all languages with *at least 1* feature, a total of 519. These numbers correspond to the ones given in the first row of Figure 2. The right-hand side of the graph shows correlations over languages which are represented by *at least 27* features in the WALS, a total of 23.[6]

Note that as we increase the minimum number of features from WALS to be included, we reduce the number of languages (indicated by the size of the dots). As can be seen from the graph, inclusion of more features results in stronger agreement between the corpus-based measures and C_{WALS}. Towards the right hand side we observe the highest values of correlations between C_{WALS} and the corpus-based measures, reaching 0.89 for C_D, 0.88 for C_{TTR}, 0.86 for C_H, and 0.70 for C_A. The intermediate cases

---

[5]Though see Koplenig (forthcoming) for an argument against hypothesis testing in corpus linguistics.

[6]This is less than the 34 languages in Table3.1 since not all of them are found in the parallel corpora.

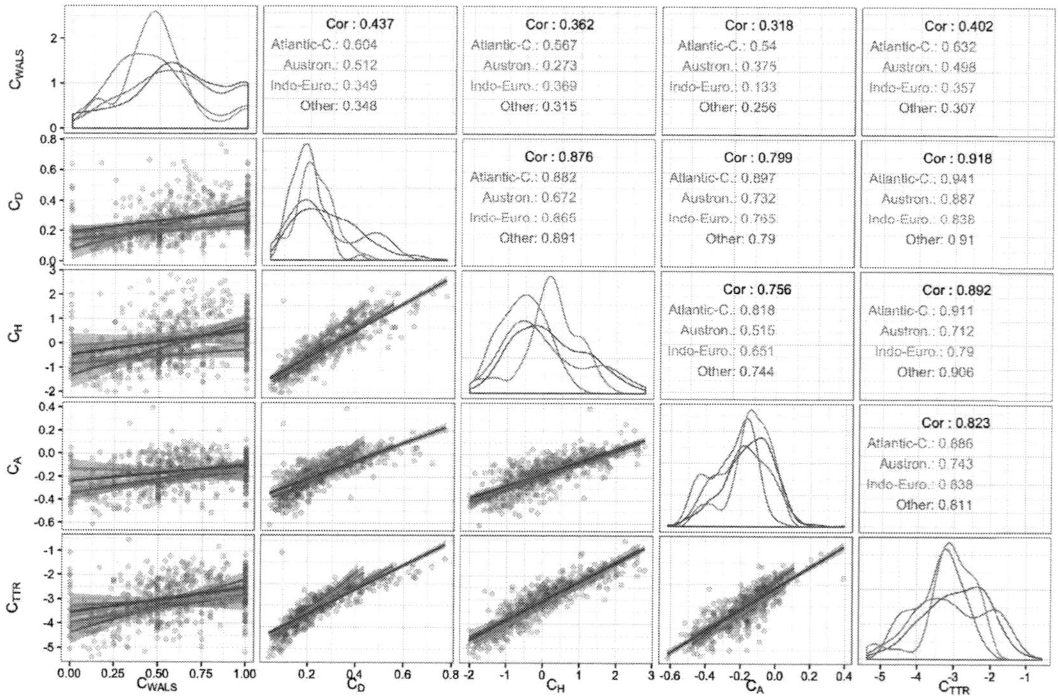

Figure 2: Pairwise correlations between all 5 complexity measures. The lower off-diagonal panels show scatterplots with fitted linear regression lines and 95% confidence intervals. The diagonal panels show density plots for the respective data set. The upper off-diagonal panels give pairwise Spearman correlations. Colours indicate the three major language families Atlantic-Congo (red), Austronesian (green), Indo-European (blue), and the rest subsumed under "Other" (purple). The correlation given in black is the overall correlation. The full data set with 519 languages is used.

have lower coverage of languages as well as less overlap of features between them. This leads to higher disagreement between the measures while they still show common trends. The results illustrate that given enough information in the WALS, C_{WALS} correlates just as good with corpus-based measures as these do amongst each other.

6 Discussion

Our results of comparing different morphological measures provide two major insights:

1. We used four vastly differing automated approaches of measuring morphological complexity (C_D, C_H, C_A, and C_{TTR}) in actual language production, i.e. parallel corpora. They all display strong correlations between each other, i.e. strong agreement on which languages are morphologically complex, and which are not. This is encouraging, since it illustrates that the judgements of these automated methods converge despite the conceptual differences.

2. Given enough feature values, the expert judgements of the WALS also converge with the automated corpus-based methods when ranking languages on a morphological complexity scale, which is reflected in Spearman correlations of up to 0.89. This is remarkable when considering how much expert knowledge and working hours go into writing of descriptive grammars, and assembling them in databases like WALS. If our sole objective is to rank languages in terms of morphological complexity, the automated methods yield high agreement with the outcome of a human expert rating.

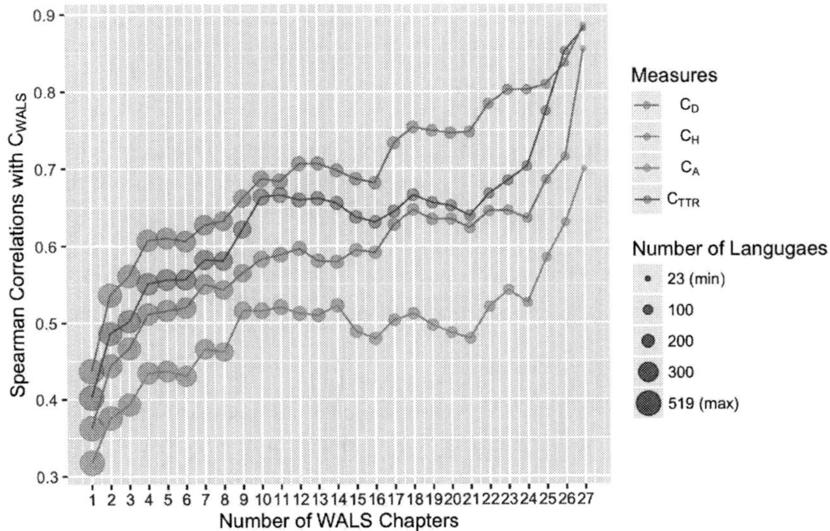

Figure 3: Spearman correlations of the corpus-based measures with C_{WALS}. The x-axis corresponds to a subcategorization of the languages included to calculate the correlations. For example, "27" means that only languages which have values in at least 27 WALS chapters are included, which is the case for 23 languages, and so on. All correlations are significant ($p < 0.001$).

Since all the measures correlate strongly, the reason for choosing either of them depends on the objective and the data limitations of a given study. In the following, we discuss some of the advantages and disadvantages of the respective measures.

6.1 Advantages and disadvantages of the measures

The objective of the WALS is to give an overview of phonetic, morphological, lexical and syntactic properties of a large and balanced sample of languages. It is a collaborative effort of dozens of experts to establish a data base that allows cross-linguistic comparisons. As such, it is a rich source for typological studies. However, by necessity it is only a coarse-grained reflection of the actual dimensions of complexity. For example, classifying a language by whether it uses 2, 3, 4, etc. nominal case markers (chapter 49) does not tell us how productive these markers are in actual language production. Note, also, that the coverage of WALS in terms of features per language is sparse. If we want to include all 28 features, then we end up with a sample of only 10 languages.

The corpus-based measures allow us to look at real instances of morphological productivity in texts across many languages. All of them can be estimated from corpora directly and efficiently, without much prior processing. The only requirement for C_H, C_D and C_{TTR} is that word types are delimited in a consistent manner, e.g. by white spaces – or other non-alphanumeric characters. Hence, these measures come without much theoretical "baggage", and are cross-linguistically comparable. At this point, they can be applied to ca. 1500 languages via massively parallel corpora like the PBC.

The simplest corpus-based measure is C_{TTR}. Once word types are defined, it is easily and straightforwardly computed from a text. However, a drawback of C_{TTR} is that it does not take into account subtle differences in the distributions of word tokens over word types. C_H is a more accurate reflection of the actual distributions. However, just like C_{TTR}, C_H does not distinguish between effects due to breadth of the base lexicon, on one hand, and word formation processes such as derivation, inflection or compounding, on the other. Also, it does not reflect differences in regular and irregular morphological processes. For example, the irregular pair *go→went* will contribute just as much to higher C_H as the regular pair *sprint→sprinted*.

C_D has the advantage of distinguishing regular from irregular processes of word formation. Regular suffixes as in the example above will introduce systematic redundancy reflected in $\hat{D}$. However, masking within-word structure requires a further processing step that might introduce biases which are not well understood yet. Also, despite picking up on regular patterns within words, C_D does still not distinguish between different types of word formation.

Likewise, C_A does – at this stage – not distinguish between different types of word formation. This could be overcome by considering alignments on the type level. Given the sum of all alignments for a word type, it is expected that the diversity of alignments will be lower for a word in a language with rich morphology, since the word types are expected to be rarer (less frequent). Therefore, a measure based on word type level alignments could distinguish between morphological and lexical diversity. Also, the influence of the choice of source language on the results needs to be clarified in future studies.

6.2 Conceptualizing morphological complexity

"Linguistic complexity" more generally, and "morphological complexity" in particular, are polysemous concepts. Here, we focused on defining and comparing different quantitative measures. They necessarily hinge upon different conceptualizations of complexity. The account based on WALS chapters is a *paradigm-based* approach. Harnessing descriptive grammars, typologists attribute a given number of paradigmatic distinctions to languages, which, in turn, reflect their complexity. Measures such as C_{TTR}, C_D and C_H, on the other hand, could be called *distribution-based*. They conceptualize complexity with reference to the distribution of word tokens over word types used in a given language. Finally, the *translation-based* account C_A is not applicable to single languages, but conceptualizes complexity via the problem of translating a concept from one language to another. Clearly, all of these are conceptualizations in their own right, with specific implications for language learning and usage. However, they turn out to be strongly correlated – across the board – since they all reflect different nuances of the same principle: linguistic complexity relates to the fundamental information-theoretic concept of *uncertainty* or *choice* when encoding and decoding a message.

7   Conclusions

We have tested four conceputally different measures of morphological complexity across more than 500 languages of 101 families. The overall results suggest that different corpus-based measures are highly consistent when ranking languages according to morphological complexity. Moreover, measures based on typological expert judgements are also converging onto similar rankings if enough language specific information is given. These findings help to establish a quantitative, empirical, and reproducible account of morphological complexity, and linguistic typology more generally.

Acknowledgements

CB was funded by a grant for international short visits of the Swiss National Science Foundation (SNSF), as well as the German Research Foundation (DFG FOR 2237: Project "Words, Bones, Genes, Tools: Tracking Linguistic, Cultural, and Biological Trajectories of the Human Past"), and the ERC Advanced Grant 324246 EVOLAEMP.

References

Matthew Baerman, Dunstan Brown, Greville G Corbett, et al. 2015. *Understanding and measuring morphological complexity*. Oxford University Press.

Christian Bentz and Dimitrios Alikaniotis. 2016. The word entropy of natural languages. *arXiv preprint arXiv:1606.06996*.

Christian Bentz and Bodo Winter. 2013. Languages with more second language speakers tend to lose nominal case. *Language Dynamics and Change*, 3:1–27.

Christian Bentz, Annemarie Verkerk, Douwe Kiela, Felix Hill, and Paula Buttery. 2015. Adaptive communication: Languages with more non-native speakers tend to have fewer word forms. *PLoS ONE*, 10(6):e0128254.

Michael Cysouw and Bernard Waelchli. 2007. Parallel texts: Using translational equivalents in linguistic typology. *STUF - Language Typology and Universals*, 60:95 – 99.

Matthew S. Dryer and Martin Haspelmath, editors. 2013. *World Atlas of Language Structures online*. Max Planck Digital Library, Munich.

Katharina Ehret and Benedikt Szmrecsanyi. 2016. An information-theoretic approach to assess linguistic complexity. In Raffaela Baechler and Guido Seiler, editors, *Complexity and Isolation*. de Gruyter, Berlin.

Joseph Harold Greenberg. 1959. A quantitative approach to morphological typology. *International Journal of American Linguistics*, 26:178–194.

Jean Hausser and Korbinian Strimmer. 2009. Entropy inference and the james-stein estimator, with application to nonlinear gene association networks. *The Journal of Machine Learning Research*, 10:1469–1484.

Patrick Juola. 1998. Measuring linguistic complexity: The morphological tier. *Journal of Quantitative Linguistics*, 5(3):206–213.

Patrick Juola. 2008. Assessing linguistic complexity. In Matti Miestamo, Kaius Sinnemäki, and Fred Karlsson, editors, *Language complexity: typology, contact, change*, pages 89–108. Amsterdam: John Benjamins.

Kimmo Kettunen. 2014. Can type-token ratio be used to show morphological complexity of languages? *Journal of Quantitative Linguistics*, 21(3):223–245.

Philipp Koehn, Franz Josef Och, and Daniel Marcu. 2003. Statistical phrase-based translation. In *Proceedings of the 2003 Conference of the North American Chapter of the Association for Computational Linguistics on Human Language Technology - Volume 1*, NAACL '03, pages 48–54. Association for Computational Linguistics.

Philipp Koehn. 2005. Europarl: A parallel corpus for statistical machine translation. In *MT summit*, volume 5, pages 79–86.

Ioannis Kontoyiannis, Paul H Algoet, Yu M Suhov, and Abraham J Wyner. 1998. Nonparametric entropy estimation for stationary processes and random fields, with applications to English text. *Information Theory, IEEE Transactions on*, 44(3):1319–1327.

Alexander Koplenig, Peter Meyer, Sascha Wolfer, and Carolin Mueller-Spitzer. 2016. The statistical tradeoff between word order and word structure: large-scale evidence for the principle of least effort. *arXiv preprint arXiv:1608.03587*.

Alexander Koplenig. forthcoming. Against statistical significance testing in corpus linguistics.

Gary Lupyan and Rick Dale. 2010. Language structure is partly determined by social structure. *PloS ONE*, 5(1):e8559, January.

Thomas Mayer and Michael Cysouw. 2014. Creating a massively parallel bible corpus. In Nicoletta Calzolari, Khalid Choukri, Thierry Declerck, Hrafn Loftsson, Bente Maegaard, Joseph Mariani, Asunción Moreno, Jan Odijk, and Stelios Piperidis, editors, *Proceedings of the Ninth International Conference on Language Resources and Evaluation (LREC-2014), Reykjavik, Iceland, May 26-31, 2014*, pages 3158–3163. European Language Resources Association (ELRA).

Matti Miestamo, Kaius Sinnemäki, and Fred Karlsson. 2008. *Language complexity: Typology, contact, change*. John Benjamins Publishing.

Marcelo A Montemurro and Damián H Zanette. 2011. Universal entropy of word ordering across linguistic families. *PLoS One*, 6(5):e19875.

Franz Josef Och and Hermann Ney. 2003. A systematic comparison of various statistical alignment models. *Computational Linguistics*, 29:19 – 51.

Robert Östling and Jörg Tiedemann. 2016. Efficient word alignment with Markov Chain Monte Carlo. *Prague Bulletin of Mathematical Linguistics*, 106, October. To appear.

Robert Östling. 2015. Word order typology through multilingual word alignment. *Proceedings of the 53rd Annual Meeting of the Association for Computational Linguistics and the 7th International Joint Conference on Natural Language Processing (Short Papers)*, pages 205 – 211.

Geoffrey Sampson, David Gil, and Peter Trudgill. 2009. *Language complexity as an evolving variable*. Oxford University Press.

Claude E. Shannon and Warren Weaver. 1949. *The mathematical theory of communication*. The University of Illinois Press, Urbana.

Richard Sproat, Bruno Cartoni, HyunJeong Choe, David Huynh, Linne Ha, Ravindran Rajakumar, and Evelyn Wenzel-Grondie. 2014. A database for measuring linguistic information content. In Nicoletta Calzolari, Khalid Choukri, Thierry Declerck, Hrafn Loftsson, Bente Maegaard, Joseph Mariani, Asuncion Moreno, Jan Odijk, and Stelios Piperidis, editors, *Proceedings of the Ninth International Conference on Language Resources and Evaluation (LREC'14)*, pages 967–974, Reykjavik, Iceland, May. European Language Resources Association (ELRA). ACL Anthology Identifier: L14-1397.

Reut Tsarfaty, Djam Seddah, Sandra Kbler, and Joakim Nivre. 2013. Parsing morphologically rich languages: Introduction to the special issue. *Computational Linguistics*, 39(1):15–22.

Bernard Waelchli and Michael Cysouw. 2012. Lexical typology through similarity semantics: Toward a semantic map of motion verbs. *Linguistics*, 50:671 – 710.

8   Appendices

8.1   Transformations of WALS features

Chapter	Name	Categories	Transformation	Final Values
22A	Inflectional Synthesis	7 (ordinal)	none	1-7
26A	Prefixing vs. Suffixing in Inflectional Morphology	6 (non-ordinal)	binarization	0-1
27A	Reduplication	3 (non-ordinal)	binarization	0-1
28A	Case Syncretism	4 (ordinal)	reorder	1-4
29A	Syncretism in Verbal Person/Number marking	3 (ordinal)	none	1-3
30A	Number of Genders	5 (ordinal)	none	1-5
33A	Coding of Nominal Plurality	9 (partially ordinal)	binarization	0-1
34A	Occurrence of Nominal Plurality	6 (ordinal)	none	1-6
37A	Definite Articles	5 (non-ordinal)	binarization	0-1
38A	Indefinite Articles	5 (non-ordinal)	binarization	0-1
49A	Number of Cases	9 (ordinal)	remove	1-8
51A	Position of Case Affixes	9 (non-ordinal)	binarization	0-1
57A	Position of Pronominal Possessive Affixes	4 (non-ordinal)	binarization	0-1
59A	Possessive Classification	4 (ordinal)	none	1-4
65A	Perfective/Imperfective Aspect	binary	none	0-1
66A	The Past Tense	4 (ordinal)	reorder	1-4
67A	The Future Tense	binary	none	0-1
69A	Position of Tense/Aspect Affixes	5 (non-ordinal)	binarization	0-1
70A	The Morphological Imperative	5 (partially ordinal)	recategorization	1-4
73A	The Optative	binary	none	0-1
74A	Situational Possibility	3 (non-ordinal)	binarization	0-1
75A	Epistemic Possibility	3 (non-ordinal)	binarization	0-1
78A	Coding of Evidentiality	6 (non-ordinal)	binarization	0-1
94A	Subordination	5 (non-ordinal)	binarization	0-1
101A	Expression of Pronominal Subjects	6 (non-ordinal)	binarization	0-1
102A	Verbal Person Marking	5 (partially ordinal)	recategorization	1-3
111A	Nonperiphrastic Causative Constructions	4 (non-ordinal)	binarization	0-1
112A	Negative Morphemes	6 (non-ordinal)	binarization	0-1

Table 2: Recoding of WALS chapters. The column "Categories" gives the type of of the original WALS variable represented in the respective chapter. "Transformations" is a short description of how the chapters where recoded. "Final Values" gives the range of ordinal values used to reflect the morphological complexity.

8.2 Convergence tests for C_A

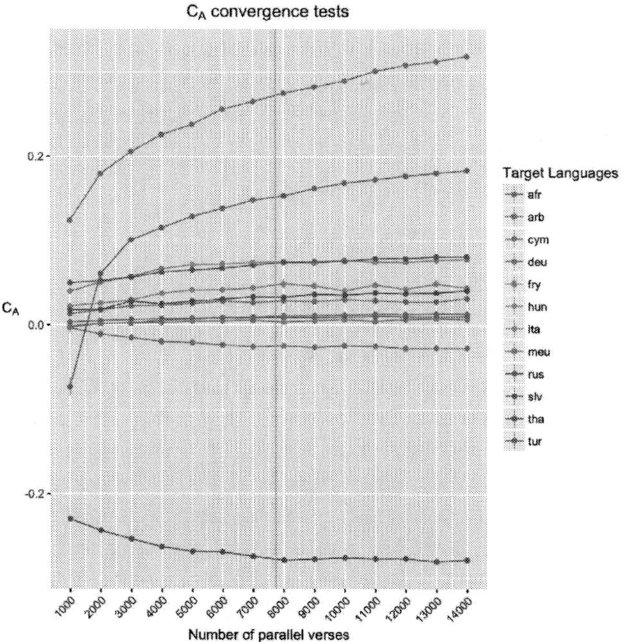

Figure 4: Convergence tests for the C_A measure. The source language for alignments is English. For each size of the verse number X the C_A measure is averaged across 50 samples with X randomly drawn parallel verses. The grey line corresponds to the average number of verses available for NT in PBC.

Similarity-Based Alignment of Monolingual Corpora for Text Simplification Purposes

Sarah Albertsson, Evelina Rennes, Arne Jönsson
SICS East Swedish ICT AB, Linköping, Sweden
Department of Computer and Information Science,
Linköping University, Linköping, Sweden
s.hantosialbertsson@gmail.com evelina.rennes@liu.se
arne.jonsson@liu.se

Abstract

Comparable or parallel corpora are beneficial for many NLP tasks. The automatic collection of corpora enables large-scale resources, even for less-resourced languages, which in turn can be useful for deducing rules and patterns for text rewriting algorithms, a subtask of automatic text simplification. We present two methods for the alignment of Swedish easy-to-read text segments to text segments from a reference corpus. The first method (M1) was originally developed for the task of text reuse detection, measuring sentence similarity by a modified version of a TF-IDF vector space model. A second method (M2), also accounting for part-of-speech tags, was developed, and the methods were compared. For evaluation, a crowdsourcing platform was built for human judgement data collection, and preliminary results showed that cosine similarity relates better to human ranks than the Dice coefficient. We also saw a tendency that including syntactic context to the TF-IDF vector space model is beneficial for this kind of paraphrase alignment task.

1 Introduction

Automatic text simplification is defined as the process of reducing text complexity, while maintaining most of the content (Chandrasekar and Srinivas, 1997; Carroll et al., 1998). While the first approaches handled the task of automatically simplifying texts by the application of hand-crafted rules, cf. Rennes and Jönsson (2015) for a recent example for Swedish, data-driven methods have gained momentum in text simplification, as in other areas within natural language processing.

By using large corpora of aligned monolingual material, it is possible to automatically extract patterns or rules but since such induction requires large amounts of aligned material, hand-crafted systems are often the only practically performable alternative for languages without such resources. To automatically collect comparable corpora would result in large-scale resources useful for deducing rules and patterns for text rewriting algorithms, particularly beneficial for less-resourced languages with sparse linguistic resources.

In this study, we hypothesized that we could extend the work of Sanchez-Perez et al. (2014), originally developed for test reuse detection, to detect paraphrased segments from two corpora; one of them containing only easy-to-read material, and the other representing the full spectra of Swedish texts. We replicated the algorithm proposed by Sanchez-Perez et al. (2014), and contrasted this method to a method that included part-of-speech tags as context. An ongoing crowdsourcing evalutation is presented, in terms of evaluation design and preliminary results.

2 Related Work

The creation of aligned comparable monolingual corpora has been suggested as a step for several tasks within the field of natural language processing, such as paraphrasing (Barzilay and Elhadad, 2003; Dolan et al., 2004), automatic text summarisation (Knight and Marcu, 2000; Jin, 2002), terminology extraction (Hazem and Morin, 2016), and automatic text simplification (Bott and Saggion, 2011; Coster and Kauchak, 2011; Klerke and Søgaard, 2012).

Proceedings of the Workshop on Computational Linguistics for Linguistic Complexity,
pages 154–163, Osaka, Japan, December 11-17 2016.

According to Nelken and Shieber (2006), the alignment task of monolingual corpora differs from the multi-lingual counterpart. While the latter exhibits conformity between source and target documents, aligned monolingual material is characterised by being similar in content, rather than linguistically, making many established methods developed for multi-lingual alignment less successful.

Since the aim of monolingual text alignment is to find similar text fragments, it forms an important subtask of applications such as text reuse detection. The method described in this paper is inspired by the approach used by Sanchez-Perez et al. (2014), originally developed for the task of text reuse detection, measuring sentence similarity by a modified version of a TF-IDF vector space model. Other approaches to monolingual text alignment have measured sentence similarity by TF-IDF. Nelken and Shieber (2006) used this similarity score, treating each individual sentence as a document, in order to estimate the probability that two sentences are aligned using logistic regression, achieving higher accuracy than previous systems. This was confirmed by Zhu et al. (2010) who showed that when comparing the TF-IDF approach by Nelken and Shieber (2006) to other similarity measures for monolingual text alignment, the former outperformed the other two measures (word overlap and maximum edit distance).

For the task of text simplification, easy-to-read material aligned to their original counterparts would be beneficial. One way to ensure that a text is easy-to-read is by applying readability metrics. For Swedish, the standard readability metric is the *Readability Index*, LIX (Björnsson, 1968), but recently, its dominance has been questioned (Mühlenbock and Johansson Kokkinakis, 2009; Heimann Mühlenbock, 2013). Another measure, often said to complement LIX for Swedish, is the *Word Variation Index*, OVIX (Hultman and Westman, 1977). The readability metrics considered in this study are further defined in section 3.3.

An automatic evaluation of paraphrases requires annotated data. Crowdsourcing enables a cheap and effective way of collecting multiple annotations from multiple annotators for one task. For annotation tasks, Snow et al. (2008) showed that crowdsourced annotations are similar to traditional annotations made by experts. The field of natural language processing has used crowdsourcing for various tasks within the NLP area, often by the use of Amazon's Mechanical Turk (Callison-burch et al., 2006). For Swedish, this is a resource that is lacking and it can be a tedious task to collect human annotated data.

3 Method

This section will describe the text resources used in this study, as well as an overview of the replicated algorithm and the experimental design of the evaluation.

3.1 Corpora

LÄSBART (Mühlenbock, 2008) is a Swedish corpus containing a collection of easy-to-read material of a total of 1.1 million tokens. Four genres are represented in the corpus; easy-to-read news texts, fiction, community information, and children's fiction.

STOCKHOLM-UMEÅ CORPUS (SUC) (Källgren et al., 2006) is a corpus of one million words of published Swedish texts written in the 1990's. The corpus is balanced according to genres and annotated with part-of-speech tags, morphological features, lemmas, and some structural and functionally interpreted tags.

Although both LÄSBART and SUC were previously tagged, the corpora were annotated again for this study, in order to create a more uniformly annotated amount of text. For this, we used STAGGER (Östling, 2013), a part-of-speech tagger based on the averaged perceptron.

3.2 Algorithm

The alignment algorithm followed the procedure described in Sanchez-Perez et al. (2014), whose original purpose was to detect text reuse. By the use of a TF-IDF vector space model, the similarity between text fragments was calculated, with a slight modification: each sentence was considered a document, and the full collection of sentences in the original document was considered the document collection. Thus, rather than an inverse document frequency measure, an inverse sentence frequency was calculated. Each pair of text fragments was given a similarity score (cosine measure and Dice coefficient), and if the score exceeded a certain threshold, originally 0.33, the text fragments were considered similar, and were thus aligned. The alignment was performed in two iterations, where the first iteration, followed the procedure given by Sanchez-Perez et al. (2014) with vectors based on lemmatised words, and the second iteration included part-of-speech tags as context information, in addition to the lemmatised lower cased words. The replicated method will henceforth be known as **M1**, and **M2** denotes the method using part-of-speech tags as context. By introducing the part-of-speech tags, we reasoned that we would improve the precision for disambiguating words and enable synonyms higher probability (Turney et al., 2010).

This algorithm was used to align one text segment originating from SUC with text segments originating from the LäSBarT corpus. The aim of this procedure was to construct the monolingual corpus consisting of reference segments (**RS**) aligned with easy-to-read segments (**ES**). The threshold of a cosine of 0.33, presented by Sanchez-Perez et al. (2014), was used as a minimum value for aligning a candidate segment. No maximum value was used, and a cosine of 1.0 was thus an admissible paraphrase candidate.

3.3 Features

To assess the algorithms' ability to produce more readable paraphrases, a number of readability measures can be used, see for instance Falkenjack et al. (2013). In this study we limit ourselves to using only a variety of commonly used readability measures, for Swedish.

N-gram overlap. An evaluation of two texts' similarity can be aided by the measure of shared n-grams between text pairs. In this evaluation, each paired segment, one RS paired to one ES, was treated as a collection of n-grams, with n ranging from 1 to 4. The proportion of intersecting n-grams in ES and RS was computed, and divided by the total number of n-grams in RS, resulting in a value ranging from 0 to 1. This value represents the overall mean n-gram overlap between the aligned segments. A value of 1 indicates that the ES is an exact copy of, or contained within, the RS. We used this measure to compare the overall n-gram overlaps between the two methods.

LIX, *readability index* (Björnsson, 1968), Equation 1. Ratio of words longer than 6 characters coupled with average sentence length. By computing this measure we were able to examine how the values differ from the original corpora's LIX, and gain a better understanding of the subset in comparison with the full set. These values were computed for M1 and M2 separately.

$$LIX = \frac{n(w)}{n(s)} + \left(\frac{n(words > 6\,chars)}{n(w)} \times 100 \right) \tag{1}$$

where $n(s)$ denotes the number of sentences and $n(w)$ the number of words.

OVIX, *word variation index*, Equation 2. Originally developed by Hultman and Westman (1977) and related to type-token ratio. Logarithms are used to cancel out type-token ratio problems with varying text length. In this paper, OVIX was computed by treating the collection of aligned cluster sentences, originating from SUC, and the aligned text segments, originating from LäSBarT, as corpora. As for LIX, this measure is taken into account for evaluating the subsets of the two corpora.

$$OVIX = \frac{log(n(w))}{log\left(2 - \frac{log(n(uw))}{log(n(w))}\right)} \tag{2}$$

where $n(w)$ denotes the number of words and $n(uw)$ the number of unique words.

Length. Measures of long documents and words have been used in readability studies (Feng, 2010) and as a baseline for evaluating new features (Pitler and Nenkova, 2008). In this paper we computed the average word length as the average characters per word, the average number of long words per segment and the average number of words per segment. As for OVIX and LIX, the measures were computed by treating each subset of the corpora, containing only RS or only ES, as its own document.

Cosine similarity, Equation 3, calculates the cosine angle between two non-zero n-dimensional vectors, as the dot product of two vectors normalised by the product of the vector lengths. The cosine similarity measure ranges between -1 and 1, where a value closer to 1 indicates a high similarity between vectors. For the purpose of aligning paraphrases, we assumed that a cosine value of 1 is unwanted since a paraphrase is defined by being syntactically different at the same time as being semantically equivalent.

$$cos(A, B) = \frac{A \cdot B}{||A|| \cdot ||B||} \tag{3}$$

The **Dice coefficient**, Equation 4, is defined as the product of 2 times the number of features in common by the sum of the length of RS and the length of ES. For M1, using lemmatised lower case words as features and for M2 by also including the part-of-speech tags as features. This value ranges from 0 to 1 and represents the similarity of two segments, where a value closer to 1 means a higher similarity between the segments. As for the cosine similarity measure, we assumed that a Dice value of 1 is undesirable for this specific paraphrasing task.

$$Dice(A, B) = \frac{2\,|A \cap B|}{|A| + |B|} \tag{4}$$

3.4   Crowdsourcing Evaluation

In this study, crowdsourcing was used to assess the two methods.The aligned items used for evaluation were chosen by only considering the RS that were paired with at least one ES at every cosine value (0.40, 0.50, 0.60, 0.70, 0.80), rounded to 2 decimals. When multiple sentences with the same cosine value were encountered, one was randomly chosen. The aim of this heuristic was to be able to better assess the cosine threshold values.

Typically, the recruitment process is managed by an employer, such as Amazon's Mechanical Turk. Since our evaluation task treated texts in Swedish, we constructed our own platform to host the tasks and collect the annotated data. For this project, the recruitment was made by public postings on Facebook and e-mails to current graduate students at a Swedish University. The recruitment post stated the aim of the tasks and contained a link to our web page. The web page presented the RS randomly to annotators followed by the (randomly ordered) aligned ES. Similarity judgements were made by rating the pair on a scale 0-4, corresponding to the following categories, as proposed in the Cross-Level Semantic Similarity Task of Semeval 2014 (Nakov and Zesch, 2014):

4. *The two items have very similar meanings and the most important ideas, concepts, or actions in the larger text are represented in the smaller text.*

3. *The two items share many of the same important ideas, concepts, or actions, but those expressed in the smaller text are similar but not identical to the most important in the larger text.*

2. *The two items have dissimilar meaning, but the shared concepts, ideas, and actions in the smaller text are related (but not similar) to those of the large text.*

1. *The two items describe dissimilar concepts, ideas and actions, but might be likely to be found together in a longer document on the same topic.*

0. *The two items do not mean the same thing and are not on the same topic.*

All categories were translated into Swedish. Even though Antoine et al. (2014) presented results that favour choosing 3 ordinal categories over 5, we believe that the nuances introduced by letting the crowdworkers annotate 5 categories will result in a richer understanding on how to choose the threshold value. The participants were not trained for the task, i.e. no example task was shown prior to the test. Studies have shown that training can render more precise results for individual workers (Le et al., 2010). As we had no experience on how the ranked categories relate to paraphrases, we chose to omit a training phase for the crowdworkers. There was no time restriction for the individual tasks, nor for the crowdsourcing test as a whole. When every aligned text item had been judged, the annotator was able to proceed. This process was repeated until reaching an end, where all aligned items had been given a ranking, or until leaving the annotation web page by choice.

4 Results

In this section, the preliminary results describing the performance of the alignment algorithm are presented and compared. As presented in Table 1, M2 resulted in higher arithmetic mean value for cosine as well as for Dice. The method produced 18,115 more aligned groups than did M1. As a result of more aligned groups, M2 contained about eight million more aligned text segments than M1. As for n-gram overlap, M1 had higher unigram overlap (0.31) than M2 (0.18), indicating that for M1, the ES is more alike the RS only considering the words, than of M2. The alignment clusters for both M1 and M2 were normally distributed with less occurrences towards the extreme values, both for cosine and Dice.

	M1	M2
Arithmetic mean Dice	0.47	0.50
Arithmetic mean cosine	0.49	0.50
Std deviation, Dice	0.13	0.13
Std deviation, cosine	0.09	0.10
Total number of aligned cluster	113,993	132,108
Total number of aligned text segments	9,294,015	17,422,338
Unigram overlap	0.31	0.18
Bigram overlap	0.05	0.04
Trigram overlap	0.01	0.01
Quadrigram overlap	0.0	0.00

Table 1: Comparison of M1 and M2 regarding descriptive features.

4.1 Alignment without context (M1)

This section presents results containing the shallow features measured for both sides of the alignment of the replicated method originally presented by Sanchez-Perez et al. (2014).

M1	SUC	LäSBarT	RS_{total}	ES_{total}	RS_{subset}	ES_{subset}
Tot. no of tokens	1,048,657	1,142,666	5,378,071	344,951,473	181	1,308
% of long words	26.55	18.03	0.09	0.14	0.05	0.02
No. of unique tokens	106,853	49,776	17,362	26,889	30	179
LIX	41.97	27.46	18.4	24.22	-*	-*
OVIX	90.9	68.83	49.22	50.04	31.93	29.33
No. of sentences	68,038	121,212	617,167	33,247,883	19	95
Avg. sentence length	15.41	9.43	10.37	8.71	6.20	6.77
Avg. word length	5.21	4.58	4.10	3.93	3.9	3.33
M2						
Tot. no of tokens	1,048,657	1,142,666	2,455,941	419,768,883	252	1,377
% of long words	26.55	18.03	0.09	0.15	0.007	0.05
No. of unique tokens	106,853	49,776	15,369	21,871	50	221
LIX	41.97	27.46	24.93	16.67	-*	-*
OVIX	90.9	68.83	49.66	49.23	21.55	32.03
No. of sentences	68,038	121,212	314,399	41,658,621	25	125
Avg. sentence length	15.40	9.43	7.80	10.07	4.30	6.25
Avg. word length	5.21	4.58	3.50	3.88	3.30	3.80

* LIX is only applicable for documents rather than unique sentences

Table 2: Feature values of corpora, alignments and subsets for M1 and M2.

In Table 2, the shallow features of the original corpora are presented, as well as the corresponding values of the aligned total (RS_{total} and ES_{total}), and the subset later evaluated by crowdsourcing (RS_{subset}

and ES$_{subset}$). The readability metric, LIX, features a lower value for the RS as well as for the ES. The OVIX value for the RS compared to SUC is lower, as well as the OVIX value for the ES, when compared to LäSBarT.

The greater number of tokens and sentences is due to the fact that the total number of sentences contains multiple copies as a result of segments which are considered candidates in different alignment setups. The average sentence length and the average word length comparing the three; full corpora, aligned total and evaluated subset, show a converging tendency for RS and ES with respect to the readability metrics as well as for the length features.

4.2 Alignment with context (M2)

The descriptive results for M2 are found in the second section of Table 2, as well as the shallow features of the full original corpora, the aligned total (RS$_{total}$ and ES$_{total}$), and the evaluated subset (RS$_{subset}$ and ES$_{subset}$). Both readability metrics for RS are lower than for the corresponding original corpus. For LIX, this also applies for ES and LäSBarT. This converging tendency is also noticeable for M2, where the RS segments might be the most easy-to-read segments in the original corpora, and vice versa for ES. As with M1, M2 resulted in an occurrence distribution similar to M1, where a lesser frequency of aligned pairs is present, as a result of an extreme value.

4.3 Evaluation

Rank	RS	ES	Cosine	Dice	Method
0	Jag vet inte, sa jag.	Jo, jag vet.	0.50	0.57	M1
	I don't know, I said	*Yes, I know.*			
1	Ja, det är du, säger Oscar.	– Ja, det säger alla!	0.60	0.60	M1
	Yes, you are, says Oscar.	*– Yes, everybody says that!*			
2	Vad är det med dig?	– Vad är det som har hänt?	0.40	0.43	M1
	What's up with you?	*– What has happened?*			
3	Vad är det?	–Vad skulle det vara?	0.80	0.86	M1
	What is it?	*– What would that be?*			
4	Jag vet inte, sa jag.	Jag vet inte.	0.70	0.55	M1
	I don't know, I said.	*I don't know.*			
0	Majsan rycker på axlarna.	Tanne ryckte tag i henne.	0.40	0.36	M2
	Majsan shrugs.	*Tanne grabbed her.*			
1	Vad menar du?	Vad hade han gjort dig?	0.60	0.60	M2
	What do you mean?	*What did he do to you?*			
2	undrar jag.	undrade hon	0.80	0.67	M2
	I wonder	*she wondered*			
3	Varför då?	Jaså, varför det?	0.50	0.44	M2
	Why?	*Oh, really? Why?*			
4	Det visste jag.	Jag visste det, fan jag visste det.	0.80	0.80	M2
	I knew that.	*I knew it, damn, i knew it.*			

Table 3: Examples sentences per rank category for sentences aligned by M1 and M2.

The heuristic rendered 220 aligned items to evaluate by crowdsourcing, each containing one RS and one ES from each cosine value. 95 of the aligned items were from M1 and the remaining 125 were from M2. Table 3 presents some examples from the alignment clusters which have been evaluated for each method. The alignments are presented with a typical rank that annotators have been giving them. The examples illustrate how the aligned sentences are loosely coupled by the words present in the sentences. The preliminary results of the mapping of cosine similarity and participant ranking is presented in Figure 1, with cosine values divided into intervals. There is a tendency of M2 scoring consistently higher than M1.

The preliminary results of the mapping of Dice similarity and participant ranking is presented in Figure 2, with Dice values divided into intervals. The results of the first and last intervals clearly differ from the remaining intervals due to skewed data, and can in this context be considered outliers. From interval 0.31–0.40 to interval 0.71–0.80, the Dice similarity seems to stabilise for values over 0.5. These prelim-

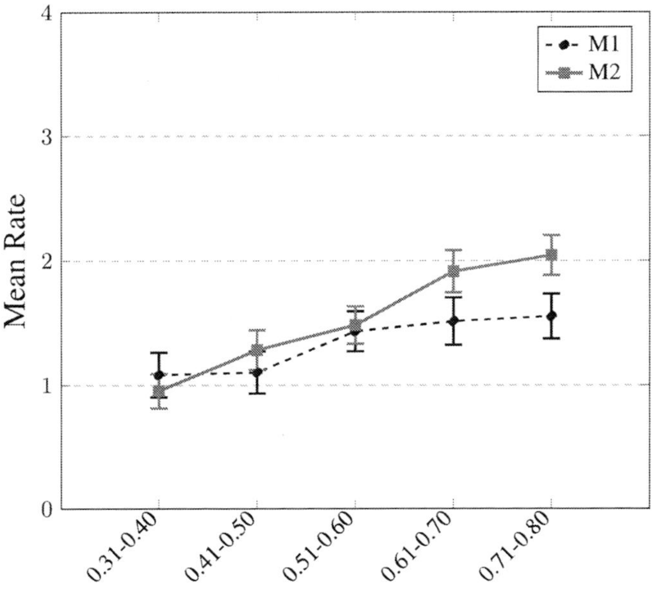

Figure 1: Mean rate for M1 and M2 over different cosine intervals

†

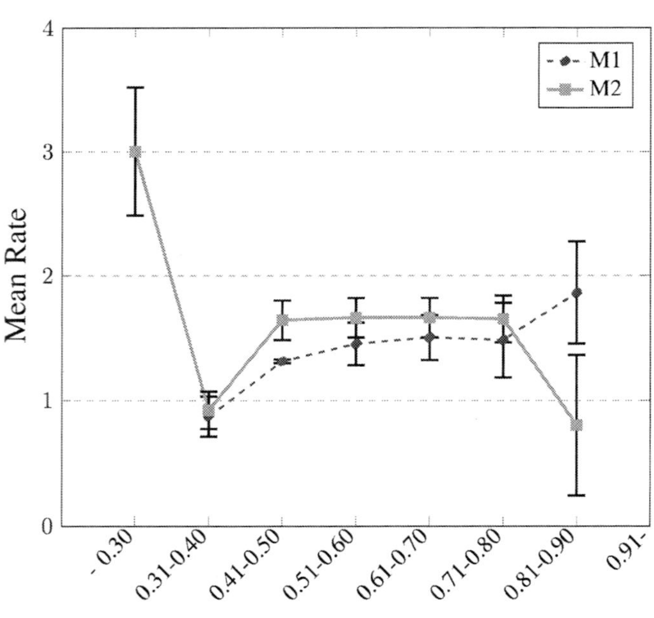

Figure 2: Mean rate for M1 and M2 over different Dice intervals

inary results propose that M2 provides a more stable relationship between the human ranked categories and the similarity measures.

5 Discussion

As the sentences in Table 3 imply, the easy-to-read segments seem syntactically alike and faithful to the reference segments on a word level. This is not always desirable for the task of extracting paraphrases. Extracting paraphrases that are dissimilar by their word usage, but semantically equivalent, enables us to achieve data that better fit the definition of paraphrases. This will be addressed in future work.

As seen in Figues 1 and 2, M2 seems to relate better to human ranking than M1. We will further explore this in a more thorough statistical analysis of a larger amount of data when available.

It is still not clear whether or not there is a limit as to how large either side of the segment should be, i.e. that a larger chunk of ES could be aligned with a smaller chunk of RS, or vice versa. The algorithm allows the aligned chunks to be expanded beyond sentence boundaries, meaning that the lengths of the resulting segments are only limited by the length of the entire document.

We presented the relationships between the annotated rankings and the cosine and Dice groups. These show trends which we believe can be used to accept a cosine higher than 0.33 as the threshold for deciding which segments to treat as candidate paraphrases.

In designing our annotator task, we chose to let annotators be new to the tasks in the sense that the crowdworkers had no intuition about how we would rate a pair of text segments. Thus, they were not primed to any systematic approach for solving the tasks, contrary to previous studies (Le et al., 2010). This has probable explanation effects on the variance in the annotated data and the possible disagreement the annotators seem to display. But it is possible that these results are only preliminary and that the gathering of more data would result in higher agreement across the categories. It would be interesting to study the alignments that people had more difficulty to agree upon, since that analysis itself could have an effect on the way we understand features of readability in text or intra class differences in peoples' ability to read and understand text segments. It might prove to be necessary to divide crowdworkers into groups based on some training task, measuring reading ability. For a language such as Swedish, there is no available platform to invite human annotators, nor is it possible to give crowdworkers any payment. There are multiple ways in which NLP can be helped by the work of human annotators, and we perceive this as an opportunity to develop and distribute a platform that could be used as portal for NLP scientists for collecting data based on peoples language skills.

6 Conclusions and future work

Data collection is ongoing, but preliminary conclusions of this study are that 1) the Dice coefficient does not seem to correspond well with human ranking, 2) the method with part-of-speech tags included (M2) provides a more stable relationship between the human ranked categories and the similarity measures and, 3) the framework developed for this study proved to be an effective tool for collecting data when crowdsourcing human rankings for a NLP task.

In this study we assumed that the corpus data would entail that the ES was easy-to-read based on the typology of the data. Future work will try to validate the readability of the aligned ES to assure that an ES is easier than its corresponding RS. At the time of writing, the data collection is ongoing, and final results from the evaluation, including a thorough statistical analysis, will be presented in future work. From the evaluation, a cosine threshold value will be estimated. The final goal is an aligned monolingual corpus, from which it is possible to deduce patterns and operations for the purpose of automatic text simplification.

Acknowledgements

This research was financed by VINNOVA, Sweden's innovation agency, and The Knowledge Foundation in Sweden.

References

Jean-Yves Antoine, Jeanne Villaneau, and Anaïs Lefeuvre. 2014. Weighted krippendorff's alpha is a more reliable metrics for multi-coders ordinal annotations: experimental studies on emotion, opinion and coreference annotation.

Regina Barzilay and Noemie Elhadad. 2003. Sentence Alignment for Monolingual Comparable Corpora. *Proceedings of the 2003 Conference on Empirical Methods in Natural Language Processing*, pages 25–32.

Carl Hugo Björnsson. 1968. *Läsbarhet[Readability]*. Liber, Stockholm.

Stefan Bott and Horacio Saggion. 2011. An unsupervised alignment algorithm for text simplification corpus construction. In *Proceedings of the Workshop on Monolingual Text-To-Text Generation*, MTTG '11, pages 20–26, Stroudsburg, PA, USA. Association for Computational Linguistics.

Chris Callison-burch, Philipp Koehn, and Miles Osborne. 2006. Improved Statistical Machine Translation Using Paraphrases. *Proceeding HLT-NAACL '06 Proceedings of the main conference on Human Language Technology Conference of the North American Chapter of the Association of Computational Linguistics*, pages 17–24.

John Carroll, Guido Minnen, Yvonne Canning, Siobhan Devlin, and John Tait. 1998. Practical simplification of English newspaper text to assist aphasic readers. In *Proceedings of the AAAI98 Workshop on Integrating Artificial Intelligence and Assistive Technology*, volume 1, pages 7–10. Citeseer.

Raman Chandrasekar and Bangalore Srinivas. 1997. Automatic Induction of Rules for Text Simplification. *Knowledge-Based Systems*, 10(3):183–190.

William Coster and David Kauchak. 2011. Simple English Wikipedia: A New Text Simplification Task. *Proceedings of the 49th Annual Meeting of the Association for Computational Linguistics: Human Language Technologies*, pages 665–669.

Bill Dolan, Chris Quirk, and Chris Brockett. 2004. Unsupervised Construction of Large Paraphrase Corpora: Exploiting Massively Parallel News Sources. *Proceedings of the 20th International Conference on Computational Linguistics (COLING '04)*, page Article No. 350.

Johan Falkenjack, Katarina Heimann Mühlenbock, and Arne Jönsson. 2013. Features indicating readability in Swedish text. In *Proceedings of the 19th Nordic Conference of Computational Linguistics (NoDaLiDa-2013), Oslo, Norway*, NEALT Proceedings Series 16.

Lijun Feng. 2010. *Automatic Readability Assessment*. Ph.D. thesis, City University of New York.

Amir Hazem and Emmanuel Morin. 2016. Improving bilingual terminology extraction from comparable corpora via multiple word-space models. In Nicoletta Calzolari (Conference Chair), Khalid Choukri, Thierry Declerck, Sara Goggi, Marko Grobelnik, Bente Maegaard, Joseph Mariani, Helene Mazo, Asuncion Moreno, Jan Odijk, and Stelios Piperidis, editors, *Proceedings of the Tenth International Conference on Language Resources and Evaluation (LREC 2016)*, Paris, France, may. European Language Resources Association (ELRA).

Katarina Heimann Mühlenbock. 2013. *I see what you mean. Assessing readability for specific target groups.* Dissertation, Språkbanken, Dept of Swedish, University of Gothenburg.

Tor G. Hultman and Margareta Westman. 1977. *Gymnasistsvenska*. LiberLäromedel, Lund.

Hongyan Jin. 2002. Using hidden markov modeling to decompose human-written summaries. *Computational Linguistics*, 28(4):527–543.

Gunnel Källgren, Sofia Gustafson-Capková, and Britt Hartmann. 2006. Manual of the stockholm umeå corpus version 2.0.

Sigrid Klerke and Anders Søgaard. 2012. Dsim, a danish parallel corpus for text simplification. In *Proceedings of the Eight International Conference on Language Resources and Evaluation (LREC'12),Istanbul, Turkey*. European Language Resources Association (ELRA).

Kevin Knight and Daniel Marcu. 2000. Statistics-Based Summarization - Step One: Sentence Compression. *AAAI-00 - 17th National Conference on Artificial Intelligence and 12th Conference on Innovative Applications of Artificial Intelligence*, pages 703–710.

John Le, Andy Edmonds, Vaughn Hester, and Lukas Biewald. 2010. Ensuring quality in crowdsourced search relevance evaluation: The effects of training question distribution. In *SIGIR 2010 workshop on crowdsourcing for search evaluation*, pages 21–26.

Katarina Mühlenbock and Sofie Johansson Kokkinakis. 2009. LIX 68 revisited - An extended readability measure. In Michaela Mahlberg, Victorina González-Díaz, and Catherine Smith, editors, *Proceedings of the Corpus Linguistics Conference CL2009*, Liverpool, UK, July 20-23.

Katarina Mühlenbock. 2008. Readable, Legible or Plain Words – Presentation of an easy-to-read Swedish corpus. In Anju Saxena and Åke Viberg, editors, *Multilingualism: Proceedings of the 23rd Scandinavian Conference of Linguistics*, volume 8 of *Acta Universitatis Upsaliensis*, pages 327–329, Uppsala, Sweden. Acta Universitatis Upsaliensis.

Preslav Nakov and Torsten Zesch, editors. 2014. *Proceedings of the 8th International Workshop on Semantic Evaluation (SemEval 2014)*.

Rani Nelken and Stuart M Shieber. 2006. Towards Robust Context-Sensitive Sentence Alignment for Monolingual Corpora. *Eacl*, pages 161–168.

Robert Östling. 2013. Stagger: An open-source part of speech tagger for swedish. *Northern European Journal of Language Technology (NEJLT)*, 3:1–18.

Emily Pitler and Ani Nenkova. 2008. Revisiting Readability: A Unified Framework for Predicting Text Quality. In *Proceedings of the 2008 Conference on Empirical Methods in Natural Language Processing*, pages 186–195, Honolulu, HI, October.

Evelina Rennes and Arne Jönsson. 2015. A tool for automatic simplification of swedish texts,. In *Proceedings of the 20th Nordic Conference of Computational Linguistics (NoDaLiDa-2015), Vilnius, Lithuania,*.

Miguel A. Sanchez-Perez, Grigori Sidorov, and Alexander Gelbukh. 2014. The winning approach to text alignment for text reuse detection at PAN 2014: Notebook for PAN at CLEF 2014. *CEUR Workshop Proceedings*, 1180:1004–1011.

Rion Snow, Brendan O'Connor, Daniel Jurafsky, and Andrew Y. Ng. 2008. Cheap and fast—but is it good?: Evaluating non-expert annotations for natural language tasks. In *Proceedings of the Conference on Empirical Methods in Natural Language Processing*, EMNLP '08, pages 254–263, Stroudsburg, PA, USA. Association for Computational Linguistics.

Peter D Turney, Patrick Pantel, et al. 2010. From frequency to meaning: Vector space models of semantics. *Journal of artificial intelligence research*, 37(1):141–188.

Zhemin Zhu, Delphine Bernhard, and Iryna Gurevych. 2010. A Monolingual Tree-based Translation Model for Sentence Simplification. *23rd International Conference on Computational Linguistics*, (August):1353–1361.

Automatic Construction of Large Readability Corpora

Jorge Alberto Wagner Filho, Rodrigo Wilkens and Aline Villavicencio
Institute of Informatics, Federal University of Rio Grande do Sul
Av. Bento Gonçalves, 9500, 91501-970, Porto Alegre, RS, Brazil
`{jawfilho,rodrigo.wilkens,avillavicencio}@inf.ufrgs.br`

Abstract

This work presents a framework for the automatic construction of large Web corpora classified by readability level. We compare different Machine Learning classifiers for the task of readability assessment focusing on Portuguese and English texts, analysing the impact of variables like the feature inventory used in the resulting corpus. In a comparison between shallow and deeper features, the former already produce F-measures of over 0.75 for Portuguese texts, but the use of additional features results in even better results, in most cases. For English, shallow features also perform well as do classic readability formulas. Comparing different classifiers for the task, logistic regression obtained, in general, the best results, but with considerable differences between the results for two and those for three-classes, especially regarding the intermediary class. Given the large scale of the resulting corpus, for evaluation we adopt the agreement between different classifiers as an indication of readability assessment certainty. As a result of this work, a large corpus for Brazilian Portuguese was built[1], including 1.7 million documents and about 1.6 billion tokens, already parsed and annotated with 134 different textual attributes, along with the agreement among the various classifiers.

1 Introduction

Text readability assessment refers to measuring how easy it is for a reader to read and understand a given text. In this context methods for automatic readability assessment have received considerable attention from the research community (DuBay, 2004). The task of attributing a readability level to a text has a wide range of applications, including support for student reading material selection (Petersen and Ostendorf, 2009) or help for clinical patients (Feng et al., 2009). It can also be used for ensuring that instructions and policies are written in an easily comprehensible way even for readers with low education (McClure, 1987). It can also contribute to the task of text simplification, evaluating the obtained version to indicate if further simplification is needed (Aluisio et al., 2010). Recently, authors such as Petersen and Ostendorf (2009), Vajjala and Meurers (2014) and Scarton et al. (2010) have started treating this task as one of text classification, using corpora manually annotated with readability classifications to train automatic learning models, based on a large set of text metrics, including deeper features, for example derived from n-gram language models and parse trees. However, an important limitation to this approach is the small availability of reliably annotated train data. Moreover, this task is known to be very subjective, and even human annotators present a high disagreement rate in their evaluations (Petersen and Ostendorf, 2009).

In this work, we aim to develop large corpora classified by readability levels. To achieve this objective we present a study of different Machine Learning approaches to the task of readability assessment of texts, focusing on Portuguese, and apply the relatively recent concept of building corpora from the Web (Bernardini et al., 2006) to automatically generate large corpora classified by readability levels. For that, we follow the framework proposed by Wagner Filho et al. (2016), where a readability classifier

---

Proceedings of the Workshop on Computational Linguistics for Linguistic Complexity,
pages 164–173, Osaka, Japan, December 11-17 2016.

was incorporated into a crawler, but changing the classifier position in the pipeline so that we can work with both low and high-cost complexity features. We also experiment with learning models trained on several different reference corpora, in both Portuguese and English, and investigate the relevance of the agreement between them.

We focus our study on two hypothesis: (H1) a learning model trained in a reference annotated corpus is able to classify a new corpus so that its classes present significant linguistic differences and (H2) the use of syntactic attributes contributes to a better classification. As a result of this work, a new Portuguese corpus of around 1.6 billion tokens was built and annotated with four different readability classifiers. This paper is structured as follows. In Section 2, we discuss some relevant work in the literature and, in Section 3, we present our materials and methods, especially our training data, features and classification algorithms and our Web corpus collection framework. In Section 4, we apply our methodology and validate our hypothesis trough a series of experiments. Finally, in Section 5 we present our conclusions and ideas for future work.

2   Related Work

Some traditional works in readability classification include, for example, Flesch and others (1946), Dale and Chall (1948), Gunning (1952), which were based in shallow textual measures. A very known example, the Flesch Reading Ease index (Flesch and others, 1946), uses the number of syllables per word and words per sentence to determine lexical and syntactic complexity. For Portuguese, Martins et al. (1996) adapted the Flesch Reading Ease index to account for language differences, and Érica Sapgnolo and Finatto (2014) analysed Brazilian news texts to generate lists of simple words.

The classical readability measures have been criticized for applying a superficial analysis of textual characteristics, ignoring, for example, that larger sentences may be clearer and more explicative than a smaller equivalent (Williams, 2004). These formulas are not able to capture several elements of cohesion and textual difficulty, according to McNamara et al. (2002), who also point that these tools force editors to modify the text to increase the calculated readability, but actually reducing cohesion. Recent studies tried to apply automatic approaches that better approximate the complexity of a text, for example using n-gram language models to identify reading ease. Petersen and Ostendorf (2009) trained Support Vector Machines using a corpus created from an educational newspaper, Weekly Reader, with different versions for four different grade levels, completed with articles for adults from the Associated Press. They worked with lexical and syntactic features and also with traditional formulas. Investigating the contribution of syntactic features, it was observed that they were not good enough separately, but contributed to the general performance. Complementarily, Vajjala and Meurers (2014) applied 152 lexical and syntactic attributes to classify a corpus of subtitles from different BBC channels for children and adults, also using SVMs. The most predictive attribute was shown to be the age of acquisition. Similar approaches were applied in multiple other languages, including Italian (Dell'Orletta et al., 2011), German (Hancke et al., 2012) and Basque (Gonzalez-Dios et al., 2014). In Portuguese, Scarton and Aluísio (2010) classified articles for children and adults from local newspapers, using a SVM trained on 48 psycholinguistic features and obtaining an F-measure of 0.944.

Wagner Filho et al. (2016) proposed a framework to take advantage of the increasing availability of language content in the Web to create large repositories of text suitable for different reading levels, incorporating a readability classifier to a pipeline similar to the one used by Baroni et al. (2009) to build a series of large Web corpora, such as the ukWaC (Baroni et al., 2009), composed by 1.91 billion tokens and 3.8 million types. This pipeline is composed by four steps: (1) identification of an appropriate set of seed URLs, (2) post crawling cleaning, (3) detection and removal of near duplicate content and (4) annotation. Considering the large corpora size made possible by these approaches and the current limitations in readability assessment, in this paper, we build on these works, experimenting with different training corpora in both English and Portuguese, and applying the resultant learning models to a large collection of documents obtained from the Web.

3 Materials and Methods

In this section, we describe the series of resources and the methodology that were applied to achieve our objective of developing large corpora classified by readability levels. Sections 3.1, 3.2 and 3.3 present, respectively, our corpora, classification models and readability features, while Section 3.4 presents the proposed Web corpora collection framework.

3.1 Corpora

We selected a series of corpora (described in Table 1) to represent different levels of readability. Aiming to avoid language specific readability issues, we explored corpora for both Portuguese (Wikilivros, ESOC, PSFL, ZH, BrEscola) and English (Wikibooks, SW, BB). *Wikilivros* (Elementary School, High School and College levels) was constructed in Wagner Filho et al. (2016). The É Só o Começo (ESOC) corpus contrasts classic literature works in Portuguese with adapted versions for modern language use. *Para o Seu Filho Ler (PSFL)* e *Zero Hora (ZH)*, corpora of news articles, were constructed by Aluisio et al. (2010), the former comparing articles for children with articles for adults, and the latter comparing original articles for adults with two different levels of simplification (natural and strong). *Brasil Escola* (BrEscola), a corpus of educational materials for children and teenagers, *Wikibooks*, a corpus of virtual books for readers of different proficiency levels (Beginner, Intermediary, Advanced and Professional), and *Britannica Biographies* (BB), a corpus of biographies with versions in three different readability levels (Elementary, Medium and High), were collected especially for this study, crawling different sections of the websites of the same names[2]. The *Simple Wikipedia* (SW) corpus was compiled by Coster and Kauchak (2011), pairing articles from the English and Simple English versions of Wikipedia[3].

In the case of the corpora Wikilivros, ZH, Wikibooks and BB, which consider more than two readability levels, tests were also done with adapted binary versions, in order to verify the impact of the number of classes in the classifier performance. For that, in Wikilivros and BB, the most simple and most difficult levels were selected. In ZH, we used the original and the natural simplification class, since the strong simplification was exaggerated for our classification purposes, and, in Wikibooks, we discarded the Beginner class, which was too small, and grouped the Advanced and Professional classes.

Language	Corpus	Classes	Documents	Sentences	Types	Tokens
PT	Wikilivros	3	78	38,865	54,462	636,309
	ESOC	2	130	21,667	32,180	442,391
	PSFL	2	259	3,075	8,628	51,963
	ZH	3	279	7,127	8,511	107,930
	BrEscola	2	9,083	200,132	95,928	3,516,097
EN	Wikibooks	4	35	65,704	24,638	897,971
	SW	2	4,480	515,230	183,824	10,384,518
	BB	3	2,385	101,149	45,687	1,747,733

Table 1: Description of the readability corpora

3.2 Classification models

We worked with the Weka Machine Learning tool (Hall et al., 2009) for generating classification models, especially with its implementations SMO, from the Sequential Minimal Optimization algorithm for SVM training (Platt, 1998), SimpleLogistic, for construction of linear logistic regression models (Landwehr et al., 2005), DecisionStump, for the one level decision tree (Iba and Langley, 1992), and RandomForest, for construction of a forest of decision trees (Breiman, 2001). All models performances were evaluated using F-measure and 10 fold cross-validation. These models represent a variety of approaches to text classification, and also allow us to evaluate any possible algorithm bias in the task.

---

[2]http://brasilescola.uol.com.br, https://en.wikibooks.org and http://school.eb.com

[3]We used here only articles that presented more than 30 sentences in both versions.

3.3 Readability features

Given our intention of assessing the contribution of different categories of language features, a large set of 134 different language attributes for Portuguese and 89 for English was selected. From basic counts, we worked with numbers of sentences, words, syllables, letters and types. We also calculated the average number of words per sentence (WPS), syllables per word (SPW) and the Type-Token Ratio, a measure of lexical diversity. The average and standard deviation of letters per word (AWL) were also used, based on the hypothesis that more complex texts are more prone to present larger words, given the more frequent presence of prefixes and suffixes, which aggregate new meaning to words.

From classical readability metrics, we used the Flesch Reading Ease (English and Portuguese versions) (Flesch and others, 1946; Martins et al., 1996), the Coleman-Liau Index (Coleman and Liau, 1975), the Flesch Grade Level, the Automated Readability Index (Senter and Smith, 1967), Fog (Gunning, 1952), SMOG (Mc Laughlin, 1969) and, for English, the Dale-Chall Formula (Dale and Chall, 1948) as well.[4]

In order to account for word ambiguity, a metric based on the hypothesis that more commonly used words, and therefore easier to understand (Vajjala and Meurers, 2014), tend to present multiple meanings in a language, we used the average number of senses from BabelNet (Navigli and Ponzetto, 2010), for Portuguese, and WordNet (Miller, 1995), for English. Moreover, following Si and Callan (2001), we worked with the average frequency in a general corpus (AFGC) and standard deviation as frequency measures, based on the hypothesis that words with higher frequencies in a general corpus tend to be more knownand, therefore, included in more levels of texts, while rarer words are more inclined to be restricted to more complex levels.

We also worked with a series of closed word lists to count word classes (*stopwords*, prepositions, articles, pronouns, personal and possessive pronouns (*PP*), conjunctions and functional words), particles (*"e"*, *"ou"* and *"se"*, in Portuguese, and their respective equivalents in English *"and"*, *"or"* and *"if"*) (McNamara et al., 2002) and simple words. For this last category, we used the lists DG and CB[5], DG+CB, CHILDES (MacWhinney, 2000) and the concatenation of all, in Portuguese. In English, we used the lists Oxford 3000, Dale-Chall (Dale and Chall, 1948), CHILDES (MacWhinney, 2000) and once again the concatenation of all of them. Simple word lists are a traditional resource in text difficulty assessment, having been notably used by Dale and Chall (1948) and also by Petersen and Ostendorf (2009), who used lists of frequent words in the lower class for a similar purpose. Finally, the incidence of unknown words (Unknown)[6] was used as a indicative of rarer, more complex vocabulary, possibly domain-specific.

Finally, we worked with counts based based in syntactic analysis, including part of speeches (18 for Portuguese and 20 for English) and dependency tags (72 for Portuguese and 27 for English), besides 7 measures of verb analysis, including verb transitivity, passive voice, average number of modifiers and average sub-categorization frame length. In Portuguese, we also analysed the incidence of verbs in the imperative mood. All these counts are frequently used as indicators of syntactic complexity, according to the online tool Coh-Metrix (McNamara et al., 2002). The parsers Palavras (Bick, 2000) and Rasp (Briscoe et al., 2006) were used to obtain these features for Portuguese and English, respectively.

Since we want to assess the contribution of different feature categories, a few specific groups were defined. The selected groups were: *sub-categorization* (transitivity, average number of modifiers, average sub-categorization frame length), classical *readability* formulas, *descriptors* (counts of sentences, words, syllables, letters and types and TTR) and *corpora-based* (incidence of unknown words, average frequency in a general corpus, lists of simple words). Moreover, we also divided our complete feature sets in three categories according to their computational costs: *shallow* (counts and lists), *medium* (part-of-speech tagging dependent) and *deep* (parsing or WordNet dependent).

---

[4]For the different versions of the Flesch formulas we computed the number of syllables in a word using, for English, an approximation based on the number of vowels and, for Portuguese, a rule-based syllabification tool (Neto et al., 2015).

[5]Available at `http://www.ufrgs.br/textecc/porlexbras/porpopular/massafiles/Lista_FINAL_MASSA.pdf` (Érica Sapgnolo and Finatto, 2014)

[6]We consider unknown words all words not present in a list (3 million words for Portuguese and 840 thousand for English).

3.4 Web corpora collection framework

In order to build a large corpus from Web content, we followed the pipeline approach from Bernardini et al. (2006), incorporating a readability classifier as in Wagner Filho et al. (2016). We followed the approach from Boos et al. (2014), submitting pairs of words with medium frequency in a general corpus to a search engine API, and obtaining the ten first results for each query. These results were then expanded collecting all the links contained in them as well. For the collection, cleaning and near duplicate content removal phases, we used the implementation provided by Ziai and Ott (2005), with some adaptations, such as the adoption of a more efficient text cleaning tool, *jusText* (Pomikálek, 2013). The Palavras (Bick, 2000) parser was used to enrich the corpus with syntactic annotation.

4 Experiments

In this section we present a comparison of different features categories (Section 4.1); evaluation of classification models (Section 4.2); and assess the generalisation of these models (Section 4.3). Finally, in Section 4.4, we create an large corpus of Web content, which we classify with our models in Section 4.5.

4.1 Feature analysis

In order to determine the most relevant features and also observe the effect of varying the training data used in our models, we worked with the entropy-based algorithm information gain[7]. We used the feature groups (defined in Section 3.3) to perform a more detailed evaluation, based in the average rank of the features when ordered decreasingly according to information gain. The results are presented in Table 2 , which corroborated to our previous observation that classical formulas have a great relevance in English but not in Portuguese, while textual descriptors presented a good classificatory power in both languages. Another noticeable pattern was that in both languages shallow features outperformed deep ones.

It was observed that most of the training corpora, in both studied languages, exhibited a large quantity of shallow attributes (e.g. basic counts) and readability formulas amongst the most predictive. Shallow attributes are indeed known to be good indicators, being this the reason for the creation of the classical formulas. However, this was especially observed in the corpora built trough manual simplification of text content (ESCO, PSFL, ZH, SW and BB), what supports McNamara et al. (2002) claims of the excessive influence of these metrics in authors of simple texts. Another possible interpretation, contrasting English and Portuguese corpora, is that the classical formulas, having been created focusing on the former, are good classifiers for it, but in Portuguese present a poorer performance. A noticeable exception to this behaviour was the pair of corpora Wikilivros and Wikibooks, which did not present almost any shallow metric amongst the twenty more relevant. This may be attributed to the collaborative approach adopted by the websites which gave origin to these corpora, resulting in a classification produced by regular users, who may consider other factors besides the language complexity in their assessments, such as the nature of the content. The great relevance of simple word lists in classifying Wikibooks also indicates the attention of users to the vocabulary. Therefore, the use of these corpora to train readability classifiers may lead to over-fitting on not necessarily relevant textual characteristics. Another factor to be considered in these corpora is that they present closer classes with fuzzy borders (more advanced High School texts and simpler College texts, for example, may be very similar), what may indicate that deep attributes are relevant to a more accurate classification.

4.2 Model performance analysis

We trained classifiers (discussed in Section 3.2), and the linear logistic regression algorithm, SimpleLogistic, presented, overall, the best results for both languages, possibly due to its built-in feature selection (Table 3 presents the F-measures for this algorithm[8]). The DecisionStump algorithm, which constructs a one-level decision tree with the most significant feature, offered an interesting baseline, achieving good results in some corpora, but not necessarily generalisable. The algorithms RandomForest, which constructs a forest of complete decision trees, and SMO, also achieved good results. As expected, the

---

[7]We used the InfoGainAttributeEval implementation available in the Weka toolkit.

[8]For reasons of space, we omit the results for the remaining ones.

	Wikil.	PSFL	ZH	BrEsc	ESOC	Avg Pt	Wikib.	SW	BB	Avg En
Shallow	49,98	39,68	41,91	43,01	43,99	43,71	25,53	33,21	32,23	30,32
Medium	24,51	54,90	28,43	40,03	71,17	43,80	73,41	55,84	53,67	60,97
Deep	83,58	82,17	86,36	83,61	77,11	82,56	50,41	51,55	53,68	51,88
Subcat.	46,53	84,00	29,60	82,90	38,62	56,33	26,18	64,45	62,45	51,03
Formulas	48,03	21,88	6,83	65,22	88,12	46,01	30,40	7,03	5,50	14,31
Descrip.	63,12	3,53	32,92	25,52	8,12	26,64	39,92	11,42	17,28	22,87
C. based	49,73	54,06	60,01	40,30	29,29	46,67	21,91	51,76	50,30	41,32

Table 2: Average rank of feature classes in the different training corpora (smaller values indicate a bigger relevance to a given class)

intermediary classes were always the most difficult to classify correctly, but still presented reasonable performance. Comparing the tests with the two versions of the ZH corpus, a great negative impact in performance was observed when considering three classes. Comparing shallow and deep attributes, we observed that the former tend to present a good classificatory power with a low computational cost but, in five out of eight scenarios, the performance was enhanced with the combination of both categories, confirming the results of François and Miltsakaki (2012) that shallow attributes are great indicators of readability while the combination with deeper attributes is positive, and also our hypothesis H2.

Lang.	Corpus	All	Shallow	Medium	Deep	Formulas	Descriptors
PT	Wikilivros	*0.71 (0.24)*	**0.75 (0.15)**	*0.67 (0.24)*	*0.69 (0.23)*	*0.59 (0.23)*	*0.59 (0.26)*
	ESOC	*0.98 (0.03)*	**0.99 (0.02)**	*0.96 (0.03)*	*0.98 (0.03)*	*0.69 (0.10)*	*0.90 (0.07)*
	PSFL	**0.99 (0.01)**	*0.98 (0.01)*	*0.81 (0.10)*	**0.99 (0.01)**	*0.80 (0.09)*	*0.98 (0.01)*
	ZH$_{2\ levels}$	**0.89 (0.08)**	*0.82 (0.13)*	*0.82 (0.06)*	*0.83 (0.04)*	*0.80 (0.10)*	*0.83 (0.12)*
	ZH$_{3\ levels}$	**0.63 (0.04)**	*0.55 (0.04)*	*0.56 (0.08)*	*0.53 (0.07)*	*0.58 (0.11)*	*0.61 (0.08)*
	BrEscola	**0.81 (0.01)**	*0.77 (0.01)*	*0.65 (0.02)*	*0.67 (0.01)*	*0.66 (0.03)*	*0.67 (0.03)*
EN	Wikibooks	*0.48 (0.25)*	*0.51 (0.26)*	*0.54 (0.33)*	*0.49 (0.15)*	**0.75 (0.24)**	*0.49 (0.28)*
	SW	**0.92 (0.01)**	*0.91 (0.01)*	*0.82 (0.02)*	*0.88 (0.01)*	*0.88 (0.01)*	*0.89 (0.01)*
	BB	**0.86 (0.02)**	*0.83 (0.03)*	*0.62 (0.02)*	*0.80 (0.02)*	*0.80 (0.02)*	*0.79 (0.02)*

Table 3: Average F-measures and standard deviations for the regression classifiers trained in different sets of features (best results are bold, and the italic if for not statistically different from best result)

4.3 Generalisation analysis

An important concern when training a classification model is how much this model will be able to be generalized beyond the training data. This is especially relevant in this context, where the training data are, by definition, very limited in volume, while the quantity of data we want to classify is very large. Initially, we analysed the compatibility between the different models. Using the lists of features ordered by information gain obtained in Section 4.1, we assessed the Spearman rank correlation between the different corpora. These results were very weak, indicating very little similarity between them. The closest corpora were Wikilivros and ZH, with a correlation of 0.62.

In a complementary analysis, we implemented projection tests, testing in a corpus a simple logistic model trained in another, in all possible combinations of our corpora in Portuguese[9]. For this tests, we worked with models trained in the binary versions of all corpora. The results indicted once again little agreement between the models, but were coherent with their individual characteristics. For example, classifiers trained in corpora with a higher complexity threshold between the classes (Wikilivros and ZH) classified most documents of corpora for children/teenagers (PSFL, BrEscola) as simple, and vice versa.

---

[9]We excluded the ESOC corpus, considering that this corpus presents language differences that are not resultant only from different complexity but also from differences between language use nowadays and the time of the original works.

The only exception for this behaviour was the projection of the model trained in BrEscola onto Wikilivros, which presented null performance in the upper level, opposed to the expected. Considering the weak agreement observed between the different models, we decided to employ the agreement between all of them in order to obtain a more generalisable classification (Enríquez et al., 2013).

4.4 Web corpus collection

Following the framework established in Section 3.4, we started with six thousand random pairs of average frequency words from a frequency list[10] obtained from several corpora from the Linguateca repository, after the removal of stopwords. These pairs were submitted to the Microsoft Bing API, and the resultant sixty thousand URLs were expanded by breadth first recursion in two levels, producing around twenty four million seeds of ".br" extension, as in Boos et al. (2014). These were then processed, resulting in corpus with 1.56 billion tokens, 4.15 million types (TTR 0.0026). All the documents were annotated with Palavras parser and the 134 different features described in Section 3.1.

4.5 Large corpus classification

In this section, we present the results of the classification of the collected Web corpus with the learning models trained in Section 4.2. We chose to apply here the models generated with the SimpleLogistic algorithm, since, besides having presented a better performance, they are easily implementable through a series of regression equations operating with the attribute values calculated by the last module of our pipeline. We work with the models trained in the whole set of attributes, and only those trained in two class scenarios, given the performance limitations observed in three class classifiers. The results are presented in Table 4, and as we already expected, considering the projection tests, the agreement between our models was small. Only 126,245 (7.5%) documents were classified as simple by all models, while only 17,634 (1%) were unanimously difficult. Discarding the BrEscola classifier, the remaining three agreed in 210,879 (12.5%) as simple and 149,279 (8.8%) as difficult[11]. This classifier presented an unexpected behaviour, since, considering its low complexity threshold (texts for children against texts for teenagers), we expected most documents to be classified as difficult. Moreover, it had already presented the poorest performance in the cross-validation tests in Section 4.2 and an unexpected behaviour in the projection tests in Section 4.3.

Model	Simple documents	Difficult documents
SimpleLogistic$_{PSFL}$	613,877 (36.4%)	1,076,173 (63.6%)
SimpleLogistic$_{ZH}$	448,199 (26.5%)	1,241,851 (73.5%)
SimpleLogistic$_{Wikilivros}$	1,413,211 (83.7%)	276,839 (16.3%)
SimpleLogistic$_{Brasil\ Escola}$	1,417,339 (83.9%)	272,711 (16.1%)

Table 4: Behaviour of the different classifiers in the collected Web corpus

Due to the size of the resulting corpus a qualitative analysis of the classification was done in terms of the behaviour of the different readability indicator features in the corpus classified with the different models presented in Table 4. Additionally we also analysed the agreement between all models. For that, all feature values were normalized to enable the comparison per feature category, as seen in Table 5. We also show the differences observed in the PSFL training data, for reference purposes. This corpus was selected due to its performance in the cross-validation tests, and because produced the most balanced document distribution. All classifiers resulted in significant differences between simple and complex documents in all categories of features (114 out of the 134 features presented statistically significant differences in all models with $p<0.01$, and 121 with $p<0.05$), confirming our hypothesis H1. It is important to note that, even though these indicators were part of our initial set of features, they were not necessarily the ones on which the model was trained, since only 10 features were selected by the simple

---

[10] http://dinis2.linguateca.pt/acesso/tokens/formas.totalbr.txt

[11] PSFL and ZH agreed in 245,431 (14%) documents as simple and 873,405 (52%) as difficult, while PSFL and Wikilivros agreed in 519,870 (31%) simple and 182,832 (11%) difficult and ZH and Wikilivros in 380,094 (22%) and 208,734 (12%).

logistic built-in feature selection. While in the individual models, the differences between the final classes were, more subtle than in the training data, considering the agreement between all classifiers, the observed differences were consistently larger. This result indicates that using more than one model can be a relevant approach for Web content classification, offering a more strict classification, less prone to over-fitting to the characteristics of a given corpus, especially considering the frequent small size of the available readability-annotated training data.

Category	PSFL train data	PSFL	ZH	Wikilivros	3-model agreement
Shallow	0.15	0.15	0.08	0.11	0.27
Medium	0.30	0.06	0.09	0.09	0.17
Deep	0.29	0.10	0.10	0.16	0.23
Sub-categorization	0.07	0.03	0.06	0.05	0.10
Formulas	0.19	0.06	0.09	0.08	0.20
Descriptors	0.16	0.62	0.27	0.11	0.82
Corpora-based	0.09	0.04	0.01	0.12	0.09

Table 5: Average difference per feature category between the simple and complex classes in the PSFL train corpus and in different classifications of our Web corpus

5   Conclusion

In this work, we presented a comparative study of different machine learning approaches to the task of readability assessment of texts in Portuguese and English, working with a framework for automatic generation of large corpora classified by readability from the Web. We observed that, as previously found in the literature for English (François and Miltsakaki, 2012), shallow, low computational cost features present a very good classificatory performance, although the complete set including deeper features outperforms them in most cases, validating our hypothesis (H2), that complex text attributes contribute to the classification according to readability levels in Portuguese. Nonetheless, in a comparison with English, we observed that classical formulas, based in these shallow features, tend to present more relevance in that language, which is explainable since they were developed focusing on its characteristics. The logistic regression presented the best classification results overall, although there was a great performance difference between classifiers for two and three levels, especially when it comes to the intermediary class, showing the difficulty of this task in a non-binary context. Finally, regarding the generalization of the classifiers, there was disagreement between the models trained in different reference corpora, reflecting the connection between the model training and the desired classification in the final corpus.

We applied the proposed methodology and the generated models in a large scale, observing significant differences between the classes in the collected Web corpus, for several indicators of readability. These differences were even greater when we considered only the documents in which three different models agreed in the classification, demonstrating the benefits of applying multiple models simultaneously to improve text classification (this will also contribute for the next phase of the project, a manual assessment by linguists). This confirmed our hypothesis (H1) that a learning model trained in a reference annotated corpus is capable of classifying a new corpus satisfactorily. The contributions of this work also include the large Web corpus produced and classified by four different learning models with different characteristics, which can contribute to further studies. As future work, new analysis must be done over the characteristics of the different documents classes in the classified corpus, including the manual sample assessment by linguists and a more fine-grained assessment of documents. Moreover, this approach can be straightforwardly expanded to develop large readability corpora for other languages.

Acknowledgements

This research was partially developed in the context of the project *Text Simplification of Complex Expressions*, sponsored by Samsung Eletrônica da Amazônia Ltda., in the terms of the Brazilian law n. 8.248/91, and by CNPq (400715/2014-7 and 312114/2015-0).

References

Sandra Aluisio, Lucia Specia, Caroline Gasperin, and Carolina Scarton. 2010. Readability assessment for text simplification. In *Proceedings of the NAACL HLT 2010 Fifth Workshop on Innovative Use of NLP for Building Educational Applications*, pages 1–9. Association for Computational Linguistics.

Marco Baroni, Silvia Bernardini, Adriano Ferraresi, and Eros Zanchetta. 2009. The wacky wide web: a collection of very large linguistically processed web-crawled corpora. *Language resources and evaluation*, 43(3):209–226.

Silvia Bernardini, Marco Baroni, and Stefan Evert. 2006. A wacky introduction. *WaCky*, pages 9–40.

Eckhard Bick. 2000. *The parsing system" Palavras": Automatic grammatical analysis of Portuguese in a constraint grammar framework*. Aarhus Universitetsforlag.

Rodrigo Boos, Kassius Prestes, Aline Villavicencio, and Muntsa Padró. 2014. brWaC: a WaCky corpus for Brazilian Portuguese. In *Computational Processing of the Portuguese Language*, pages 201–206. Springer.

Leo Breiman. 2001. Random forests. *Machine learning*, 45(1):5–32.

Ted Briscoe, John Carroll, and Rebecca Watson. 2006. The second release of the rasp system. In *Proceedings of the COLING/ACL on Interactive presentation sessions*, pages 77–80. Association for Computational Linguistics.

Meri Coleman and Ta Lin Liau. 1975. A computer readability formula designed for machine scoring. *Journal of Applied Psychology*, 60(2):283.

William Coster and David Kauchak. 2011. Simple English Wikipedia: a new text simplification task. In *Proceedings of the 49th Annual Meeting of the Association for Computational Linguistics: Human Language Technologies: short papers-Volume 2*, pages 665–669. Association for Computational Linguistics.

Edgar Dale and Jeanne S Chall. 1948. A formula for predicting readability. *Educational research bulletin*, pages 37–54.

Felice Dell'Orletta, Simonetta Montemagni, and Giulia Venturi. 2011. Read-it: Assessing readability of italian texts with a view to text simplification. In *Proceedings of the second workshop on speech and language processing for assistive technologies*, pages 73–83. Association for Computational Linguistics.

WH DuBay. 2004. The principles of readability. *Costa Mesa, CA: Impact Information (2004)*.

Fernando Enríquez, Fermín L Cruz, F Javier Ortega, Carlos G Vallejo, and José A Troyano. 2013. A comparative study of classifier combination applied to nlp tasks. *Information Fusion*, 14(3):255–267.

Érica Sapgnolo and Maria José B. Finatto. 2014. Buscando delinear um vocabulário básico: comparaço de duas listas de frequencia de palavras - jornais populares e linguagem geral. *Available at http://www.ufrgs.br/textecc/porlexbras/porpopular/massafiles/Lista_FINAL_MASSA.pdf*.

Lijun Feng, Noémie Elhadad, and Matt Huenerfauth. 2009. Cognitively motivated features for readability assessment. In *Proceedings of the 12th Conference of the European Chapter of the Association for Computational Linguistics*, pages 229–237. Association for Computational Linguistics.

Rudolf Franz Flesch et al. 1946. *Art of Plain Talk*. Harper.

Thomas François and Eleni Miltsakaki. 2012. Do nlp and machine learning improve traditional readability formulas? In *Proceedings of the First Workshop on Predicting and Improving Text Readability for target reader populations*, pages 49–57. Association for Computational Linguistics.

Itziar Gonzalez-Dios, María Jesús Aranzabe, Arantza Díaz de Ilarraza Sánchez, and Haritz Salaberri. 2014. Simple or complex? assessing the readability of basque texts. In *COLING*, pages 334–344.

Robert Gunning. 1952. The technique of clear writing.

Mark Hall, Eibe Frank, Geoffrey Holmes, Bernhard Pfahringer, Peter Reutemann, and Ian H Witten. 2009. The weka data mining software: an update. *ACM SIGKDD explorations newsletter*, 11(1):10–18.

Julia Hancke, Sowmya Vajjala, and Detmar Meurers. 2012. Readability classification for german using lexical, syntactic, and morphological features. In *COLING*, pages 1063–1080.

Wayne Iba and Pat Langley. 1992. Induction of one-level decision trees. In *Proceedings of the ninth international conference on machine learning*, pages 233–240.

Niels Landwehr, Mark Hall, and Eibe Frank. 2005. Logistic model trees. *Machine Learning*, 59(1-2):161–205.

Brian MacWhinney. 2000. *The CHILDES project: The database*, volume 2. Psychology Press.

Teresa BF Martins, Claudete M Ghiraldelo, Maria das Graças Volpe Nunes, and Osvaldo Novais de Oliveira Junior. 1996. *Readability formulas applied to textbooks in brazilian portuguese*. Icmsc-Usp.

G Harry Mc Laughlin. 1969. Smog grading-a new readability formula. *Journal of reading*, 12(8):639–646.

Glenda M McClure. 1987. Readability formulas: Useful or useless? *Professional Communication, IEEE Transactions on*, (1):12–15.

Danielle S McNamara, Max M Louwerse, and Arthur C Graesser. 2002. Coh-metrix: Automated cohesion and coherence scores to predict text readability and facilitate comprehension. Technical report, Technical report, Institute for Intelligent Systems, University of Memphis, Memphis, TN.

George A Miller. 1995. Wordnet: a lexical database for english. *Communications of the ACM*, 38(11):39–41.

Roberto Navigli and Simone Paolo Ponzetto. 2010. Babelnet: Building a very large multilingual semantic network. In *Proceedings of the 48th annual meeting of the association for computational linguistics*, pages 216–225. Association for Computational Linguistics.

Nelson Neto, Willian Rocha, and Gleidson Sousa. 2015. An open-source rule-based syllabification tool for brazilian portuguese. *Journal of the Brazilian Computer Society*, 21(1):1–10.

Sarah E Petersen and Mari Ostendorf. 2009. A machine learning approach to reading level assessment. *Computer speech & language*, 23(1):89–106.

J. Platt. 1998. Fast training of support vector machines using sequential minimal optimization. In B. Schoelkopf, C. Burges, and A. Smola, editors, *Advances in Kernel Methods - Support Vector Learning*. MIT Press.

J Pomikálek. 2013. justext: Heuristic based boilerplate removal tool. *Available: Google code, online http://code. google. com/p/justext*.

Carolina Evaristo Scarton and Sandra Maria Aluísio. 2010. Análise da inteligibilidade de textos via ferramentas de processamento de língua natural: adaptando as métricas do coh-metrix para o português. *Linguamática*, 2(1):45–61.

Carolina Scarton, Caroline Gasperin, and Sandra Aluisio. 2010. Revisiting the readability assessment of texts in portuguese. In *Advances in Artificial Intelligence–IBERAMIA 2010*, pages 306–315. Springer.

RJ Senter and Edgar A Smith. 1967. Automated readability index. Technical report, DTIC Document.

Luo Si and Jamie Callan. 2001. A statistical model for scientific readability. In *Proceedings of the tenth international conference on Information and knowledge management*, pages 574–576. ACM.

Sowmya Vajjala and Detmar Meurers. 2014. Exploring measures of "readability" for spoken language: Analyzing linguistic features of subtitles to identify age-specific tv programs. In *Proceedings of the 3rd Workshop on Predicting and Improving Text Readability for Target Reader Populations (PITR)@ EACL*, pages 21–29.

Jorge Wagner Filho, Rodrigo Wilkens, Leonardo Zilio, Marco Idiart, and Aline Villavicencio. 2016. Crawling by readability level. In *Proceedings of 12th International Conference on the Computational Processing of Portuguese (PROPOR)*.

Sandra Williams. 2004. *Natural Language Generation (NLG) of discourse relations for different reading levels*. Ph.D. thesis, University of Aberdeen.

Ramon Ziai and Niels Ott. 2005. Web as corpus toolkit: User's and hacker's manual. *Lexical Computing Ltd., Brighton, UK*.

Testing the Processing Hypothesis of word order variation using a probabilistic language model

Jelke Bloem
Amsterdam Center for Language and Communication
University of Amsterdam
Spuistraat 134, 1012 VB Amsterdam, Netherlands
`j.bloem@uva.nl`

Abstract

This work investigates the application of a measure of surprisal to modeling a grammatical variation phenomenon between near-synonymous constructions. We investigate a particular variation phenomenon, word order variation in Dutch two-verb clusters, where it has been established that word order choice is affected by processing cost. Several multifactorial corpus studies of Dutch verb clusters have used other measures of processing complexity to show that this factor affects word order choice. This previous work allows us to compare the surprisal measure, which is based on constraint satisfaction theories of language modeling, to those previously used measures, which are more directly linked to empirical observations of processing complexity. Our results show that surprisal does not predict the word order choice by itself, but is a significant predictor when used in a measure of uniform information density (UID). This lends support to the view that human language processing is facilitated not so much by predictable sequences of words but more by sequences of words in which information is spread evenly.

1   Introduction

According to functionalist theories of language, the way humans process language has shaped the grammars of natural languages (Hawkins, 2014). While it is not always clear whether a particular grammatical rule or construction can be viewed as a consequence of general language processing mechanisms, there is certainly evidence suggesting that processing efficiency plays a role — speakers may choose to use different constructions in more complex contexts. This is particularly clear in contexts where grammatical variation is possible. Sometimes a speaker can choose between different constructions to express a similar meaning. A well-known example of two such near-synonymous constructions in English is the dative alternation: [SUBJ *gave* DO *to* IO] or [SUBJ *gave* IO DO]. When a ditransitive verb is used, a speaker can almost always choose between those two constructions. For this particular alternation, and others like it, many studies have shown that a wide range of factors affect the choice (Gries, 2001; Bresnan et al., 2007; Colleman, 2009; Wasow et al., 2011), including factors related to language processing, and that the choice is not random.

These near-synonymous constructions are a particularly interesting case for the study of language processing, because other factors that may affect linguistic form, such as (most aspects of) meaning and grammaticality, are the same across both constructions. Nevertheless, usage differences can be observed between the two alternatives, even when produced by the same speaker. What remains to explain these differences is other factors such as information structure, other pragmatic factors or (relative) processing complexity. To be able to take such factors into account, near-synonymous constructions are often studied using (large) text corpora and multifactorial statistical models. A range of variables that are considered to be empirical operationalizations of relevant factors (e.g. a factor such as DEFINITENESS, which can be related to information structure or processing complexity) are measured for each instance of the

Proceedings of the Workshop on Computational Linguistics for Linguistic Complexity,
pages 174–185, Osaka, Japan, December 11-17 2016.

construction in the corpus, and modeled statistically. The model can then show how much each of those variables contributes to explaining the variation. This approach was first taken by Gries (2001) for English optional particle movement, studying the alternation between constructions where the particle 'up' is placed before or after the noun phrase:

(1) John picked *up* the book.

(2) John picked the book *up*.

The dative alternation was also studied using this method, by Bresnan et al. (2007). The variables that are found to be significant predictors in these multifactorial corpus studies are often related to language processing. Finding that construction (1) is preferred in contexts that are more difficult to process, Gries (2001) proposed the Processing Hypothesis for particle movement:

> The multitude of variables (most of which are concerned with the direct object NP) that seems to be related to Particle Movement can all be related to the processing effort of the utterance. (Gries, 2001)

However, the definition of processing effort or processing complexity used in these studies is generally quite broad. A wide variety of measures and features that can be linked to processing complexity are used, as well as theoretical notions applying to various domains of language. While the results of this approach are interesting, it is difficult to generalize over the factors discussed in such studies when so many different things constitute processing complexity. There are also more specific theories of language processing that are internally consistent and that have been used to account for a range of phenomena. While they may not cover all domains of linguistic complexity, they help to make the notion of processing effort more directly quantifiable. This means that they can be used as a single measure, that they can therefore be tested on large corpora.

In this work, we test such a specific theory. We test a basic implementation of constraint satisfaction models of language processing by applying an n-gram language model to a case of grammatical variation between near-synonymous constructions. We use this n-gram model as a measure of surprisal, which, according to constraint satisfaction models of language processing, is a measure of processing complexity. This particular case of variation, Dutch verb clusters, has previously been studied using the type of multifactorial statistical model just described, and significant effects of processing complexity were found in these studies (De Sutter, 2007; Bloem et al., in press). By comparing our results to the results of these studies, our study can serve as a test of n-gram language models as a measure of processing complexity, and perhaps even of the surprisal theory it is based on.

We will start by introducing our case study of Dutch verb clusters in section 2. Section 3 will address models of language processing and how language processing has been argued to affect grammatical variation in previous work. Section 4 describes our data, in section 5 we describe our language model, and in section 6 we present our results. The results are discussed in section 7.

2 The case of Dutch two-verb clusters

Just like other Germanic languages, Dutch expresses properties such as tense and aspect by means of auxiliary verbs. As Dutch is (mostly) verb-final, these verbs end up clustered together at the end of the sentence. But unlike in other Germanic languages, these verb clusters allow a high degree of word order variation. Even in two-verb clusters, both logical word orders are possible in almost all cases:

(3) Zij zei dat ze het **gelezen had**
    She said that she it   read   had
    'She said that she has read it.'

(4) Zij zei dat ze het **had gelezen**
     She said that she it   had read
     'She said that she has read it.'

The difference in word order is generally assumed not to correspond to a meaning difference, so we can consider these constructions to be near-synonymous. As in other instances of near-synonymous constructions, a wide variety of factors has been shown to correlate with this alternation (De Sutter et al., 2007) and several generalizations over these factors have been proposed: sentence rhythm (De Schutter, 1996), information weight (De Sutter et al., 2007) and also minimizing processing complexity (De Sutter, 2005; Bloem et al., in press). Bloem et al. argue that the order in example (4), called the ascending order, is easier to process than the alternative order (3), called the descending order, because it correlates with features that are considered to be more difficult to process. This is similar to how Gries (2001) argued that the construction in example (1) is easier to process. Additional evidence comes from the claim that the ascending order is also acquired earlier by children (Meyer and Weerman, 2016).

In Bloem et al.'s (in press) study, factors that are expected to correlate with the verb cluster word order variation are tested using a multifactorial model, and it is argued that those factors relate to processing complexity (besides the ones that mark different constructions). As an example, a factor relates to processing complexity when some psycholinguistic study has measured that a particular factor is more difficult to process. A set of such factors can be viewed as an a measure of processing complexity. However, another approach to measuring processing complexity is also possible and has been used in other corpus studies of grammatical variation phenomena: to implement a theoretical model of language processing, and test that on instances of the constructions of interest extracted from a corpus. The next section will elaborate upon these two methods of measuring processing complexity, and discuss studies that used them.

3 Processing complexity

Processing complexity, from a human subjects perspective, refers to the amount of cognitive effort required to produce or comprehend an utterance. Speakers prefer to minimize their use of cognitive resources, formulating sentences in a way that minimizes processing complexity when multiple ways to express something are available. Listeners seem to process complex sentences more slowly and make more comprehension errors (Jaeger and Tily, 2011). This human subjects definition of complexity has also been called 'relative complexity', in contrast to 'absolute complexity' which is the formal complexity of the linguistic system (i.e. grammar) being used. Generally, only relative complexity is invoked in studies of grammatical variation.

There are at least two ways in which the notion of processing complexity can be invoked to account for grammatical variation in a corpus. Firstly, one can take a theoretical model of language processing, and apply it to instances the constructions under study from a corpus. The model might predict that one construction is more difficult to process than the other, or perhaps only in certain contexts. Secondly, one can use empirical measures of processing complexity, based on psycholinguistic experiments. If experiments have shown that people exhibit slower reading times or make more errors in sentences with feature A than with feature B, this can be taken to mean that feature A is more difficult to process. One can then test in a corpus whether the constructions under study occur more with the 'easy' feature or the 'complex' feature. This section will discuss these two approaches.

3.1 Theoretical models

Among theoretical models of language processing, two main approaches can be identified: constraint-satisfaction models, and resource-limitation (or memory-based) models (Levy, 2008).

Resource-limitation models focus on the idea that there is some limited cognitive resource, such as memory, that limits people's capacity to process and produce language. Gibson's (1998) Dependency Locality Theory is a prominent example of this approach. In this theory, among other constraints, longer-distance dependencies are dispreferred because they require more memory, and are therefore considered more difficult to process. Another such model, which is frequently referred to in linguistics, is formed by the efficiency principles of Hawkins (2004; 2014). The first principle in his theory is Minimize Domains, which states that dependency relations in the smallest possible domains are the most efficient. These principles are argued to play an important role in shaping what is grammatical, though they can be applied to the study of grammatical variation as well. Wiechmann and Lohmann (2013) applied this theoretical model in their multifactorial corpus study of prepositional phrase ordering, an alternation in English where the order of a verb's two PP arguments (an adjunct and a complement) is free:

(5)   The astronomer gazed [into the sky] [through his telescope].

(6)   The astronomer gazed [through his telescope] [into the sky].

One factor they derive from the theory is that a shorter PP argument might prefer the first position, following the principle of Minimize Domains (the phrasal combination domain would be shorter with that ordering). Their model did not have a very high predictive accuracy over the corpus data. This is a common finding in these studies, as not every factor can be included in the model — factors such as prosody and information structure are difficult to test using a standard annotated corpus. Nevertheless, they found that the constraints theorized by Hawkins (2004) held for the corpus data they studied. However, they do not compare the effect of these constraints to other factors that often affect variation, such as empirical measures of processing complexity. Only the additional factor 'information status' is discussed.

Furthermore, these principles cannot easily be applied to every case of grammatical variation. The Wiechmann and Lohmann study discusses a case of interconstituent alternations, involving the ordering of constituents. However, in our case study of Dutch two-verb clusters, the alternation takes place within the verb phrase domain, and is therefore an intraconstituent alternation. As noted by De Sutter (2009, p. 226–227), principles like Minimize Domains do not necessarily apply here. So, we will look to the other main approach to modeling language processing.

The other approach, **constraint satisfaction** models, uses information from various domains of language (i.e. lexical, pragmatic) to consider various parallel alternative interpretations or parses of a sentence during processing. Furthermore, they relate processing difficulty to expectation, which is often grounded in probability theory (Jurafsky, 2003) or relatedly, measures of surprisal (Hale, 2001; Levy, 2008). Therefore, this has also been called the Surprisal framework. In Hale's surprisal theory, log-probability is considered a measure of the difficulty of a word. More surprising sequences of words or structures (that have lower probability) are considered to be more difficult to process and therefore more complex. These measures have been used to make various predictions about processing complexity that were verified using empirical data from psycholinguistic experiments. The concept of minimizing surprisal has also been called uniform information density (UID). This term is frequently used in linguistic studies, for example by Levy and Jaeger (2007). This UID measure measures the same thing as the perplexity measure, which is often used by computational linguists to evaluate language models. Levy and Jaeger (2007) studied it in the context of syntactic reduction, namely the possible omission of 'that' as a relativizer, which can also be considered a form of grammatical variation. In their study, an n-gram language model is a significant predictor of relativizer omission, as well as more syntactic features that are considered to have predictive power. This n-gram model was trained on a version of the Switchboard corpus in which all optional relativizers were omitted. However, no comparison with empirical measures of processing complexity is made. The UID measure has also been found to predict variation in other domains of language, such as discourse connective omission (Asr and Demberg, 2015). Therefore, this approach links probabilistic models of language that are typically used in natural language processing, to processing complexity.

3.2 Empirical measures

We have just seen some examples of corpus studies of grammatical variation in which a particular theoretical model of processing complexity is used as the basis of the analysis, but usually, processing
complexity is defined more broadly. An example of such a definition of processing complexity can be
found in the first multifactorial corpus study of grammatical variation, where Gries (2001) states: "My
idea of the notion of processing effort is a fairly broad one: it encompasses not only purely syntactic
determinants, but also factors from other linguistic levels". He lists phonologically indicated processing cost, morphosyntactically determined processing cost, semantically conditioned processing cost, and
discourse-functionally determined processing cost.

In De Sutter's (2007) variational corpus study of verb clusters, he interprets five factors that have
previously been linked to verb cluster order variation in terms of cognitive cost. For example, the factor
'frequency' is interpreted as an indicator of cognitive cost, since psycholinguistic studies (i.e. reaction
time studies) have shown that lower-frequency words are processed more slowly. In a subsequent corpus
study, Bloem et al. (in press) provide an overview of nine such factors that correlate with the word order
variation in a large corpus. Just as other corpus studies of variation, this study is operationalized as a
logistic regression model predicting which of the two orders is likely to be used, given the factors as
predictors or independent variables. These factors are shown in Table 1. In this table, they are ranked
by their information gain as measured in the stepwise regression procedure performed by Bloem et al.
(in press). In this procedure, one starts with an empty model, and adds the most informative factor each
time, measuring the information gain. This measure is expressed as an Akaike Information Criterion
(AIC) value, which measures information loss. A higher AIC means that more information is lost by the
model, compared to the original data set. Therefore, the highest-ranked factors account for the largest
amount of variation.

Rank	Factor	AIC	Decrease
0	(none)	463279	—
1	Type of auxiliary	382538	80741
2	Priming	378185	4353
3	'te'-infinitive	374378	3807
4	Extraposition	371413	2965
5	Length of middle field	369817	1596
6	Frequency of the main verb	368744	1073
7	Information value	367806	938
8	Morphological structure of the main verb	366870	936
9	Multi-word units	366162	708
10	Structural depth	365674	488
11	Definiteness	365461	213

Table 1: List of factors in the Bloem et al. (in press) model of verb cluster order variation, ranked by
information gain.

Factors 1 and 3 are control variables. Using a different auxiliary verb changes the meaning of a verb
cluster construction and different auxiliary verbs have different word order preferences, so this factor
obviously predicts word order in this kind of model, even though it is not a processing complexity factor.
For the other factors, Bloem et al. discuss how they can be linked to results from psycholinguistic
studies in which the factors, or similar ones, are measured, as well as to verb cluster order variation.
Several of these factors are the ones that De Sutter (2007) also discussed. FREQUENCY is also included
here (6th in the table), as well as syntactic PRIMING (2nd), which is argued to ease processing on the
basis of priming studies. The LENGTH OF THE MIDDLE FIELD of the sentence (5th) is also discussed,
where a longer middle field is argued to be more difficult to process due to longer dependencies. The
factor EXTRAPOSITION (4th) indicates whether a prepositional phrase was extraposed and positioned

after the verb cluster, which has been argued to ease processing, and the factor INFORMATION VALUE (7th) measures the information value of the word before the verb cluster (i.e. whether it is a function word or content word). The factor MORPHOLOGICAL STRUCTURE OF THE MAIN VERB (8th) refers to seperable verbs, such as *afwassen* 'wash up' — such verbs appear to have a strong preference for the ascending order. The MULTIWORD UNIT factor (9th) indicates whether the verb cluster is (part of) a fixed expression, and STRUCTURAL DEPTH (10th) refers to the depth of the verb cluster in the syntactic tree of the sentence. Lastly, as for the factor DEFINITENESS of the last word before the verb (11th), definiteness is argued to be more difficult to process on the basis of a study with language-impaired children, among other work. More detailed descriptions of the factors, their link to the notion of processing complexity and their effect on word order are provided by Bloem et al. (in press).

All of the factors listed in Table 1 are statistically significant predictors of verb cluster word order, and they are all linked to processing complexity. In the present study, we will use this study as a basis of comparison for our probabilistic language model based on the constraint-satisfaction theory of language processing. Outside of the world of multifactorial corpus studies, processing complexity is also often defined in terms of empirical psycholinguistic measures, as evidenced by Bach et al.'s (1986) study on the processing complexity of larger verb clusters, where processing complexity is measured in terms of error rate and comprehensibility judgements.

4   Data

For reasons of comparison, we use the same corpus that was used by Bloem et al. (in press), which is the Wikipedia section of the Lassy Large corpus (van Noord, 2009). This corpus consists of a 145 million word dump of the Dutch-language Wikipedia in August 2011, and among these words, we can find 827.709 two-verb verbal clusters in total. The corpus has been automatically annotated with full syntactic dependency trees by the Alpino parser for Dutch (van Noord et al., 2006). While we do not need the annotation to train our language model, we do need it to automatically find and extract verb cluster constructions — extracting any sequence of two verbs is not sufficient. Furthermore, the annotation was used to extract the empirical measures of processing complexity used by Bloem et al. (in press), used as factors in their model. The corpus was split into a training set (90%) and test set (10%), and from each set, the verb clusters and the factors were extracted. We also extracted plaintext, but tokenized, versions of the training and test sets for creating the language model.

5   Language model

To model the surprisal or predictability of a verb cluster, we trained a trigram language model on the plaintext corpus. We used Colibri Core (van Gompel and van den Bosch, 2016) to implement the language model efficiently. Colibri Core's compression and counting algorithms enabled the modeling of this fairly large corpus without requiring excessive amounts of memory. The model was trained by having Colibri count n-grams and storing them as an unindexed pattern model. We used 3 as the maximum construction length ($n = 3$) and no minimum length (to get trigrams, bigrams and unigrams), and no skipgrams. The construction threshold was set to 2, i.e. n-grams that only occur once are not included in the language model. Because we use an automatically annotated corpus, including such hapax legomena would be likely to result in the inclusion of many tokenization errors at the cost of more memory.

A Colibri unindexed pattern model stores frequencies, but not probabilities. We perform maximum likelihood estimation (MLE) on the model over the training data to obtain probabilities during the test procedure. When testing, we iterate through all verb clusters extracted from the test set portion of the corpus, and estimate their probability and perplexity using frequency counts from the Colibri pattern model. For each of the two verbs in a cluster, we use linear interpolation to include trigram, bigram and unigram construction counts in the estimate. Furthermore, we use generalized additive smoothing, over the unigram constructions only, to account for out of vocabulary words in the test set. Therefore, our maximum likelihood estimation for a single verb is performed as follows:

$$\hat{P}(w_n|w_{n-1}w_{n-2}) = \lambda_1 P(w_n|w_{n-1}w_{n-2})$$
$$+ \lambda_2 P(w_n|w_{n-1}) \tag{1}$$
$$+ \lambda_3 P(w_n) \qquad \text{where } P(w_n) = \frac{\delta + c(w_n)}{\delta|V| + c(N)}$$

λ_1, λ_2 and λ_3 refer to the interpolation weights of trigram, bigram and (smoothed) unigram probabilities respectively. δ is the smoothing parameter. V refers to the vocabulary size (or, the number of types in the language model), N to all tokens, and $c()$ refers to counts. We can now use perplexity per word (PPW) as a measure of surprisal for individual verbs or verb types. Perplexity is a measure of predictability or surprisal and it is generally used to compute how well a language model predicts a word in a sequence, or a sequence of words. We compute PPW as follows:

$$PP(W) = 2^{-log_2(P(V1)P(V2))} \tag{2}$$

$p(V1)$ and $p(V2)$ are the estimated probabilities of the two verbs in the cluster (as estimated in Equation 1).

However, we would also like to have a measure of the predictability of the verb cluster as a whole. To this end, we also compute the perplexity per word over both words in the verb cluster:

$$PP(C) = 2^{-\frac{1}{2}log_2(P(V1)P(V2))} \tag{3}$$

The log probabilities of $P(V1)$ and $P(V2)$ are multiplied by $1/2$ because the verb cluster can be regarded as a sequence of length 2.

As noted, this measure is similar to Uniform Information Density as defined in previous work. We did not evaluate our language model in detail, because the goal of this study is not to have an optimal model for natural language processing. Rather, it is an attempt to see whether a basic form of a constraint-satisfaction model of language processing can account for verb cluster order variation, so we aim to make as few assumptions about the nature of the language model as possible.

6 Results

We ran the testing procedure to obtain perplexity values for each verb cluster with a range of parameter settings. We decided on a set of parameters to use based on two criteria. Firstly, regarding the construction length, we wanted the linear interpolation weights to be somewhat balanced between unigram, bigram and trigram probabilities in order to have a representative trigram model that does not rely too much on unigram or bigram probabilities. Longer construction lengths seem more cognitively plausible. Secondly, even though we do not consider a well-performing language model to be essential for this study, we chose parameter settings that resulted in a low overall perplexity per word, computed over all verbs within the clusters. This resulted in a model with the interpolation weights set at $\lambda_1 = 0.3$, $\lambda_2 = 0.45$, $\lambda_3 = 0.25$, and a smoothing parameter of $\delta = 0.5$. We take perplexity to be an indicator of complexity following (Hale, 2001) who took log-probability as an indicator of complexity, as well as subsequent work in constraint-based models of language processing.

As a reminder, we repeat examples (3) and (4), showing the two possible word orders. Example (7) is in the **descending** order, where the main verb comes first and the auxiliary verb, in this case *hebben* 'to have', comes last. Example (8) is in the **ascending** order, which is the opposite:

(7) Zij zei dat ze het **gelezen had**
     She said that she it read   had

     'She said that she has read it.'

(8) Zij zei dat ze het **had gelezen**
    She said that she it   had read

    'She said that she has read it.'

Word order	Perplexity
Ascending order clusters	1681.2
Descending order clusters	1675.8
Overall PPW	1679.8

Table 2: Perplexity per word (PPW) results for the two word orders, over all test-set clusters.

Table 2 shows that the perplexity per word of clusters in the ascending order, which is the more frequent order, is slightly higher than that of clusters in the descending order. At first sight, this seems to confirm the processing hypothesis of Bloem et al. (in press) — the ascending order occurs in contexts of higher surprisal, and therefore lower predictability. This would confirm their idea that the ascending order is easier to process — to minimize surprisal and maintain uniform information density, one would use the less complex construction in the more complex context.

The difference seems small though, only 5.4 units of perplexity. We can test the predictive power of this measure for predicting word order by defining a logistic regression model over this data. In this model, word order is the dependent variable, a binary outcome variable that can be either 'ascending' or 'descending', and verb cluster perplexity (as defined in Equation 3) is the predictor variable. In this model, the perplexity factor is significant ($p < 0.05$), with a z-score of 2.2. As for the effect size, according to the model, for a one unit increase in perplexity, the log odds of the cluster being in the ascending order increases by 0.00000000035 (3.5e−10). In other words, the effect size is tiny. For confirmation, we also tested the predictive power of the model by computing the concordance index (c-index). A c-index of 0.5 indicates chance level prediction, while 1 is perfect. This model's c-index, based on 100 bootstrap repetitions, is 0.493, while multifactorial models of verb cluster order variation had c-indexes of 0.803 (De Sutter, 2005) and 0.765 (Bloem et al., 2014). Therefore, we cannot consider this result to be reliable.

Condition	Value	Perplexity
Linear position	First verb	2264.9
	Second verb	1245.8
Verb type	Auxiliary verb in cluster	714.0
	Main verb in cluster	3952.0
Position and type	Auxiliary verb in descending cluster	178.2
	Main verb in descending cluster	15763.5
	Auxiliary verb in ascending cluster	2445.8
	Main verb in ascending cluster	1155.6
-	Overall PPW	1679.8

Table 3: Perplexity per word (PPW) results for various conditions, over all test-set clusters.

To analyze this negative result, we can look at the perplexity per word values of individual verbs, for different verb types and verb positions. These different conditions are listed in table 3. We can distinguish two conditions here: the position of the verb in the linear order of the sentence (does it come first or last), and whether the verb is an auxiliary verb or a main verb. These are essentially two features of the two word orders: in the ascending order, the first verb is the auxiliary verb while the second verb is the main verb, while the reverse is true for the descending order.

As for the linear position, we can observe that the first verb of a cluster is less predictable than the second verb. This seems logical, because in a two-verb cluster, the first verb is always followed by another verb. As for the verb type, we observe a bigger difference in perplexity between auxiliary verbs and main verbs — auxiliary verbs are much more predictable than main verbs. This can also be expected, because there is a limited number of auxiliary verbs (including any verbs that select another verb in a cluster), while main verbs can be anything and may include unknown words. This shows that linear position and verb types are both confounding factors in computing verb cluster surprisal. However, these observations do not control for the fact that the ascending order is more frequent, and therefore main verbs more often occur in the second position in linear order.

Therefore, it may be more informative to look at perplexity values for both linear position and verb type, as shown in table 3. This shows that perplexity is distributed quite differently in both orders. In the descending order, the main verb comes first. The perplexity for this is very high — the descending main verb is very surprising both because main verbs are more surprising, and because verbs in the first position are more surprising. Conversely, the auxiliary verb, which comes second, has very low surprisal. In the ascending orders, the two factors balance each other out — the auxiliary verb (low surprisal factor) comes first (which is a high surprisal factor). The main verb (high surprisal) comes last (low surprisal). In other words, instances of the ascending order have a more uniform information density.

Based on this result, we define a measure of verb cluster information density, which is the absolute difference between the log probabilities of both verbs in the cluster:

$$UID(C) = |log_2(P(V1)) - log_2(P(V2))| \tag{4}$$

Again, $P(V1)$ and $P(V2)$ are the estimated probabilities of the two verbs in the cluster (as estimated in Equation 1). Putting this factor in a logistic regression model gives us a c-index of 0.686 according to the procedure described for the previous model (except that the measure from Equation 4 is used, instead of that in Equation 3). This is of course a lot better than 0.493, especially for a model with a single predictor. The effect of the factor is also highly significant. We can now test whether this UID-effect holds when we also include the nine empirical measures of processing complexity (and the control variables) from the study of Bloem et al. (in press). This would tell us if our cluster-UID-measure measures the same thing as the empirical measures from that study.

This can be done by adding the UID measure from Equation 4 to the multifactorial regression model of Bloem et al. as a predictor variable. To do so, we created a regression model that includes all of the factors listed in Table 1 as predictors, as well as our UID measure, and that has word order as the dependent variable. We found that adding UID to the Bloem et al. model significantly improves it. A global comparison of the original model and the model with the UID factor using the χ^2-test shows that the residual deviance drops from 54880 to 48795, and this is statistically significant ($p < 0.001$). We also observe that the UID-measure is highly significant in this model, with an odds ratio is 0.788, indicating a decrease in the odds of observing an ascending order when the UID-measure is higher (which is when the density is less uniform). Furthermore, if we perform stepwise regression with this model to measure information gain, the UID factor is ranked second after the control factor TYPE OF AUXILIARY. In Table 1, which lists information gain for the Bloem et al. model, it would be listed second. It is therefore the most informative factor related to processing complexity in the new model. However, the predictive value of the model does not improve — the original model has a predictive value of $c = 0.7897$, and adding our UID-measure gives us $c = 0.7896$, a negligible difference.

Surprisingly, there is no multicollinearity in this model. The variance inflation factor (VIF) for each factor is very low (< 1.2, 1.203 for the UID factor). This indicates that the UID-measure does not correlate with the factors from the Bloem et al. model, but is complentary to them instead.

7 Discussion

Our results show that perplexity-per-word as a measure of surprisal does not predict word order variation in two-verb clusters, even though it has been argued that processing complexity predicts word order. The perplexity values computed on the basis of the probabilities from the n-gram language model that we used cannot be considered a measure of processing complexity. However, a derived measure of uniform information density (UID), which measures a *difference* in surprisal within the verb cluster construction on the basis of the same language model, does predict the word order variation. We furthermore showed that this UID measure improves upon a previous model, that was based on empirical measures of processing complexity. Therefore, our UID measure can be viewed as complementary to these measures when accounting for word order variation in two-verb clusters.

This result indicates that part of the variation that the empirical measures account for, is also accounted for by the UID measure, but not all of it. Furthermore, not all of the variation that the UID measure accounts for, is accounted for by the empirical measures. More broadly, human subject measures and a computational measure of complexity were combined, and this combination lead to an improvement in explanatory power for this grammatical variation. We chose to use a measure in the Surprisal framework, or constraint satisfaction modeling approach, because Dependency Locality Theory is not so clearly applicable to verb cluster order variation, which is an intraconstituent alternation.

Our analysis also showed that verb clusters in the ascending order generally have a more uniform information density than verb clusters in the descending order. This is because both linear position and the type of verb affect the predictability of a verb, and in the ascending word order, these two factors balance each other out. Under the assumption made by Levy and Jaeger (2007) that uniform information density indeed facilitates processing, our findings seem to support the processing hypothesis for Dutch verb cluster order. However, the direction of the effect is not clear - it can either be argued that the ascending order is easier to process because it has a more uniform information density, or it can be argued that the ascending order is more difficult to process, because speakers use it in more predictable contexts (that are less difficult to process). In future work, this ambiguity could be clarified by studying the information density of not only the verbs themselves, but also the words before and after the verbs.

While we believe that Dutch verb cluster word order is a typical case of near-synonymous word order variation, this raises the question of whether these findings would hold for other cases of grammatical variation. Our result does not necessarily mean that surprisal measures are not representative of processing complexity in general. Surprisal has been shown to be informative in other studies of other phenomena, for example to discover contexts in which a relativizer is preferred (Levy and Jaeger, 2007). Furthermore, surprisal can be and has been measured in a variety of ways. We implemented it in a very basic way. Hale (2001) measured surprisal using a probabilistic parser rather than an n-gram language model. Perhaps a measure of surprisal that takes more structure or syntax into account would be more predictive of verb cluster order variation or other alternations. The measure can and has been implemented on the basis of other structural elements rather than words, such as constructions, part-of-speech sequences, topic models, or any other level of structure that one could train a language model over In future work, it would be interesting to try computing surprisal in the same way as Hale (2001), to compute it at a different level of structure, or to use more elaborate language models containing larger chunks or skipgrams. A delexicalized n-gram model could be used to make the measures we used more sensitive to structure. For our particular case it would also be interesting to define our prediction task in a different way — to learn more about the word order variation, it would be interesting to adapt the language model such that it only predicts the order of the cluster, rather than the specific words in it. This might tell us more about how predictable the cluster orders are, regardless of the specific lexical items involved.

Nevertheless, our findings do provide evidence that uniform information density may be a better operationalization of constraint satisfaction models of language processing than plain surprisal, when one is studying an alternation involving multiple words. Uniform information density should be considered as a measure of processing complexity, particularly in multifactorial corpus studies of grammatical variation.

References

Fatemeh Torabi Asr and Vera Demberg. 2015. Uniform information density at the level of discourse relations: Negation markers and discourse connective omission. *IWCS 2015*, page 118.

Emmon Bach, Colin Brown, and William Marslen-Wilson. 1986. Crossed and nested dependencies in German and Dutch: A psycholinguistic study. *Language and Cognitive Processes*, 1(4):249–262.

Jelke Bloem, Arjen Versloot, and Fred Weerman. 2014. Applying automatically parsed corpora to the study of language variation. In Jan Hajic and Junichi Tsujii, editors, *Proceedings of COLING 2014, the 25th International Conference on Computational Linguistics: Technical Papers*, pages 1974–1984, Dublin, August. Dublin City University and Association for Computational Linguistics.

Jelke Bloem, Arjen Versloot, and Fred Weerman. in press. Verbal cluster order and processing complexity. *Language Sciences*.

Joan Bresnan, Anna Cueni, Tatiana Nikitina, and R. Harald Baayen. 2007. Predicting the dative alternation. In G. Bouma, I. Kraemer, and J. Zwarts, editors, *Cognitive foundations of interpretation*, pages 69–94. KNAW, Amsterdam.

Timothy Colleman. 2009. Verb disposition in argument structure alternations: a corpus study of the dative alternation in Dutch. *Language Sciences*, 31(5):593–611.

G De Schutter. 1996. De volgorde in tweeledige werkwoordelijke eindgroepen met voltooid deelwoord in spreek- en schrijftaal. *Nederlandse taalkunde*, 1:207–220.

Gert De Sutter, Dirk Speelman, and Dirk Geeraerts. 2007. Luisteren schrijvers naar hun innerlijke stem? De invloed van ritmische factoren op de woordvolgorde in geschreven werkwoordelijke eindgroepen. *Neerlandistiek*, 2007.

Gert De Sutter. 2005. *Rood, groen, corpus! Een taalgebruiksgebaseerde analyse van woordvolgordevariatie in tweeledige werkwoordelijke eindgroepen*. Ph.D. thesis, University of Leuven.

Gert De Sutter. 2007. Naar een corpusgebaseerde, cognitief-functionele verklaring van de woordvolgordevariatie in tweeledige werkwoordelijke eindgroepen. *Nederlandse Taalkunde*, 12(4):302–330.

Gert De Sutter. 2009. Towards a multivariate model of grammar: The case of word order variation in Dutch clause final verb clusters. In A Dufter, J Fleischer, and G Seiler, editors, *Describing and Modeling Variation in Grammar*, pages 225–255. Walter De Gruyter.

Edward Gibson. 1998. Linguistic complexity: Locality of syntactic dependencies. *Cognition*, 68(1):1–76.

Stefan T Gries. 2001. A multifactorial analysis of syntactic variation: Particle movement revisited. *Journal of quantitative linguistics*, 8(1):33–50.

John Hale. 2001. A probabilistic Earley parser as a psycholinguistic model. In *Proceedings of the second meeting of the North American Chapter of the Association for Computational Linguistics on Language technologies*, NAACL '01, pages 1–8. Association for Computational Linguistics.

John A Hawkins. 2004. *Efficiency and complexity in grammars*. Oxford University Press.

John A Hawkins. 2014. *Cross-linguistic variation and efficiency*. OUP Oxford.

T Florian Jaeger and Harry Tily. 2011. On language 'utility': Processing complexity and communicative efficiency. *Wiley Interdisciplinary Reviews: Cognitive Science*, 2(3):323–335.

Dan Jurafsky. 2003. Probabilistic modeling in psycholinguistics: Linguistic comprehension and production.

Roger P Levy and TF Jaeger. 2007. Speakers optimize information density through syntactic reduction. In *Advances in neural information processing systems*, pages 849–856.

Roger Levy. 2008. Expectation-based syntactic comprehension. *Cognition*, 106(3):1126–1177.

Caitlin Meyer and Fred Weerman. 2016. Cracking the cluster: The acquisition of verb raising in Dutch. *Nederlandse Taalkunde*, 21(2):181–212.

Maarten van Gompel and Antal van den Bosch. 2016. Efficient n-gram, skipgram and flexgram modelling with Colibri Core. *Journal of Open Research Software*, 4(1).

G.J.M. van Noord, P Mertens, C Fairon, A Dister, and P Watrin. 2006. At Last Parsing Is Now Operational. In *TALN06. Verbum Ex Machina. Actes de la 13e conference sur le traitement automatique des langues naturelles*, pages 20–42. Leuven University Press.

G.J.M. van Noord. 2009. Huge parsed corpora in LASSY. In F. Van Eynde, A. Frank, K. De Smedt, and G. van Noord, editors, *Proceedings of the Seventh International Workshop on Treebanks and Linguistic Theories (TLT 7)*, volume 12, pages 115–126. LOT.

Thomas Wasow, T Florian Jaeger, and David Orr. 2011. Lexical variation in relativizer frequency. In Horst J. Simon and Heike Wiese, editors, *Expecting the unexpected: Exceptions in grammar*, pages 175–195. Walter de Gruyter, Berlin.

Daniel Wiechmann and Arne Lohmann. 2013. Domain minimization and beyond: Modeling prepositional phrase ordering. *Language Variation and Change*, 25(01):65–88.

Temporal Lobes as Combinatory Engines for both Form and Meaning

Jixing Li
Cornell University
jl2939@cornell.edu

Jonathan Brennan
University of Michigan
jobrenn@umich.edu

Adam Mahar
Cornell University
ajm348@cornell.edu

John Hale
Cornell University
jthale@cornell.edu

Abstract

The relative contributions of meaning and form to sentence processing remains an outstanding issue across the language sciences. We examine this issue by formalizing four incremental complexity metrics and comparing them against freely-available ROI timecourses. Syntax-related metrics based on top-down parsing and structural dependency-distance turn out to significantly improve a regression model, compared to a simpler model that formalizes only conceptual combination using a distributional vector-space model. This confirms the view of the anterior temporal lobes as combinatory engines that deal in both form (see e.g. Brennan et al., 2012; Rogalsky and Hickok, 2009) and meaning (see e.g., Wilson et al., 2014). This same characterization applies to a posterior temporal region in roughly "Wernicke's Area."

1 Introduction

Processing complexity in human language comprehension remains a central challenge for computational psycholinguistics. Investigations of this essentially biological phenomenon typically rely on formalized complexity metrics. These metrics reflect some aspect of the language being comprehended: some are form-based in the sense of syntactic structure while others are meaning-based in the sense of conceptual information.

But what is the biological basis of the processing that these metrics index? The clinical syndrome semantic dementia suggests that the anterior temporal lobes (ATLs) perform some sort of conceptual combination (for a review, see Patterson et al., 2007). But it remains unclear whether this conceptual processing overlaps or is separate from form-based processing e.g. based on syntactic phrase structure.

To disentangle the influence of form and meaning in sentence processing in different brain regions, we used stepwise regression against freely-available ROI timecourses (Brennan et al., 2016). The regressors in these statistical models are incremental complexity metrics formalizing several different cognitive and linguistic theories about processing difficulty in form and meaning. The pattern of improvements across these steps suggests a role for syntactic processing, above and beyond conceptual combination. This result is consistent with the experimental work of Rogalsky and Hickok (2009) as well as the correlational work of Brennan et al. (2012) on which we build. The remainder of the paper is organized into four sections: Section 2 reviews our syntactic and semantic complexity metrics; Section 3 describes the material and data analysis methods; Section 4 presents the results and Section 5 discusses the implications of the results and concludes the paper.

2 Quantifying complexity factors

We quantify two different aspects of syntactic complexity: Structural Distance and Node Count (this latter metric previously investigated in Brennan et al., 2016), and we use vector-space model to quantify semantic complexity as Lexical-Semantic Coherence. In evaluating the contribution of these complexity metrics, we control for linear order in two ways: Lexical sequences from Google Book ngrams (Michel, 2011), and the linear order of parts of speech using the same POS trigram model in Brennan et al. (2016).

Proceedings of the Workshop on Computational Linguistics for Linguistic Complexity,
pages 186–191, Osaka, Japan, December 11-17 2016.

2.1 Structural Distance

One form-related aspect of processing difficulty derives from memory load induced by integration of two syntactically dependent words (Wanner and Maratsos, 1978; O'Grady, 1997; Gibson, 1998). Following Baumann (2014), we quantify this load as Structural Distance, i.e., the number of phrase-structural tree nodes between two dependent words. We obtained both phrase structures and dependency relations for every sentence using the Stanford Parser (Klein and Manning, 2003; de Marneffe et al., 2006). Structural Distance is then the number of nodes traversed between the head and the dependent in the phrase structural tree. We considered only the rightmost word in any dependency relation. For words in multiple dependency relations, we summed the structural distances.

2.2 Node Count

Another form-based complexity metric is Node Count, which is the number of phrase structural nodes in between successive words in a sentence. This expresses a form of Yngve's (1960) Depth hypothesis (see also Frazier, 1985). We examined X-bar structures generated by Minimalist Grammars in the sense of Stabler (1997). These structures reflect grammatical analysis by Van Wagenen et al. (2014). We counted the number of nodes in these trees that would be visited by a top-down parser (see Hale, 2014).

2.3 Lexical-Semantic Coherence

Our meaning-based metric Lexical-Semantic Coherence is built on vector-space models. Vector-space models represent word meaning based on co-occurrence statistics from a large text corpus (e.g., Baroni et al., 2014; Erk, 2012). Cosine similarity between the word vectors have been found to influence eye-fixation times (Pynte et al., 2008), word pronunciation duration (Sayeed et al., 2015), and fMRI activation patterns (Mitchell et al., 2008). We used latent semantic analysis (LSA; Landauer and Dumais, 1997) to build our semantic vector space model. The training data were the whole book of *Alice in Wonderland*. We first built the type-by-document matrix where the rows are all the words in the book and the documents are all the paragraphs. The input vector space was transformed by singular value decomposition (SVD), and truncated to a *100*-dimensional vector space. The context vector is the average of the previous 10 word vectors. We used negative cosine between the target word vector and the context vector to represent lexical-semantic coherence: higher negative cosine value indicates less semantic coherence.

2.4 Linear Order

Our control predictors include the lexical and POS trigram models. Linear order of words, as reflected in a Markov chain, has been successful in modeling human reading performance (Frank and Bod, 2011; Frank et al., 2015). We used the freely-available trigram counts from the Google Books project (see e.g. Michel, 2011) and restricted consideration to publication years 1850-1900, i.e., the year surrounding the publication of *Alice in Wonderland*. We backed off to lower-order grams where necessary: coverage was 1725/2045 for trigrams and 1640/1694 for bigrams. The POS trigram regressor from ?) served as an additional control. We then used surprisal of the trigram probabilities to link the probability of a word in its left-context to BOLD signals (see Hale, 2001; 2016).

3 Methods

3.1 Data acquisition

The ROI timecourses from Brennan et al. (2016) come from twenty-five native English speaker (17 female, 18-24 years old, right-handed) listening to a story while in the scanner. The story was the first chapter of *Alice in Wonderland*, lasting for about 12.4 minutes. Participants completed twelve multiple-choice questions after scanning. The detailed imaging parameters and preprocessing procedures are described in Brennan et al. (2016).

3.2 Regions of interest

Six regions of interest (ROIs), including the left anterior temporal lobe (LATL), the right anterior temporal lobe (RATL), the left inferior frontal gyrus (LIFG), the left posterior temporal lobe (LPTL), the left inferior parietal lobe (LIPL) and the left premotor region (LPreM).

Both functional and anatomic criteria guided the precise positioning of these ROIs. . The functional criterion derives from an atheoretical Word Rate regressor, which has value 1 at the offset of each word in the audio stimulus, and 0 elsewhere. This localizer identified regions whose BOLD signals were sensitive to word presentation. Each ROI sphere (10 mm radius) was centered on a peak t-value of at least 2.0 within the anatomical areas.

3.3 Data analysis

3.3.1 Estimating hemodynamic response

Following Just and Varma (2007), we convolved each complexity metric's time series with SPM12's canonical hemodynamic response function (HRF). These time series are made orthogonal to the convolved Word Rate vector since it is our localizer for defining the ROIs.

3.3.2 Stepwise regression

We tested the unique contribution of each model by conducting stepwise model comparisons against the ROI timecourses. The null model included fixed effects for head movements (dx, dy, dz, rx, ry, rz) and word rate; We also included fixed effects for word frequency, f0, and root mean square (RMS) intensity of the speech into our null model, which were also convolved with the same HRF. word frequency was based on the SUBTLEXus corpus (Brysbaert and New, 2009), which contains 51 million words from the subtitles of American films and television series. The random effects included a random intercept by participant and a random slope for word rate:

$$BOLD_{null} = BOLD \sim dx + dy + dz + rx + ry + rz + rate + f0 + intensity + frequency(1 + rate|subject) \quad (1)$$

We then added regressors in a particular order: surprisal of trigram lexical, negative cosine similarity between word vector and context vector (semantic coherence), surprisal of trigram pos, top-down node count and structural distance between dependent words. Model fit was assessed using chi-square tests on the log-likelihood values to compare different models. Both the predictors were converted to z-scores before statistical analysis. Statistical significance was corrected for multiple comparisons across six ROIs with the Bonferroni method (the adjusted alpha-level is 0.05/6=0.0083).

4 Results

4.1 Correlation between predictors

The correlation matrix shows highest values for word rate and intensity ($r = 0.58$). This is expected as word rate tracks the presentation of a word, which is generally higher in intensity than silences. Similarly, f0 is also moderately correlated with intensity ($r = 0.39$) and word rate ($r = 0.37$). semantic coherence and word frequency have a correlation coefficient of 0.38; no other two parameters has a correlation coefficient higher than 0.3.

4.2 Model comparison

The complexity parameters are subsequently added to the six baseline models. In the ATLs, an improvement in the goodness of fit is obtained for Lexical-Semantic Coherence, but Structural Distance is also significant for the RATL. All the parameters are highly significant for the LPTL, roughly corresponding to the traditional "Wernicke's area". Lexical-Semantic Coherence and Structural Distance also significantly improve model fit in the LIPL. However, only the linear order lexical and POS trigram models are significant for the LIFG. The statistical details for the model comparisons are shown in Table 1.

(a) Step-wise model comparison results for LATL.

	Parameter	df	LogLik	χ^2	p
$\emptyset$		15	-11661		
A	trigram lexical	16	-11625	71.3	**<.001**
B	semantic coherence	17	-11614	22.8	**<.001**
C	trigram pos	18	-11608	12.7	**<.001**
D	node count	19	-11605	4.3	0.04
E	structural distance	20	-11605	0.9	0.34

(b) Step-wise model comparison results for RATL.

	Parameter	df	LogLik	χ^2	p
$\emptyset$		15	-11221		
A	trigram lexical	16	-11210	23.1	**<.001**
B	semantic coherence	17	-11202	15.2	**<.001**
C	trigram pos	18	-11196	11.6	**<.001**
D	node count	19	-11196	1.9	0.2
E	structural distance	20	-11189	13.3	**<.001**

(c) Step-wise model comparison results for LIFG.

	Parameter	df	LogLik	χ^2	p
$\emptyset$		15	-10653		
A	trigram lexical	16	-10648	9.3	**0.002**
B	semantic coherence	17	-10647	2.5	0.11
C	trigram lexical	18	-10639	16.5	**<.001**
D	node count	19	-10636	6.5	0.011
E	structural distance	20	-10635	0.2	0.657

(d) Step-wise model comparison results for LPTL.

	Parameter	df	LogLik	χ^2	p
$\emptyset$		15	-11898		
A	trigram lexical	16	-11867	62	**<.001**
B	semantic coherence	17	-11851	32	**<.001**
C	trigram pos	18	-11821	60	**<.001**
D	node count	19	-11810	22	**<.001**
E	structural distance	20	-11800	19	**<.001**

(e) Step-wise model comparison results for LIPL.

	Parameter	df	LogLik	χ^2	p
$\emptyset$		15	-12027		
A	trigram lexical	16	-12027	0.0	0.853
B	semantic coherence	17	-12022	9.1	**0.003**
C	trigram pos	18	-12019	5.8	0.016
D	node count	19	-12017	5.8	0.016
E	structural distance	20	-12000	34.0	**<.001**

(f) Step-wise model comparison results for LPreM.

	Parameter	df	LogLik	χ^2	p
$\emptyset$		15	-12133		
A	trigram lexical	16	-12125	15.8	**<.001**
B	semantic coherence	17	-12121	9.0	**0.003**
C	trigram lexical	18	-12120	2.1	0.143
D	node count	19	-12119	0.9	0.348
E	structural distance	20	-12117	4.3	0.039

Table 1: *Step-wise model comparison results for all regions of interest.*

5 Discussion & Conclusions

The meaning-based metric Lexical-Semantic Coherence is a significant predictor across a broad network of regions including the ATLs, LPTL, LIPL and LPreM. This is consistent with previous findings implicating bilateral ATL in conceptual combination (Rogalsky and Hickok, 2009; Wilson et al., 2014; Pylkkänen, 2015). The form-related metric Structural Distance accounts for the RATL activity even on top of Lexical-Semantic Coherence, suggesting that the ATLs are also involved in syntactic computation (Humphries et al., 2006; Brennan et al., 2012; Brennan et al., 2016).

The LPTL activity is highly correlated with all the syntactic and semantic complexity metrics. As shown in Wehbe et al. (2014), multiple regions spanning the bilateral temporal cortices represent both syntax or semantics. Our results further confirms their suggestion that syntax and semantics might be non-dissociated concepts.

No semantic or syntactic metric is significantly correlated with the LIFG, or the "Broca's area". This fails to support traditional models derived from the deficit-lesion studies that have long associated syntactic computation with the LIFG (e.g., Ben-Shachar et al., 2003; Caplan et al., 2008; Just et al., 1996; Stromswold et al., 1996). .

To sum up, our correlational results from fMRI suggest that the temporal lobes perform a kind of computation that is both syntactic in the classical sense of phrase structure, and semantic in the sense of word-embeddings. One set of questions this work leaves open is the precise relationships between these two predictors – for instance, temporal precedence. Other methods, such as MEG, may provide further insight here as suggested by van Schijndel et al. (2015).

6 Acknowledgements

This material is based upon work supported by the National Science Foundation under Grant No. 1607441. The authors thank Brian Roark for his assistance with OpenGrm.

References

M. Baroni, R. Bernardi, and R. Zamparelli. 2014. Frege in space: A program of compositional distributional semantics. *Linguistic Issues in language technology.*, 9:241–346.

P. Baumann. 2014. Dependencies and hierarchical structure in sentence processing. In *Proceedings of CogSci 2014*, pages 152–157.

M. Ben-Shachar, T. Hendler, I. Kahn, D. Ben-Bashat, and Y. Grodzinsky. 2003. The neural reality of syntactic transformations: Evidence from fmri. *Psychological Science*, 14:433–440.

J. Brennan, Y. Nir, U. Hasson, R. Malach, D. Heeger, and L. Pylkkänen. 2012. Syntactic structure building in the anterior temporal lobe during natural story listening. *Brain and Language*, 120:163–173.

J. Brennan, E. Stabler, S. Van Wagenen, W. Luh, and J. Hale. 2016. Abstract linguistic structure correlates with temporal activity during natrualistic comprehension. *Brain and Language*, 157-158:81–94.

M. Brysbaert and B. New. 2009. Moving beyond kučera and francis: A critical evaluation of current word frequency norms and the introduction of a new and improved word frequency measure for american english. *Behavior Research Methods*, 41:977–990.

D. Caplan, E. Chen, and G. Water. 2008. Task-dependent and task-independent neurovascular responses to syntactic processing. *Cortex*, 44:257–275.

M. de Marneffe, B. MacCartney, and C. Manning. 2006. Generating typed dependency parses from phrase structure parses. In *LREC 2006*.

K. Erk. 2012. Vector space models of word meaning and phrase meaning: A survey. *Language and Linguistics Compass.*, 6:635–653.

S. Frank and R. Bod. 2011. Insensitivity of the human sentence-processing system to hierarchical structure. *Psychological Science*, 22:829–834.

S. Frank, L. Otten, G. Galli, and G. Vigliocco. 2015. The erp response to the amount of information conveyed by words in sentences. *Brain and Language*, 140:1–11.

L. Frazier. 1985. Syntactic complexity. In D. Dowty, L. Karttunen, and A. Zwicky, editors, *Natural language parsing: Psychological, computational, and theoretical perspectives*, pages 129–189. Cambridge: Cambridge University Press.

E. Gibson. 1998. Syntactic complexity: Locality of syntactic dependancies. *Cognition*, 68:1–76.

J. Hale. 2001. A probabilistic earley parser as a psycholinguistic model. In *Proceedings of NAACL*, volume 2, pages 159–166.

J. Hale. 2014. *Automaton theories of human sentence comprehension.* CSLI Publications.

J. Hale. 2016. Information-theoretical complexity metrics. *Language and Linguistics Compass.*, 10:397–412.

C. Humphries, J. Binder, D. Medler, and E. Liebenthal. 2006. Syntactic and semantic modulation of neural activity during audiotry senntece comprehension. *Journal of Cognitive Neuroscience*, 18:665–679.

M. Just and S. Varma. 2007. The organization of thinking: What functional brain imaging reveals about the neuroarchitecture of complex cognition. *Cognitive, Affective, and Behavioral Neuroscience*, 7:153–191.

M. Just, P. Carpenter, T. Keller, W. Eddy, and K. Thulborn. 1996. Brain activation modulated by sentence comprehension. *Science*, 274:114–116.

D. Klein and C. Manning. 2003. Accurate unlexicalized parsing. In *Proceedings of the 41st Meeting of the association for computational linguistics.*, pages 423–430.

T. Landauer and S. Dumais. 1997. A solution to plato's problem: The latent semantic analysis theory of acquisition, induction, and representation of knowledge. *Psychological Review*, 104:211–240.

J. et al. Michel. 2011. Quantitative analysis of culture using millions of digitized books. *Science*, 331:176–182.

T. Mitchell, S. Shinkareva, A. Carlson, K. Chang, V. Malave, R. Mason, and M. Just. 2008. Predicting human brain activity associated with the meanings of nouns. *Science*, 320:1191–1195.

W. O'Grady. 1997. *Syntactic development*. Chicago, IL: University of Chicago Press.

K. Patterson, P. Nestor, and T. Rogers. 2007. Where do you know what you know? the representation of semantic knowledge in the human brain. *Nature Reviews Neuroscience*, 8:976–987.

L. Pylkkänen. 2015. Composition of complex meaning: Interdisciplinary perspectives on the left anterior temporal lobe. In G. Hickok and S. Small, editors, *Neurobiology of language*, pages 621–631. Academic Press.

J. Pynte, B. New, and A. Kennedy. 2008. A multiple regression analysis of syntactic and semantic influences in reading normal text. *Journal of Eye Movement Research*, 2:1–11.

C. Rogalsky and G. Hickok. 2009. Selective attention to semantic and syntactic features modulates setence processing networks in anterior temporal cortex. *Cerebral Cortex*, 19:786–796.

A. Sayeed, S. Fischer, and V. Demberg. 2015. Vector-space calculation of semantic surprisal for vector-space calculation of semantic surprisal for predicting word pronunciation duration. In *Proceedings of the 53rd annual meeting of the association for computational linguistics and the 7th international joint conference on natural language processing.*, volume 1, pages 763–773.

T. Snijders, T. Vosse, G. Kempen, J. Van Berkum, K. Petersson, and P. Hagoort. 2009. Retrieval and unification of syntactic structure in sentence comprehension: An fmri study using word-category ambiguity. *Cerebral Cortex*, 19:1493–1503.

E. Stabler. 1997. Derivational minimalism. In Retoré, editor, *Logical aspects of Logical aspects of computational linguistics*, pages 68–95. Springer.

K. Stromswold, D. Caplan, N. Alpert, and S. Rauch. 1996. Localization of syntactic comprehension by positron emission tomography. *Brain and Language*, 52:452–473.

M. van Schijndel, B. Murphy, and W. Schuler. 2015. Evidence of syntactic working memory usage in MEG data. In *Proceedings of CMCL 2015*, pages 79–88.

S. Van Wagenen, J. Brennan, and E. Stabler. 2014. Quantifying parsing complexity as a function of grammar. In C. Schütze and L. Stockall, editors, *UCLA working papers in linguistics.*, volume 18, pages 31–47. UCLA Linguistics Department.

E. Wanner and M. Maratsos. 1978. An atn approach to comprehension. In M. Halle, J. Bresnan, and G. Miller, editors, *Linguistics theory and psychological reality*. The MIT Press.

L. Wehbe, B. Murphy, P. Talukdar, A. Fyshe, A. Ramdas, and T. Mitchell. 2014. Simutaneously uncovering the patterns of brain regions involved in different story reading subprocesses. *PLoS ONE*, 9:e112575.

S. Wilson, A. DeMarco, M. Henry, B. Gesierich, M. Babiak, M. Mandelli, B. Miller, and M. Gorno-Tempini. 2014. What role does the anterior temporal lobe play in sentence-level processing? neural correlates if syntactic processing in sematic ppa. *Journal of Cognitive Neuroscience*, 26:970–985.

V. Yngve. 1960. A model and a hypothesis for language structure. In *Processings of the American Philosophical Society.*, volume 104, pages 444–466.

Automatic Speech Recognition Errors as a Predictor of L2 Listening Difficulties

Maryam Sadat Mirzaei, Kourosh Meshgi, Tatsuya Kawahara
Graduate School of Informatics, Kyoto University
Yoshida-Honmachi, Sakyo-ku, Kyoto 606-8501, Japan
`maryam@sap.ist.i.kyoto-u.ac.jp`

Abstract

This paper investigates the use of automatic speech recognition (ASR) errors as indicators of the second language (L2) learners' listening difficulties and in doing so strives to overcome the shortcomings of Partial and Synchronized Caption (PSC) system. PSC is a system that generates a partial caption including difficult words detected based on high speech rate, low frequency, and specificity. To improve the choice of words in this system, and explore a better method to detect speech challenges, ASR errors were investigated as a model of the L2 listener, hypothesizing that some of these errors are similar to those of language learners' when transcribing the videos. To investigate this hypothesis, ASR errors in transcription of several TED talks were analyzed and compared with PSC's selected words. Both the overlapping and mismatching cases were analyzed to investigate possible improvement for the PSC system. Those ASR errors that were not detected by PSC as cases of learners' difficulties were further analyzed and classified into four categories: homophones, minimal pairs, breached boundaries and negatives. These errors were embedded into the baseline PSC to make the enhanced version and were evaluated in an experiment with L2 learners. The results indicated that the enhanced version, which encompasses the ASR errors addresses most of the L2 learners' difficulties and better assists them in comprehending challenging video segments as compared with the baseline.

1 Introduction

Automatic speech recognition technology has formed the integral part of many language learning tools and CALL systems particularly for evaluating, training and improving L2 pronunciation and speaking skill (Neri et al., 2003; Witt, 2012; Thomson and Derwing, 2014). However, this technology has rarely been used for developing listening skill. When it comes to listening skill, instructors are often disadvantaged by the lack of readily available information about the challenges and difficulties of the audio/visual input. Therefore, they suggest the use of assistive tools, such as caption, to help the learners overcome their listening difficulties (Danan, 2004; Winke et al., 2010).

It is criticized, however, that captioning can allow the learner to comprehend the speech by reading the text even without listening (Pujolà, 2002; Vandergrift, 2011). In this view, captioning cannot serve the purpose of promoting the use of listening skill for language learners. To assist L2 learners in training listening skill, an alternative captioning tool called partial and synchronized caption (PSC) was developed (Mirzaei et al., 2016b). The system attempts to realize effective listening by presenting difficult words in the caption and hiding easy ones. PSC employs ASR technology to synchronize each word to the corresponding speech segment in order to allow text-to-speech mapping. It then selects difficult words based on the speech rate, frequency, and specificity of the words (Figure 1). These three factors are accounted for the major causes of L2 listening difficulties according to many studies (Griffiths, 1992; Révész and Brunfaut, 2013). However, there are a number of other factors such as hesitation, distortion, breached boundaries, etc. that play equal roles in making L2 listening challenging for language learners (Field, 2003; Bloomfield et al., 2010). To investigate such factors, this paper attempts to use the ASR

Proceedings of the Workshop on Computational Linguistics for Linguistic Complexity,
pages 192–201, Osaka, Japan, December 11-17 2016.

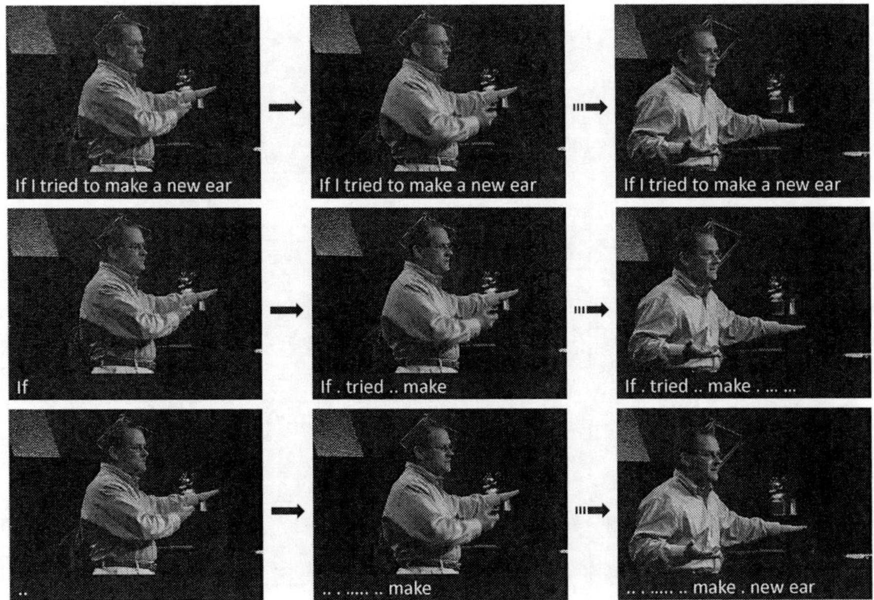

Figure 1: Caption types: (top) Full caption, (mid) Baseline partial and synchronized caption(PSC), (bottom) Enhanced PSC. TED talk by Alan Russell: The potential of regenerative medicine

technology in order to detect the problematic speech segments and to improve the choice of words in the PSC system.

Spontaneous speech such as TED talks presents numerous challenges to both ASR systems and L2 listeners. These challenges often lead to the erroneous performance of the ASR systems (Radha and Vimala, 2012; Goldwater et al., 2010). Such errors potentially involve useful information on the difficulties of speech. Accordingly, the main idea of the paper is to consider the ASR system as a potential model for L2 learners, which will encounter similar difficulties in the perception of the speech and transcription of the audio, thereby could be an indicative of areas of learner difficulties in listening.

Previous studies have compared the ASR systems performance with native and non-native speakers (but not L2 learners) of the target language. These studies are known as ASR-HSR (human speech recognition) research (Meyer et al., 2006; Scharenborg, 2007; Vasilescu et al., 2011). The majority of these studies conclude that HSR outperforms ASR especially in spontaneous speech and suggest different methods to improve the quality of the ASR output and reduce the word error rate (Moore and Cutler, 2001; Scharenborg, 2007). In this study, however, rather than considering ASR errors as major drawbacks of these systems, we are focusing on them as a rich source that elucidates the difficulties of speech. In this view, ASR errors and PSC selected words share some cases as they both refer to similar sources of difficulties. Nevertheless, the ASR errors include a wider range of factors and can introduce undiscovered features, hence can be complementary for the PSC system. In this regard, in an earlier study, we compared the ASR errors with L2 learners' mistakes on transcribing the audio in a contrastive analysis of ASR and L2SR (second language speech recognition). To this end, an in-depth error analysis was performed between the ASR systems and L2 learners (Mirzaei et al., 2015). The results of this study confirmed that some parts of the input were difficult to decode by both ASR systems and language learners and these often led to the erroneous performance of both. Thus, it was concluded that ASR errors could provide insights on detecting challenging speech segments.

To further investigate this concept, in this study, ASR errors and PSC's selected words are compared to specify the degree of overlap and differences. Through this analysis, those ASR errors, which were not included in the PSC's selected words, were detected. Next, the underlying factors that associated with the emergence of these groups of errors were investigated. Drawing upon literature, it was found that some of these root-cause factors lead to listening difficulties for L2 listeners (Field, 1998; Field, 2003). This

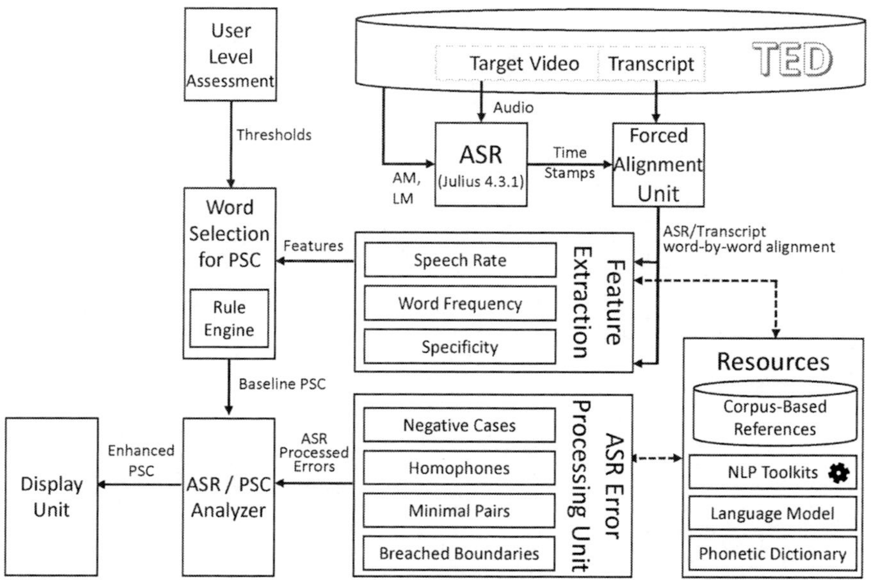

Figure 2: Schematic of the PSC system architecture. Julius ASR system was trained using 780 hours of TED talks and used to transcribe the given video. Via a word-level forced-alignment procedure, the original transcript is synchronized with the speaker's utterance. Several features are extracted for each word in the Feature Extraction module. Considering the user's proficiency level, the Rule Engine marks difficult words and generates the Baseline PSC. The ASR errors, on the other hand, signals other types of listening difficulties, which are extracted using ASR Error Processing Unit. These instances are included to the Baseline PSC to generate the Enhanced PSC.

indicates that these errors can provide useful hints for detecting difficult words or phrases. Accordingly, the aim of the present paper is to detect those parts of the speech that cause listening difficulties for L2 learners by attending to the ASR errors and incorporating them into PSC to provide better assistance for the L2 learners. Moreover, ASR correct cases that were contrarily detected to be difficult by PSC's features, were utilized as a signal for relatively easier segments of speech and used to remove too easy words from the PSC (Figure 2). The enhanced PSC will then build on the baseline system, employing the ASR clues. This enhanced version aims to outperform the baseline PSC in providing essential clues for recognition of the listening tasks to the L2 learners.

2   Method

52 TED talks (approximately 15 hours) were used in this study. `Julius 4.3.1` ASR system (Lee and Kawahara, 2009) was employed to generate the transcripts for these talks. This ASR system was trained using 780 hours of TED talks based on the lightly-supervised training approach (Naptali and Kawahara, 2012). Human-annotated transcripts for these talks were readily available from the TED website and used to evaluate the ASR output. Using forced alignment method, the two transcripts were aligned in word-level to enable error detection. Next, the errors were classified into deletion, insertion and substitution categories as shown in Table 1. ASR error rate was 19.8% with the majority of errors belonging to substitution categories.

2.1   Comparison of ASR Output and PSC Selection

PSC was generated for these videos controlling for high speech rate, low frequency, and specific or academic words. The selected words to be shown in the PSC based on the above categories were compared with the ASR errors to find the degree of overlap. We assumed that ASR errors and PSC's selected words should share some cases, as both refer to the difficult words. Table 2 indicates that 3.7 percent of the

Categories	Frequency	(%)
Total Words	145,663	
ASR Correct	116,807	(80.2%)
ASR Errors	28,856	(19.8%)
ASR Error Substitution	24,269	(16.7%)
ASR Error Insertion	2,928	(2.0%)
ASR Error Deletion	1,659	(1.1%)

Table 1: ASR error analysis

	ASR Correct (80.2%)	ASR Errors (19.8%)
PSC shown words (17.7%)	**(a)** 14.0%	**(b)** 3.7%
PSC hidden words (82.3%)	**(c)** 66.2%	**(d)** 16.1%

Table 2: ASR performance versus baseline PSC's choice of words. In **(a)** PSC categorized the words as difficult cases based on its three features, but ASR managed to correctly recognize them. Cell **(b)** indicates difficult sections according to both PSC and ASR, whereas cell **(c)** accounts for easy regions of the speech. Cell **(d)** counts the challenging words for ASR that PSC missed to select. The proposed enhancement on PSC aims to utilize ASR errors for hiding too easy words and showing the difficult words that the baseline PSC missed, i.e., to move words from **(a)** to **(c)** and from **(d)** to **(b)**.

cases are common between ASR errors and PSC shown words, however, 16.1 percent of the ASR errors could not be explained by PSC's features.

To better understand the results, the ASR errors were further analyzed taking PSC's features into account, i.e. frequency, speech rate and specificity features. Similar to PSC, the speech rate of the ASR errors were calculated in syllables per second, the frequency was estimated based on the corpus of contemporary American English - COCA (Gardner and Davies, 2013) and the specific words were detected by referring to the Academic Word List (Coxhead, 2000) and academic corpus of COCA. Figure 3 illustrates the comparison between ASR errors with PSC selection.

Figure 3(a) depicts the distribution of the mutual cases between the ASR errors and PSC's selected words based on the speech rate, frequency, and specificity. As the figure suggests speech rate is the primary factor that selects the words for PSC and is also the major factor that leads to the emergence of the ASR errors (58%). The frequency factor shows 20 percent of overlap between the PSC shown words and the ASR errors. Finally, specific words are by default set to be always shown in the PSC system, yet only a small number of these words cause ASR errors (6%).

2.2 Analysis of ASR Correct Cases

While our assumption is that ASR errors can indicate problematic speech segments for L2 listeners, ASR correct cases can specify easy items, which may not be necessarily needed to appear in PSC. Looking back to Table 2, our analysis reveals that 14.0% of the ASR correct cases are categorized as difficult words by PSC and are shown in the caption. To explore these cases, we made similar analysis considering the speech rate, frequency and specificity factors. Figure 3(b) demonstrates how these three features are responsible for words in this category, i.e. PSC shown words and ASR correct output. As the figure shows, speech rate (43%) is still the main reason to show these words in PSC, while many of the words brought by the speech rate factor could be correctly transcribed by our ASR system; indicating that these words were not too difficult. Examples include the words such as *one, every, open, look,* etc., which have high frequency and can be simply excluded from PSC without causing a barrier for L2 listeners. Thus, the findings notify the importance of refining our speech rate threshold on ASR correct cases to prevent the inclusion of difficult cases in PSC.

On the other hand, our investigation revealed that few instances of the words shown in PSC based on the frequency feature seem to be unnecessary. For instance, words such as *dystopia, piggybacking,*

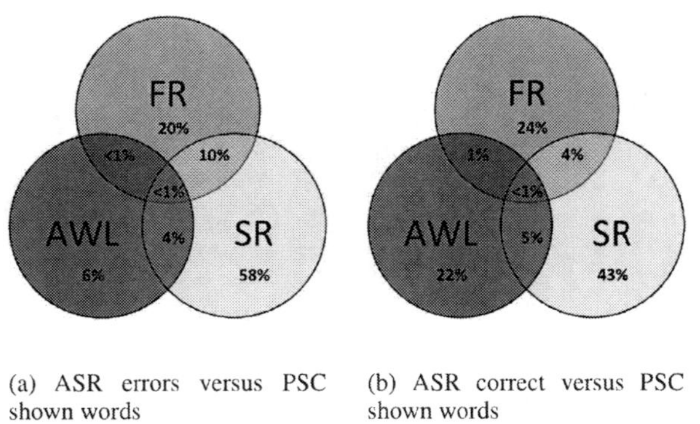

(a) ASR errors versus PSC shown words

(b) ASR correct versus PSC shown words

Figure 3: Feature analysis of PSC shown words regarding the correctness of ASR output

pandemic, larceny, abyss, could be correctly transcribed by the ASR, but are infrequent to many L2 listeners and hence likely to be unknown.

Based on our findings, while specific words are always shown in PSC, many of them are not infrequent. For example, words such as *positive, science* and *research* are categorized as academic terms. However, these words are very frequent and the majority of L2 listeners should have no problem with them. Likewise, highly frequent Proper nouns (e.g. *China* and *Obama*) could be simply omitted from or repeated less in the PSC. Meanwhile, our ASR system could also correctly transcribe these words. These findings suggest that frequency of specific words and proper nouns should be considered when deciding on their inclusion in PSC.

2.3 Analysis of ASR Erroneous Cases

The strategies to refine the choice of words in PSC based on excluding easy cases are taken for granted in this study. However, a thorough investigation is needed to ensure that segments including ASR errors are actually difficult for L2 learners. Our earlier experiment with L2 listeners, who were asked to transcribe ASR erroneous cases, revealed that learners have substantial difficulties in transcribing segments that include ASR errors (Mirzaei et al., 2016a).

Based on these results, we augmented the baseline PSC to automatically detect these groups of errors (ASR errors not shown in PSC). We have limited the scope of the automation in this stage to the nine categories of **homophones, minimal pairs, negatives, breached boundaries, verb inflections, determiners, prefixes/suffixes, possessives and plural cases**, since the root-causes of other ASR errors were difficult to discover, hence these categories were discarded in this study. Our earlier study (Mirzaei et al., 2016a) showed that from among all categories, four of them are beneficial for L2 learners: homophones, minimal pairs, breached boundaries and negative cases.

Verb inflections and prefix/suffix derivations of the words are detected using word lemmatizers and COCA word stem list, while language-specific grammar rules are used to detect possessives and plurals. Detecting homophones and minimal pairs rely on word-to-phone mappings empowered by CMU Pronouncing Dictionary. The dictionary allows mappings from words to their pronunciations in the ARPAbet phoneme set, which in turn enables us to detect homophones and minimal pairs. Homophones are defined as two words with different writings, but identical ARPAbet transcripts (e.g., *blue* /B L UW/ and *blew* /B L UW/). In the case of ASR substitution errors, we select the closest pronunciation of a word in the transcript to its ASR-hypothesized utterance. Some special cases are handled, for instance, American and British spelling differences were considered.

Two words are minimal pairs if their phonetics has a Levenshtein distance of one, and they have distinct meaning. This distance enables the detection of different types of minimal pairs: initial consonant (e.g., *rot* /R AA T/ and *lot* /L AA T/), vowels (e.g., *pen* /P EH N/ and *pan* /P AE N/), and final consonant (e.g., *hat* /HH AE T/ and *had* /HH AE D/). Miniml pairs are found to be difficult to distinguish for the L2 learners (e.g., *lay* /L EY/ and *clay* /C L EY/) (Weber and Cutler, 2004). This category also includes the third person in the present tense and past tense for regular verbs, which we preferred to exclude from the list.

Wrong boundary detection can be attributed to numerous factors, many of which are rare or hard to regulate. In this sense, some of the most studied phenomena are considered that may lead to wrong boundary detection in L2 listening. One of these rules is the frequency rule (Field, 2008; Cutler, 1990), which is built upon the idea that listeners tend to associate what the speaker says to high-frequency words when the speaker actually uses less frequent or unknown word (e.g., *dusty senseless drilling* → *thus he sent his drill in*). This is in line with what happens in ASR system when facing out-of-vocabulary words (Chen et al., 2013). To implement this rule, the average of ASR-hypothesized error phrase on the false boundary is calculated and compared to the average of the original phrase. Function words are excluded from calculations for having an excessive high frequency, as argued in (Cutler, 1990).

Another pattern that elicits breached boundary is a special arrangement of strong and weak syllables within one word or consecutive words (Cutler, 1990). Strong syllables typically signal for the beginning of the word, which explains why learners tend to insert a boundary when they encounter a strong syllable (e.g., *it was illegal* → *it was a legal*). On the other hand, learners often remove the boundaries and combine the words when they encounter a week syllable (e.g., *paint with a brush* → *paint without rush*). Attending to these rules, we tried to detect such boundary cases in our algorithm.

Resyllabification (Field, 2003) is another rule which often refers to the attachment of final consonant to the following syllable (e.g., *last hour* → *glass tower*).

Assimilation (Cruttenden, 2014) is another common phenomenon, in which one sound becomes similar or more like a nearby sound (e.g., *did you go?* → *di due go*). Assimilation patterns are restricted in English. Therefore, we followed the standard patterns in (Cruttenden, 2014) to detect such cases.

Accordingly, we calculate the Levenshtein distance of the phonetic representations of the transcript and ASR-hypothesized phrase. If the distance doesn't exceed a pre-defined threshold (e.g., four differences), we proceed to examine the frequency of the words. If the flagged ASR error involved words with higher frequency (obtained by COCA corpus), then we may have a breached boundary. Along with the frequency check, we draw upon the stress pattern, syllabification, and assimilation rules to precisely detect the misrecognized boundary cases.

Finally, there are numerous situations where acoustic artifacts and speaker disfluencies or high speech rate prevent the listener from hearing the words accurately. Negative forms, in this regard, are the most likely ones to be misrecognized, while they are important to distinguish for understanding the meaning of the sentence. Given the difference between *can and can't*, for example, is a subtle one, these cases are frequently misrecognized by many L2 listeners. Other instances such as *legal and illegal* are equally important as their misrecognition can thoroughly change the meaning. To assist learners in this regard, we detected all the negative forms, which were among the ASR errors to include in the PSC system.

3 PSC Enhancement

To enhance the PSC system we apply the clues derived from the investigation of ASR errors and PSC selected word. The analysis provided us with useful insights on removing easy cases from the baseline PSC in order to provide room for inclusion of more difficult words in the enhanced version. To this end, the frequency of specific words (academic terms) was taken into account in the enhanced version. Referring to COCA academic word corpus, we could retrieve the frequency of these words and by determining a threshold based on an expert suggestion, we aimed to exclude trivial specific words in the enhanced version. The same strategy was used for highly frequent proper nouns *(e.g. America, Paris)*. In the enhanced PSC, the frequency of these cases is based on the frequency of their occurrences in TED corpus. Another enhancement on the exclusion of the easy cases regards the speech rate threshold, which was refined by defining a secondary threshold. In the case of ASR correct output, a stricter threshold was applied to prevent the speech rate factor from bringing in too many easy words. Through these improvements, many of the easy cases were excluded from the enhanced version. In the next step, difficult cases, which were detected based on ASR erroneous output were embedded into the PSC. These cases, which include homophones, minimal pair, breached boundaries and negatives were automatically detected and incorporated into the PSC system to foster L2 listening for the learners. Table 3 presents the distribution of shown and hidden words in the enhanced PSC based on ASR correct and erroneous cases. As the table shows, using ASR clues, we could successfully move some of the easy cases (3.6%) from **(a)** to **(b)**, i.e exclude trivial words from PSC shown to PSC hide. More importantly, our enhanced version encompasses more of the ASR errors (cases were moved from **(d) to (b)** to provide an effective scaffold for L2 listeners (7.1%). It should be noted that a comparable number of shown words in both the baseline and enhanced version were maintained (the enhanced version includes an even lower amount of words) in order to enable a fair comparison.

	ASR Correct (80.2%)	ASR Errors (19.8%)
PSC shown words (17.5%)	**(a)** 11.4%	**(b)** 7.1%
PSC hidden words (82.5%)	**(c)** 69.8%	**(d)** 12.7%

Table 3: ASR performance versus Enhanced PSC's choice of words

4 Experimental Evaluation

While some improvement could be anticipated based on these enhancements, an experiment was conducted in order to confirm our hypothesis that the enhanced PSC is more helpful to the learners than the baseline.

4.1 Participants

The participants of this study were 38 Japanese and Chinese students who enrolled in CALL courses at Kyoto University. They were undergraduates, majoring in different fields such as engineering, law, science, etc. All participants had TOEIC ITP scores between 450 to 560, notifying that they were beginners to pre-intermediates. There were 8 females and 30 male students.

4.2 Material

20 TED videos were selected for this experiment. All talks were delivered by native American English speakers. We excluded the effect of other accents such as British English in our experiment. From these videos, those segments in which there was a difference between the baseline and the enhanced PSC were extracted. These segments included ASR error – PSC hide cases i.e. they involved one of the four categories of minimal pair, homophone, breached boundary, and negative.

4.3 Procedure

Two type of questions were designed for this experiment:

Transcribing: The participants were asked to watch a series of video segments, each segment lasting from 25 to 35 seconds. Once a video paused, the participants were supposed to transcribe the last few words that they have heard. Each segment ended with 4~6 words, including the target word(s), all replaced by a blank. Videos were paused at irregular intervals and the participants were not aware of the exact time of the pause in order to simulate real-life listening. Moreover, the target word(s) was among the words to be transcribed and the participants had no clue about it. A timer was set for each question and the participants were supposed to transcribe the words right after the pause without having excess time to overthink or analyze, but to type down exactly what they have recognized. It was anticipated that immediately after the transcription, the participants could recognize their difficulties and misrecognitions, therefore immediately after transcribing the audio, the participants received two types of captions (baseline and enhanced PSC) to choose from. They were supposed to select the caption that included more of their misrecognized words, i.e., the ones that can better assist them to overcome their listening difficulties. Both the baseline and the enhanced versions included the same number of words, but different choices to make a fair comparison.

Paraphrasing: To make a more quantitative analysis, students were randomly assigned into two groups. One group received the baseline PSC, whereas the other one received the enhanced version.

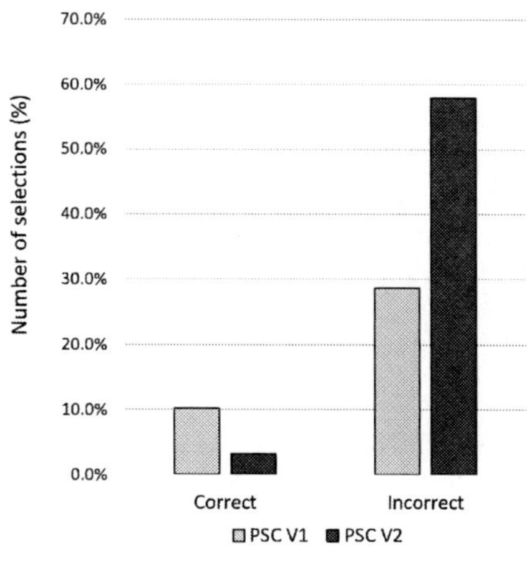
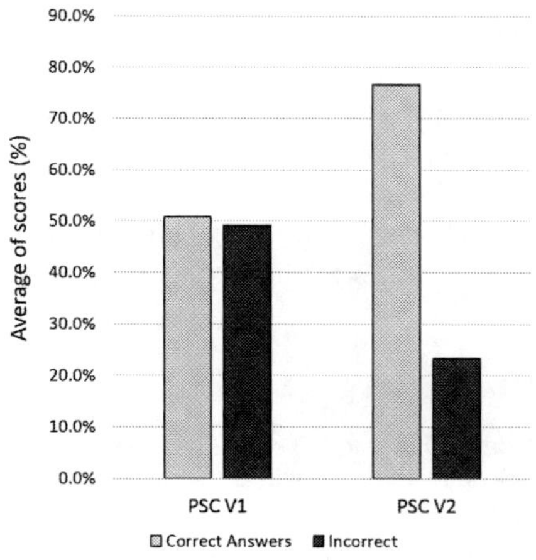

(a) Part 1: Transcribing and choosing from baseline and enhanced PSC – the graph shows the number of participants who chose baseline PSC (PSC V1) versus Enhanced PSC (PSC V2).

(b) Part 2: Paraphrasing based on the type of caption received in each group: baseline (PSC V1) vs. enhanced (PSC V2) – The graph shows the paraphrasing scores in the two groups.

Figure 4: Experimental results

They were asked to watch the videos with the assigned type of caption and paraphrase the last sentence of each segment whenever the video was paused. Paraphrase test focuses on the recognition of a specific part of listening material thus the participants' answers on paraphrasing the last segment are based on the caption clues they have received in each group. It was assumed that the group who received the enhanced PSC had better hints to disambiguate the sentence and select the best paraphrasing choice.

5   Results

The results of this experiments should be explained in two parts: (1) the number of times the enhanced PSC was chosen over the baseline PSC after the transcription task (qualitative analysis) and (2) the scores of the participants on paraphrasing the last sentence based on the type of the caption they had received (quantitative analysis).

Figure 4(a) shows the analysis of the results on participants' preferences regarding the selection between the baseline and the enhanced PSC. As the figure shows the number of times the participants preferred the enhanced PSC is significantly higher than the baseline version (61% versus 39%).

Our quantitative analysis on the participants' paraphrasing scores illustrated in figure 4(b) demonstrates that the students in the enhanced PSC group gained statistically higher scores than their peers in the baseline group (based on a t-test analysis). While the baseline PSC group answered the questions chance-like (50.9% correct versus 49.1% incorrect), the enhanced PSC group could choose the correct answer 76% of the time.

The results reveal that some of the ASR errors signal problematic speech segments and ASR clues could be used for facilitating recognition and comprehension of the input. Moreover, our findings identified that some improvements are realized in the enhanced PSC, which makes it more preferable to the L2 listeners. Furthermore, the enhanced version, which encompasses useful ASR errors, can better assist the L2 listeners compared to the baseline.

6   Conclusion

The study investigated the use of ASR errors in detecting problematic speech segments and improving the word selection criteria in PSC. Following a thorough analysis, it was found that several categories in the ASR errors signal the difficulties for the L2 listeners. These categories include homophones, minimal pairs, negative, and breached boundaries. Our baseline PSC system was extended to detect these cases and generate the enhanced PSC drawing upon these clues. On the other hand, analysis of these errors provided some insights on how to refine PSC's selection by omitting too easy cases.

Experiment with the L2 listeners confirmed this hypothesis that some of these errors can predict L2 listening difficulties; hence the enhanced PSC, which includes these cases, can effectively assist the L2 listeners. To conclude our in-depth analysis on the ASR errors revealed that ASR systems epitomize a model of an L2 listener, shedding light on both easy and difficult words and phrases in the input, which can be directly used to enhance the PSC system in order to foster L2 listening.

References

Amber Bloomfield, Sarah C Wayland, Elizabeth Rhoades, Allison Blodgett, Jared Linck, and Steven Ross. 2010. What makes listening difficult? factors affecting second language listening comprehension. Technical report, DTIC Document.

Wei Chen, Sankaranarayanan Ananthakrishnan, Rohit Kumar, Rohit Prasad, and Prem Natarajan. 2013. Asr error detection in a conversational spoken language translation system. In *2013 IEEE International Conference on Acoustics, Speech and Signal Processing*, pages 7418–7422. IEEE.

Averil Coxhead. 2000. A new academic word list. *TESOL quarterly*, 34(2):213–238.

Alan Cruttenden. 2014. *Gimson's pronunciation of English*. Routledge.

Anne Cutler. 1990. Exploiting prosodic probabilities in speech segmentation.

Martine Danan. 2004. Captioning and subtitling: Undervalued language learning strategies. *Meta: Journal des traducteursMeta:/Translators'Journal*, 49(1):67–77.

John Field. 1998. Skills and strategies: Towards a new methodology for listening. *ELT journal*, 52(2):110–118.

John Field. 2003. Promoting perception: Lexical segmentation in l2 listening. *ELT journal*, 57(4):325–334.

John Field. 2008. Bricks or mortar: which parts of the input does a second language listener rely on? *TESOL quarterly*, 42(3):411–432.

Dee Gardner and Mark Davies. 2013. A new academic vocabulary list. *Applied Linguistics*, page amt015.

Sharon Goldwater, Dan Jurafsky, and Christopher D Manning. 2010. Which words are hard to recognize? prosodic, lexical, and disfluency factors that increase speech recognition error rates. *Speech Communication*, 52(3):181–200.

Roger Griffiths. 1992. Speech rate and listening comprehension: Further evidence of the relationship. *TESOL quarterly*, 26(2):385–390.

Akinobu Lee and Tatsuya Kawahara. 2009. Recent development of open-source speech recognition engine julius. In *Proceedings: APSIPA ASC 2009: Asia-Pacific Signal and Information Processing Association, 2009 Annual Summit and Conference*, pages 131–137. Asia-Pacific Signal and Information Processing Association, 2009 Annual Summit and Conference, International Organizing Committee.

Bernd Meyer, Thorsten Wesker, Thomas Brand, Alfred Mertins, and Birger Kollmeier. 2006. A human-machine comparison in speech recognition based on a logatome corpus. In *Speech Recognition and Intrinsic Variation Workshop*.

Maryam Sadat Mirzaei, Kourosh Meshgi, Yuya Akita, and Tatsuya Kawahara. 2015. Errors in automatic speech recognition versus difficulties in second language listening. In *Critical CALL–Proceedings of the 2015 EURO-CALL Conference, Padova, Italy*, page 410. Research-publishing.net.

Maryam Sadat Mirzaei, Kourosh Meshgi, and Tatsuya Kawahara. 2016a. Leveraging automatic speech recognition errors to detect challenging speech segments in ted talks. In *CALL Communities and Culture-Proceedings of the 2016 EUROCALL Conference, Limmasol, Cyprus*. Research-publishing.net.

Maryam Sadat Mirzaei, Kourosh Meshgi, and Tatsuya Kawahara. 2016b. Partial and synchronized captioning: A new tool to assist learners in developing second language listening skill. *ReCALL (in press)*.

Roger K Moore and Anne Cutler. 2001. Constraints on theories of human vs. machine recognition of speech. In *Workshop on Speech Recognition as Pattern Classification (SPRAAC)*, pages 145–150. Max Planck Institute for Psycholinguistics.

Welly Naptali and Tatsuya Kawahara. 2012. Automatic transcription of ted talks. IWSLT.

Ambra Neri, Catia Cucchiarini, and Wilhelmus Strik. 2003. Automatic speech recognition for second language learning: how and why it actually works. In *Proc. ICPhS*, pages 1157–1160.

Joan-Tomàs Pujolà. 2002. Calling for help: Researching language learning strategies using help facilities in a web-based multimedia program. *ReCALL*, 14(02):235–262.

V Radha and C Vimala. 2012. A review on speech recognition challenges and approaches. *doaj. org*, 2(1):1–7.

Andrea Révész and Tineke Brunfaut. 2013. Text characteristics of task input and difficulty in second language listening comprehension. *Studies in Second Language Acquisition*, 35(01):31–65.

Odette Scharenborg. 2007. Reaching over the gap: A review of efforts to link human and automatic speech recognition research. *Speech Communication*, 49(5):336–347.

Ron I Thomson and Tracey M Derwing. 2014. The effectiveness of l2 pronunciation instruction: A narrative review. *Applied Linguistics*, page amu076.

Larry Vandergrift. 2011. Second language listening. *Handbook of research in second language teaching and learning*, 2:455.

Ioana Vasilescu, Dahbia Yahia, Natalie D Snoeren, Martine Adda-Decker, and Lori Lamel. 2011. Cross-lingual study of asr errors: On the role of the context in human perception of near-homophones. In *INTERSPEECH*, pages 1949–1952.

Andrea Weber and Anne Cutler. 2004. Lexical competition in non-native spoken-word recognition. *Journal of Memory and Language*, 50(1):1–25.

Paula Winke, Susan Gass, and Tetyana Sydorenko. 2010. The effects of captioning videos used for foreign language listening activities. *Language Learning & Technology*, 14(1):65–86.

Silke M Witt. 2012. Automatic error detection in pronunciation training: Where we are and where we need to go. *Proc. IS ADEPT*, 6.

Quantifying sentence complexity based on eye-tracking measures

Abhinav Deep Singh, Poojan Mehta, Samar Husain, Rajakrishnan Rajkumar
Indian Institute of Technology Delhi
New Delhi, India
{abhinav1010.ads, poojanmehta8994}@gmail.com
{samar, raja}@hss.iitd.ac.in

Abstract

Eye-tracking reading times have been attested to reflect cognitive processes underlying sentence comprehension. However, the use of reading times in NLP applications is an underexplored area of research. In this initial work we build an automatic system to assess sentence complexity using automatically predicted eye-tracking reading time measures and demonstrate the efficacy of these reading times for a well known NLP task, namely, readability assessment.

We use a machine learning model and a set of features known to be significant predictors of reading times in order to learn per-word reading times from a corpus of English text having reading times of human readers. Subsequently, we use the model to predict reading times for novel text in the context of the aforementioned task. A model based only on reading times gave competitive results compared to the systems that use extensive syntactic features to compute linguistic complexity. Our work, to the best of our knowledge, is the first study to show that *automatically predicted* reading times can successfully model the difficulty of a text and can be deployed in practical text processing applications.

1 Introduction

Quantifying the complexity of a sentence has been one of the central goals of psycholinguistics (Gibson, 2000; Lewis, 1996; Levy, 2008). Decades of experimental research has shown us that certain kinds of syntactic patterns are more complex than others. For example, in English, object relative clause is generally assumed to be more difficult than the active counterpart e.g. (Gibson, 2000). Similarly center-embeddings lead to more complexity (Lewis and Vasishth, 2005). Such experiments try to establish a causal link between complex linguistic pattern and processing difficulty. The difficulty is manifested in slower response of a measurable variable (e.g. reaction time, gaze duration, etc.). The eye-tracking experimental paradigm is known to capture processing difficulty during naturalistic reading (Just and Carpenter, 1980; Frazier and Rayner, 1982; Clifton et al., 2007).

Deploying insights from eye-movement research for Natural Language Processing (NLP) tasks is an upcoming area of research. Previous works have used fixation durations (and saccades) as features in their prediction models. For example, eye-movement data has been used to model translation difficulty (Mishra et al., 2013), sentiment annotation complexity (Joshi et al., 2014), and sarcasm detection (Mishra et al., 2016). Recent works have also incorporated eye-tracking data as features in sequence models for part-of-speech tagging (Barrett et al., 2016; Barrett and Søgaard, 2015).

In this exploratory work, we build an automatic system to assess sentence complexity using *automatically predicted* eye-tracking reading time measures and demonstrate the efficacy of these reading times for READABILITY ASSESSMENT. **Readability assessment** is the task of automatically classifying text into different levels of difficulty (Petersen and Ostendorf, 2009; Feng, 2010; Vajjala and Meurers, 2014). One use of such difficulty assessment could be to evaluate text simplification, e.g. to automatically simplify Wikipedia text for the English L2 learners (Zhu et al., 2010; Woodsend and Lapata, 2011; Coster and Kauchak, 2011; Wubben et al., 2012; Siddharthan and Mandya, 2014). There is also a large

Proceedings of the Workshop on Computational Linguistics for Linguistic Complexity,
pages 202–212, Osaka, Japan, December 11-17 2016.

body of work that has attempted to quantify and automatically compute the complexity of a text using various linguistic features (Kincaid et al., 1975; Flesch, 1948; Gunning, 1968; Si and Callan, 2001). See Vajjala Balakrishna (2015) for an extensive review. Such quantification becomes necessary for tasks such as text simplification (Siddharthan, 2014) and for L2 learners' systems (Schwarm and Ostendorf, 2005). So far previous work in text simplification (and more generally in NLP) has not explored directly using various eye-tracking reading time measures while quantifying linguistic complexity. Clearly, such reading times are not available for new text and hence need to be automatically predicted. For machine translation evaluation, Mishra et al. (2013) formulate a translation difficulty index which is computed using eye-movement data, but they do not directly predict reading time measures.

Our work, to the best of our knowledge, is the first study to show that automatically predicted reading times can successfully model the difficulty of a text and can be deployed in practical text processing applications. We use a machine learning model and a set of features known to be significant predictors of reading times in order to learn per-word reading times from a corpus of English text having reading times of human readers. Subsequently, we use the model to predict reading times for novel text for readability assessment. For this task, a model based only on reading times gave competitive results compared to the systems that use extensive syntactic features. Our best-performing model, which combines learned reading times with other sentence-level features, comes close to state-of-the-art results reported previously for the dataset used in this work (Ambati et al., 2016; Vajjala and Meurers, 2016).

The paper is organized as follows. Section 2 provides an overview of our two-level hierarchical system. Section 3 describes our model to automatically predict per-word reading time using a wide range of lexical as well as syntactic features. Subsequently, Section 4 reports on our readability assessment experiments using predicted reading times from the above model. Finally, we conclude the paper in Section 5.

2   Approach

Our approach comprises of two modules:

1. **Reading time (RT) prediction**: System-1 using lexical and syntactic features to predict the reading times (RTs) of each word in the sentence

2. **Sentence level prediction**: System-2 using predicted reading times (outputted by System-1) and other sentence-level features for the task of readability assessment.

Supervised learning algorithms were employed to train both systems (1) and (2).

2.1   Motivation: Why predict RTs?

An obvious question that could be asked about our approach is 'Why build a two-step system?' or 'Why use predicted RTs when one can use linguistic features directly?'. Several reasons present themselves in support of our approach:

1. We would like to explore the extent to which behavioural measure of processing difficulty can be used to predict sentential complexity.

2. It is known from the experimental psycholinguistic literature that eye-tracking RTs can reflect increased linguistic complexity (Clifton et al., 2007; Vasishth et al., 2012). A model that predicts RTs for each word in a sentence can contribute to a fine-grained picture of reading difficulty at various points in a sentence, in contrast to sentence-level features.

3. Finally, previous works cited in the introduction have demonstrated the efficacy of using RTs for various NLP applications. Many of these works, e.g. (Mishra et al., 2016), have used gold RTs (reading times collected from participants). Clearly, if one needs to use RTs for large amount of novel text, they have to be automatically predicted.

3   System 1 - Predicting Reading Times

In this section we discuss the features that can impact reading time prediction. We do this using an ablation study and using Pearson's coefficient. Only those features which cause an increase in R^2 goodness score are selected for the final model.

3.1   Data Set

The Dundee eye-tracking corpus (Kennedy, 2003) was used to train the reading time prediction system. It has eye-movement record of 10 participants on a large collection of newspaper text. We used 2378 sentences (50597 words) from the Dundee corpus. We randomly divided the data (at sentence level, and not word level) into training (60%), development (20%) and test (20%) splits. RTs for all the subjects were pooled into one set.[1]

Our task is to predict the reading times of each word in a sentence. We will focus on 4 types of measures – first fixation duration, first pass duration, regression path duration and total duration. Together these measures represent the 'early' and 'late' measures and are known to reflect sentence processing difficulty (Clifton et al., 2007). *First fixation duration* (FFD) is the duration of the first fixation on a region. *First pass duration* (FPD) is the sum of all the fixations on a region from the time it was first entered until it was left. *Regression path duration* (RPD) is the sum of all the fixations on a region from the time it was first entered until moving to the right of the region. *Total fixation duration* (TD) of a region is the sum of all fixations on a region including re-fixations after it was left. All these measures, of course, assume that the region in question has been fixated.

3.2   Feature Set

The features used in the model have been attested to influence lexical and syntactic processing reading and it has been established conclusively that all these features are significant predictors of reading times (Rayner, 1998; Juhasz and Rayner, 2003; Demberg and Keller, 2008; Clifton et al., 2007; van Schijndel and Schuler, 2015). We use both low level predictors like word length, sentence length, word frequency and age of acquisition (in years) as well as high level predictors like surprisal.

Word length has been taken as it is from the Dundee corpus. *Sentence length* is the number of words in a sentence. *Word frequency* is the unigram frequency in the entire English Wikipedia text. The *age of acquisition* gives the average age and standard deviation at which a word is learnt (Kuperman et al., 2012). This reflects the familiarity of a word, which has been shown to affect lexical processing (Juhasz and Rayner, 2006). These features have previously been shown to be helpful in predicting the difficulty in reading (Vajjala Balakrishna, 2015). British National Corpus (BNC) (Aston and Burnard, 1998) was used to calculate *forward transition probability* – $P(w_k|w_{k-1})$ and *backward transition probability* – $P(w_k|w_{k+1})$ for each word.

In addition, we also added *surprisal* (Hale, 2001; Levy, 2008), *entropy reduction* (Hale, 2006), *embedding depth* and *embedding difference* (Wu et al., 2010) computed by an incremental probabilistic left-corner parser (van Schijndel et al., 2013). *Surprisal* models comprehension difficulty where words which are more predictable in a given syntactic or lexical context are read faster (lower surprisal values) compared to less predictable words (higher surprisal values). Mathematically, surprisal at word k+1, $S_{k+1} = -\log P(w_{k+1}|w_1...w_k)$. In our incremental left-corner probabilistic parser, strings of a language are assumed to be generated by Probabilistic Context Free Grammars (PCFGs). So each word w_k has a prefix probability computed by summing the probabilities of all trees T in the span of words w$_1$ to w$_k$. Surprisal is estimated as the difference in the prefix probabilities at successive words. Both syntactic and lexical surprisal are standout predictive measures for reading times regardless of word class (Wu et al., 2010).

Entropy reduction at word index = i is defined as: $\max\{0, H_i - H_{i-1}\}$, where H_i is the entropy function. So, it is the reduction in (syntactic) uncertainty at the appearance of word at index = i. *Embedding depth* is a quantitative measure reflecting memory load caused due to center embeddings (left branching parse tree nodes contained within right branching ones). A weighted version of this measure obtained

---

[1] For more details regarding the Dundee corpus, kindly refer to section 2.1 in Kennedy and Pynte (2005)

by multiplying with the parse probability is also used. *Embedding difference* is defined as the difference between the embedding depth at the current beam and the previous beam (Wu et al., 2010). (Howcroft, 2015) also uses the features from Wu et al (2010) for readability assessment and shows that they induce modest gains over other features. However, that work does not use reading times as features. In addition, we added eight more features emitted by the left-corner parser. These represent hierarchical structure decisions made by the parser and encode memory operations like cue activation, initiation, termination and wait. For more details, please refer to (van Schijndel and Schuler, 2013).

3.3 Model

We used linear regression using python-sklearn (Pedregosa et al., 2011) to predict the reading times. All features were standardized.

3.4 Experiments

Pearson's Coefficients Study

We calculated Pearson's coefficient for each of the features w.r.t. the four reading times, *first fixation duration, first pass duration, regression path duration,* and *total fixation duration*. Almost all correlations reported are significant at $p<0.01$.[2]. These results can be seen in Table 1. We find that most of the features show low correlation with the 4 duration measures in question (first fixation, first pass, regression and total fixation duration). However, as expected the word length and surprisals is found to have high positive correlation while frequency and familiarity (mean age of acquisition - AoA) have negative correlations with RT. We move forward with the ablation study with first fixation duration, as among the four durations features seem to be most correlated with first fixation in general.

S. No.	Features	First Fixation Duration	First Pass (Gaze) Duration	Regression Duration	Total Fixation Duration
1	Word Length	0.765	0.722	0.700	0.668
2	Sentence Length	-0.009	-0.008	-0.010	-0.011
3	Wikipedia Frequency	-0.142	-0.133	-0.129	-0.126
4	Mean AoA (in years)	0.048	0.032	0.028	0.021
5	Standard Dev. in AoA	-0.048	-0.058	-0.059	-0.067
6	Total Surprisal	0.369	0.368	0.365	0.358
7	Lexical Surprisal	0.372	0.372	0.369	0.363
8	Syntactical Surprisal	-0.067	-0.074	-0.073	-0.072
9	Entropy Reduction	-0.008	-0.013	-0.008	-0.013
10	Embedding Depth	0.102	0.092	0.086	0.084
11	Embedding Difference	0.051	0.046	0.043	0.045

Table 1: Pearson's Correlation Coefficient of features w.r.t. different reading times.

Ablation Study

We did an ablation study to select the best features for the model that predicts first fixation duration. The results can be seen in Table 2. In total there were 20 features in the model. Instead of exploring all (20!) orders, features were added incrementally based on the following rationale. At first, we added all the low-level predictors of reading times described in previous work (Demberg and Keller, 2008). In the case of the remaining features, we added the frequency-based predictors of reading difficulty next and finally memory-based predictors. This distinction was based on Collin Phillips' theory of grounding (Phillips, 2013), which characterizes memory load costs as predictors of comprehension difficulty after frequency-based costs have already been taken into account. If the goodness of the learned regression curve improved, the feature was retained in the final model[3]. The process helped in ascertaining the

---

[2]Except in case of sentence length w.r.t. first fixation and first pass, where p-value is 0.03 and 0.02 respectively.

[3]Issues related to multicollinearity have also been sidestepped in this initial analysis. We intend to address these issues in the future work.

relevance of individual feature in the model. We find that the word frequency, age of acquisition, total and syntactic surprisals lead to largest increase in the goodness score. Interestingly, lexical surprisal does not appear to be a significant contributor, probably because, word frequency already captures much of the effect (cf. Demberg and Keller, 2008).

S.No.	Features	R^2 score	S.No.	Features	R^2 score
1	Word Length	0.267	7	Lexical Surprisal	0.575
2	Sentence Length	0.500	8	Syntactical Surprisal	0.579
3	Word Frequency	0.504	9	Entropy Reduction	0.579
4	Mean Age of Acquisition (AoA)	0.532	10	Embedding Depth	0.580
5	Standard Deviation in AoA	0.533	11	Embedding Difference	0.580
6	Total Surprisal	0.576	12	Hierarchical structure feats	0.585

Table 2: Ablation study done on features by adding them incrementally to the FFD regression model.

Implementation and Results

We trained our model for all the four reading times, i.e. RTs for all the subjects were pooled into one set. The results can be seen in Table 3. R^2 score gives the goodness of the model. A closer look at the predicted reading times showed that on a number of occasions the regression model predicted very low non-zero reading times which were non-existent in the Dundee corpus. Therefore, we set a threshold (84 ms) for predicted reading times (for Fixed Fixation Duration), and any prediction less than this threshold was reduced to 0.0 ms. The threshold was fixed on the development set. As can be seen from table 3, using a threshold led to an improvement.

Reading Times	R^2 score	
First Fixation Duration	**0.585**	**0.649** [84 ms]
First Pass (Gaze) Duration	0.549	0.600 [88 ms]
Regression Path Duration	0.521	0.570 [91 ms]
Total Fixation Duration	0.510	0.516 [98 ms]

Table 3: Performance of System 1 on different eye-tracking measures. The number inside [] shows the threshold value.

3.5 Discussion

Predictions for first fixation duration are consistently better than other eye-tracking measures. The post hoc addition of threshold improved the performance significantly, and we see that R^2 score reaches upto 0.649 for first-fixation duration. First-fixation durations are known to reflect both low-level lexical processing (Clifton et al., 2007) as well as syntactic processes (Vasishth et al., 2012).

We were unable to do equally well on other measures such as first pass duration, regression path duration and total fixation duration compared to first fixation duration. So, while the current results are promising, more experiments with regards to alternative models need to be explored. In particular, it will be interesting to investigate if feature selection differs from one eye-movement to the other. This will shed some light on the feature-measure mapping. In addition, alternative/additional features that could correlate better with these measures need to be tried out. Finally, other measures such as regression probability, etc. need to investigated. These issues will be taken up as part of future work.

4 System 2 - Readability Assessment

The task that we evaluate the system discussed in the previous section is readability assessment. The exact task of readability assessment is the following:

Given a pair of two sentences (Sentence1, Sentence2) identify which one belongs to standard Wikipedia and which to simple Wikipedia. Sentence 1 and sentence 2 are paraphrases of the same idea.

Vajjala and Meurers (2016) have previously built a system to accomplish this task using various linguistic features. They used features produced by a non-incremental syntactic parser and found them to be useful in the task. They also used lexical semantic properties from WordNet, features encoding morphosyntactic properties of lemmas, word-level psycholinguistic features such as concreteness, meaningfulness and imageability extracted from the MRC psycholinguistic database as well as age of acquisition (AoA). Their model achieved an accuracy of 74.58%.

Motivated by the incremental nature of human sentence processing, Ambati et al. (2016) use features extracted from an incremental Combinatory Categorical Grammar (CCG) parser to achieve higher accuracy on this task. Their feature set included sentence length, height of the CCG derivation, the final number of constituents, CCG rule counts and complexity of CCG category. Their model achieved an accuracy of 78.87%.

Our system is also motivated by human sentence processing. However, unlike Ambati et al. (2016), we directly use predicted reading times to model complexity of a sentence. As discussed in section 3, the model that predicts reading times is based on psycholinguistically motivated lexical and syntactic features.

4.1 Data Set

The dataset used for evaluation is the dataset released by Ambati et al. (2016). This is a cleaned subset of the parallel sentence pairs collected by Hwang et al. (2015). The data contains 150K sentence pairs of standard Wikipedia (WIKI) and simple Wikipedia (SIMPLEWIKI). Ambati et al. (2016) further removed pairs containing identical sentences which resulted in 117K clean pairs. We randomly divided the data into training (60%), development (20%) and test (20%) splits.

4.2 Feature Set

Sentence-1 features	Sentence-2 features
sentence1_word1: 169	sentence2_word1: 189
sentence1_word2: 110	sentence2_word2: 309
sentence1_word3: 215	sentence2_word3: 85
sentence1_word4: 219	sentence2_word4: 85
...	...
...	...

Table 4: Example features in a sentence pair (each column contains the feature name and value separated by a space). The features values are in milliseconds.

Vajjala and Meurers (2016) formulated the readability assessment task as a ranking task, instead of a classification task. In our model we simply classify within a pair of sentences. For a sentence, we first predict reading time for each word (using System 1). The features are of the form "Word Position:Predicted RT". "Word Position" is the feature name and corresponds to the position of a word in a sentence, and predicted RT (which models first fixation duration) is its value. We define a sample as a pair of sentences. To avoid using same feature name for each sentence we simply concatenate "sentence1" or "sentence2" before all the feature names. For example, consider the following sentence pair from the dataset:

1. *With a higher humidity, the rate of evaporation is less.*

2. *Under conditions of high humidity, the rate of evaporation of sweat from the skin decreases.*

Assuming the following reading times for words in the first sentence – "with: 169ms", "a: 110ms", "higher: 215ms", "humidity: 219ms", "the: 149ms" and so on, the features for our 'Base RT' model are depicted in Table 4. The features from both the sentences together are then used to train the classification system. So the total number of features equal to twice the number of words in the longest sentence in our corpus as we work with sentence pairs.

The 'Base RT' model uses only these word-level features. We also experimented with a model that uses sentence-level features in addition to the base model features. This 'Extended RT' model contained the following additional features: sentence length, normalized (w.r.t. sentence length) sum of predicted reading time of the sentence. The incremental probabilistic left-corner parser (van Schijndel et al., 2013) was used to further add the following features: sum of total surprisal of all words, sum of lexical surprisal of all words, sum of syntactical surprisal of all words and log of parse probability of the entire sentence.

4.3 Model

As discussed in section 4.2, the pair of sentences are represented as a multiset of its features. We use a bag of words unigram model, except the features we use are not just words the sentences have, but 'wordposition:predicted RT'. The model assumes that relevant properties of the syntactic structure have already been captured by System-1 (discussed in section 3) to predict the reading time. Logistic regression classifier, using python-sklearn (Pedregosa et al., 2011) was used for the classification task. We also experimented with SVM (Hearst et al., 1998) and SVM^{rank} (Joachims, 2006), used by Vajjala and Meurers (2016), but these models were unable to outperform the logistic regression model. [4]

4.4 Results

A 10 fold cross-validation was done to obtain the accuracies. We evaluated the model with all four predicted durations (first fixation, first pass, regression and total). The best results were obtained with predicted first fixation duration therefore we show only those figures in Table 5.

Model	Accuracy (%)
Vajjala and Meurers, 2016 (Baseline)	74.58
Ambati et.al, 2016 (State-of-the-art)	78.87
System 2 (Base RT model) - SVM^{rank}	73.79
System 2 (Base RT model) - Pairwise Classification	73.82
System 2 (Extended RT model) - SVM^{rank}	75.09
System 2 (Extended RT model) - Pairwise Classification	75.21

Table 5: Performance of models with predicted first fixation duration.

Table 5 depicts 74.58% as the classification accuracy of Vajjala and Meurers (2016). It needs to be noted that the Vajjala and Meurers (2016) paper reports an accuracy of 82.7% on their evaluation data. The number 74.58% is taken from the Ambati et. al (2016) paper. This figure was obtained by Ambati and colleagues as a result of running the Vajjala and Meurers code on their evaluation data[5]. As mentioned before, we used the same evaluation data as Ambati et. al (2016). Hence Table 5 results are all based on the same dataset and thus directly comparable.

4.5 Discussion

We tested our model with the both SVM^{rank} strategy as used by Vajjala and Meurers (2016) and the pairwise classification strategy discussed in section 4.2. In both cases, pairwise classification performs slightly better than SVM^{rank}.

The Base RT model using just the predicted reading times and the word positions achieves an accuracy of 73.82%. This shows that predicted reading time alone can be successfully employed as a predictor

---

[4]Time taken by the system - Incremental Parser: The data set was divided into 100 sections and parsing was done in parallel. Each section took almost 10 hours. Final training: Takes around 5 min for around 120K sentences pairs.

[5]See Footnote 7 of Ambati et al 2016

to compute sentence complexity. Our Extended RT model achieves an accuracy of 75.21% which is marginally better than the Vajjala and Meurers (2016) model. The Ambati et al. (2016) system is still the best performing system. To see how much do reading times contribute to our system, we ran a model with just sentence level features from extended model and no Base RT features, which had the accuracy of 73.6% (1.6 points lower). This indicates that reading times do contribute to boost our model accuracy.

Note that, similar to Ambati et al. (2016), our RT prediction model (discussed in section 3) uses many syntactic features. These features include surprisal, entropy reduction, embedding depth, embedding difference, etc. The syntactic features in the Ambati et al. (2016) model (such as CCG rule counts, CCG categories) are much more fine-grained in terms of the different syntactic phenomenon that they capture. In would be very interesting to see if these fine-grained features can lead to improvement in a model that predicts eye-movement reading measures. We plan to test this out as part of our future work. Also, our results are based on just one eye-tracking measure, i.e. first fixation duration. Future work can try to improve this performance by exploring multiple measures in a single model.

5   Conclusion

We used a machine learning model and a set of features known to be significant predictors of reading times in order to learn per-word reading times from a corpus of English text having reading times of human readers. Subsequently, we used the model to predict reading times for novel text in the context of *readability assessment*. For this task, a model based only on reading times gave competitive results compared to the systems that use extensive syntactic features.

Notwithstanding the debate on strict vs loose connection between parsing processes and eye movements (Just and Carpenter, 1980) (also see, Vasishth et al., 2012), it has been conclusively established that sentence parsing events are manifested in reading times. Since automatic quantification of complexity is required in a number of NLP tasks/evaluations, models based on automatically predicted reading times present themselves as an attractive alternatives to the current methods. Our work, to the best of our knowledge, is the first study to show that such a model is indeed viable. We demonstrated that it can be used to successfully model the difficulty of a text and can be deployed in practical text processing applications. In addition to technological advances in field of NLP, we also envisage that our system can potentially facilitate scientific inquiries in human sentence processing. Prior to running behavioural experiments involving human subjects, our method can be used to formulate precise hypothesis by generating reading times for the test sentences.

Acknowledgement

We thank the three anonymous reviewers for their insightful comments. Their feedback has helped us improve the paper. Any errors that remain are our own.

References

Bharat Ram Ambati, Siva Reddy, and Mark Steedman. 2016. Assessing relative sentence complexity using an incremental CCG parser. In *Proceedings of the North American Chapter of the Association for Computational Linguistics on Language technologies, California, USA*.

Guy Aston and Lou Burnard. 1998. *The BNC handbook: exploring the British National Corpus with SARA*. Capstone.

Maria Barrett and Anders Søgaard. 2015. Reading behavior predicts syntactic categories. In *Proceedings of the Nineteenth Conference on Computational Natural Language Learning*, pages 345–349, Beijing, China, July. Association for Computational Linguistics.

Maria Barrett, Joachim Bingel, Frank Keller, and Anders Søgaard. 2016. Weakly supervised part-of-speech tagging using eye-tracking data. In *Proceedings of the 54th Annual Meeting of the Association for Computational Linguistics (Volume 2: Short Papers)*, pages 579–584, Berlin, Germany, August. Association for Computational Linguistics.

C. Clifton, A. Staub, and K. Rayner. 2007. Eye movements in reading words and sentences. In R. Van Gompel, M. Fisher, W. Murray, and R. L. Hill, editors, *Eye movements: A window on mind and brain*, chapter 15. Elsevier.

William Coster and David Kauchak. 2011. Simple English Wikipedia: a new text simplification task. In *Proceedings of the 49th Annual Meeting of the Association for Computational Linguistics: Human Language Technologies*.

Vera Demberg and Frank Keller. 2008. Data from eye-tracking corpora as evidence for theories of syntactic processing complexity. *Cognition*, 109(2):193–210.

Lijun Feng. 2010. *Automatic readability assessment*. City University of New York.

R. Flesch. 1948. A new readability yardstick. *Journal of Applied Psychology*, 32(3):221.

L. Frazier and K. Rayner. 1982. Making and correcting errors during sentence comprehension: Eye movements in the analysis of structurally ambiguous sentences. *Cogn Psychol*, 14:178–210.

Edward Gibson. 2000. The dependency locality theory: A distance-based theory of linguistic complexity. *Image, language, brain*, pages 95–126.

R. Gunning. 1968. *The Technique of Clear Writing*. McGraw-Hill Book Company, 2nd ed.

John Hale. 2001. A probabilistic Earley parser as a psycholinguistic model. In *Proceedings of the second meeting of the NAACL*, pages 1–8. Association for Computational Linguistics.

John Hale. 2006. Uncertainty about the rest of the sentence. *Cognitive Science*, 30:643–672.

Marti A. Hearst, Susan T Dumais, Edgar Osman, John Platt, and Bernhard Scholkopf. 1998. Support vector machines. *IEEE Intelligent Systems and their Applications*, 13(4):18–28.

David Howcroft. 2015. Ranking sentences by complexity. Master's thesis, Saarland University.

William Hwang, Hannaneh Hajishirzi, Mari Ostendorf, and Wei Wu. 2015. Aligning sentences from standard wikipedia to simple wikipedia. In *Proceedings of the 2015 Conference of the North American Chapter of the Association for Computational Linguistics (NAACL)*.

Thorsten Joachims. 2006. Training linear SVMs in linear time. In *Proceedings of the 12th ACM SIGKDD international conference on Knowledge Discovery and Data Mining*, pages 217–226. ACM.

Aditya Joshi, Abhijit Mishra, Nivvedan Senthamilselvan, and Pushpak Bhattacharyya. 2014. Measuring sentiment annotation complexity of text. In *Proceedings of the 52nd ACL*, pages 36–41, June.

Barbara J Juhasz and Keith Rayner. 2003. Investigating the effects of a set of intercorrelated variables on eye fixation durations in reading. *Journal of Experimental Psychology: Learning, Memory, and Cognition*, 29(6):1312.

Barbara J Juhasz and Keith Rayner. 2006. The role of age of acquisition and word frequency in reading: Evidence from eye fixation durations. *Visual Cognition*, 13(7-8):846–863.

Marcel Adam Just and Patricia A. Carpenter. 1980. A theory of reading: from eye fixations to comprehension. *Psychological Review*, 87:329–354.

Alan Kennedy and Joël Pynte. 2005. Parafoveal-on-foveal effects in normal reading. *Vision research*, 45(2):153–168.

A Kennedy. 2003. The Dundee Corpus [CD-ROM]. *Psychology Department, University of Dundee*.

J. Peter Kincaid, Lieutenant Robert P. Jr. Fishburne, Richard L. Rogers, and Brad S. Chissom. 1975. Derivation of new readability formulas (Automated Readability Index, Fog Count and Flesch Reading Ease Formula) for navy enlisted personnel.

Victor Kuperman, Hans Stadthagen-Gonzalez, and Marc Brysbaert. 2012. Age-of-acquisition ratings for 30,000 English words. *Behavior Research Methods*, 44(4):978–990.

Roger Levy. 2008. Expectation-based syntactic comprehension. *Cognition*, 106(3):1126 – 1177.

Richard L Lewis and Shravan Vasishth. 2005. An activation-based model of sentence processing as skilled memory retrieval. *Cognitive science*, 29(3):375–419.

R. L. Lewis. 1996. Interference in short-term memory: The magical number two (or three) in sentence processing. *Journal of Psycholinguistic Research*, 25(1):93–116.

Abhijit Mishra, Pushpak Bhattacharyya, and Michael Carl. 2013. Automatically predicting sentence translation difficulty. In *Proceedings of the 51st ACL*, pages 346–351, August.

Abhijit Mishra, Diptesh Kanojia, and Pushpak Bhattacharyya. 2016. Predicting readers' sarcasm understandability by modeling gaze behavior. In *Proceedings of the Thirtieth AAAI Conference on Artificial Intelligence, Phoenix, Arizona, USA.*, pages 3747–3753.

F. Pedregosa, G. Varoquaux, A. Gramfort, V. Michel, B. Thirion, O. Grisel, M. Blondel, P. Prettenhofer, R. Weiss, V. Dubourg, J. Vanderplas, A. Passos, D. Cournapeau, M. Brucher, M. Perrot, and E. Duchesnay. 2011. Scikit-learn: Machine learning in Python. *Journal of Machine Learning Research*, 12:2825–2830.

Sarah E Petersen and Mari Ostendorf. 2009. A machine learning approach to reading level assessment. *Computer Speech & Language*, 23(1):89–106.

Colin Phillips. 2013. Some arguments and non-arguments for reductionist accounts of syntactic phenomena. *Language and Cognitive Processes*, 28:156–187.

Keith Rayner. 1998. Eye movements in reading and information processing: 20 years of research. *Psychological Bulletin*, 124(3):372.

S. Schwarm and M. Ostendorf. 2005. Reading level assessment using support vector machines and statistical language models. In *Proceedings of the 43rd Annual Meeting of the Association for Computational Linguistics*.

L. Si and J. Callan. 2001. A statistical model for scientific readability. In *Proceedings of the 10th International Conference on Information and Knowledge Management (CIKM)*, pages 574–576.

Advaith Siddharthan and Angrosh Mandya. 2014. Hybrid text simplification using synchronous dependency grammars with hand-written and automatically harvested rules. In *EACL*, pages 722–731.

A. Siddharthan. 2014. A survey of research on text simplification. *International Journal of Applied Linguistics: Special issue on Recent Advances in Automatic Readability Assessment and Text Simplification*, 165(2):259–298.

Sowmya Vajjala and Detmar Meurers. 2014. Assessing the relative reading level of sentence pairs for text simplification. In *EACL*, pages 288–297.

Sowmya Vajjala and Detmar Meurers. 2016. Readability-based sentence ranking for evaluating text simplification. *arXiv preprint arXiv:1603.06009*.

Sowmya Vajjala Balakrishna. 2015. *Analyzing Text Complexity and Text Simplification: Connecting Linguistics, Processing and Educational Applications*. Ph.D. thesis, Universität Tübingen.

Marten van Schijndel and William Schuler. 2013. An analysis of frequency- and memory-based processing costs. In *Proceedings of the 2013 Conference of the North American Chapter of the Association for Computational Linguistics: Human Language Technologies*, pages 95–105, Atlanta, Georgia, June. Association for Computational Linguistics.

Marten van Schijndel and William Schuler. 2015. Hierarchic syntax improves reading time prediction. In *Proceedings of the 2015 Conference of the North American Chapter of the Association for Computational Linguistics: Human Language Technologies*, pages 1597–1605, Denver, Colorado, May–June. Association for Computational Linguistics.

Marten van Schijndel, Andy Exley, and William Schuler. 2013. A model of language processing as hierarchic sequential prediction. *Topics in Cognitive Science*, 5(3):522–540.

Shravan Vasishth, Titus von der Malsburg, and Felix Engelmann. 2012. What eye movements can tell us about sentence comprehension. *Wiley Interdisciplinary Reviews: Cognitive Science*, pages 125–134.

Kristian Woodsend and Mirella Lapata. 2011. WikiSimple: Automatic simplification of wikipedia articles. In *AAAI*.

Stephen Wu, Asaf Bachrach, Carlos Cardenas, and William Schuler. 2010. Complexity metrics in an incremental right-corner parser. In *Proceedings of the 48th Annual Meeting of the Association for Computational Linguistics*, pages 1189–1198. Association for Computational Linguistics.

Sander Wubben, Antal Van Den Bosch, and Emiel Krahmer. 2012. Sentence simplification by monolingual machine translation. In *Proceedings of the 50th Annual Meeting of the Association for Computational Linguistics*.

Zhemin Zhu, Delphine Bernhard, and Iryna Gurevych. 2010. A monolingual tree-based translation model for sentence simplification. In *Proceedings of the 23rd International Conference on Computational Linguistics*, pages 1353–1361. Association for Computational Linguistics.

Upper Bound of Entropy Rate Revisited —A New Extrapolation of Compressed Large-Scale Corpora—

Ryosuke Takahira[1]   **Kumiko Tanaka-Ishii**[2]   **Łukasz Dębowski**[3]

[1]Graduate School of Information Science and Electrical Engineering, Kyushu University, Japan
`takahira@limu.ait.kyushu-u.ac.jp`
[2]Research Center for Advanced Science and Technology, University of Tokyo, Japan
`kumiko@cl.rcast.u-tokyo.ac.jp`
[3]Institute of Computer Science, Polish Academy of Sciences, Poland
`ldebowsk@ipipan.waw.pl`

Abstract

The article presents results of entropy rate estimation for human languages across six languages by using large, state-of-the-art corpora of up to 7.8 gigabytes. To obtain the estimates for data length tending to infinity, we use an extrapolation function given by an ansatz. Whereas some ansatzes of this kind were proposed in previous research papers, here we introduce a stretched exponential extrapolation function that has a smaller error of fit. In this way, we uncover a possibility that the entropy rates of human languages are positive but 20% smaller than previously reported.

1 Introduction

Estimation of the entropy rate of natural language is a challenge originally set up by Shannon (Shannon, 1948; Shannon, 1951). The entropy rate quantifies the complexity of language, precisely the rate how fast the amount of information grows in our communication with respect to the text length. Today, the entropy rate provides an important target for data compression algorithms, where the speed of convergence of the compression rate to the entropy rate is an informative benchmark. Measuring the entropy rate is also the first step in answering what kind of a stochastic process can model generation of texts in natural language, an important question for many practical tasks of natural language engineering.

An important theoretical question concerning the entropy rate, which has also been noted in the domains of computational linguistics (Genzel and Charniak, 2002) and speech processing (Levy and Jaeger, 2007), is whether the entropy rate of human language is a strictly positive constant. The overwhelming evidence collected so far suggests that it is so—in particular, the amount of information communicated per unit time in English text is generally agreed to be about 1 bpc (bit per character) (Shannon, 1951; Cover and King, 1978; Brown et al., 1983; Schümann and Grassberger, 1996). Although this is what we might intuitively expect, Hilberg formulated a hypothesis that the entropy rate of natural language is zero (Hilberg, 1990). Zero entropy rate does not imply that the amount of information in texts is not growing, but that it grows with a speed slower than linear. From this perspective we want to provide as exact estimates of the entropy rate for natural language as possible.

Precise estimation of the entropy rate is a challenging task mainly because, mathematically speaking, the sought parameter is a limit for text length tending to infinity. To alleviate this problem, previous great minds proposed estimation methods based on human cognitive testing (Shannon, 1951; Cover and King, 1978). Since human testing is costly, however, such attempts remain limited in terms of the scale and number of tested languages. In contrast, although any conceivable data size can only be finite, today's language data have become so large in scale that we may reconsider estimation of the entropy rate using big data computation. This point was already raised by (Shannon, 1948), which led to important previous works such as (Brown et al., 1983) in the domain of computational linguistics. Both of these articles and many other that followed, however, mostly considered the English language only.

In contrast, in this article, we present the results of entropy rate estimation using state-of-the-art large data sets in six different languages, including up to 7.8 gigabytes of data in English. We try to estimate the entropy rate by compressing these data sets using the PPM algorithm and extrapolating the data points with a carefully selected ansatz function. Whereas a couple of ansatz functions were previously

213

Proceedings of the Workshop on Computational Linguistics for Linguistic Complexity,
pages 213–221, Osaka, Japan, December 11-17 2016.

proposed in (Hilberg, 1990; Crutchfield and Feldman, 2003; Ebeling and Nicolis, 1991; Schümann and Grassberger, 1996), here we introduce another function, which is a stretched exponential function and enjoys the same number of parameters as previous proposals. The new functions yields a smaller error of fit. As a result, we arrive at the entropy rate estimates which are positive but 20% smaller than previously reported.

2 Entropy Rate

Let X_1^∞ be a stochastic process, i.e., an infinite sequence of random variables $X = X_1, X_2, X_3, \ldots$ with each random variable X_i assuming values $x \in \mathbb{X}$, where $\mathbb{X}$ is a certain set of countably many symbols. For natural language, for instance, $\mathbb{X}$ can be a set of characters, whereas X_1^∞ is an infinite corpus of texts. Let X_i^j, where $i \leq j$, denote a finite subsequence $X_i^j = X_i, X_{i+1}, \ldots, X_j$ of X_1^∞ and let $P(X_i^j = x_i^j)$ denote a probability function of the subsequence X_i^j. The Shannon entropy of a finite subsequence X_i^j is defined as:

$$H(X_i^j) = -\sum_{x_i^j} P(X_i^j = x_i^j) \log_2 P(X_i^j = x_i^j), \tag{1}$$

where sequences x_i^j are instances of X_i^j (Shannon, 1948). In contrast, the entropy rate of the infinite sequence X is defined as (Cover and Thomas, 2006):

$$h = \lim_{n \to \infty} \frac{H(X_1^n)}{n}. \tag{2}$$

The entropy rate is the amount of information per element for the data length tending to infinity.

Let us note that the entropy rate quantifies the asymptotic growth of the number of possible values of an infinite sequence X_1^∞. Roughly speaking, there are effectively only 2^{nh} possible values for a subsequence X_1^n, where n is the sequence length. In other words, condition $h > 0$ is tantamount to an exponential growth of the number of possible sequences with respect to n. Value $h = 0$ need not mean that the number of possibilities does not grow. For instance, for a sequence X_1^n whose number of possibilities grows like $2^{A\sqrt{n}}$, as supposed by Hilberg (1990), we have $h = 0$. Although the number of possibilities for such a sequence of random variables grows quite fast, the speed of the growth cannot be properly measured by the entropy rate.

The entropy rate thus quantifies, to some extent, the degree of randomness or freedom underlying the text characters to follow one another. For human languages, the occurrence of a linguistic element, such as a word or character, depends on the previous elements, and there are many long repetitions. This results in a lower value of the entropy rate than for a random sequence, but the ultimate degree of randomness in natural language is hard to simply guess. Whereas Hilberg (1990) supposed that $h = 0$ holds for natural language, this is only a minority view. According to the overwhelming experimental evidence the entropy of natural language is strictly positive (Shannon, 1951; Cover and King, 1978; Brown et al., 1983; Schümann and Grassberger, 1996). We may ask however whether these known estimates are credible. In fact, if convergence of $H(X_1^n)/n$ to the entropy rate is very slow, this need not be so. For this reason, while estimating the entropy rate, it is important to investigate the speed of the estimate convergence.

3 Direct estimation methods

There are several methods to estimate the entropy rate of natural language. These can be largely divided into methods based on human cognitive testing and methods based on machine computation. Estimation via human cognitive testing is mainly conducted by showing a substring of a text to a human examinee and having him or her guess the character to follow the substring. This method was introduced by Shannon (1951). He tested an unmentioned number of examinees with the text of Dumas Malone's "Jefferson the Virginian" and obtained $h \approx 1.3$ bpc. This method was improved by Cover and King (1978) as a sort of gambling. The results with 12 examinees produced an average of $h \approx 1.34$ bpc. Human cognitive testing has the advantage over methods based on machine computations that the estimates of entropy rate converge faster. Unfortunately, such human cognitive testing is costly, so the number of examinees involved is small and the samples are rather short. It is also unclear whether human examinees guess the text characters according to the true probability distribution.

In contrast, today, estimation of the entropy rate can be performed by big data computation. For this paradigm, two specific approaches have been considered so far.

1. The first approach is to estimate the probabilistic language models underlying formula (2). A representative classic work is (Brown et al., 1983), who reported $h \approx 1.75$ bpc, by estimating the probability of trigrams in the Brown National Corpus.

2. The second approach is to compress the text using a data compression algorithm. Let $R(X_1^n)$ denote the size in bits of text X_1^n *after* the compression. Then the code length per unit, $r(n) = R(X_1^n)/n$, is always larger than the entropy rate (Cover and Thomas, 2006),

$$r(n) \geq h. \tag{3}$$

We call $r(n)$ the *encoding rate* in the rest of this article.

In the following we will apply the second approach. In fact, there are various algorithms to compress texts. Within our context we are interested in *universal* methods. A universal text compressor guarantees that the encoding rate converges to the entropy rate, provided that the stochastic process X_1^∞ is stationary and ergodic, i.e., equality

$$\lim_{n \to \infty} r(n) = h \tag{4}$$

holds with probability 1. Among the important known universal compressors we can name: the Lempel-Ziv (LZ) code (Ziv and Lempel, 1977), the PPM code (Bell et al., 1990), and a wide class of grammar-based codes (Kieffer and Yang, 2000), with many particular instances such as SEQUITUR (Nevill-Manning and Witten, 1997) and NSRPS (Non-Sequential Recursive Pair Substitution) (Ebeling and Nicolis, 1991; Grassberger, 2002). Whereas all these codes are universal, they are not equal. Let us briefly describe some properties of these compressors. First of all, they are based on different principles. The LZ code and the grammar-based codes compress texts roughly by detecting repeated substrings and replacing them with shorter identifiers. A proof of universality of the LZ code can be found in (Cover and Thomas, 2006), whereas the proof of universality of grammar-based codes can be found in (Kieffer and Yang, 2000). In contrast, the PPM code is an n-gram based language modeling method (Bell et al., 1990) which applies variable length n-grams and arithmetic coding. The PPM code is guaranteed to be universal when the length of the n-gram is considered up to infinity (Ryabko, 2010).

A very important question for our application is the scaling of the encoding rate of universal codes for finite real data. Since the probabilistic model of natural language remains unknown, the notion of universality may serve only as a possible standard to obtain a stringent upper bound. One may raise some doubt that natural language is strictly stationary since the word probabilities do vary across time, as indicated by (Baayen, 2001). Moreover, many off-the-shelf compressors are not strictly universal, since they are truncated in various ways to gain the computational speed. Therefore, a suitable compressor can only be chosen through experimental inspection.

Among state-of-the-art compressors, we have considered zip, lzh, tar.xz, and 7-zip LZMA for the LZ methods and 7-zip PPMd for the PPM code. In Figure 1 (right panel) we show how the encoding rate depends on the data length for a Bernoulli process with $p = 0.5$ (left panel, listed later in the first line of the third block of Table 1) and for natural language data of Wall Street Journal corpus (right panel, listed in the third line of the third block of Table 1). First, let us consider the Bernoulli process, which is a simple artificial source. Formally, the Bernoulli process is a sequence of independent random variables taking the value of 1 with probability p and 0 with probability $1 - p$. There are two known theoretical results for this process: The theoretically proven encoding rate of the LZ code is as much as

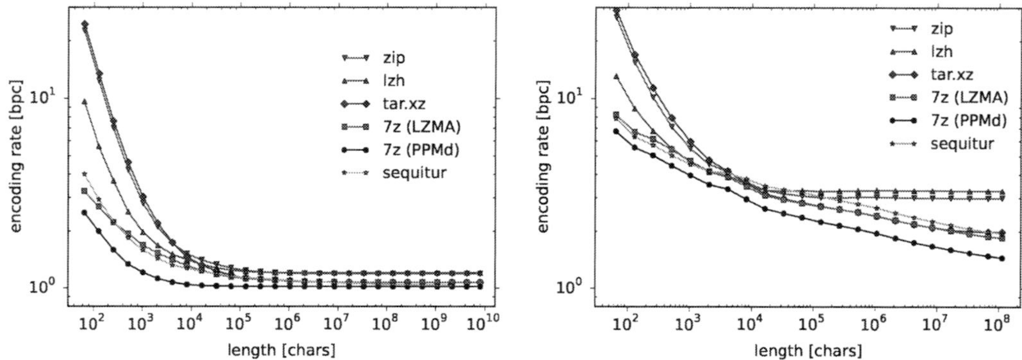

Figure 1: Compression results for a Bernoulli process ($p = 0.5$, left panel) and Wall Street Journal (right panel) for LZ, PPM, and SEQUITUR.

$r(n) = A/(\log n) + h$ (Louchard and Szpankowski, 1997), whereas the encoding rate for the PPM code is proved to be only $r(n) = A(\log n)/n + h$ (Barron et al., 1998; Atteson, 1999). Thus the convergence is extremely slow for the LZ code and quite fast for the PPM code. This exactly can be seen in Figure 1 (left panel), where all data points for the LZ code remain way above 1.0 bpc, the true entropy rate, while the data points for the PPM code practically converge to 1.0 bpc.

As for natural language data, whereas the empirical speed of convergence is much slower for the Wall Street Journal, the gradation of the compression algorithms remains the same. Algorithms such as zip and lzh get saturated probably because they are truncated in some way, whereas SEQUITUR, 7-zip LZMA and 7-zip PPMd gradually improve their compression rate the more data they read in. Since the encoding rate is visibly the smallest for 7-zip PPMd, in the following, we will use this compressor to estimate the entropy rate for other natural language data.

4 Extrapolation Functions

Many have attempted to estimate the entropy rate via compression. For example, paper (Bell et al., 1990) reported $h \approx 1.45$ bpc for the collected works of Shakespeare in English. Majority of the previous works, however, reported only a single value of the encoding rate for the maximal size of the available data. Whereas any computation can handle only a finite amount of data, the true entropy rate is defined in formula (2) as a limit for infinite data. The later fact should be somehow taken into consideration, especially if convergence (4) is slow, which is the case of natural language. One way to fill this gap between the finite data and the infinite limit is to use extrapolation. In other words, the encoding rate $r(n)$ is calculated for many n and the plots are extrapolated using some function $f(n)$. Since the probabilistic model of natural language is unknown, function $f(n)$ has been considered so far in form of an ansatz.

Previously, two ansatzes have been proposed, to the best of our knowledge. The first one was proposed by Hilberg (1990). He examined the original paper of (Shannon, 1951), which gives a plot of some upper bounds of $H(X_1^n)/n$. Since Hilberg believed that the entropy rate vanishes, $h = 0$, his ansatz was

$$f_0(n) = An^{\beta-1},\tag{5}$$

with $\beta \approx 0.5$, according to Hilberg. If we do not believe in a vanishing entropy rate, the above formula can be easily modified as

$$f_1(n) = An^{\beta-1} + h,\tag{6}$$

so that it converges to an arbitrary value of the entropy rate, cf., (Crutchfield and Feldman, 2003). Another ansatz was given in papers (Ebeling and Nicolis, 1991) and (Schümann and Grassberger, 1996). It reads

$$f_2(n) = An^{\beta-1}\ln n + h.\tag{7}$$

Table 1: Data used in this work, its size, its encoding rate, entropy rate and the error

Text	Language	Size (chars)	encoding rate (bit)	$f_1(n)$ h (bit)	$f_1(n)$ error $\times 10^{-2}$	$f_3(n)$ h (bit)	$f_3(n)$ error $\times 10^{-2}$
Large Scale Random Document Data							
Agence France-Presse	English	4096003895	1.402	1.249	1.078	1.033	0.757
Associated Press Worldstream	English	6524279444	1.439	1.311	1.485	1.128	1.070
Los Angeles Times/Washington Post	English	1545238421	1.572	1.481	1.108	1.301	0.622
New York Times	English	7827873832	1.599	1.500	0.961	1.342	0.616
Washington Post/Bloomberg	English	97411747	1.535	1.389	1.429	1.121	0.991
Xinhua News Agency	English	1929885224	1.317	1.158	0.906	0.919	0.619
Wall Street Journal	English	112868008	1.456	1.320	1.301	1.061	0.812
Central News Agency of Taiwan	Chinese	678182152	5.053	4.459	1.055	3.833	0.888
Xinhua News Agency of Beijing	Chinese	383836212	4.725	3.810	0.751	2.924	0.545
People's Daily (1991-95)	Chinese	101507796	4.927	3.805	0.413	2.722	0.188
Mainichi	Japanese	847606070	3.947	3.339	0.571	2.634	0.451
Le Monde	French	727348826	1.489	1.323	1.103	1.075	0.711
KAIST Raw Corpus	Korean	130873485	3.670	3.661	0.827	3.327	1.158
Mainichi (Romanized)	Japanese	1916108161	1.766	1.620	2.372	1.476	2.067
People's Daily (pinyin)	Chinese	247551301	1.850	1.857	1.651	1.667	1.136
Small Scale Data							
Ulysses (by James Joyce)	English	1510885	2.271	2.155	0.811	1.947	1.104
À la recherche du temps perdu (by Marcel Proust)	French	7255271	1.660	1.414	0.770	1.078	0.506
The Brothers Karamazov (by Fyodor Dostoyevskiy)	Russian	1824096	2.223	1.983	0.566	1.598	0.839
Daibosatsu toge (by Nakazato Kaizan)	Japanese	4548008	4.296	3.503	1.006	2.630	0.875
Dang Kou Zhi (by by Wan-Chun Yu)	Chinese	665591	6.739	4.479	1.344	2.988	1.335

Using this ansatz, paper (Schümann and Grassberger, 1996) obtained $h \approx 1.7$ bpc for the collected works of Shakespeare and $h \approx 1.25$ bpc for the LOB corpus of English.

We have used up to 7.8 gigabytes of data for six different languages and quite many plots were available for fitting, as compared to previous works. As will be shown in §6.1, function $f_1(n)$ does not fit well to our plots. Function $f_1(n)$, however, is no more than *some* ansatz. If we can devise another ansatz that fits better, then this should rather be used to estimate the entropy rate. In fact we have come across a better ansatz. The function we consider in this article is a stretched exponential function,

$$f_3(n) = \exp(An^{\beta-1} + h'), \tag{8}$$

which embeds function $f_1(n)$ in an exponential function and yields the entropy rate $h = \exp h'$. In fact, function $f_3(n)$ converges to h slower than $f_1(n)$. In a way, this is desirable since slow convergence of the encoding rate is some general tendency of the natural language data. As a by-product, using function $f_3(n)$ we will obtain smaller estimates of the entropy rate than using function $f_1(n)$.

5 Experimental Procedure

5.1 Data preparation

Table 1 lists our data, including each text, its language and size in the number of characters, its encoding rate using the full data set (the minimal observed encoding rate), and the extrapolation results for the entropy rate h, including the error of the estimates—as defined in §5.2 and analyzed later. We carefully chose our data by examining the redundancies. Many of the freely available large-scale corpora suffer from poor quality. In particular, they often contain artificially long repetitions. Since such repetitions affect the entropy rate estimates, we have only used corpora of a carefully checked quality, making sure that they do not contain large chunks of a repeated text.

The table contains two blocks. The first block contains state-of-the-art large-scale corpora of texts. As will be shown in our experiments, the plots for the raw corpora often oscillated due to the topic change. To overcome this problem we have performed randomization and averaging. First, we have shuffled the corpora at the level of documents and, second, we have averaged ten different random permutations for each corpus. The experimental results shown from the 4th column to the last one of Table 1 pertain to so processed language data. As for the Japanese and Chinese data, in addition to the original texts of the Mainichi and People's Daily newspapers, the Romanized versions were generated.[1] In contrast, the second block of Table 1 contains long literary works in five different languages. These data have not been randomized. The data in the first and second blocks encompass six different languages.

5.2 Detailed procedure

To estimate the entropy rate, we have used the 7-zip compressor, which implements the PPMd algorithm. As discussed in §3, this compressor seems the best among state-of-the-art methods. It compresses best not only the real Wall Street Journal corpus but also the artificial Bernoulli process. For this reason, we have used this compressor. Further detailed options of the PPMd algorithm were carefully chosen. Since the 7-zip program compresses by recording statistics for file names as well, the input text was fed to the compressor via a Unix pipe so that the compression was conducted *without* a file name. We also carefully excluded the *header* of the compressed file (which includes the name of the compressor etc.). This header is included in the compressed file but does not count to the proper compression length.

Another important option of the 7-zip program concerns the maximal n-gram length used by the PPM, called here MAX. As noted in §3, when MAX is infinite the compression method is universal. But the larger MAX is, the slower the compression procedure becomes. Therefore, any available compressor sets an upper bound on MAX, whereas the user can choose the MAX value smaller than this bound (the bound equals 32 in the case of 7-zip PPMd). However, even within this preset range, it was not always the case that a larger MAX resulted in a better encoding rate. Therefore, in our work, for each full data set, we searched for the value of MAX that achieved the best encoding rate and consistently used those best encoding rates for different subsets of the full data set.

Having clarified these specific issues, our detailed experimental procedure, applied to each data set from Table 1, was as follows. First, for every $n = 2^k$, where $k = 6, 7, \ldots, \log_2(\text{data size})$, the first n characters of the full text were taken. This subsequence, denoted X_1^n, was then compressed using the 7-zip program, and its size $R(X_1^n)$ in bits was measured to calculate the encoding rate $r(n) = R(X_1^n)/n$. The obtained encoding rates for different n were fitted to the ansatz functions $f(n) = f_j(n)$, where $j = 1, 2, 3, 4$. When encoding rates $r(n_i) = R(X_1^{n_i})/n_i$ for K distinct values of n_i were obtained, the fit was conducted by minimizing the square error as follows:

$$error = \sqrt{\frac{\sum_{i=1}^{K} (\ln r(n_i) - \ln f(n_i))^2}{K}}. \tag{9}$$

The logarithm was taken here to ascribe a larger weight to the errors of the larger n, since we were particularly interested in the tail behavior of the data points.

6 Experimental Results

6.1 Fitting Results

Figure 2 shows our results for the Wall Street Journal (WSJ) corpus (Table 1, first block, seventh line), which is the benchmark corpus most typically used in the computational processing of human language. The figure shows the encoding rate $r(n)$ (vertical axis) as a function of the text size in characters n (horizontal axis). The left panel of Figure 2 shows the results obtained from the original text. The encoding rates tend to oscillate, which is due to topic changes in the corpus. Such oscillation is visible in majority of the natural language data, where some data can oscillate much worse than WSJ. In the context of entropy rate estimation such oscillation was already reported in paper (Schümann and Grassberger, 1996). Some possible way to cope with this problem is to shuffle the text at the level of documents. The right panel of Figure 2 shows the average encoding rate for the data 10-fold shuffled by documents. The data points in the right panel oscillate less than in the left panel. At the same time, since shuffling the documents introduces some randomness, the entropy rate estimate is about 1% larger for the randomized data

---

[1] KAKASI and Pinyin Python library software were used to Romanize Japanese and Chinese, respectively.

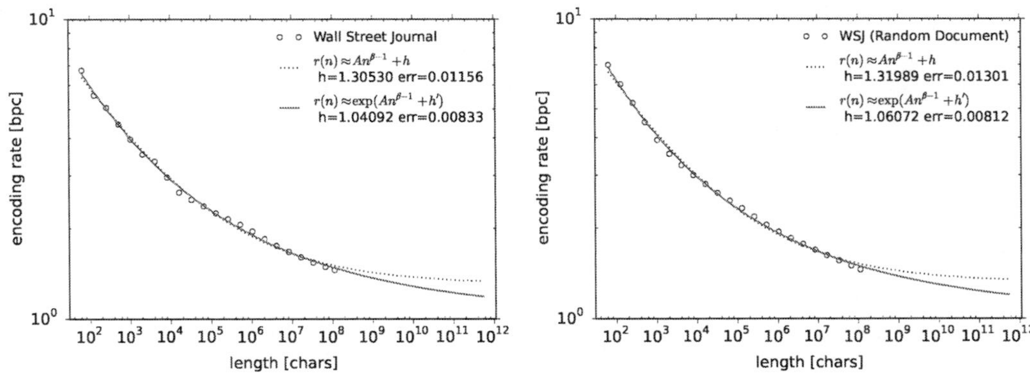

Figure 2: Encoding rates for the Wall Street Journal corpus (in English). The left panel is for the original data, whereas the right panel is the average of the data 10-fold shuffled by documents. To these results we fit functions $f_1(n)$ and $f_3(n)$.

than for the original corpus. Both panels of Figure 2 show two fits of the encoding rate, to extrapolation functions $f_1(n)$ and $f_3(n)$—given by formulae (6) and (8), respectively. Whereas, visually, it is difficult to say which of the functions fits better, we can decide on that using the value of error (9). The estimates of the entropy rate are $h = 1.32$ with $error$ being 0.0130 for $f_1(n)$ and $h = 1.061$ with $error$ being 0.00812 for $f_3(n)$. We can suppose that function $f_3(n)$ yields both a smaller entropy rate estimate and a smaller fitting error.

This hypothesis can be confirmed. We conducted the analogous fitting to all our data sets for three ansatz functions $f_1(n)$, $f_2(n)$, and $f_3(n)$. The fitted values of h and $error$ for $f_1(n)$ and $f_3(n)$, for both 10-fold randomized corpora and non-randomized texts are listed in Table 1 in the last four columns. The average values of the $error$ for $f_1(n)$, $f_2(n)$ and $f_3(n)$ were 0.0113, 0.0194, and 0.00842 across all data sets, respectively. The plots therefore fit the best to $f_3(n)$. Among the three ansatz functions, function $f_2(n)$ is the worst choice. In contrast, the stretched exponential function $f_3(n)$ seems better than the modified Hilberg function $f_1(n)$ and it consistently yields smaller estimates of the entropy rate.

6.2 A Linear Perspective

If the exponent β does not depend on a particular corpus of texts, i.e., if it is some language universal, then for all three functions $f_1(n)$, $f_2(n)$, and $f_3(n)$ we can draw a diagnostic linear plot with axes: $Y = r(n)$ and $X = n^{\beta-1}$ for $f_1(n)$, $Y = r(n)$ and $X = n^{\beta-1}\ln n$ for $f_2(n)$, and $Y = \ln r(n)$ and $X = n^{\beta-1}$ for $f_3(n)$, respectively. In these diagnostic plots, the entropy rate corresponds to the intercept of the straight line on which the data points lie approximately. Since we observe that exponent β is indeed some language universal, we use these plots to compare different text corpora.

In these plots, ansatzes $f_1(n)$, $f_2(n)$, and $f_3(n)$ can be analyzed as a form of linear regression. Let us focus on $f_3(n)$, the function that yields the minimal fitting error. If we put $Y = \ln r(n)$ as the vertical axis and $X = n^{\beta-1}$ as the horizontal axis where $\beta = 0.884$, the average value for the fit to $f_3(n)$, then the plots for all large scale natural language data (first block of Table 1) can be transformed as shown in Figure 3. It can be seen that each set of data points is roughly assembled in a linear manner.

In Figure 3, the black points are English, the white ones are Chinese, and the gray ones are other languages including Romanized Chinese and Japanese. Two main groups of plots can be seen in Figure 3, one lower and one upper, where the lower plots in black are for English and the upper plots in white are for Chinese . The results for other languages, shown in gray, are located somewhere between English and Chinese. The gray plots appearing amidst the lower group indicate Romanized Japanese and Chinese. These results show that the script type distinguishes the amount of information per character.

Two straight lines were obtained in Figure 3 for the English and Chinese groups by least squares fitting to all data points from each group, respectively. Since the horizontal axis indicates variable $X = n^{\beta-1}$, condition $n \to \infty$ corresponds to condition $X = 0$. The intercept of a fitted straight line is thus the

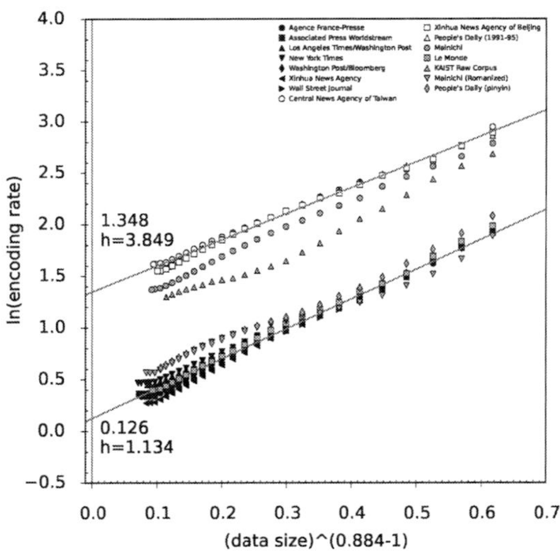

Figure 3: All large scale natural language data (first block of Table 1) from a linear perspective for function $f_3(n)$.

logarithm of the entropy rate. The intercepts are $h' = 0.126$ and $h' = 1.348$, with the corresponding entropy rates $h = 1.134$ bpc and $h = 3.849$ bpc, for the English and Chinese groups, respectively. Compared to the values reported previously, the entropy rate estimate h is smaller by 20%. Interestingly, a similar analysis can be conducted for ansatz $f_1(n)$. For this function, by using the average of $\beta = 0.789$, the final h was found to be 1.304 and 4.634 for English and Chinese, respectively, which is similar to previous reports. Therefore, the estimate of the entropy rate depends on the used ansatz, with the better fitting ansatz yielding estimates smaller than generally agreed.

Given our results, we may revisit the question whether the entropy rate of natural language is a strictly positive constant. Our estimates of the entropy were obtained through extrapolation. Thus, the possibility of a zero entropy rate cannot be completely excluded but it seems highly unlikely in view of the following remark. Namely, if the entropy rate is zero, then the data points should head towards negative infinity in Figure 3. However, the plots do not show such a rapid decrease for data size of the order of several gigabytes. On the contrary, all endings of the plots for large data sizes are slightly bent upwards. Hence we are inclined to believe that the true entropy rate of natural language is positive and close to our estimates. Of course, a far larger amount of data would be required to witness the behavior of the plots in the margin between the infinite limit and the largest data size considered in our experiment.

7   Conclusion

In this article, we have evaluated the entropy rates of several human languages by means of a state-of-the-art compression method. Compared to previous works, our contribution can be summarized as follows. First, we have calculated the compression rates for six different languages by using state-of-the-art corpora with sizes of up to 7.8 gigabytes. Second, we have extrapolated the empirical compression rates to some estimates of the entropy rate using a novel ansatz, which takes form of a stretched exponential function. This new ansatz function fits better than the previously proposed ansatzes and predicts smaller entropy rates than reported before. Especially for English, where the vast majority of previous works suggested an entropy rate around 1.3 bpc, our new results suggest the possibility of a value around 1.1 bpc. Some future extension of our work might be to simply enlarge the data, but it will not be trivial to obtain a uniform corpus of a larger scale. Hence, in the future work, it may be advisable to look for other computational approaches to the problem of entropy estimation.

The complete version of this article is available at (Takahira et al., 2016)

Acknowledgements

We like to thank Japan Science and Technology Agency (JST, Precursory Research for Embryonic Science and Technology) for financial support.

References

K. Atteson. 1999. The asymptotic redundancy of Bayes rules for Markov chains. *IEEE Transactions on Information Theory*, 45:2104–2109.

R. H. Baayen. 2001. *Word Frequency Distributions*. Kluwer Academic Publishers.

A. Barron, J. Rissanen, and B. Yu. 1998. The minimum description length principle in coding and modeling. *IEEE Transactions on Information Theory*, 44:2743–2760.

T. C. Bell, J. G. Cleary, and I. H. Witten. 1990. *Text Compression*. Prentice Hall.

P. F. Brown, S. A. Della Pietra, V. J. Della Pietra, J. C. Lai, and R. L. Mercer. 1983. An estimate of an upper bound for the entropy of English. *Computational Linguistics*, 18(1):31–40.

T. M. Cover and R. C. King. 1978. A convergent gambling estimate of the entropy of English. *IEEE Transactions on Information Theory*, 24:413–421.

T. M. Cover and J. A. Thomas. 2006. *Elements of Information Theory*. Wiley-Interscience.

J. P. Crutchfield and D. P. Feldman. 2003. Regularities unseen, randomness observed: The entropy convergence hierarchy. *Chaos*, 15:25–54.

W. Ebeling and G. Nicolis. 1991. Entropy of symbolic sequences: The role of correlations. *Europhysics Letters*, 14(3):191–196.

D. Genzel and E. Charniak. 2002. Entropy rate constancy in text. In *Annual Meeting of the Association for the ACL*, pages 199–206.

P. Grassberger. 2002. Data Compression and Entropy Estimates by Non-sequential Recursive Pair Substitution. *ArXiv Physics e-prints*, July.

W. Hilberg. 1990. Der bekannte Grenzwert der redundanzfreien Information in Texten — eine Fehlinterpretation der Shannonschen Experimente? *Frequenz*, 44:243–248.

John C. Kieffer and Enhui Yang. 2000. Grammar-based codes: A new class of universal lossless source codes. *IEEE Transactions on Information Theory*, 46:737–754.

R. Levy and T. F. Jaeger. 2007. Speakers optimize information density through information density through syntactic reduction. In *Annual Conference on Neural Information Processing Systems*.

G. Louchard and W. Szpankowski. 1997. On the average redundancy rate of the Lempel-Ziv code. *IEEE Transactions on Information Theory*, 43:2–8.

C. G. Nevill-Manning and I. H. Witten. 1997. Identifying hierarchical structure in sequences: A linear-time algorithm. *Journal of Artificial Intelligence Research*, 7:67–82.

B. Ryabko. 2010. Applications of universal source coding to statistical analysis of time series. In Isaac Woungang, Sudip Misra, and Subhas Chandra Misra, editors, *Selected Topics in Information and Coding Theory*, Series on Coding and Cryptology. World Scientific Publishing.

T. Schümann and P. Grassberger. 1996. Entropy estimation of symbol sequences. *Chaos*, 6(3):414–427.

S. Shannon. 1948. A mathematical theory of communication. *Bell System Technical Journal*, 30:379–423,623–656.

C. Shannon. 1951. Prediction and entropy of printed English. *Bell System Technical Journal*, 30:50–64.

Ryosuke Takahira, Kumiko Tanaka-Ishii, and Łukasz Dębowski. 2016. Entropy rate estimates for natural language—a new extrapolation of compressed large-scale corpora. *Entropy*, 18(10):364, Oct.

J. Ziv and A. Lempel. 1977. A universal algorithm for sequential data compression. *IEEE Transactions on Information Theory*, 23(3):337–343.

Learning pressures reduce morphological complexity: Linking corpus, computational and experimental evidence

Christian Bentz
University of Tübingen
DFG Center for Advanced Study
Rümelinstraße 23
Tübingen, 72074, Germany
chris@christianbentz.de

Aleksandrs Berdicevskis
UiT The Arctic University of Norway
Department of Language and Culture
Postbox 6050 Langnes
9037 Tromsø, Norway
aleksandrs.berdicevskis@uit.no

Abstract

The morphological complexity of languages differs widely and changes over time. Pathways of change are often driven by the interplay of multiple competing factors, and are hard to disentangle. We here focus on a paradigmatic scenario of language change: the reduction of morphological complexity from Latin towards the Romance languages. To establish a causal explanation for this phenomenon, we employ three lines of evidence: 1) analyses of parallel corpora to measure the complexity of words in actual language production, 2) applications of NLP tools to further tease apart the contribution of inflectional morphology to word complexity, and 3) experimental data from artificial language learning, which illustrate the learning pressures at play when morphology simplifies. These three lines of evidence converge to show that pressures associated with imperfect language learning are good candidates to causally explain the reduction in morphological complexity in the Latin-to-Romance scenario. More generally, we argue that combining corpus, computational and experimental evidence is the way forward in historical linguistics and linguistic typology.

1 Introduction

Languages inevitably change over time. Sounds are added or removed from phoneme inventories, morphological markers are grammaticalized or lost, word orders permute in historical variants. Causal explanations for these phenomena are often complex – or lacking all together – since they have to cope with the interplay of learning and usage in a multitude of social settings, at different times, in different places.

We here focus on a prominent change from Latin towards the Modern Romance languages: the systematic loss of *morphological markers* in all descendant languages of the common proto-language over hundreds and thousands of years. Latin marked grammatical functions by means of inflectional variants of the same word root, thus displaying complex word forms. For example, the Latin word for "brother" *frater* was inflected to yield *fratres, fratribus, fratris, fratrum, fratri, fratre*, etc. according to singular/plural and case distinctions. This complexity is considerably reduced in Modern Romance languages, where there are often simpler singular/plural distinctions as in Italian *fratello/fratelli*, French *frère/frères*, and Spanish *hermano/hermanos*.

A theory currently gaining ground at the interface of historical linguistics, linguistic typology and sociolinguistics maintains that reduction in morphological complexity might be driven by learning pressures, namely *imperfect learning* by non-native adults (McWhorter, 2002; McWhorter, 2011; Trudgill, 2011; Wray and Grace, 2007). Adults learning a foreign language often lack the breadth of exposure to the target language that a native speaker would have. Thus, they only partially learn the range of inflectional variants of a word, and omit morphological markers in their language production (Papadopoulou et al., 2011; Haznedar, 2006; Gürel, 2000). If non-native speakers represent a considerable part of the overall speaker population, they might drive the language towards morphological simplification.

This line of reasoning was recently backed by quantitative analyses. Across different language families and areas it was shown that languages spoken by more people (a proxy for the proportion of non-native

Proceedings of the Workshop on Computational Linguistics for Linguistic Complexity,
pages 222–232, Osaka, Japan, December 11-17 2016.

speakers) tend to have lower morphological complexity (Lupyan and Dale, 2010), that languages with more non-native speakers have less complex morphological case marking (Bentz and Winter, 2013), and that languages with more non-native speakers have fewer word forms more generally (Bentz et al., 2015).

Our hypothesis is that imperfect language learning might also explain the loss of inflections from Classical Latin towards the Romance languages. These formed as the Roman empire expanded into the European continent, and later evolved into modern day Romance languages. In the process of expansion, Vulgar Latin varieties must have "recruited" considerable numbers of non-native speakers, which might have reduced the range of word forms in usage across the whole population of speakers (Herman, 2000; Bentz and Christiansen, 2010; Bentz and Christiansen, 2013). Over several generations, this mechanism can lead to considerable loss of morphological marking. We here present three lines of evidence to give such language change hypotheses an empirical and quantitative foundation.

1. A growing number of *diachronic and synchronic corpora* (see Cysouw & Wälchli (2007)) are available to measure patterns of change, rather than using single, isolated examples. Typological analyses based on corpora have the advantage of reflecting actual language production and usage, rather than expert judgement only. They are reproducible and transparent. In line with a range of earlier studies (Juola, 1998; Milin et al., 2009; Moscoso del Prado, 2011; Bentz et al., accepted; Ehret and Szmrecsanyi, 2016; Wälchli, 2012; Wälchli, 2014), we here apply corpus-based methods to measure morphological complexity.

2. NLP tools allow us to automatically and efficiently analyze large collections of texts. This is here illustrated with *lemmatization*, i.e. neutralization of inflected word forms to their base forms, also called *lemmas*. Thus we can tease apart the effect of inflections from other factors influencing the complexity of words.

3. Psycholinguistic experiments elicit the learning pressures that drive language change. So-called *iterated learning* experiments are particularly helpful to understand multiple factors shaping information encoding strategies in artificial languages (Kirby et al., 2008; Kirby et al., 2015). We here reanalyse data gathered in an artificial language learning experiment where inflectional marking is transmitted over several generations of "normal" and "imperfect" learners (Berdicevskis and Semenuks, forthcoming).

We would argue more generally that an integration of corpus, computational and experimental evidence is a valid strategy for understanding changes in any other set of languages and their phonological, morphological and syntactic features.

2 Methods

2.1 Corpora

To control for constant content across languages, we use two sets of parallel texts: 1) the *Parallel Bible Corpus* (PBC) (Mayer and Cysouw, 2014),[1] and 2) the *Universal Declaration of Human Rights* (UDHR) in unicode.[2] Details about the corpora can be seen in Table 1. The general advantage of the PBC is that it is bigger in terms of numbers of word tokens per language (ca. 280K), compared to the UDHR (ca. 1.8K). They represent two different registers: religious writing and transcribed speeches. This is important to ensure that the trends observed extrapolate to different text types. In our analyses, we focus on the Romance languages available in these corpora.

2.2 Estimating the Complexity of Words

We apply an information-theoretic measure of word complexity. Imagine a language that repeats the same word over and over again. This language is maximally redundant, each instance (token) of the same word (type) does essentially not store any information, hence this language has minimum word

---

[1] Last accessed on 09/03/2016
[2] http://unicode.org/udhr/

Parallel Corpus	Size	∅ Size	Texts	Lang.
PBC	$\approx 420M$	$\approx 280K$	1471	1083
UDHR	$\approx 650K$	$\approx 1.8K$	356	333

Table 1: Information on the parallel corpora used.

complexity. In contrast, a language with an infinite number of different words, expressing an infinite number of concepts, packs a lot of information into words, i.e. has maximum word complexity. Natural languages range in between these extremes (Bentz et al., 2015), displaying a variety of distributions of word tokens over word types. Such differences in type-token distributions can be measured by calculating their entropies. The classic Shannon entropy (Shannon and Weaver, 1949) is defined as

$$H = -K \sum_{i=1}^{r} p_i \, log_2(p_i). \tag{1}$$

Where K is a positive constant determining the unit of measurement (which is bits for K=1 and log to the base 2), r is the number of ranks (or different word types) in a word frequency distribution, and p_i is the probability of occurrence of a word of ith rank.

According to the maximum likelihood account, the probability p_i is simply the frequency of a type divided by the overall number of tokens in a text. However, it has been shown that this method underestimates the entropy, especially for small texts (Hausser and Strimmer, 2009). To estimate entropies reliably, the *James-Stein shrinkage* estimator (Hausser and Strimmer, 2009) is used here instead. According to this approach the estimated probability per type is

$$\hat{p}_i^{shrink} = \lambda \hat{p}_i^{target} + (1 - \lambda)\hat{p}_i^{ML}, \tag{2}$$

where $\lambda \in [0, 1]$ is the shrinkage intensity and $\hat{p}_i^{target}$ is the so-called "shrinkage target". Hausser & Strimmer (2009) suggest to use the maximum entropy distribution as a target, i.e. $\hat{p}_i^{target} = \frac{1}{V}$. This yields

$$\hat{p}_i^{shrink} = \frac{\lambda}{V} + (1 - \lambda)\hat{p}_i^{ML}. \tag{3}$$

The idea here is that the estimated probability $\hat{p}_i^{shrink}$ consists of two additive components, λ/V and $(1 - \lambda)\hat{p}_i^{ML}$ respectively. In the full shrinkage case ($\lambda = 1$), Equation 3 yields $\hat{p}_i^{shrink} = 1/V$, i.e. the maximum entropy. In the no shrinkage case ($\lambda = 0$), Equation 3 yields $\hat{p}_i^{shrink} = \hat{p}_i^{ML}$, i.e. the ML estimation that is biased towards low entropy. Given empirical data, the true probability is very likely to lie somewhere in between these two cases and hence $0 < \lambda < 1$. The optimal shrinkage can be found analytically. Finally, the probability p_i^{shrink} plugged into the original entropy equation yields

$$\hat{H}^{shrink} = -K \sum_{i=1}^{r} \hat{p}_i^{shrink} log_2(\hat{p}_i^{shrink}). \tag{4}$$

$\hat{H}^{shrink}$ is a robust approximation of the word entropy calculated from a text collection. It reflects the shape of type-token distributions. A long-tailed distribution will have higher $\hat{H}^{shrink}$, i.e. higher overall word complexity, while a short tailed distribution will have lower $\hat{H}^{shrink}$, i.e. lower overall word complexity. We use the R package *entropy* for shrinkage entropy estimations (Hausser and Strimmer, 2014).

Language	Tokens	unknown	%
Latin	11427	266	2.5
Italian	15314	888	5.8
French	17602	983	5.6
Spanish	15581	907	5.8

Table 2: Information on number and percentage of tokens unknown to the TreeTagger in a combined corpus of the PBC and UDHR. Note that only verses of the PBC which are parallel across several hundred languages were taken into account here. This explains the relatively low number of tokens.

2.3 Lemmatization and Inflectional Complexity

Note that the overall complexity of words is driven by a range of factors. Consider the example of the Latin lexeme *frater* "brother" again, which is frequently used in the Bible. As is illustrated in Figure 1, in Latin we get a whole range of inflectional variants, while in Italian, French and Spanish this range is reduced to the singular/plural forms. However, inflection is but one process besides derivation, compounding, contraction and others that shape type-token distributions (Bentz et al., accepted).

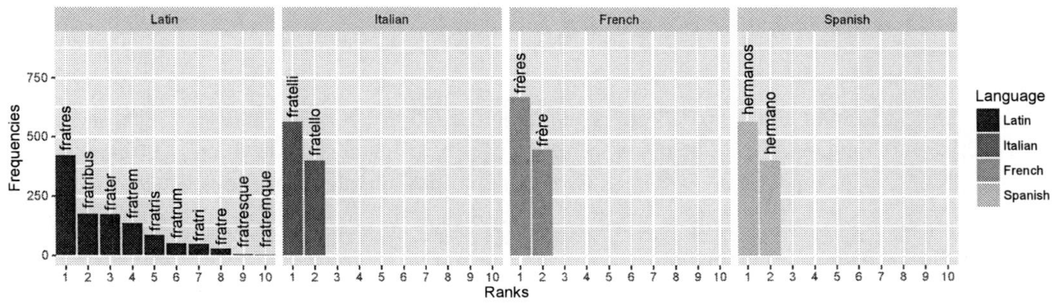

Figure 1: Reduction of inflectional variants from Latin to the Romance languages. Here exemplified with the occurrence of the word for "brother" in the Latin, Italian, French and Spanish texts of the PBC.

To tease apart *inflectional complexity* (C_{infl}) we can estimate the difference in entropy before (H_{raw}) and after lemmatization (H_{lem}):

$$C_{infl} = \Delta H = H_{raw} - H_{lem} \qquad (5)$$

This requires automatic (or manual) neutralization of inflectional variants of the same word root in a corpus, i.e. lemmatization (see Moscoso del Prado (2011) for a similar account). In the following, this process is outlined for both the natural and artificial languages used here.

Natural Languages: Word types of some natural languages can be lemmatized using the *TreeTagger* (Schmid, 1994). It first associates the respective word type with a POS tag (and case indication if relevant), and then derives the most likely lemma, thus outputting *wordType/POS/lemma*. For example, for the Latin proper noun *fratrem* "brother.ACC.SG" the TreeTagger outputs: *fratrem/N:acc/frater*. Likewise, for an inflected verb such as *creavit* "create.3P.SG.PST" it outputs *creavit/V:IND/creo* (where *creo* "create.1P.SG.PRES" is taken as the default lemma instead of the infinitive *creare*).

The TreeTagger is based on a statistical model trained on samples of manually lemmatized text. It provides high accuracy on words already seen in the training set (close to 100%). The words that are unknown to the tagger result in higher error rates. Table 2 shows the percentage of unknown word types for each language. We use the PBC for lemmatization, since it is the bigger corpus in number of tokens. The Romance languages that can be lemmatized using the TreeTagger are: Latin, Italian, French, and Spanish.

Artificial Languages: The morphological structure of the artificial language used in our analyses is outlined in Section 2.4, and illustrated in Appendix 6.1. Note that descendant languages usually preserve much of this structure. We lemmatize the artificial languages by the following rules:

1. Only if two word forms occur at the same place in the utterance (i.e. first or second), can they be neutralized to the same lemma.

2. Moreover, word forms have to adhere to the following similarity criteria to be neutralized to the same lemma:

   - Words that occur at the first place are "nouns", they always denote an entity. For nouns, the similarity criterion is the normalized Levenshtein distance between the two forms, which has to be smaller than 0.50. In the initial languages, noun stems consisted of three letters, with a plural marker being a one-letter ending. However, more complicated systematic ways to mark number emerged in some descendant languages, which is why the threshold is 0.50 instead of 0.25.

   - Words that occur at the second place are "verbs", they always denote an event. For verbs, the first letter has to be the same. In the initial languages, verb forms always consisted of two letters, the first of which was a stem, the second an agreement marker. In the descendant languages, the stem letter is usually preserved, while the agreement marker can undergo various changes.

3. The shortest form of a given paradigm is chosen as the lemma. For example, the nouns *seg* and *segl* (PL.) are lemmatized to *seg*. If there are several forms of equal length, the most frequent one of these is chosen as the lemma. If there is a tie, the first form the algorithm comes across is chosen.[3]

2.4   Iterated Learning Experiments

The experimental data are taken from an *iterated learning experiment* (Berdicevskis and Semenuks, forthcoming). In the experiment, an artificial miniature-language called "epsilon" is learned and transmitted from one participant to the next in an online setting. 15 isomorphic variants of epsilon are created to be transmitted in 15 separate chains. "Isomorphic" here means that the grammatical structure of the variants is the same, but the vocabulary is different. Thus, phrases are built based on a selection of two nouns (e.g. *seg*, *fuv*) and three verb roots: e.g. *m-* "to fall apart", *r-* "to grow antlers", *b-* "to fly". Morphological features include number marking on nouns (e.g. SG: -∅, PL: -*l*) and agreement on verbs (e.g. agreement with *seg*: -*o*, agreement with *fuv*: -*i*). Phrases consisting of nouns and verbs have to be learned based on visual scenes of moving objects. For example, the phrase *segl bo* would be paired with a picture where several *seg* objects fly. Overall, this leads to 15 epsilon variants made up of 16 possible phrases matching 16 possible scenes (see Appendix 6.1).

Transmission chains consist of 10 generations (one participant per generation). There are 45 transmission chains, 15 for the *normal* learning condition (there are no imperfect learners in the population), 15 for what is called a *temporarily interrupted* condition (there are imperfect learners in generations 2-4) and 15 for a *permanently interrupted* condition (there are imperfect learners in generations 2-10). Note that the same 15 epsilon variants were used for all three conditions.

Imperfect (non-native) learning is simulated via less exposure. "Native" learners have six training blocks to learn the artificial language epsilon, whereas "non-native" imperfect learners have only half of the training blocks.

For further analyses, we collapse the 15 transmission chains per condition to one "corpus" consisting of the word tokens produced in each generation. This yields around 280 tokens (noun and verb forms) used in each generation of 10 learners. Finally, there were 450 participants (45 chains times 10 generations), all of them native speakers of Russian.

---

[3]Sometimes an utterance does not contain a verb, even though there is an event occurring on the stimulus image. We do not posit empty tokens for these cases, which means that there is some variation in the corpus size across languages, both for the lemmatized and non-lemmatized versions. If a participant produced one verb-less utterance, it means that their output language will lack one word form which it might have had if the participant chose to name every event.

3 Results

3.1 Corpus Analyses

First, we want to measure the exact difference in word complexities between Latin and the Romance languages. To this end, we use the shrinkage entropy estimation method (Section 2.2) applied to our parallel corpora. As is illustrated in Figure 2 for both the PBC and the UDHR, Modern Romance languages have systematically lower word entropies. While Latin has a word entropy of ~ 10.5 (PBC) and ~ 8.5 (UDHR) respectively, Modern Romance languages fall below 9.75 and 8.2. Note that for some languages we get different translations (e.g. 6 translations into Portuguese in the PBC), and hence a range of entropy values. This variation is indicated by 95% confidence intervals in Figure 2 and also Figure 3. Overall, these analyses illustrate that in the ca. 2000 years since Latin was last spoken as a native language, the word entropy of its daughter languages systematically declined by around 10-15%.[4]

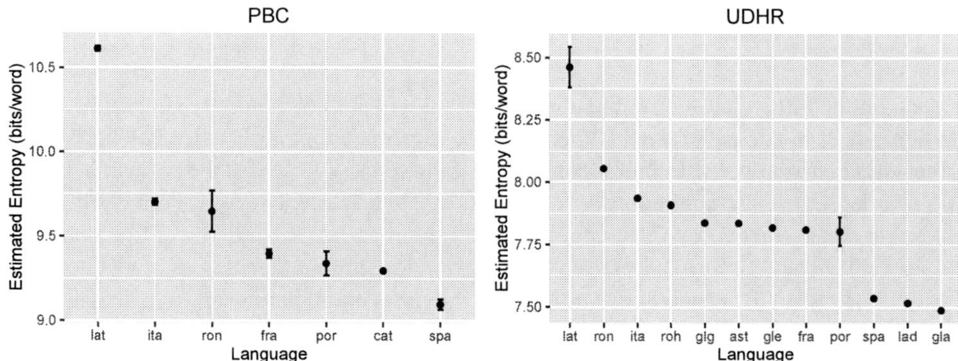

Figure 2: Reduction of word entropy from Latin to the Romance languages in two parallel corpora (PBC and UDHR). ISO 639-3 codes are given on the x-axis: Latin (lat), Italian (ita), Romanian (ron), French (fra), Portuguese (por), Catalan, (cat), Spanish (spa), Romansh (roh), Galician (glg), Asturian (ast), Ladino (lad).

3.2 Inflectional Complexity Reduction: Latin to Romance

Secondly, to pin down the reduction in inflectional complexity, we apply the lemmatization method outlined in Section 2.3. The results of this analysis for Latin, Italian, French and Spanish can be seen in Figure 3. Grey dots indicate the word complexities for the raw texts (H_{raw}), black dots indicate the word complexities after lemmatization (H_{lem}). The difference between these indicates the inflectional complexity of each language, or in other words, how much information is stored in inflectional variants of word roots. This is highest for Latin ($C_{infl} = \Delta H \sim 2.5$), and systematically lower for Italian, French and Spanish ($C_{infl} = \Delta H \sim 1.5$). Hence, the complexity of inflectional marking has systematically dropped in the 2000 years between Latin and its descendant languages. Namely, around 1 bit of information – formerly stored in inflectional marking – is now either lost or replaced by another level of encoding (Ehret and Szmrecsanyi, 2016; Koplenig et al., 2016; Moscoso del Prado, 2011).

3.3 Iterated Learning Experiments

The missing link to explain the entropy reduction in natural languages is the actual behaviour of language learners and users. Their impact on word entropy is illustrated here with data gathered from epsilon. Figure 4 gives an overview of the entropy change in the aggregated epsilon variants over 10 generations of transmission. The left panel shows the word entropy change in the three different learning conditions (normal, temporarily interrupted, permanently interrupted), while the right panel shows lemma entropy change (words neutralized for inflections).

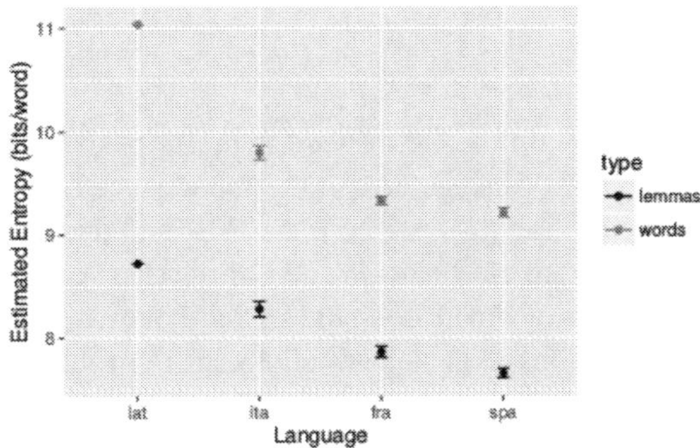

Figure 3: Differences in entropies before and after lemmatization (*words* and *lemmas*) in Latin, Italian, French and Spanish.

Focusing on the left panel first: in the normal condition (black), the entropy slightly decreases (from 7.23 to 7.15, i.e. ca. -1.1%) over 10 generations. For the temporarily interrupted condition (light grey), the word entropy decreases more sharply by 7.23 to 6.93 (-4.1%). In the permanently interrupted condition (dark grey), it also continuously drops from 7.23 to 6.95, i.e. by -3.9%. The right panel further illustrates – as we would expect – that entropy drops for lemmas compared to words, namely from 7.23 to 6.23, i.e. by 1 bit or -14% (in generation 0). However, for lemmas there is less of a systematic pattern in entropy change over 10 generations. In fact, for the normal and permanently interrupted conditions there is almost no change at all. Only for the temporarily interrupted condition does the lemma entropy drop somewhat from 6.23 to 6.09 (-2.2%).

In other words, the entropy drop in word forms over 10 generations of learning is mainly due to loss of morphological markers (e.g. losing plural marking -*l*, or agreement marking -*o* and -*i*), rather than a change in the base vocabulary (e.g. replacing vocabulary or using the noun *seg* where *fuv* should actually be used).

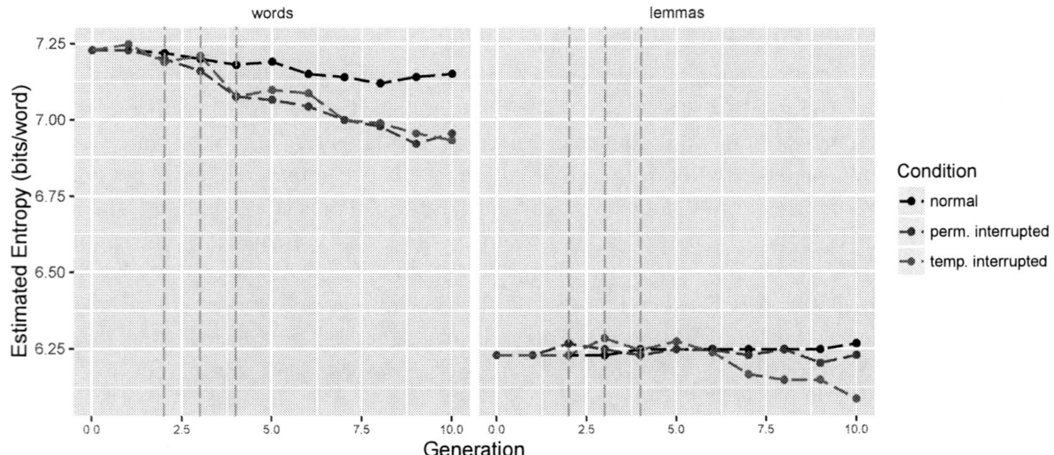

Figure 4: Entropy changes in the artificial language epsilon over 10 generations for both the original words produced by participants (left panel), and the lemmatized version (right panel). The languages were either transmitted via normal exposure (black), with temporary interruption (light grey), or with permanent interruption (dark grey). The vertical dashed lines indicate the generations of interruption in the "temporarily" interrupted condition.

4   Discussion

The word entropy/complexity of *all* Modern Romance languages represented in the PBC and UDHR parallel texts is lower than that of Classical Latin, which represents an earlier stage of the Romance genus. Namely, across 10 different descendants the word entropy is reduced by ca. 10-15%. Since this is a trend found in two independent parallel corpora, it is very unlikely due to effects of register or style of translation.

Instead, this pattern derives to a large extent from the loss of morphological marking witnessed in the ca. 2000 years since Romance languages evolved from Vulgar Latin. This is most clearly illustrated by means of lemmatization. Systematically neutralizing inflectional variants reduces the word entropy in Latin by around 2.5 bits, but in Spanish, French and Italian only by around 1.5 bits. Put differently, there is 1 bit less information stored in word forms of these three Modern Romance languages compared to Latin. Note that this information is not necessarily entirely lost, but potentially traded off for other means of information encoding beyond the word, e.g. word order (Ehret and Szmrecsanyi, 2016; Koplenig et al., 2016; Moscoso del Prado, 2011).

A potential caveat of our approach is that we infer grammatical structures used in spoken language production from analysing written texts. Classical Latin, as represented in the PBC and UDHR texts, is generally not considered the spoken proto-language of Modern Romance languages. Hence, a careful interpretation is that our analyses hold for written Latin and written Modern Romance. Written records are probably more conservative than spoken varieties, and reflect the spoken languages used at an earlier stage. Having said that, a mechanism for morphological loss in (written) language usage is starting to emerge from artificial language learning experiments. The data examined here illustrate that morphological marking can be learned and successfully transmitted under sufficient exposure. That is, the word type entropy of the artificial language epsilon was largely maintained in the "normal" condition of learning and transmission. However, when learning pressure is increased by reducing the exposure, imperfect learning effects kick in, and morphological distinctions are lost, which causes the word entropy to drop by around 4%, depending on the number of generations of imperfect learners.

These numbers seem relatively small, but over several centuries and millennia they can accumulate to considerable changes in the morphological structure of languages. Remarkably, the percentages of reduction from artificial languages also make sense – as an approximation – in the natural language context. If we assume generations of 30 years for a timespan of 2000 years, we arrive at ca. 66 generations. The word entropy reduction in epsilon (for the temporarily and permanently interrupted conditions) is approximately $\frac{0.3}{10} = 0.03$ bits per generation. If we multiply this by 66 we predict a reduction of ~ 2 bits, which is around -18%. This is close to – but somewhat higher than – the 10% to 15% word entropy reduction we actually find across 10 Modern Romance languages.

5   Conclusion

We have reported three lines of evidence – based on natural language corpora, NLP tools, and experimental data – to support the hypothesis that changes in morphological complexity from Latin to Romance languages were driven by imperfect learning scenarios. This suggests more generally that integrating corpora, computational tools, and experiments is a worthwhile strategy to model and explain complex scenarios of language change.

First, corpus data of historical and synchronic varieties are a source to help us observe general trends, rather than cherry-picking examples fitting our hypotheses. This was here illustrated by measuring the exact word entropy reduction between Latin and Modern Romance languages. Second, computational tools, such as entropy estimators and lemmatizers, allow us to quantify and further tease apart the effects in question. In our case study, we established that morphological loss is the main driver for entropy reduction. Third, psycholinguistic experiments elicit the potential learning pressures at play under different scenarios of language transmission. The systematic loss of morphological distinctions in the artificial language epsilon, driven by "non-natives", i.e. learners with less exposure, helps to understand the exact mechanisms of change. They might be subtle when looked at in isolation, but can have considerable effects when accumulated over time.

Thus, it is conceivable that elaborate corpus analyses in conjunction with iterated learning experiments (with several, separate points of interruption, and with artificial languages closely modelled after specific natural languages) could – for the first time – give us a model of language change "in real time".

Acknowledgements

CB was funded by the German Research Foundation (DFG FOR 2237: Project "Words, Bones, Genes, Tools: Tracking Linguistic, Cultural, and Biological Trajectories of the Human Past"), and the ERC Advanced Grant 324246 EVOLAEMP.

AB was funded by the Norwegian Research Council (grant 222506, "Birds and Beasts") and the CLEAR research group (Faculty of Humanities, Social Sciences and Education, UiT The Arctic University of Norway).

References

Christian Bentz and Morten H Christiansen. 2010. Linguistic adaptation at work? The change of word order and case system from Latin to the Romance languages. In Thomas C. Scott-Phillips, Monica Tamariz, Erica A. Cartmill, and James R Hurford, editors, *The evolution of language. Proceedings of the 8th international conference (EVOLANG8)*, pages 26–33, Singapore. World Scientific.

Christian Bentz and Morten H Christiansen. 2013. Linguistic Adaptation: The trade-off between case marking and fixed word orders in Germanic and Romance languages. In *East Flows the Great River: Festschrift in Honor of Prof. William S-Y. Wang's 80th Birthday*, pages 46–58.

Christian Bentz and Bodo Winter. 2013. Languages with more second language speakers tend to lose nominal case. *Language Dynamics and Change*, 3:1–27.

Christian Bentz, Annemarie Verkerk, Douwe Kiela, Felix Hill, and Paula Buttery. 2015. Adaptive communication: Languages with more non-native speakers tend to have fewer word forms. *PLoS ONE*, 10(6):e0128254.

Christian Bentz, Tanja Samardžić, Dimitrios Alikaniotis, and Paula Buttery. accepted. Variation in word frequency distributions: Definitions, measures and implications for a corpus-based language typology. *Journal of Quantitative Linguistics*.

Aleksandrs Berdicevskis and Arturs Semenuks. forthcoming. Imperfect language learning eliminates morphological overspecification: experimental evidence.

Michael Cysouw and Bernhard Wälchli. 2007. Parallel texts. Using translational equivalents in linguistic typology. *Sprachtypologie & Universalienforschung STUF*, 60.2.

Katharina Ehret and Benedikt Szmrecsanyi. 2016. An information-theoretic approach to assess linguistic complexity. In Raffaela Baechler and Guido Seiler, editors, *Complexity and Isolation*. de Gruyter, Berlin.

Ayse Gürel. 2000. Missing case inflection: Implications for second language acquisition. In Catherine Howell, Sarah A. Fish, and Thea Keith-Lucas, editors, *Proceedings of the 24th Annual Boston University Conference on Language Development*, pages 379–390, Somerville, MA. Cascadilla Press.

Jean Hausser and Korbinian Strimmer. 2009. Entropy inference and the james-stein estimator, with application to nonlinear gene association networks. *The Journal of Machine Learning Research*, 10:1469–1484.

Jean Hausser and Korbinian Strimmer, 2014. *entropy: Estimation of Entropy, Mutual Information and Related Quantities*. R package version 1.2.1.

Belma Haznedar. 2006. Persistent problems with case morphology in l2 acquisition. *Interfaces in multilingualism: Acquisition and representation*, pages 179–206.

József Herman. 2000. *Vulgar Latin*. The Pennsylvania State University Press, University Park, PA.

Patrick Juola. 1998. Measuring linguistic complexity: The morphological tier. *Journal of Quantitative Linguistics*, 5(3):206–213.

Simon Kirby, Hannah Cornish, and Kenny Smith. 2008. Cumulative cultural evolution in the laboratory: An experimental approach to the origins of structure in human language. *Proceedings of the National Academy of Sciences*, 105(31):10681–10686.

Simon Kirby, Monica Tamariz, Hannah Cornish, and Kenny Smith. 2015. Compression and communication in the cultural evolution of linguistic structure. *Cognition*, 141:87–102.

Alexander Koplenig, Peter Meyer, Sascha Wolfer, and Carolin Mueller-Spitzer. 2016. The statistical tradeoff between word order and word structure: large-scale evidence for the principle of least effort. *arXiv preprint arXiv:1608.03587*.

Gary Lupyan and Rick Dale. 2010. Language structure is partly determined by social structure. *PloS ONE*, 5(1):e8559, January.

Thomas Mayer and Michael Cysouw. 2014. Creating a massively parallel bible corpus. In Nicoletta Calzolari, Khalid Choukri, Thierry Declerck, Hrafn Loftsson, Bente Maegaard, Joseph Mariani, Asunción Moreno, Jan Odijk, and Stelios Piperidis, editors, *Proceedings of the Ninth International Conference on Language Resources and Evaluation (LREC-2014), Reykjavik, Iceland, May 26-31, 2014*, pages 3158–3163. European Language Resources Association (ELRA).

John H McWhorter. 2002. What happened to English? *Diachronica*, 19(2):217–272.

John H McWhorter. 2011. *Linguistic simplicity and complexitiy: Why do languages undress?* Mouton de Gruyter, Boston.

Petar Milin, Victor Kuperman, Aleksandar Kostic, and R Harald Baayen. 2009. Paradigms bit by bit: An information theoretic approach to the processing of paradigmatic structure in inflection and derivation. *Analogy in grammar: Form and acquisition*, pages 214–252.

F Moscoso del Prado. 2011. The mirage of morphological complexity. In *Proc. of the 33rd Annual Conference of the Cognitive Science Society*, pages 3524–3529.

D. Papadopoulou, S. Varlokosta, V. Spyropoulos, H. Kaili, S. Prokou, and a. Revithiadou. 2011. Case morphology and word order in second language Turkish: Evidence from Greek learners. *Second Language Research*, 27(2):173–204, February.

Helmut Schmid. 1994. Probabilistic part-of-speech tagging using decision trees. In *Proceedings of the International Conference on New Methods in Language Processing*, volume 12, pages 44–49.

Claude E. Shannon and Warren Weaver. 1949. *The mathematical theory of communication*. The University of Illinois Press, Urbana.

Peter Trudgill. 2011. *Sociolinguistic typology: social determinants of linguistic complexity*. Oxford University Press, Oxford.

Bernhard Wälchli. 2012. Indirect measurement in morphological typology. In A Ender, A Leemann, and Bernhard Wälchli, editors, *Methods in contemporary linguistics*, pages 69–92. De Gruyter Mouton, Berlin.

Bernhard Wälchli. 2014. Algorithmic typology and going from known to similar unknown categories within and across languages. *Aggregating Dialectology, Typology, and Register Analysis: Linguistic Variation in Text and Speech*, 28:355.

Alison Wray and George W Grace. 2007. The consequences of talking to strangers: Evolutionary corollaries of socio-cultural influences on linguistic form. *Lingua*, 117:543–578.

6 Appendices

6.1 Appendix A. Meaning space used in iterated learning experiment.

		event: none	event: fall apart	event: grow antlers	event: fly
agent: round animal	number: singular	 seg_N	 seg_N m_V-o_{AGR}	 seg_N r_V-o_{AGR}	 seg_N b_V-o_{AGR}
	number: plural	 seg_N-l_{PL}	 seg_N-l_{PL} m_V-o_{AGR}	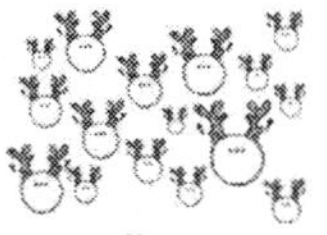 seg_N-l_{PL} r_V-o_{AGR}	 seg_N-l_{PL} b_V-o_{AGR}
agent: square animal	number: singular	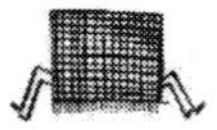 fuv_N	 fuv_N m_V-i_{AGR}	 fuv_N r_V-i_{AGR}	 fuv_N b_V-i_{AGR}
	number: plural	fuv_N-l_{PL}	 fuv_N-l_{PL} m_V-i_{AGR}	 fuv_N-l_{PL} r_V-i_{AGR}	 fuv_N-l_{PL} b_V-i_{AGR}

Figure 5: The meaning space of one of the initial input languages with the corresponding signals. Subscript N denotes noun stems, V - verb stems, PL - plural marker, AGR - agreement marker. Morphemes are hyphenated for illustration purposes. Reproduced with permission from Berdicevskis and Semenuks (under revision).

Author Index